THE WRITING PROCESS

A Guide for ESL Students

THE WRITING PROCESS:
A Guide for ESL Students

A WORKBOOK TO ACCOMPANY

The HarperCollins Concise Handbook for Writers

AMY TICKLE

Michigan State University

HarperCollinsCollegePublishers

Executive Editor: Jane Kinney
Project Editor: Ellen MacElree
Design Manager: Lucy Kirkorian
Text Designer: Eriben Graphics Inc.
Cover Designer: Kay Petronio
Cover Painting: *Orfeo* by Orlando Agudelo-Botero, 1949. Multi-media painting on papier
   d'Arches, 29" × 4". Courtesy of Ergman International, Laguna Beach, CA.
Art Studio: Vantage Art, Inc.
Manufacturing Manager: Willie Lane
Compositor: BookMasters, Inc.
Printer and Binder: RR Donnelley & Sons Company
Cover Printer: RR Donnelley & Sons Company

For permission to use copyrighted material, grateful acknowledgment is made to the copyright holders on pp. 443–445, which are hereby made part of this copyright page.

The Writing Process: A Guide for ESL Students
A Workbook to Accompany *The HarperCollins Concise Handbook for Writers*

Copyright © 1996 by HarperCollins College Publishers

Library of Congress Cataloging-in-Publication Data

Tickle, Amy.
   The writing process : a guide for ESL students: a workbook to
accompany the HarperCollins concise handbook for writers / Amy
Tickle.
      p.   cm.
   Includes index.
   ISBN 0–06–502022–7
   1. English language—Textbooks for foreign speakers.   2. English
language—Rhetoric—Problems, exercises, etc.   I. Tickle, Amy.
HarperCollins concise handbook for writers.   II. Title.
[PE1128.T49   1996]
808'.042—dc20   94-26071
                                                 CIP

94 95 96 97   9 8 7 6 5 4 3 2 1

 # CONTENTS

Preface   *xx*

PART I   The Writing Process   1

1   WRITING PROCESSES   3

1a Why You Write 3
ACTIVITY 1.1   Writing Situations   3
ACTIVITY 1.2   Differences between Speaking and Writing   4

1b Writing in Different Languages 4
ACTIVITY 1.3   Is Writing in English Different?   4

1c How Writers Write 5
ACTIVITY 1.4   Identifying and Evaluating Your Composing Process   5

2   PLANNING: THE WRITING CONTEXT   8

2a The Assignment 8

2b Deciding on a Topic 8

2c Narrowing a Topic 9
ACTIVITY 2.1   Using Brainstorming to Narrow a Topic   10
ACTIVITY 2.2   Practice with Invention Techniques   14

2d Purpose 15
ACTIVITY 2.3   Understanding Different Purposes   16

2e Audience 17
ACTIVITY 2.4   Writing with a Similar Purpose for Different Audiences   17
ACTIVITY 2.5   Applying the Concepts of Purpose and Audience to Writing   19

2f Collecting Information 20
ACTIVITY 2.6   Differentiating between Primary and Secondary Sources   20

v

3   DRAFTING AND REVISING   21

3a   The Drafting Process   21
ACTIVITY 3.1   Understanding Drafting   21
3b   Revision and Editing Overview   23
ACTIVITY 3.2   What Are Revision and Editing?   23
3c   Large-scale and Small-scale Revision   23
ACTIVITY 3.3   Revising for Content, Purpose, and Audience   24
3d   Peer Review   29
ACTIVITY 3.4   Peer Review   29

PART II   Revising for Organization   37

4   ACHIEVING PARAGRAPH STRUCTURE   39

4a   Topic Sentences   39
ACTIVITY 4.1   Evaluating Topic Sentences   39
ACTIVITY 4.2   Matching Topic Sentences to Paragraphs   40
ACTIVITY 4.3   Recognizing Topic Sentences   41
ACTIVITY 4.4   Writing Topic Sentences   41
4b   Formatting Paragraphs   42
ACTIVITY 4.5   Are Headings Appropriate?   42
4c   Sticking to the Point (Unity)   42
ACTIVITY 4.6   Identifying Irrelevant Information   43
4d   Coherence in a Paragraph   43
ACTIVITY 4.7   Using Transitions Appropriately   44
ACTIVITY 4.8   Writing Appropriate Repetitions   45
ACTIVITY 4.9   Using Demonstratives   46
ACTIVITY 4.10 Revising for Paragraph Coherence   47
4e   Sentence Variety   47
ACTIVITY 4.11 Identifying Tools for Sentence Variety   47
ACTIVITY 4.12 Achieving Sentence Variety   48
4f   Paragraph Length   49
ACTIVITY 4.13 Breaking Paragraphs Appropriately   50
ACTIVITY 4.14 Putting It All Together   51

5   DEVELOPING IDEAS   52

5a   Types of Support   52
ACTIVITY 5.1   Recognizing Types of Support   52
ACTIVITY 5.2   Generating Details   53
ACTIVITY 5.3   Writing Supporting Details   53
5b   Arranging Supporting Material   54
ACTIVITY 5.4   Recognizing Language Used in Spatial Organization   54
ACTIVITY 5.5   Writing Paragraphs Using Spatial Organization   54
ACTIVITY 5.6   Organizing Paragraphs Chronologically   55
ACTIVITY 5.7   Writing Paragraphs according to Time or Sequence   55

ACTIVITY 5.8   Recognizing General Ideas and Specific Details in
                Paragraphs   56
ACTIVITY 5.9   Defining, Recognizing, and Using Patterns of
                Development   56

6 WRITING INTRODUCTIONS AND CONCLUSIONS 59

6a   Purpose of Introductions   59
ACTIVITY 6.1   Identifying the Parts of an Introduction   59
6b   Thesis Statements   61
ACTIVITY 6.2   Critiquing Thesis Statements   61
ACTIVITY 6.3   Writing Thesis Statements   63
6c   Techniques for Writing Introductions   63
ACTIVITY 6.4   Recognizing Introduction Techniques   64
6d   Techniques for Writing Conclusions   64
ACTIVITY 6.5   Recognizing Conclusion Techniques   65
ACTIVITY 6.6   Identifying Introductions and Conclusions   66
ACTIVITY 6.7   Writing Introductions and Conclusions   67

PART III Revising for Effective Sentences and Word Use 71

7 AVOIDING UNNECESSARY SHIFTS 73

7a   Avoiding Shifts in Tense
ACTIVITY 7.1   Explaining Shifts in Tense   73
ACTIVITY 7.2   Revising Paragraphs for Tense Consistency   74
7b   Avoiding Shifts in Person and Number   75
ACTIVITY 7.3   Revising Paragraphs for Consistency in Person and
                Number   76
ACTIVITY 7.4   Editing Sentences for Consistency in Person and
                Number   76
7c   Avoiding Shifts in Mood   77
ACTIVITY 7.5   Editing Sentences for Shifts in Mood   77
7d   Avoiding Shifts in Voice   78
ACTIVITY 7.6   Editing Sentences for Shifts in Voice   78
7e   Avoiding Shifts between Direct and Indirect Quotation   78
ACTIVITY 7.7   Editing Sentences for Shifts in Discourse   79

8 FORMING COMPOUND AND COMPLEX SENTENCES USING COORDINATION AND SUBORDINATION 80

8a   Diagnostic Activity: Coordination and Subordination   80
ACTIVITY 8.1   How Much Do You Know?   80

8b Understanding the Terminology 81

8c Forming Compound Sentences Using Coordination 81

8d About Coordination 82

ACTIVITY 8.2 Identifying the Function of Coordinating Conjunctions and Conjunctive Adverbs 83

ACTIVITY 8.3 Forming Compound Sentences 83

8e Avoiding Comma Splices and Fused Sentences 85

ACTIVITY 8.4 Revising Fused Sentences 85

ACTIVITY 8.5 Identifying and Correcting Fused Sentences and Comma Splices 86

8f Forming Complex Sentences Using Subordination 86

8g Forming Adjective Clauses 86

ACTIVITY 8.6 Forming Adjective Clauses 90

ACTIVITY 8.7 Omitting Relative Pronouns 91

ACTIVITY 8.8 Using Adjective Clauses 91

8h Forming Adverb Clauses 92

ACTIVITY 8.9 Using Subordinating Conjunctions 93

ACTIVITY 8.10 Writing Sentences Using Adverb Clauses 94

8i Forming Noun Clauses 94

ACTIVITY 8.11 Writing Sentences Using Noun Clauses 95

8j Finding and Revising Fragments 96

ACTIVITY 8.12 Identifying and Correcting Fragments 97

8k About Subordination 98

ACTIVITY 8.13 Emphasizing Important Ideas through Subordination 99

8l Forming Compound and Complex Sentences Using Coordination and Subordination: Comprehensive Check 99

ACTIVITY 8.14 Diagnostic Retest 99

ACTIVITY 8.15 Putting It All Together 99

9 USING PARALLEL STRUCTURES FOR PARALLEL IDEAS 101

9a Diagnostic Activity: Parallelism 101

ACTIVITY 9.1 How Much Do You Know? 101

9b Parallelism with Coordinating Conjunctions 102

ACTIVITY 9.2 Creating Parallel Sentences Using Coordinating Conjunctions 103

ACTIVITY 9.3 Combining Sentences Using Coordinating Conjunctions 104

9c Parallelism with Correlative Conjunctions 104

ACTIVITY 9.4 Writing Parallel Sentences with Correlative Conjunctions 105

ACTIVITY 9.5 Writing Parallel Sentences Using Both Coordinating and Correlative Conjunctions 105

9d Parallelism with Items in a Series 106

ACTIVITY 9.6 Completing Series with Parallel Items 106

9e   Parallelism with Comparisons   107
ACTIVITY 9.7   Parallelism with Comparisons Using *than* or *as*   107
9f   Parallelism in Lists and Outlines   108
ACTIVITY 9.8   Parallelism in Outlines   108
ACTIVITY 9.9   Parallelism in Lists   109
9g   Repeating Key Words in Parallel Structures   109
ACTIVITY 9.10 Repetition of Key Words in Parallel Structures   110
9h   Parallelism: Comprehensive Check   110
ACTIVITY 9.11 Diagnostic Retest   110
ACTIVITY 9.12 Putting It All Together   110

10   AVOIDING MIXED OR INCOMPLETE CONSTRUCTIONS   112
10a   Diagnostic Activity: Avoiding Mixed Constructions   112
ACTIVITY 10.1 How Much Do You Know?   112
10b   Revising Mixed Grammatical Constructions   113
ACTIVITY 10.2 Revising Mixed Grammatical Constructions   114
10c   Revising Mixed Meaning   114
ACTIVITY 10.3 Revising Sentences with Mixed Meaning   115
10d   Revising Sentences of the Pattern "My brother, he . . ."   115
ACTIVITY 10.4 Revising Sentences of the Pattern "My brother, he . . ."   116
10e   Revising Errors with *in which*   116
ACTIVITY 10.5 Revising Errors with *in which*   117
10f   Revising Incomplete Sentences   117
ACTIVITY 10.6 Recognizing and Correcting Incomplete Sentences   119
10g   Mixed Constructions: Comprehensive Check   121
ACTIVITY 10.7 Diagnostic Retest   121
ACTIVITY 10.8 Putting It All Together   121

11   AVOIDING MISPLACED AND DANGLING MODIFIERS   122
ACTIVITY 11.1 Recognizing Modifiers in a Sentence   122
11a   Diagnostic Activity: Misplaced and Dangling Modifiers   123
ACTIVITY 11.2 How Much Do You Know?   123
11b   Placing Modifiers Near the Words Modified   124
ACTIVITY 11.3 Recognizing and Correcting Misplaced Modifiers   124
11c   Locating Limiting Modifiers   125
ACTIVITY 11.4 Placing Limiting Modifiers Appropriately in a Sentence   125
11d   Avoiding Dangling Modifiers   126
ACTIVITY 11.5 Revising Sentences with Dangling Modifiers   126
11e   Avoiding Split Infinitives   127
ACTIVITY 11.6 Recognizing and Revising Sentences with Split Infinitives   128

11f   Misplaced and Dangling Modifiers: Comprehensive Check   128
ACTIVITY 11.7   Diagnostic Retest   128
ACTIVITY 11.8   Putting It All Together   128

12   CHOOSING THE RIGHT WORDS   130

12a   Diagnostic Activity: Word Choice   130
ACTIVITY 12.1   How Much Do You Know?   130
12b   Confusing Word Choices   131
ACTIVITY 12.2   Using *do* and *make*   131
ACTIVITY 12.3   Using *another, other, the other, each other*, and *one
                          another*   133
ACTIVITY 12.4   Using *yet* and *still*   134
ACTIVITY 12.5   Using *already, yet,* and *still*   134
ACTIVITY 12.6   Where Have You Been?   135
12c   Avoiding Mistakes in Usage   135
ACTIVITY 12.7   Avoiding Mistakes in Usage   137
12d   Conciseness   138
ACTIVITY 12.8   Avoiding Redundancy   139
ACTIVITY 12.9   Avoiding Excessive Intensifiers   140
ACTIVITY 12.10 Avoiding *there* and *it*   140
12e   Using Language Appropriately   140
ACTIVITY 12.11 Avoiding Excessive Humility   141
ACTIVITY 12.12 Avoiding Sexist Language   142
12f   Being Aware of Connotation   143
ACTIVITY 12.13 Recognizing Positive and Negative Connotations   143
ACTIVITY 12.14 Making Sentences More Neutral   144
12g   Word Choice: Comprehensive Check   144
ACTIVITY 12.15 Diagnostic Retest   144
ACTIVITY 12.16 Putting It All Together   145

PART IV   Editing for Grammar and Usage   147

13   FINDING AND REVISING ERRORS WITH VERB FORM   149

13a   Diagnostic Activity: Verb Forms   149
ACTIVITY 13.1   How Much Do You Know?   149
13b   Regular and Irregular Verb Forms   150
ACTIVITY 13.2   Using Regular and Irregular Verbs   152
13c   Phrasal Verbs   153
ACTIVITY 13.3   Understanding Common Intransitive Phrasal Verbs   155
ACTIVITY 13.4   Understanding Common Transitive Phrasal Verbs   157

ACTIVITY 13.5   Using the Correct Particle with Phrasal Verbs   158
ACTIVITY 13.6   Writing Sentences Using Transitive Phrasal Verbs   159
ACTIVITY 13.7   Editing for Usage of Phrasal Verbs   160

13d   Modals   160
ACTIVITY 13.8   Using Modals for Giving Advice   163
ACTIVITY 13.9   Using Modals with Permission and Requests   164
ACTIVITY 13.10   Using Perfective Modals of Advice   165
ACTIVITY 13.11   Using Modals Expressing Degrees of Certainty   167
ACTIVITY 13.12   Writing Sentences Using Modals Expressing Degrees
                 of Certainty   167
ACTIVITY 13.13   Using Modals of Ability and Events in the Past   168

13e   Verb Forms: Comprehensive Check   169
ACTIVITY 13.14   Diagnostic Retest   169
ACTIVITY 13.15   Recognizing the Meaning of Modals and
                 Periphrastic Modals   169
ACTIVITY 13.16   Editing Sentences for Modals   170

**14   FINDING AND REVISING ERRORS WITH VERB
       TENSE AND VOICE   171**

14a   Diagnostic Activity: Verb Tense and Voice   171
ACTIVITY 14.1   How Much Do You Know?   171

14b   The English Tense System   172

14c   Present Time   173
ACTIVITY 14.2   Identifying the Uses of the Simple Present Tense   173
ACTIVITY 14.3   Using the Simple Present and the Present Progressive   175
ACTIVITY 14.4   More Simple Present and Present Progressive   175

14d   Past Time   176
ACTIVITY 14.5   Choosing between the Simple Past and the Present
                 Perfect   178
ACTIVITY 14.6   Using Past Time Tenses   180
ACTIVITY 14.7   Using Present and Past Time Tenses   180
ACTIVITY 14.8   Writing Situation   181

14e   Future Time   181
ACTIVITY 14.9   Using Future Tenses   182
ACTIVITY 14.10   Editing Sentences for Tense   183
ACTIVITY 14.11   Using Tenses Correctly   183

14f   Active and Passive Voice   184
ACTIVITY 14.12   Use of the Passive Voice   185
ACTIVITY 14.13   Editing Sentences for Use of the Passive Voice   185
ACTIVITY 14.14   Further Practice with Forming the Passive   186
ACTIVITY 14.15   Using Tense and Voice   186

14g   Verb Tense and Voice: Comprehensive Check   187
ACTIVITY 14.16   Diagnostic Retest   187

15 FINDING AND REVISING ERRORS WITH CONDITIONALS, HYPOTHETICALS, AND THE SUBJUNCTIVE   189

15a   Diagnostic Activity: Conditionals, Hypotheticals, and the Subjunctive   189
ACTIVITY 15.1   How Much Do You Know?   189

15b   Conditionals   190
ACTIVITY 15.2   Using Conditionals   191
ACTIVITY 15.3   Editing Sentences for Correct Usage of Conditionals   191

15c   Hypotheticals   192
ACTIVITY 15.4   Writing Hypothetical Statements   193
ACTIVITY 15.5   Writing Conditional and Hypothetical Statements   193
ACTIVITY 15.6   Hypotheticals with Inverted Word Order   194

15d   Subjunctive Mood   194
ACTIVITY 15.7   Using the Subjunctive   196
ACTIVITY 15.8   The Subjunctive   196

15e   Conditionals, Hypotheticals, and the Subjunctive: Comprehensive Check   197
ACTIVITY 15.9   Diagnostic Retest   197
ACTIVITY 15.10 Putting It All Together   197

16 FINDING AND REVISING ERRORS WITH VERBALS   199

16a   Diagnostic Activity: Verbals   199
ACTIVITY 16.1   How Much Do You Know?   199

16b   Identifying Infinitives, Gerunds, and Participles   199

16c   Function of Infinitives and Gerunds   200
ACTIVITY 16.2   Identifying the Function of Verbals   201

16d   Choosing between Infinitives and Gerunds   201
ACTIVITY 16.3   Editing Sentences for Infinitives and Gerunds   203
ACTIVITY 16.4   Choosing between Infinitives and Gerunds   204

16e   Participles   204
ACTIVITY 16.5   Using the Right Participle   205
ACTIVITY 16.6   Reduced Adjective and Adverb Clauses   206

16f   Verbals: Comprehensive Check   207
ACTIVITY 16.7   Diagnostic Retest   207
ACTIVITY 16.8   Putting It All Together   207

17 FINDING AND REVISING SUBJECT-VERB AGREEMENT ERRORS   208

17a   Diagnostic Activity: Subject-Verb Agreement   208
ACTIVITY 17.1   How Much Do You Know?   208

17b   Basic Subject-Verb Agreement   210
ACTIVITY 17.2   Basic Rule   210

17c   Subject-Verb Agreement with *I* and *you* as the Subject   210
ACTIVITY 17.3   Subject-Verb Agreement with *I* and *you*   211
17d   Subject-Verb Agreement with the Verb *be*   211
ACTIVITY 17.4   Writing Sentences with the Verb *be*   211
ACTIVITY 17.5   Editing for Subject-Verb Agreement with the Verb *be*   212
17e   Subject-Verb Agreement with Helping Verbs   213
ACTIVITY 17.6   Editing for Subject-Verb Agreement with Helping
Verbs   213
17f   Subject-Verb Agreement with Past and Future Tenses   214
ACTIVITY 17.7   Using Past and Future Tenses with Correct
Agreement   214
**17g   Subject-Verb Agreement with Intervening Phrases and
Compound Subjects   215**
ACTIVITY 17.8   Identifying and Editing Sentences for Subject-Verb
Agreement   216
ACTIVITY 17.9   Editing for Subject-Verb Agreement   216
17h   Subject-Verb Agreement with Collective Nouns   217
ACTIVITY 17.10 Using the Correct Verb with Collective Nouns   217
**17i   Subject-Verb Agreement When the Subject Follows
the Verb   218**
ACTIVITY 17.11 Subject-Verb Agreement in Sentences Beginning with
there   218
ACTIVITY 17.12 Subject-Verb Agreement in Sentences Beginning with a
Prepositional Phrase   219
17j   Subject-Verb Agreement with Linking Verbs   219
ACTIVITY 17.13 Identifying Subjects and Verbs in Sentences with
Linking Verbs   220
**17k   Subject-Verb Agreement When the Subject Is Plural in Form
but Singular in Meaning   220**
ACTIVITY 17.14 Recognizing Singular Subjects in Plural Form   220
17l   Subject-Verb Agreement with Indefinite Pronouns   221
ACTIVITY 17.15 Subject-Verb Agreement with Indefinite Pronouns   222
**17m   Subject-Verb Agreement in Clauses Beginning with *who,
which,* or *that*   222**
ACTIVITY 17.16 Subject-Verb Agreement with Relative Pronouns   223
ACTIVITY 17.17 Subject-Verb Agreement with Relative Pronouns   224
ACTIVITY 17.18 Using the Correct Form of the Verb with Relative
Pronouns   224
17n   Subject-Verb Agreement: Comprehensive Check   225
ACTIVITY 17.19 Diagnostic Retest   225
ACTIVITY 17.20 Putting It All Together   225

**18   FINDING AND REVISING PRONOUN
AGREEMENT AND REFERENCE ERRORS   226**
18a   Diagnostic Activity: Pronoun Agreement and Reference   226
ACTIVITY 18.1   How Much Do You Know?   226

18b Basic Pronoun Agreement   227
ACTIVITY 18.2   Editing for Number, Person, and Gender   228
18c Avoiding Sexism with Pronouns   229
ACTIVITY 18.3   Three Methods of Avoiding Sexism with Pronouns   229
ACTIVITY 18.4   Eliminating Sexism in Writing   230
18d Pronoun Agreement with Compound Antecedents   230
ACTIVITY 18.5   Editing for Pronoun Agreement with Compound Antecedents   231
18e Pronoun Agreement with Indefinite Pronoun Antecedents   232
ACTIVITY 18.6   Revising Sentences for Pronoun Agreement with Singular Indefinite Pronoun Antecedents   232
ACTIVITY 18.7   Revising Sentences for Pronoun Agreement with Indefinite Pronoun Antecedents   233
18f Pronoun Reference   234
ACTIVITY 18.8   Identifying Pronoun Referents   234
ACTIVITY 18.9   Editing for Pronoun Reference Errors   235
18g Pronoun Agreement and Reference: Comprehensive Check   235
ACTIVITY 18.10 Diagnostic Retest   235
ACTIVITY 18.11 Putting It All Together   235

19   FINDING AND REVISING PRONOUN CASE ERRORS   237
19a Diagnostic Activity: Pronoun Case   237
ACTIVITY 19.1   How Much Do You Know?   237
19b Subjects versus Objects   238
ACTIVITY 19.2   Using Pronouns in the Subjective and Objective Cases   239
19c Subjective Case after Linking Verbs   239
ACTIVITY 19.3   Using the Subjective Case after Linking Verbs   239
19d Case in Compound Structures   240
ACTIVITY 19.4   Choosing Correct Pronoun Case in Compound Structures   240
19e Case in Appositives   241
ACTIVITY 19.5   Using Correct Pronoun Case with Appositives   241
19f *We* and *us* before a Noun   241
ACTIVITY 19.6   Using Pronoun Case Correctly in Sentences with *we* and *us* before a Noun   242
19g Case in Sentences with *than* and *as*   242
ACTIVITY 19.7   Using the Correct Form of the Pronoun in Sentences with *than* and *as*   243
19h *Who* and *whom*, *whoever* and *whomever*   243
ACTIVITY 19.8   Determining When to Use *who* and *whom*   243
ACTIVITY 19.9   Choosing between *who* and *whom*, *whoever* and *whomever*   244

19i   Case before a Gerund   244
ACTIVITY 19.10 Using Pronoun Case Correctly with Gerunds   245
19j   Pronoun Case: Comprehensive Check   245
ACTIVITY 19.11 Diagnostic Retest   245
ACTIVITY 19.12 Putting It All Together   245

**20   FINDING AND REVISING ADJECTIVE AND
          ADVERB ERRORS   247**
20a   Diagnostic Activity: Adjectives and Adverbs   247
ACTIVITY 20.1   How Much Do You Know?   247
20b   Distinguishing between Adjectives and Adverbs   248
ACTIVITY 20.2   Identifying and Using the Correct Form of Adjectives
                  and Adverbs   249
20c   Using Adjectives after Linking Verbs   249
ACTIVITY 20.3   Recognizing Linking and Action Verbs with Adjectives
                  and Adverbs   250
ACTIVITY 20.4   Common Mistakes with Adjectives and Adverbs Used
                  with Linking and Action Verbs   250
20d   Using Comparative and Superlative Forms   251
ACTIVITY 20.5   Choosing the Correct Form of Comparatives and
                  Superlatives   253
ACTIVITY 20.6   Using Comparatives and Superlatives   253
ACTIVITY 10.7   Editing for Correct Usage of Comparatives and
                  Superlatives   254
20e   Avoiding Double Negatives   255
ACTIVITY 20.8   Avoiding Double Negatives   255
20f   Determining the Order of Adverbs and Adjectives   256
ACTIVITY 20.9   Putting Adjectives and Adverbs in Order   257
20g   Adjectives and Adverbs: Comprehensive Check   257
ACTIVITY 20.10 Diagnostic Retest   257
ACTIVITY 20.11 Putting It All Together   258

**21   FINDING AND REVISING ERRORS WITH
          ARTICLES   259**
21a   Diagnostic Activity: Articles   259
ACTIVITY 21.1   How Much Do You Know?   259
21b   Determiners   260
21c   Choosing between *a* and *an*   261
ACTIVITY 21.2   Choosing between *a* and *an*   261
21d   Article Usage with Proper Nouns   261
ACTIVITY 21.3   Using Articles with Proper Nouns   262
**21e   Article Usage with Countable and Noncountable Singular and
         Plural Common Nouns   263**
ACTIVITY 21.4   Identifying Noncountable Nouns   263
ACTIVITY 21.5   Using Irregular Plural Nouns   266

**21f   Article Usage with Definite, Generic, and Indefinite
        Common Nouns   267**
    ACTIVITY 21.6   Identifying the Criteria for Using the Definite Article   267
    ACTIVITY 21.7   Differentiating among Generic, Definite, and Indefinite
                    Usage of Articles   268
21g   Rules for Use of Articles with Common Nouns   269
**21h   Exceptions to the Rules for the Use of Articles with
        Common Nouns   269**
21i   Articles: Comprehensive Check   271
    ACTIVITY 21.8   Diagnostic Retest   271
    ACTIVITY 21.9   Putting It All Together   271

**22   FINDING AND REVISING ERRORS WITH
      PREPOSITIONS   276**
22a   Diagnostic Activity: Prepositions   276
    ACTIVITY 22.1   How Much Do You Know?   276
22b   The Nine Most Common Prepositions   277
22c   Prepositions of Time and Space   278
    ACTIVITY 22.2   Using the Appropriate Preposition of Time   278
    ACTIVITY 22.3   Using the Appropriate Preposition of Space   279
    ACTIVITY 22.4   Writing Directions Using Prepositions of Space   280
22d   Prepositions Showing Logical Relationships   281
    ACTIVITY 22.5   Identifying the Meaning of Prepositions Showing Logical
                    Relationships   281
    ACTIVITY 22.6   Using Prepositions That Show Logical Relationships   282
22e   Three Common Errors with Prepositions   282
    ACTIVITY 22.7   Identifying Errors with Prepositions   283
22f   Ending Sentences with Prepositions   283
    ACTIVITY 22.8   Revising Sentences That End with Prepositions   284
22g   Choosing between *of* and *'s* for Possessives   284
    ACTIVITY 22.9   Choosing between *of* and *'s* for Possessives   285
22h   Verb + Preposition Combinations   286
22i   Prepositions: Comprehensive Check   287
    ACTIVITY 22.10 Diagnostic Retest   287
    ACTIVITY 22.11 Putting It All Together   287

PART V   Punctuation, Mechanics, and Spelling   289

**23   EDITING FOR COMMAS, SEMICOLONS,
      APOSTROPHES, AND QUOTATION MARKS   291**
**23a   Diagnostic Activity: Commas, Semicolons, Apostrophes, and
        Quotation Marks   291**
    ACTIVITY 23.1   How Much Do You Know?   291

23b   **Commas and Semicolons   292**
ACTIVITY 23.2   Using Commas with Introductory Elements and Commas
and Semicolons with Items in a Series   293
ACTIVITY 23.3   Forming Sentences with Two Independent Clauses   293
ACTIVITY 23.4   Using Commas with Restrictive and Nonrestrictive
Elements   295
ACTIVITY 23.5   Editing for Comma Usage   297
ACTIVITY 23.6   Using Commas and Semicolons   298
23c   **Apostrophes   298**
ACTIVITY 23.7   Forming Possessives   300
ACTIVITY 23.8   Editing for Apostrophe Usage   302
23d   **Quotation Marks   303**
ACTIVITY 23.9   Using Quotation Marks with Direct Quotations   306
ACTIVITY 23.10   Distinguishing between Direct and Indirect
Quotations   306
ACTIVITY 23.11   Using Quotation Marks with Dialogue   307
23e   **Commas, Semicolons, Apostrophes, and Quotation Marks:
Comprehensive Check   307**
ACTIVITY 23.12   Diagnostic Retest   307
ACTIVITY 23.13   Putting It All Together   307

24   **EDITING FOR OTHER PUNCTUATION   309**
24a   **Diagnostic Activity: Other Punctuation Marks   309**
ACTIVITY 24.1   How Much Do You Know?   309
24b   **Using Periods, Exclamation Points, and Question Marks to
End Sentences   310**
ACTIVITY 24.2   Using End Punctuation   310
24c   **Colons   311**
ACTIVITY 24.3   Editing for Use of Colons   313
ACTIVITY 24.4   Writing Sentences Using Colons   314
24d   **Ellipses   314**
ACTIVITY 24.5   Using Ellipses   316
24e   **Parentheses   316**
24f   **Dashes   317**
24g   **Brackets   317**
24h   **Slashes   318**
ACTIVITY 24.6   Using Parentheses, Dashes, Brackets, and Slashes   318
24i   **Other Punctuation: Comprehensive Check   319**
ACTIVITY 24.7   Diagnostic Retest   319
ACTIVITY 24.8   Putting It All Together   319

25   **MECHANICS   322**
25a   **Diagnostic Activity: Mechanics   322**
ACTIVITY 25.1   How Much Do You Know?   322

25b   Capitalization   323
   ACTIVITY 25.2   Editing Sentences for Capitalization   326
   ACTIVITY 25.3   Writing Sentences with Capitalized Words   326
   ACTIVITY 25.4   Using Capitals   327
25c   Abbreviations and Acronyms   327
   ACTIVITY 25.5   Using Abbreviations and Acronyms   330
25d   Italics   330
   ACTIVITY 25.6   Using Italics   332
25e   Hyphens   332
   ACTIVITY 25.7   Using Hyphens to Divide Words at the End of a
                   Line   334
   ACTIVITY 25.8   Using Hyphens   334
25f   Numbers   335
   ACTIVITY 25.9   Using Numbers   336
25g   Mechanics: Comprehensive Check   336
   ACTIVITY 25.10   Diagnostic Retest   336
   ACTIVITY 25.11   Putting It All Together   337

26   SPELLING   338
26a   Diagnostic Activity: Spelling   338
   ACTIVITY 26.1   How Much Do You Know?   338
26b   Pronunciation and Spelling   338
26c   Words Commonly Misspelled or Confused   340
   ACTIVITY 26.2   Editing for Commonly Misspelled Words   345
   ACTIVITY 26.3   Using Homonyms and Near Homonyms Correctly   346
   ACTIVITY 26.4   Writing Sentences with Homonyms or Near
                   Homonyms   347
26d   Spelling Rules   347
   ACTIVITY 26.5   Using Spelling Rules   349
26e   Strategies for Improving Spelling   349
26f   American versus British Spelling   351
**26g   How to Find Words in a Dictionary When You Don't Know
         How to Spell Them   351**
26h   Using Computer Spelling Checkers   352
   ACTIVITY 26.6   Checking Up on the Spelling Checker   352
26i   Spelling: Comprehensive Check   353
   ACTIVITY 26.7   Diagnostic Retest   353

PART VI   Writing a Research Paper   355
**27   USING AND DOCUMENTING MATERIAL FOR A
         RESEARCH PAPER   357**
27a   Review: Writing a Research Paper   357
   ACTIVITY 27.1   What Is a Research Paper?   357

27b   **Using Information from Other Sources in Your Paper**   **358**

ACTIVITY 27.2   Distinguishing between Direct Quotations and
                               Paraphrases   358

27c   **Deciding What Needs to Be Documented in Your Paper**   **359**

ACTIVITY 27.3   Deciding What Information Needs to Be
                               Documented   359

27d   **Paraphrasing**   **361**

ACTIVITY 27.4   Recognizing Techniques for Paraphrasing   361

ACTIVITY 27.5   Recognizing Acceptable and Unacceptable Paraphrases
                               362

ACTIVITY 27.6   Writing Paraphrases   364

27e   **Documenting Sources in a Text**   **364**

ACTIVITY 27.7   Using In-Text Citations   366

27f   **The List of Works Cited**   **368**

ACTIVITY 27.8   Writing References for the Works Cited List   369

27g   **Manuscript Preparation**   **370**

Answer Key   *371*
Credits   *443*
Index   *447*

PREFACE

The Writing Process: A Guide for ESL Students: A Workbook to Accompany The HarperCollins Concise Handbook for Writers is designed for advanced learners of English as a Second Language (ESL) enrolled in university degree programs or intensive English programs.

The text can be utilized in several ways. First, teachers can use it as a supplement to their composition courses by assigning individual chapters addressing areas that students may need to work on further. Teachers can also use this text as a primary resource for a writing or grammar class, with supplementary readings and classroom activities. Finally, students may use this text independently to work on areas in writing or grammar where they need more practice.

Like the handbook, the workbook's philosophy is based on the idea that writing is a recursive process. Writers do not move linearly from point A to point B, but instead weave back and forth between the stages of planning, drafting, and revising. The workbook encourages students to examine their own writing process and to develop new skills that may improve their strategies for the various stages of writing. It also provides thorough coverage of two areas of writing that are particularly difficult but very important for ESL students: revision and editing (helping the students recognize errors in their own and others' writing), and avoiding plagiarism through techniques of documentation.

The points of grammar included in this text originated in an extensive survey I conducted to determine errors that advanced ESL students make in their writing. Most chapters begin with a diagnostic activity to help students focus on their specific problems with the points of grammar covered. The students are then encouraged to retake the diagnostic at the end of the chapter to check their progress and see what they still need to work on.

As in *The HarperCollins Concise Handbook for Writers,* the discussions and activities are presented primarily in an inductive format, which encourages students to generate *themselves* how or why a particular form is used. This "active" discovery helps students retain the information more easily. However, I have also included activities that require simple manipulation of the form, without any relation to meaning. These activities are important because they ensure that students understand the rules, which will help increase writing accuracy.

I have used authentic materials wherever possible, although some of these passages have had to be adapted slightly, and some are more difficult or more interesting than others. Despite these drawbacks, I feel it is essential that ESL students at this level see how English is used in the "real" world.

Many people were instrumental in helping this project get through the various stages of planning, drafting, and revising, and I would like to express my sincere appreciation. First, this text never would have happened without Peter Adams, author of *The HarperCollins Concise Handbook for Writers,* who had this great idea in the first place, and Jane Kinney, the acquisitions editor at HarperCollins, who coordinated the search for an ESL specialist to work on the project. Carla Samodulski, the developmental editor, was invaluable in her fantastic, detailed, and incredibly efficient feedback. Laurie Connole also provided insightful comments on the manuscript. The revision process, a most important step, was possible only with the help of the following reviewers: Gwen Bindas, Northeastern University; Ellen Bitterman, State University of New York, New Paltz; Jacqueline George, Seattle Central College; Christine Jensen, University of Kansas; Mary McGann, University of Indianapolis; Bill Newmiller, United States Air Force Academy; Nancy Rosen, Broward Community College; Robert Rubin, Wright State University; and Mara Ann Thorson, University of Arizona. The project editor Ellen MacElree and the rest of the staff at HarperCollins deserve special thanks as well.

Three people deserve particular mention for their contributions to the book. Cheryl Delk and Sharon Cavusgil both helped me cowrite four chapters in the text, and Larry Kuiper helped prepare the answer key with his witty responses, which sometimes, unfortunately, had to be edited. I'd also like to thank my parents, "the gang" (Tom, India, John, Sabine, Stefan, Cheryl, and Wayne), and Sue Gass for their incredible support. Finally, I want to thank my sister Laura, Lotte Marcus, and Kathi Bailey, who convinced me I could.

AMY TICKLE

THE WRITING PROCESS

A Guide for ESL Students

THE WRITING PROCESS

1 Writing Processes

2 Planning: The Writing Context

3 Drafting and Revising

WRITING PROCESSES

I don't know what the movie will be before I sit down. Certainly I have certain ideas in my mind. I have ideas about the whole paper but not the pictures to describe my ideas. I discover these pictures while I am writing.

ESL student in V. Zamel, "The Composing Processes of
Advanced ESL Students"

When we think of past writing experiences in academic settings in our first language (L1) and our second language (L2), most of us can recall the marks on our papers and not having a clear idea about why we received these marks or what to do differently the next time. In other words, the emphasis was primarily on the end product. Writing teachers are now developing new ideas for teaching students how to write. The most important change has been the focus on understanding *how* we write and not just *what* we write. In other words, it will help our writing ability if we think about not only the product of writing but also the process of getting to the end result.

Notice that the title of this chapter is plural. That's because there are many successful writing processes. Good writers do not all use the same process; in fact, good writers often follow different writing processes when they are involved in different writing tasks. The best way to go about a particular writing task depends on both the task and the writer.

To understand your writing process better, it is important to become aware of why you write, the differences between writing in your first and second languages, and how you reach the final written product.

1a WHY YOU WRITE

ACTIVITY 1.1 Writing Situations

Make a list of all the situations in which you write. Two examples are provided.

> Filling in a a job application
> Writing a note to a friend

As you can see, you use writing for many different purposes and vary your writing depending on who or what you are writing for. All of these situations, however, have one thing in common, the reason for writing things down: to communicate.

Writing Is Communication

This is perhaps the most important idea to keep in mind when you are writing in any situation. It is easy to lose sight of this detail when you are pressured to turn in a paper for a grade.

Another important way to communicate is through speaking. These two forms of communication have similarities and differences that are important to remember.

ACTIVITY

1.2 | Differences between Speaking and Writing

Think about each of the following statements. After each statement, indicate whether it is true for speaking ("S"), writing ("W"), or both ("B").

1. A permanent record of the communication remains. _____

2. The idea can be changed if the original message is unclear. _____

3. The idea can be changed before the audience receives the message. _____

4. Immediate feedback indicates that the message has been received. _____

5. A message is communicated. _____

6. More formal language is *usually* used. _____

7. Incomplete sentences are *usually* acceptable. _____

1b WRITING IN DIFFERENT LANGUAGES

ACTIVITY

1.3 | Is Writing in English Different?

Write a paragraph in English describing any animal that you know about. Then write about the same animal in your *native* language. When you are finished, rate the various aspects of the two writing experiences on the chart, using the following scale: 1 = excellent, 2 = very good, 3 = good, 4 = fair, 5 = poor. Compare your ratings.

	NATIVE LANGUAGE	ENGLISH
Comfort	_____	_____
Quality of content (interest, relevance)	_____	_____
Organization	_____	_____
Vocabulary	_____	_____
Grammar	_____	_____
Punctuation	_____	_____
Spelling	_____	_____

What are your writing problems in your first language? In your second language? Most people tend to rate their vocabulary and sentence-level matters (grammar, punctuation, and spelling) lower in English than in their native language. Is this true for you? If so, this lower rating might be due to the emphasis that was placed on these aspects when you were being taught written English. Some writing teachers think that these areas are the only written differences between languages. However, that is not true. Writing in English is different at all levels from writing in other languages. As a result, many ESL students have not recognized the importance of larger issues such as content and organization.

In some senses, therefore, it is necessary to "start from scratch" when writing in English. For example, if you always put the introduction on the second page of a paper in your country, you will have to realize that that might not be appropriate when writing a paper in English. In fact, research has shown that your native language may actually inhibit your ability to write in English!

One area of writing in your first language that you should *not* ignore when writing in English is your composing process. We will look at this next.

1c HOW WRITERS WRITE

ACTIVITY
1.4   **Identifying and Evaluating Your Composing Process**

Whether you are a beginner or an expert writer, you have developed your own composing process (how you go about writing) both in your first language and in English. In this activity, you will describe that process and evaluate it.

Imagine that in your composition class, you have just been given an assignment to write a research paper. What process do you go through, from start to finish? Consider questions 1 through 4. Then, on a separate sheet of paper, write a few paragraphs about your composing process in your first language and in English.

1. What do you do first? (go to the library, make notes, think, begin writing a draft, talk to other people, etc.)
2. What do you do when you begin writing? (write the entire paper before any revision, revise after every sentence, revise after every paragraph, revise after every page or couple of pages, etc.)
3. If you revise, how many times do you reread your paper? (once or twice, several times, etc.)
4. When do you revise your paper for content? For organization? For grammar and spelling?

When you have finished writing, answer question 5.

5. How is your writing process in English similar to or different from that in your first language?

For some writers, their composing process may be completely different in their L1 and L2; for others, it might be just the same. Studies show that successful composing strategies in your L1 can be applied to help your L2 writing. For example, if you are effective at planning and revising in your L1, you will probably be successful at these in your L2. If you feel that your writing is successful in your L1, see that you use the same process in your L2. If you aren't producing effective writing even in your L1, you might consider some different approaches.

Examine the following summary of the writing process. Then compare your writing process with that of the experts.

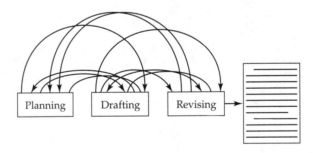

Writers engage in three different activities, but *not* in three discrete steps. Instead, we weave back and forth among the three activities in a fairly unpredictable order, doing whatever seems to need doing at a particular point. At first glance, it would seem that the process by which we write is so irregular that there is nothing to be taught to beginning writers. But research has revealed some interesting patterns.

Research into both L1 writing and L2 writing has turned up three principal differences between expert and beginning writers. First, researchers discovered that different writers devote different percentages of time to planning, drafting, and revising. When researchers added up the *total* amount of time spent in each of the three activities, they found that expert writers spent considerably more time in planning and revising than beginners did. Second, expert writers do very little editing of grammar, punctuation, and spelling until they have almost finished writing. While drafting and making initial revisions, they work on sharpening their focus, improving their organization, gauging their audience, and developing support for their argument. Finally, beginners tend to limit their revising to editing for errors in grammar, punctuation, and spelling; experts do this and much more. They revise by changing the tone of their writing, tightening the focus, clarifying the organization, and adding support for their arguments.

How does your writing process compare with that of experts?

_____

_____

_____

_____

Again, if your composing process is different from that of the experts, you might try to go about writing in a different way. A good first step would be to spend more time planning your writing. Chapter 2 will give you some useful strategies for planning your papers.

 **PLANNING: THE WRITING CONTEXT**

At the beginning, I have some order in my mind, but I don't really know what's going to happen.

ESL student in V. Zamel, "The Composing Processes of
Advanced ESL Students"

Planning does not necessarily involve writing anything down. In fact, planning often involves *thinking* rather than writing. Spend some time before you begin any writing project thinking about the writing context—**the assignment, the choice of topic, the purpose of your writing, and the audience.**

2a THE ASSIGNMENT

It is important that you understand exactly what an assignment requires. Things to consider include these:

- **Topic.** Does the topic you chose match the assignment? It is worthwhile to ask your teacher if the topic you have selected is appropriate.
- **Length.** If the teacher has not designated the length, ask how long your paper should be. If there is a designated length, find out how flexible the teacher is willing to be about it.
- **Due date.** What is your teacher's policy on late papers, if they are allowed at all?
- **Task.** Often the assignment will include words like *compare, explain, analyze, describe,* or *define.* Pay attention to these words. If the assignment asks you to describe a spider and instead you define one, you may not do well.

2b DECIDING ON A TOPIC

A good topic has the following characteristics:

- It satisfies the assignment.
- It is something you find interesting to write about.
- It is something you know enough about or can find out enough about to write a paper of the required length.
- It is not too broad for the length specified.
- It is not too narrow to write a significant paper about.
- It is not a subject that has been discussed so many times that you will be unlikely to say anything that your audience hasn't heard before.

NARROWING A TOPIC

Invention Techniques

Imagine that you have been asked to submit a ten-page paper on any environmental problem. After visiting the library and talking with a friend in the biology department on campus, you decide that you are interested in learning more about acid rain. But how do you get started? You could easily write a thirty-page paper on acid rain!

A number of "invention techniques" may help you either find a good topic with suitable characteristics or narrow down a topic that you have already chosen. Try some of these out. You will probably find that some of them work better for you than others, especially for certain kinds of writing. Remember there is no "right" way to narrow your focus. It is important to choose a process that works for you.

Brainstorming. Let your brain just come out with ideas like a volcano. Write them down in any form that makes sense; a list is probably the easiest form. You are aiming for quantity and creativity. Don't censor. Don't worry about whether you spell something wrong. Just get those ideas down as fast as possible. When you run out of ideas, don't stop. Force yourself to think harder. Sometimes the best ideas are the ones that come after you've listed all the obvious ones. Because you are trying to get as much information down as quickly as you can, you should try to write quick words and phrases rather than complete sentences.

The following is what a student wrote on acid rain during a five-minute brainstorming session.

Acid Rain

odor   long time   short time
taste
comes from   to man   industrial
effect   animal   cost
dangerous   plant
protection   environment
chemical components   etc.
Who found?   sex, lake
What part of the world?
How to measure severity?
treatment
whose responsibility?   Government?
                    international problem

ACTIVITY
2.1   **Using Brainstorming to Narrow a Topic**

Once you have a list of brainstormed ideas like the one on acid rain, you can use it to help narrow your focus. Review the brainstorming on acid rain. What are some possible topics this student could write about? Which ideas in this list relate to that topic? An example is provided below.

TOPIC	RELATED IDEA
Solutions to acid rain	Protection, treatment, responsibility — government, international problem

Freewriting. Freewriting is writing without rules, without constraints, without even a goal. Instead, put your pen to the paper and write everything that comes to your mind. Of course, you don't worry about spelling or punctuation or even making sense. You just write whatever occurs to you. The only restraint is to write freely without stopping, without correcting, just writing whatever occurs to you. Some people feel it helps to establish a time limit—perhaps five minutes—during which time you must keep writing without pause. Do not lift your pen from the paper. If you cannot think of anything, write, "I can't think of anything."

If you are freewriting on the computer, you might want to try a trick. Get everything ready to begin freewriting, with the cursor right where you want it. Then turn the *screen* (not the computer) off and start typing. You won't be able to edit your writing because you won't be able to see it. After your five or ten minutes are up, you can turn your screen back on and edit what you have written.

The following example of freewriting was written in a five-minute time period on the subject of overpopulation. Can you find any topics in this freewriting to write about?

Like ~~Main~~ Chia, overpopulation enforces the
                                              rule
government to make ~~rule~~ the ~~policy~~ of "one baby"
policy. People who want ~~girl~~ boy will kill the girl
baby in order to have chace to born another baby.

~~I~~ Overpopulation make the country crowded
and it's a big burden to rearrange natural resources
to so many people. Usually, the country which have
the overpopulation problem is associated with war,
hungry, poor, and ~~no~~ dirty.

Journalistic Questions. To gather ideas for a story, journalists often ask the following questions: who, what, when, where, why, and how? The following example shows a writer's response to journalistic questions on American Expatriot Writers.

American Expatriate Writers

Who: Ernest Hemingway
F. Scott Fitzgerald

What: Left America during World War II
Wrote about people and their problems
Simple style
The Sun Also Rises
A Farewell to Arms
Tender Is the Night
The Great Gatsby
Characters drank a lot and were depressed
Escapism

When: Early 1920s

Where: Paris (France), Spain

Why: Did not like American ideas during the war.
Wanted to escape what they didn't like by moving and by drinking.

How: Authors moved at different times;
wrote in a simple style

Cubing. In the cubing process, you take your subject and do the following:

1. *Describe:* What does it feel, look, smell, taste, and sound like?
2. *Compare:* What is it similar to or different from?
3. *Associate:* What is it associated with?
4. *Analyze:* What is it made of, and can it be broken down?
5. *Apply:* How can it be used?
6. *Argue:* Are you for or against it and why?

You will end up with six "sides" of information about your subject. Decide which side would make an interesting topic for a paper.

Second Language Learning

Describe-

SLL isn't something you can touch, see, etc., but it's a great feeling (in my opinion) to "hear" someone attempt to speak a foreign language.

Compare-

-similiar to learning any new skill — riding a bike becomes much easier the more you do it, and after a while, you don't even think about it anymore unless you drive over new terrain and then you think more about it.

Associate-

-frustration for a while

-feeling of success when you say something and people respond so well to you.

Analyze-

-composed of different learning processes.

-composed by taking all different parts of your learning.

-part of the whole culture, and when you've done it well, you feel part of the culture.

Apply-

-used to communicate, to understand the culture, and to understand the literature, music, art, and people.

Argue-

-everyone should learn a new second language because of its importance in mutual understanding, and we also understand our own language better.

Mapping. Mapping is a highly visual technique that leads you to think about many different aspects of a topic. To start mapping, write your subject in the center of a blank piece of paper and draw a circle around it. Then think of the main subideas that make up or support your subject; write those around the subject, draw circles around them, and draw lines connecting them to the subject. Continue in this fashion until you have a rich diagram of the topic you intend to write about. The following illustrates a mapping diagram:

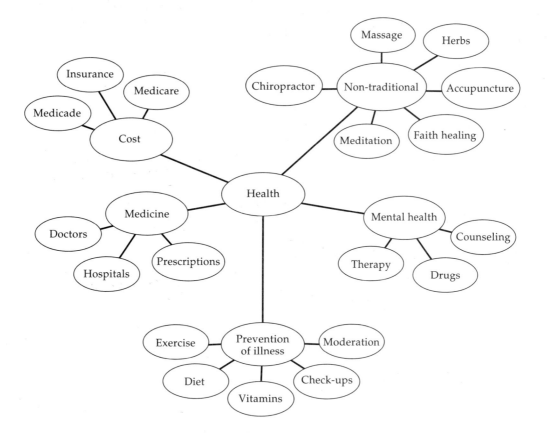

Such a diagram of your ideas can serve as a map when you begin to write. It allows you to see relationships between ideas and helps you narrow your focus.

Working Outline. The working outline provides a framework to identify the main ideas and supporting details of your paper. It provides an overall view of your paper, letting you see where to add more information or how ideas are tied together. The outline is tentative—as you move along in the writing process, your ideas may change, and you will add and delete information.

To make a working outline, proceed as follows:

1. Write your purpose and audience at the top of the paper.
2. Write the main idea of your paper.
3. Write a tentative introduction and thesis for your paper.
4. Write supporting ideas and details you will use.
5. Write a tentative conclusion.

Purpose: To tell about the differences between Japanese and American culture, and teach Jap. + Am. so they can understand each other better.

Audience: Americans who are not so familiar with Japanese culture and Japanese who are not so familiar with American culture and anyone who might be interested.

Introduction:

> In recent decades, there have been more interactions between cultures. In particular, Japanese + American cultures are facing each other more and more. These groups of people should learn about the differences in their culture to improve relations.

> Personality?
> Group vs. individual

> Work-
> Top-down vs. bottom-up management
> lifetime employment

> Society-
> Religion
> Family

Conclusion:

> Understanding cultural differences will improve relationships and harmony among Japanese + Americans.

ACTIVITY 2.2 **Practice with Invention Techniques**

Use one or two invention techniques to discover more about a topic. You can choose a topic from the list below or write about a different topic that interests you.

Nuclear power	Gun control	Slavery
Terrorism	Communism	Prayer in schools
Psychic healing	Immigration quotas	Medical insurance

Keeping a Journal. You may find yourself writing in a journal for several different reasons. Often writing teachers ask students to write in journals to build fluency and confidence in writing and to maintain communication between student and teacher. Writing in journals will also assist you in the writing process if you write down good ideas that occur to you as you read, as you fall asleep at night, as you talk with others, as you listen to the news on television, or at any other time when you are likely to come up with interesting ideas. You can also use a journal to practice invention techniques or to keep records of articles related to the topic of a paper you are working on.

The following page is an example of a journal entry. The grammar has not been corrected.

The Old Japanese Professor

It was the Sunday morning when I happen to meet that old Japanese professor. I was eating breakfast at that time when the old man in the deck of Owen cafeteria. I saw him taking a couple of picture of east wing of dormitory with a smile on his face. After a little while, he turned his face to me and asked me "are you a student at MSU?" I answered to him "Yes sir I am MBA student from Korea." Then he shared my table. Introduce himself to me that he was a MSU student exactly thirty years ago and he lived east wing of Owen for two years. In addition, he showed me a really old student ID and meal card which are issued thirty years ago by MSU. He looks very happy to come back to Michigan even though it is probably short to enjoy the old memories.

He told me he was teaching the food engineering in Tokyo University in Japan and he was really proud of being an alumnus of MSU. I hoped I can be happy as much as the old man has after thirty years from graduation.

2d PURPOSE

Once you have identified a topic, you must discover your reason for writing about it—the purpose of your essay. In other words, when readers are finished with your paper, what do you want them to do with the information?

There are several purposes for writing, and often one piece of writing will have several purposes. For example, a student's primary purpose may be to answer a question about the laws concerning gambling. The student may find, however, that another purpose develops during the writing process. As a result of research, the student decides to convince readers that gambling should be outlawed everywhere.

ACTIVITY
2.3

Understanding Different Purposes

Match each paragraph to its most probable purpose. Write the letter indicating the purpose in the blank at the start of the paragraph.

Purpose

a. To **express feeling** through writing in a diary, a journal, or a letter.
b. To **entertain** through such writing as poetry, songs, or humor.
c. To **show similarities or differences** through **comparison.**
d. To **define** or to **describe.**
e. To **explain a process.**
f. To **persuade** or attempt to change the opinion of the reader or urge to action through editorials, political slogans, or propaganda.

_a_ 1. Last year, I went to a certain piano concert that was given by a girl who is now drawing the world's attention because she is giving concerts at the age of only twelve. She made herself famous in Japan through mass media. That is why the concert cost almost $40. But as soon as the performance began, I became disappointed and felt like leaving because I found she was just a twelve-year-old girl, not a genuine pianist. [Masaya Yoshimoto, Japan]

_d_ 2. Biomechanics is a field of science that describes the motion undergone by the various body segments and the forces acting on these body parts during normal daily activities. [Hai Gu, China]

_f_ 3. Alcohol-related crashes are the leading cause of death for young Americans between sixteen and twenty-four years of age. On the average, approximately three Americans are killed and eighty are injured by drunk drivers every hour of every day. It is clear that society needs stricter laws and more education dealing with drunk driving. [Ronnie Hsu, Taiwan]

_e_ 4. The acceleration of an electric vehicle follows a very simple procedure. When the driver accelerates, the battery's direct current goes to the inverter, where it is converted into three separate alternating current sources with distinct frequencies. The alternating current is used by the vehicle's electric motors to move the wheels of the car. [Hans Schneewind, Ecuador]

_c_ 5. My new puppy is very much like the dog I used to own named Shane. They both have white paws and a white spot on their noses, and they are both golden in color. My puppy also likes to chase the ball like Shane did. Fortunately, Kira doesn't like to chew things like Shane did, but she definitely needs more attention.

_b_ 6. Was there ever a more wonderful wedding? Marge said we made her believe in romance again. But whatever possessed us to go on this transformational wilderness backpacking retreat? It was a package deal— promising higher consciousness and body awareness through mountain climbing and transcendental trout fishing. Money back guaranteed; the brochure said we would find ourselves. Not only did we *not* find *ourselves*, we lost contact with the rest of the group and spent our wedding night in the woods sleeping on a bed of leaves that turned out to be poison ivy. [Jane Wagner, *The Search for Signs of Intelligent Life in the Universe*]

Remember that you may discover your purpose as you move along in the writing process, or you may find that your original purpose will change. Be flexible and allow your purpose to develop naturally. It is very unusual for writers to know what they are going to say before they begin writing!

2e AUDIENCE

Now that you have something to say (your topic) and a reason to say it (your purpose), you must have someone to say it to—your audience. Most likely in college your audience will be your teacher. However, you will face many different writing situations in your life, and it is important to consider the audience to communicate your message effectively. Perhaps you could ask your teacher to serve as a different "specified" audience.

Once you have identified your audience, you will need to adapt your writing style to match your readers' expectations and knowledge level. Your writing style will depend on who your readers are, what they already know, and your relationship to them.

ACTIVITY 2.4 Writing with a Similar Purpose for Different Audiences

A.   Read both of the following business memos. Fill in the purpose, which is the same for both memos, and the audience, which is different.

DATE: April 23

TO: _____ (audience)

FROM: Tom Bird

SUBJECT: _____ (purpose)

I would like to ask your opinion of my suggested itinerary for Stefan Hannuschke's visit from Germany. He will be met at the airport in the company limousine by two of our finest sales-people, Mr. Donald Busman and Ms. Krystyna Rumisek. They will escort him to lunch at the club and then bring him at 2:00 to your office, where we can meet to discuss the proposal. Please let me know if these arrangements are suitable.

DATE: 4/23

TO: _____ (audience)

FROM: Tom

SUBJECT: _____ (purpose)

Hannuschke's plane arrives at 11:00 a.m. on Monday. Meet him in the company limo. Take him to the club for lunch (make sure it goes on our tab) and then bring him to Mr. Rodini's of-fice, where the three of us—Rodini, Hannuschke, and I—will meet to discuss the proposal.

Underline the writing differences in these memos.

B.   Now read the following two pieces of writing by a student named Tasanee Puttaporn. The first piece is an in-class essay in response to the assignment *"Convince someone to study abroad."*

In the coming decades, the world will become a global village. Studying abroad will be a tremendous asset to any individuals to promote their language and cultural understanding and to understand themselves.

Studying abroad will obviously help to increase your language ability in the language of the country. It is important, however, that the individual create opportunities to speak and interact in that language, instead of finding fellow foreigners to spend time with. Going to movies, joining a club, and living with a native roommate will all help increase language ability.

A second important reason for studying abroad is to promote cultural understanding both of the individuals' country and the country they are visiting. It is often necessary to experience a different culture before one can truly understand one's own. Reading books and watching films in your native country will certainly enhance your knowledge, but to really understand another culture, one must live there.

Finally, an experience studying abroad will help people understand themselves better. In particular, they will learn how well they can adapt to challenging and difficult situations and how tolerant they are at accepting differences.

In conclusion, an opportunity to study abroad is one of the richest experiences a person can have.

The following is a letter from Tasanee intended to convince her sister to study in the United States.

Things here are going well at college, but I have to be honest and admit that they certainly can be frustrating at times! I really think you should come and study here. You will get so much better at speaking English. I can't believe how quickly I am picking it up, compared to studying at home. I joined a drama club and am really trying to hang around with Americans. I think that is why my English is improving so much. It's also amazing what you'll learn about our culture and the American culture. I had no idea how open and expressive Americans are compared to our culture, and it's really made me think how restricted things are at home. I'm really starting to understand myself better since coming to the USA. I used to think I was so easygoing, but I'm finding out that I don't do well when things don't go exactly my way. It gets so frustrating trying to do something simple like wash my clothes. But all in all, I wouldn't trade this experience for anything. I really think you should come!

Love,
Tasanee

Both of Tasanee's pieces of writing have the same purpose. How are they different? Fill in the chart using examples or descriptions. One comparison has been provided already.

Differences in Writing	Essay	Letter
Content (details, examples)		
Organization		
Sentence structure		
Word choice	*"increase your language ability"*	*"get so much better at speaking English"*
Use of pronouns		
Other differences (if any)		

ACTIVITY

2.5   **Applying the Concepts of Purpose and Audience to Writing**

A.   Pick a favorite type of candy, and write an advertisement for it, targeting the following audiences:

Children   Teenagers

Couples in their twenties and thirties   Grandparents

B.   Imagine that you are studying at a college in your native country. You read an advertisement that describes a travel grant for a program to study abroad. Write a statement of purpose to the organization explaining why you want to go abroad and why it should choose you. Then write a letter to your parents convincing them to allow you to go.

1. Your audiences: _____

2. Your purpose: _____

C.   When you have finished, compare the writing you did for part A and then part B for similarities and differences, using charts like the one in Activity 2.4.

2f   COLLECTING INFORMATION

Once you have identified your topic, you need to begin collecting information on which to base a first draft. Chapter 45c in *The HarperCollins Concise Handbook for Writers* discusses in detail how to use the library; however, don't be limited to this source of information. You can gather information for your paper from many different places and people.

In general, information is of two types, primary and secondary. **Primary information** consists of raw data that are collected by the writer. **Secondary information** is someone else's analysis and interpretation of data from primary sources.

ACTIVITY
2.6   Differentiating between Primary and Secondary Sources

A.   Look at the following list of information sources. Put a "P" next to the item that is a primary source or an "S" if it is a secondary source.

1. A brochure from a government agency on AIDS _____

2. An interview with a man who lived in a concentration camp _____

3. An article in the newspaper about President Clinton _____

4. A questionnaire on nutrition that you develop and analyze _____

5. A visit to Costa Rica to write about rain forests _____

6. A scholarly journal on learning a second language _____

B.   List other primary and secondary sources that will help you write your paper.

DRAFTING AND REVISING

The first draft is for getting the ideas down. The second is for finding the way to say it the way I want. . . . I enjoy the first draft because I don't have to worry about correct grammar and vocabulary.

I get angry at myself when I cross out an entire paragraph after spending so much time on it, but I know I have to do it if it doesn't make sense.

ESL students in V. Zamel, "The Composing Processes of
Advanced ESL Students"

3a THE DRAFTING PROCESS

Understanding Drafting

Quickly scan the following text about drafting. Choose the main idea of each section from the list, and write it in the blank at the beginning of each paragraph. Finally, reread the text carefully for detail.

> Keeping the plan in mind
> Definition of drafting
> Drafting on the computer
> Postponing editing

1._____

Drafting implies that later you will go back and revise what you have drafted. It is this idea that what you are doing is "just getting your thoughts down on paper" that we want you to keep in mind while drafting. When drafting a piece of writing, you should try to keep in mind the tentative nature of what you are doing. Unless you have put this writing off too long, there will be plenty of time later to revise what you have written. So the important thing at the drafting stage is to get your ideas down on paper.

2._____

It is important while drafting to remind yourself occasionally of the writing context: the assignment, the subject, the purpose, and the audience. While writing, if you periodically think back over this context, your writing is less likely to wander into areas outside those defined by the context.

On the other hand, you may find as you draft that you change your mind about some elements of the context. You might change the thesis or the audience or the purpose of the writing. It is unlikely that you will have the latitude to change the assignment, but if you have been given several options to write about, you might find yourself switching from one to another. Changing your mind about any of this is fine; in fact, that's the kind of fluidity that produces good writing. But you should make these changes deliberately and not accidentally; otherwise, the results may be confusing to your reader.

In addition, if you have completed some of the planning techniques suggested in Chapter 2 before you started drafting, make use of that plan, whether it is an outline, a mapping diagram, a brainstormed list, some freewriting, or a particular organizational mode, to guide your drafting. But *guide* is the important word here: you should not feel obligated to stick with your original plan; in fact, you will undoubtedly modify it as you write. Keeping it nearby to *guide* you as you write your first draft is a good idea, however.

3._____

Have you ever tried to pat your stomach and rub your head at the same time? Either of these actions is fairly easy by itself, but most people have difficulty doing both at once. The human mind seems to do a better job if it can focus on one task at a time. This is just as true of writing as it is of patting and rubbing. Your mind will work more effectively if you can structure your writing process so that you are not trying to do more than one task at the same time.

When drafting, you are trying to get ideas into words and down on paper in a coherent order; that's a lot. If on top of that you attempt to worry about the thousands of intricacies of English grammar, punctuation, and spelling, you are unlikely to do either task well. For this reason, you will produce better writing if you postpone concern about errors until you've gotten at least a first draft down on paper. Errors in grammar, punctuation, and spelling are important, of course, but you will do a better job of eliminating them if you work on them after you've gotten your ideas down on paper. In addition, time spent in correcting surface errors at the early stages of drafting may be wasted because you may rewrite completely as you revise.

4._____

One of the major reasons we recommend that you try to do your writing on a computer is that the fluidity of the computer environment—the ease with which things can be changed—encourages the attitude toward drafting that we have been discussing in this chapter. If you know that you can later make changes easily, you are probably going to be much more willing to write paragraphs with the kind of openness and experimentation that leads to creativity. If you can change the wording of a sentence just by typing over it, you are going to be more experimental in the wording you try out as you write.

Some writers even find themselves trying out several ways of saying the same thing when they write on a computer. Then they can look at the different versions and eliminate all but the most effective.

The next section gives an example of a draft and shows how to revise it.

3b REVISION AND EDITING OVERVIEW

ACTIVITY
3.2 What Are Revision and Editing?

Decide if the following questions about revising are true or false. (In the blank, write "T" for true or "F" for false.) Then quickly scan the reading that follows to see if your answers are correct.

1. You should revise your paper only once. _____

2. It is best to revise your paper for large-scale revision first. _____

3. The best time to revise your paper is immediately after you have written it. _____

4. Small-scale revision involves revising for organization. _____

Revision

Sometimes beginning writers think of revising as nothing more than reading a paper over and correcting any errors they find. We're using the term to describe a much more complex activity, one that usually involves reading a paper over several times, looking for a different set of problems with each reading.

Revision can be divided into two types of activities. During **large-scale revision,** you worry about the big picture—the overall organization, focus, and development of your argument. You should always begin with large-scale revision, as it is likely that your paper will change as it develops. Imagine how frustrating it would be to take the time to correct a section of your paper for grammatical errors, only to decide later that the section doesn't contain enough relevant or interesting information. Only during **small-scale revision,** sometimes called **editing** or **proofreading,** should you pay attention to the details as you improve the wording and the correctness of the paper.

When you revise your paper, it is best to wait some time after you have written it before trying to make any changes. This means that you have to allow yourself plenty of time to work on a paper—you can't wait a day or two between drafts if you start your paper the night before!

3c LARGE-SCALE AND SMALL-SCALE REVISION

Read through the following guidelines for large-scale and small-scale revision. Refer to these guidelines often as you draft your papers.

Large-scale Revision

Content. Is the content interesting? Thoughtful? Or have you merely repeated arguments everyone is familiar with?

Purpose. Will the paper accomplish the purpose you intend? Have you changed your mind about the purpose since you began drafting? If so, has that change caused any inconsistencies in the paper? Is the purpose clear to the reader? Is it clear what the reader should do or think after reading the paper?

Audience. Is the paper appropriate for the audience that will read it? Is the voice too formal and stuffy? Is it too informal and personal? Is the voice too brief and businesslike? How about the technical aspects of the paper? Have you used terminology that your audience won't understand? Have you explained concepts that your readers may not be familiar with? Have you explained too much? Have you forgotten how knowledgeable your audience is about this subject?

Thesis and Unity. Does the paper have a single clear thesis? Is the thesis consistent throughout, or does it change somewhat from the beginning to the end of the paper? Does everything in the paper support the thesis? It is not enough that everything be about the *subject;* everything also should support the *thesis.*

Organization. What are the main points in your essay? Are they presented in a logical order? Would a different order be more effective? Is the amount of attention you devote to each point proportional to its importance in the paper? Do you have an effective introduction and conclusion?

Development of Ideas. Does each point in the essay have sufficient, relevant, and interesting supporting details to convince the intended audience? Are there places where additional concrete details or specific examples would make the paper more convincing or clearer?

Small-scale Revision

Word Choice. Are there places where the wording is awkward? Unclear? Wordy? Redundant? Vague? Unnecessarily abstract? Incorrect?

Grammar, Punctuation, and Mechanics. As a final step, review the paper for errors in grammar, punctuation, and mechanics. You may be aware of certain types of errors that you are particularly prone to make; if so, you may want to read the paper once again looking just for these.

ACTIVITY

3.3 ### Revising for Content, Purpose, and Audience

Up to this point in this workbook, you have learned how to choose and narrow a topic and determine the purpose and audience for your paper. These are large-scale revisions which usually involve adding, deleting, or moving text. In this activity, we will focus on revising papers for these concerns. In future chapters, you will learn how to revise for other features of the paper, such as thesis and unity, organization, and development of ideas.

This activity focuses on a paper written by Anders Nordin, a Swedish student. Anders was given an assignment to write a paper about any natural disaster. Having lived through the 1989 San Francisco earthquake, he knew immediately that he wanted to write about earthquakes. Anders began his writing process by going to the library to research his topic. He read through several books and articles and referred to the journal he kept after the earthquake.

A.   The following paper is Anders's first draft. At this stage in his writing, he wasn't completely sure of his focus, but he wanted to get his ideas on paper. Read Anders's essay about earthquakes, and answer the questions that follow it. (The grammar has been corrected to allow you to focus on the issues of topic, audience, and purpose.)

Earthquakes are very dangerous natural disasters because they occur suddenly and without warning. Once an earthquake begins, it usually builds to an intensity over ten to fifteen seconds, and there is little chance to escape or prepare adequately. Approximately ten thousand people die each year from this disaster.

Earthquakes are caused by movement of continental plates. There are four basic regions of earthquake occurrence. One is along the mid-ocean ridges. The second is along transform fault zones, such as the San Andreas Fault in California. This fault was involved in the earthquake in San Francisco in 1989, which measured 7.1 on the Richter scale. The third occurrence of earthquakes is shallow-focus earthquakes, which extend from the Himalayas to the Alps, and the fourth are deep-sea trenches and volcanic island arcs that surround the Pacific Ocean.

The primary effects of an earthquake are ground shaking, fault ruptures, the creation of tidal waves, and landslides. Secondary effects include falling debris from buildings and the ignition of fires from dislodged fuel and electrical systems. In the San Francisco earthquake, ground shaking caused the upper level of Interstate 880 to collapse onto the lower level, killing more than forty people. One girl was killed when a building fell on her in Santa Cruz. A fire was ignited in the Marina district in San Francisco that destroyed twelve apartment buildings. Living through the San Francisco earthquake was a very frightening experience.

In summary, earthquakes can cause a lot of damage and heartache because they occur so suddenly and without warning. Perhaps people should think twice about where they choose to live!

Purpose

1. What do you think is the purpose of this paper? In other words, what does the writer want the reader to know or do after finishing this paper?

You can never be exactly sure what the purpose of a first draft is, so it is helpful to ask the writer. Anders would tell you that his purpose was to discuss his experience in the San Francisco earthquake in order to convince people to think about whether they should live where earthquakes occur.

2. Now that you know the purpose, what suggestions do you have to help Anders make his purpose clearer? Be very specific about where he could add text, delete text, or move text.

Audience

Anders would also tell you that he wrote this paper to everyone who has never lived through an earthquake.

3. With this audience in mind, answer the following questions based on the revision guidelines: Is the paper appropriate for the intended audience? Why or why not? How about the technical aspects of the paper? Has Anders used terminology that his audience won't understand? Has he explained concepts that his readers may not be familiar with? Has he explained too much? Has he forgotten how knowledgeable his audience is about this subject? Be specific.

B.   Based on feedback from his teacher, Anders wrote a second draft. Read this draft carefully. Did he incorporate any of the changes you suggested?

Earthquakes are very dangerous natural disasters because they occur suddenly and without warning. Once an earthquake begins, it usually builds to an intensity over ten to fifteen seconds, and there is little chance to escape or prepare adequately. Approximately ten thousand people die each year from this disaster. Living through an earthquake can be a very frightening experience. People should think carefully about whether they want to live where earthquakes are common.

First, it is important to know where most earthquakes occur. There are four basic regions of earthquake activity.

One is along the mid-ocean ridges out in the middle of the ocean. The second is along transform fault zones--where one section of the earth's crust is sliding by another--such as the San Andreas Fault in California or the Anatolian Fault in northern Turkey. Shallow-focus earthquakes are the third type; they occur from the Himalayas to the Alps. These types of earthquakes are the most dangerous because they are the most numerous and release the greatest amount of energy. The last earthquake area is the deep-sea trenches and volcanic island arcs that surround the Pacific Ocean.

The effects of an earthquake can be very devastating. The primary effects are ground shaking, fault ruptures, the creation of tidal waves, and landslides. Secondary effects include falling debris from buildings and the ignition of fires from dislodged fuel and electrical systems. The intensity of the earthquake and its location will determine what kind of effect the earthquake will have.

On October 17, 1989, I experienced my first, and, I hope, last, earthquake in San Francisco, California. This earthquake was centered on the San Andreas Fault and measured 7.1 on the Richter scale. As with any earthquake, there was no warning, and although it lasted only fifteen seconds, it caused tremendous physical and emotional damage.

The primary effect of ground shaking caused the upper level of Interstate 880 to collapse onto the lower level, killing more than forty people. Secondary effects included people dying from falling building debris and a fire that was ignited in the Marina district in San Francisco, which destroyed twelve apartment buildings.

I was lucky in that nothing physically happened to me or my apartment, other than a few cracks in the wall. Emotionally, however, I will never be quite the same. After the earthquake stopped, there was total silence. Radios didn't work, traffic lights were out, and people were walking around in a daze, wondering if it was really over. Soon people ran to the grocery stores, which had merchandise all over the floors and no lights. Employees were allowing only a few people in at a time to avoid theft. Everyone was discussing what happened elsewhere. In

particular, I had relatives living to the north, and there were
rumors that the Bay Bridge had collapsed and downtown San
Francisco was destroyed. It was a long, long night, sitting by
candlelight, waiting to hear news of what really happened. I
realized that there were much bigger forces than myself.

   In summary, earthquakes can cause a lot of damage and
heartache because they occur so suddenly and without warning.
People should really consider where they choose to live, if they
don't want to wake to a shaking surprise.

1. What was deleted from the text?

2. What was added to the text?

3. What was moved within the text?

C.   Now that Anders seems to have a clear purpose and has adjusted his paper to his audience, he can consider the content of the paper.

1. Does all of the content relate to his purpose? Should anything be added or taken out?

2. Is the content interesting? Is there anything more that you would like to know after reading Anders's essay?

Once Anders has made sure that his content is relevant and interesting, his purpose is clear, and his audience has been considered, he is ready to begin looking at the other matters in the revision guidelines. These aspects of the paper will be discussed in later chapters.

3d PEER REVIEW

In a writing class, teachers will often have students read one another's papers and ask them to give feedback. This process is called **peer review** or **peer editing.**

Although a student may not be as knowledgeable as a teacher, peer review has many benefits. Most important, it lets you check with a real audience to see if your message is being communicated. You will also learn about different writing styles from reading other students' papers, and your own critical skills for analyzing writing will be developed. Finally, learning how to give and receive feedback is a process used by many people in the real world, and you may find it a tool that is extremely helpful to you.

There are many ways to approach peer review; the process will vary, depending on your teacher. Here we provide some general guidelines to use in any peer review session.

When you are asked to revise a peer's paper, keep in mind the order of things you should revise for. If the first step is not accomplished, there is no need to comment on the remaining steps; if the second step is not accomplished, do not comment on the third; and so on.

1. Does the paper identify a clear purpose and audience?
2. Does the content match the purpose and the audience? Is the content interesting?
3. Is the paper well organized? Is the material presented in a logical order? Do paragraphs have clear topic sentences and relevant, interesting, and sufficient supporting details? Dos the paper have an effective introduction and an effective conclusion?
4. Are there any grammatical problems? When checking for grammar, look first for any sentences that you cannot understand because of grammar problems and for any grammar errors that the student makes repeatedly.
5. Are there any problems with punctuation or mechanics?

ACTIVITY 3.4 Peer Review

A.   Read the following first draft about black mortality rates in the United States, written by Mowli Salehin Kamal from Bangladesh. Because this is a first draft, read only to see if the writer has identified a clear purpose and audience. The grammar has not been corrected.

```
     Death is a normal thing for every living creature.  Man is

not immortal.  In order to live long everybody need some facilities

such as health care, nutrition, hospital service.  Though the

United States has all the facilities still black mortality rate

is higher than any other developed nation.  It has been found

that mortality rate among blacks is twice that of whites.
```

Racism is a totally biological concept that promotes
the ordering of human variations. Humans are classified on
genetically determined anatomical and chemical features. The
modern fallacy that races differ genetically from the other is
not justified scientifically. God has created us in different
ways. All of us have different looks. But beneath our skin all
of us are same. To be racist is harmful to society.

Infant mortality in the United States during 1989 was the
lowest it has ever been, but it is still higher than in other
developed countries. In 1989, the infant mortality rate for
blacks was twice that of whites, and infant deaths among blacks
have decreased at a much slower rate than among whites. Between
1988 and 1989, the main causes of infant death were premature
birth and low birth weight, respiratory distress syndrome, and
complications associated with pregnancy. Black infants have over
twice the risk of dying in their first year of life compared to
white infants. Prematurity is the primary cause of newborn
deaths and illness, and poverty and unplanned pregnancies are
important causes of preterm births. Teenagers, unmarried black
women, and those receiving Medicaid are at greatest risk for
both poverty and unplanned pregnancy.

The leading cause of death among young black males is
homicide and "legal intervention"--in other words, being shot by
police officers. These two causes accounted for 98.9 per 100,000
deaths of black males aged 24 to 34 in 1987. For white males of
the same age, the rate was 13.2 per 100,000. The probability of
a black male being killed is 500 percent greater than for whites
their age.

The United States has the best health care system in the
world technologically but is lacking measurements of good health
care service. Services are not easily available, nor are health
care resources used efficiently. The United States spends 40
percent more than Canada for health care and much more than
England, though England's level of health care is equivalent of
the US. There is not distributional equity. A specific level of
health care is not available to all citizens.

High mortality rate for a nation is always bad. The white

people are using their powers over the black people. As a result,
the black people are being deprived from their rights. It is
always wise to find out the key reason of any problem. Because it
helps a person to solve the problem in a meaningful way.

You can respond to your peer in writing, verbally, or in both ways. The two major issues to consider when you are giving feedback to peers are how to express your feedback and the quality of that feedback.

Look at the following worksheet a student filled out after reading Mowli's paper.

---

1. What do you think the purpose of this paper is?

I don't know —high black mortality?

---

2. Who do you think the audience is?

Not sure.

---

3. Is there any content you think the writer should take out? Why? Is there any information that needs to be added?

Maybe the stuff on health in the United States—it seems stupid.

No.

---

4. Do you have any other suggestions for this writer?

No.

Now, look at an improved version of this same worksheet.

---

1. What do you think the purpose of this paper is?

I'm not sure. You talk about high black mortality and show facts for infant mortality and black males.

Then you talk about racism. Do these two things relate? How? How does the health care system in

the US relate?

2. Who do you think the audience is?

Everything seems pretty general so I guess everybody? Unless you are trying to convince a certain

audience of something?

3. Is there any content you think the writer should take out? Why? Is there any information that needs to be added?

In the 3rd paragraph you talk about causes of infant death. I'm not sure how this fits in.

In the 5th paragraph you mention a distributional inequity. What citizens do not get health care

and why? Maybe you mean blacks? I think you might need more statistics there.

Your conclusion says that black people are deprived of their rights but you never really mention this

in your paper.

4. Do you have any other suggestions for this writer?

It's a great paper with lots of interesting information! I think you might want to show the relationship

between black mortality, racism, and the health care system.

1. What are the differences in this worksheet in terms of how the feedback is expressed and the quality of the feedback?

B. Based on peer feedback, Mowli revised her paper. Here is her second draft. Much of the grammar is still not corrected.

Death is a normal thing for every living creature. In order to live long everybody need some facilities such as health care, nutrition, hospital service. Though the United States has all the facilities still black mortality rate is higher than any other developed nation. It has been found that mortality rate among blacks is twice that of whites. Racism is a significant contributing factor to the higher black mortality rate.

Racism is a totally biological concept that promotes the ordering of human variations. Humans are classified on genetically determined anatomical and chemical features. The modern fallacy that races differ genetically from the other is not justified scientifically. God has created us in different ways. All of us have different looks. But beneath our skin all of us are same. To be racist is harmful to society.

Infant mortality in the United States during 1989 was the lowest it has ever been, but it is still higher than in other developed countries. In 1989, the infant mortality rate for blacks was twice that of whites, and infant deaths among blacks have decreased at a much slower rate than among whites. Black infants have over twice the risk of dying in their first year of life compared to white infants.

Between 1988 and 1989, the main causes of infant death were premature birth and low birth weight, respiratory distress

syndrome, and complications associated with pregnancy.
Prematurity is the primary cause of newborn deaths and illness,
and poverty and unplanned pregnancies are important causes of
preterm births. Teenagers, unmarried black women, and those
receiving Medicaid are at greatest risk for both poverty and
unplanned pregnancy.

It seems that racism is a contributing factor to the high
infant mortality rate. Poor black women who have no education
and cannot get the same health care as whites are giving birth
to these premature babies. Black women are often the victims of
a national policy that prevents them from receiving information
about family planning, including ready availability of
contraceptives. Poverty, illiteracy, and unplanned pregnancy
was responsible for premature births.

The United States has the best health care system in the
world technologically but is lacking in measurements of good
health care service. Services are not easily available, nor are
health care resources used efficiently. The United States spends
40 percent more than Canada for health care and much more than
England, though England's level of health care is equivalent of
the US. There is not distributional equity. A specific level of
health care is not available to all citizens. This inequity of
distribution is the leading cause of high mortality rate. As we
know, that inequality prevails when there remains several races.
We can say that black people are not getting the facilities
because they are black. Blacks living in urban areas of the US
are generally more disadvantaged in economic, social, and health
care areas than whites. Blacks are more likely to be sick and
disabled and to have lower incomes and education levels. The
differences in the quality of health care among people in the
United States are persistent and often substantial, with
considerable disparity between white and black people. Infant
mortality among blacks is twice that of whites, and whites can
expect to live an average of six years longer. Differences also

exist in need for and access to health care. It appears that
even when blacks are treated, they are less likely to receive
certain kinds of treatment. Treatment of some conditions, such
as pneumonia, was found to be more aggressive for white people.
Differences in the rates of cesarean sections were noted, with
more being performed for white women. Here racial prejudice is
probably the factor.

The leading cause of death among young black males is
homicide and "legal intervention"--in other words, being shot by
police officers. These two causes accounted for 98.9 per 100,000
deaths of black males aged 24 to 34 in 1987. For white males of
the same age, the rate was 13.2 per 100,000. The probability of
a black male being killed is 500 percent greater than it is for
his white counterpart.

In this case, racism is also a factor. In most of the cases,
the blacks are being shot without any reason. Sometimes the police
officers killed black people only under suspicion. As the blacks
have no power or very little power against the whites, the
police officers are killing these people without any hesitations.
Because they know that they are not going to be charged.

The main problem of the high black mortality rates is
because of racism. Poverty, illiteracy, lack of health care, and
inequity in hospital service are some of the racial prejudices.
High mortality rate for a nation is always bad. The white people
are using their powers over the black people. As a result, the
black people are being deprived from their rights. It is always
wise to find out the key reason of any problem. Because it helps
a person to solve the problem in a meaningful way. It is really
very unfortunate that a country like the United States has high
black mortality rate due to racism.

Fill in the worksheet on the following page with comments to Mowli. Think
carefully about how to express your opinions and the quality of your comments.

1. What do you think the purpose of this paper is?

_____

_____

_____

2. Who do you think the audience is?

_____

_____

_____

3. Is there any content you think the writer should take out? Why? Is there any information that needs to be added?

_____

_____

_____

4. Do you have any other suggestions for this writer?

_____

_____

_____

PART II

REVISING FOR ORGANIZATION

4 Achieving Paragraph Structure

5 Developing Ideas

6 Writing Introductions and Conclusions

4 ACHIEVING PARAGRAPH STRUCTURE

In this chapter you will learn about paragraphs, the building blocks of the essay. Paragraphing clarifies the structure of a piece of writing. When readers come to a paragraph break, they know that one section of the discussion has ended and a new section is beginning. These paragraph boundaries make the discussion easier to follow.

4a TOPIC SENTENCES

The topic sentence is the sentence that states the main point of the paragraph. Topic sentences will help you, the writer, keep your writing focused. They help the reader understand quickly what the paragraph will be about.

ACTIVITY 4.1 **Evaluating Topic Sentences**

A. Look at the following topic sentences, and predict what each paragraph will be about.

1. Sushi can be classified into three types.

I expect the paragraph to be about _____

_____

2. Sushi is made with fish, rice, vinegar, and seaweed.

I expect the paragraph to be about _____

_____

3. Sushi is very delicious.

I expect the paragraph to be about _____

_____

B. Why are sentences 2 and 3 poor topic sentences?

ACTIVITY
4.2   Matching Topic Sentences to Paragraphs

Read the following paragraphs about factors that influence the behavior and living conditions of animals. Several topic sentences are listed. Write the appropriate topic sentence in the blank at the beginning of each paragraph. (One topic sentence does not fit any paragraph.)

Temperature can act as a limiting factor.

Light affects animals directly as they perceive their prey or detect their enemies.

During the winter, some mammals become dormant; that is, they *hibernate*.

Temperature may have a significant effect on the appearance of organisms.

Animals that maintain themselves at their optimum temperature are warm-blooded, or *homeothermal*, animals.

1._____

_____. At this time, the body temperature (normally about 100°F) falls to 45°F or even lower. The heartbeat of a ground squirrel drops from a summer average of over 200 beats per minute to an average of less than 20 beats per minute in the winter.

2._____

_____. For example, the distribution of the polar bear is limited to regions in which the temperature averages no higher than 32°F. By contrast, the malarial parasite does not develop when the temperature goes below 77°F.

3._____

_____. In other words, the weather outside can change, but they will keep the same temperature. If this "temperature regulator" doesn't work, however, the animal will die. If humans are kept in cold weather for too long, their body temperature will fall from 98.6°F to 65°F. At this point, the heart will fail.

4._____

_____. The Himalayan rabbit is mostly white but has black ears, tail, and feet. If the hair is taken from a white area, it will grow back white if the animal is kept at room temperature (68°F). However, if the animal is kept at a temperature below 50°F, the hair will grow back black. [Adapted from Ralph Buchsbaum and Mildred Buchsbaum, *Basic Ecology*]

The topic sentence does not have to be the first sentence in the paragraph. However, placing it first ensures that the reader is aware of the point of the paragraph from the beginning. This is the most straightforward and clearest means of organizing a paragraph. Another approach is to place the topic sentence at the end of the paragraph. This variation is especially helpful when the topic sentence is controversial, and presenting some evidence first may prepare the reader to be more receptive to the idea. Withholding the topic sentence until the end of a paragraph can also build a little suspense and therefore interest. It can also provide some variety. Finally, writers sometimes place topic sentences after one or two transitional sentences that link the paragraph to what has gone before.

ACTIVITY

4.3 **Recognizing Topic Sentences**

Read the following paragraphs, and underline the topic sentence for each.

1. Many argue that Holland State Park has one of the best beaches in Michigan. The 150-foot-wide park beach, with its sugar-like sand, extends 1800 feet along Lake Michigan and is crowned by "Big Red," the distinctively red Holland Harbor Lighthouse that was built in 1907 and is located across the channel. The beautiful beach and the scenic lighthouse have made Holland a very, very popular park. [Jim Du Fresne, *Michigan State Parks*]

2. Another important piece of the communication picture is nonverbal communication. A researcher named Birdwhistell asserts that "probably no more than 30 to 35 percent of the social meaning of a conversation or an interaction is carried by the words" (Leathers, 1976: 4). Some researchers estimate that 93 percent of total communication is nonverbal. [Susan Gass and Natalie Lefkowitz, *Varieties of English*]

3. For Japanese in their late sixties and seventies, the discovery that they must live apart from their children is a wrenching experience. And until recently, the choices open to elderly Japanese were dismal. They could either spend their final days in unwelcome solitude or take refuge in a cheerless government nursing home for the poor. Now, a small but growing minority of elderly Japanese are settling in American-style retirement communities. [Robert C. Christopher, *The Japanese Mind*]

ACTIVITY

4.4 **Writing Topic Sentences**

Write an appropriate topic sentence for each of the following paragraphs.

1._____

_____. Voters can get directly in touch with candidates; moreover, they can compare the merits and demerits of each candidate. Voters use presidential debates as an opportunity to judge the candidates side by side, evaluating their issue positions and leadership qualifications. [Seong Yong Shin, South Korea]

2._____

_____. In fact, statistics show that the probability of a black male being killed is 500 percent greater than it is for his white counterpart.

In 1987, 98.9 per 100,000 deaths of black males aged 24 to 34 were caused by homicide, while the rate for white males of the same age was 13.2 per 100,000. [Mowli Salehin Kamal, Bangladesh]

3._____

_____. By 1985 the higher-income developing countries had reached literacy rates of 85 percent or more for adult males and 70 percent or more for females. In the lower income groups, less than 65 percent of the adult males and less than 40 percent of the adult females were literate. [United Nations, *Global Outlook 2000*]

4b FORMATTING PARAGRAPHS

There are two ways to indicate that you are starting a new paragraph. The more common way, and the one you will use for most personal and college writing, is to indent the first word of a new paragraph five spaces if you are typing or one inch if you are writing by hand. The alternative method, more appropriate for business correspondence, is not to indent but to leave a blank line between paragraphs. In both formats, a topic sentence is necessary.

For longer pieces of writing such as master's theses, monographs, and business reports, you may want to use headings to indicate the content of various sections of the writing. The phrase "Formatting Paragraphs" above is such a heading. In most academic writing, especially writing that is less than ten pages long, such headings are inappropriate. In no circumstance would it be correct to use such headings as substitutes for the topic sentences of paragraphs.

ACTIVITY 4.5 Are Headings Appropriate?

The following examples come from a research paper on environmental problems in China. Which format is more appropriate for this type of academic paper? Place a check next to the more appropriate one.

_____ 1. **Pollution of Cities**
Cities in China are so crowded with dust and noise that it is uncomfortable to live in them. According to Zhang (1992), life in modern Chinese cities is similar to that in Europe in the nineteenth and early twentieth centuries.

_____ 2. Pollution in cities is another serious environmental problem China faces today. Cities in China are so crowded with dust and noise that it is uncomfortable to live in them. According to Zhang (1992), life in modern Chinese cities is similar to that in Europe in the nineteenth and early twentieth centuries. [Di Wang, China]

4c STICKING TO THE POINT (UNITY)

Each paragraph must focus on one point or main idea. Everything in the paragraph must support that main point and relate to it in some apparent way.

Identifying Irrelevant Information

Read the following paragraphs. In each, underline the sentence that does not belong.

1. When teaching your dog something new, eliminate as many distractions as possible. Take your dog to a quiet place, either in your home or in your fenced yard. Make sure the dog has been fed and watered, so that it is able to concentrate on the tasks at hand. Reward the dog with treats for positive behavior. Most important, avoid working where there are other people or animals. [Adapted from Barbara Handler, *Positively Obedient*]

2. Many different types of musical activities can have therapeutic benefits for mentally retarded individuals. The rhythmic movement to music can help patients improve their motor coordination skills. Knowledge of body parts and concepts of directionality can be learned and reinforced in dances, action songs, and musical movement games. Choosing these musical pieces can be fun for the trained volunteers who work with the mentally retarded. Finally, special song lyrics can be written to help patients learn and memorize sequences and procedures for self-help skills like dressing and brushing their teeth. [Eunjoo Lee, South Korea]

3. It is worth travelling to Turkey just to eat. Turkish cuisine is the very heart of eastern Mediterranean cooking, which demands excellent, fresh ingredients and careful, even laborious preparation. The ingredients are often very simple, but are of the highest quality. Turkish farmers, herders and fishermen bring forth a wealth of truly superb produce from this agriculturally rich land. This land has rolling hills and pleasant landscapes, making Turkey a beautiful place to visit. Being one of only seven countries on earth which produce a surplus of food, the Turks have enough good produce to feed everyone here. [Tom Brosnahan, *Turkey*]

4d COHERENCE IN A PARAGRAPH

Coherence is the quality that allows writing to stick together and to flow smoothly. Problems with coherence can make a piece of writing difficult for the reader to follow. The organization and development of a well-unified paragraph contribute to the coherence of a piece of writing.

There are three principal tools to make your writing coherent: the use of transitional expressions (logical connectors), the repetition of key words and phrases, and the use of demonstratives *(this, that, these, those).*

Providing Transitions

The accompanying box lists the most common transitional expressions, grouped by function. A word of caution is in order. Once you get accustomed to using transitional expressions, you may fall into a common habit: overuse. You may find yourself starting nearly every sentence with a transitional expression, and your writing may consequently become so clotted with these expressions that they slow down readers rather than assist them. Use transitional expressions when they are needed to indicate relations between ideas, events, or objects in your writing, but **do not overuse them.** (For a brief discussion of another way to indicate relationships between ideas, see Chapter 8, on coordination and subordination.)

TRANSITIONAL EXPRESSIONS

To give examples:

for example	in fact	specifically	to illustrate
for instance			

To indicate that you are going to give additional information:

and	besides	furthermore	moreover
also	further	in addition	too

To indicate where information fits in a sequence:

and then	in the first place	last	second
again	in the second place	next	third
finally			
first			

To indicate how ideas are related in time:

after	earlier	later	soon
after a while	finally	meanwhile	then
afterward	formerly	next	thereafter
at last	immediately	now	until
at length	in the meantime	presently	when
at that time	in the past	shortly	while
before	lately	simultaneously	

To indicate that one idea is similar to another (comparison):

also	in the same way	likewise	similarly
in the same manner			

To indicate that one idea conflicts with or contradicts another (contrast):

but	in contrast	nonetheless	regardless
even so	instead	on the contrary	still
for all that	nevertheless	on the other hand	yet
however			

To indicate that you are summarizing or concluding:

all in all	in short	therefore	to summarize
in brief	in summary	to conclude	to sum up
in conclusion			

To indicate how things are related physically in space:

above	farther on	there	to the right
below	here	to the east	to the south
beyond	nearby	to the left	to the west
elsewhere	opposite	to the north	

To indicate that one idea or event is caused by another:

accordingly	consequently	so	to this end
as a result	hence	therefore	

ACTIVITY 4.7   **Using Transitions Appropriately**

Fill in each blank in the following sentences with an appropriate transitional word. There are often several correct choices. Be creative by using different options!

1. Colorado, which is located _____ Wyoming, has a more developed ski industry. _____, tourism is higher in this state.

2. On May 15, 1989, with a big handshake in front of the cameras, Soviet president Mikhail Gorbachev and Chinese party chairman Deng Xiaoping agreed that "the problem of the past should be gone with the wind." _____ the two major reformers of the Communist world ended thirty years of enmity between their countries.

3. The movement of art called Surrealism is a product of Dada and the traumas of the First World War. _____, a painting by Max Ernst called *The Horde,* evoked the image of a terrifying group of strangers. _____ to Ernst's threatening piece, Joan Miró in 1931 created a small assemblage called *Sculpture-Object* that was light and poetic.

4. Some ecologists say that the world's most gorgeous reefs are being destroyed by divers. _____, a diver's weight belt can unbuckle, dropping ten pounds of lead onto the coral below. _____, a diver can whack a coral sea fan with an errant fin.

5. American manufacturers are discarding billions of dollars in investment they made in the 1980s to adopt Japanese manufacturing ideas. One reason is that American companies went overboard in copying Japanese automation. Federal-Mogul, _____, mistakenly surmised that the Japanese got a major cost advantage from computers, robots, and other automated equipment. _____, the company revamped its Lancaster [Pennsylvania] auto parts plant in 1987 with state-of-the-art automation. _____, Federal-Mogul found that although the plant turned out parts faster than before, it couldn't shift gears quickly. _____, switching from a small clutch bearing to a larger one required many changes. _____, the complex machinery required extensive maintenance. _____ the automation not only failed to lower costs, but it _____ created a serious problem. [Amal Kumar Naj, "Some Manufacturers Drop Efforts to Adopt Japanese Techniques"]

Repeating Key Words and Phrases

Another way to achieve coherence in a paragraph is through the repetition of key words and phrases. Notice how the italicized words in the following paragraph serve to repeat the main subject of the paragraph and remind the reader of it.

My *briefcase* is a marvelously well designed contraption. It is first of all a *satchel* for carrying primarily papers but also books, clipboards, tablets, and the like. In addition, this *briefcase* includes numerous pockets just right for other items. I keep my computer disks in the outer pocket of the *bag,* sealed shut by Velcro. Inside, three pockets carry my eyeglasses, my business cards, and my appointment book. And the *briefcase* also includes a series of tubelike pockets where I keep my supply of pens and pencils. There is even a strap with a clip on the end to which I attach my Swiss army knife. My *briefcase* is perfectly designed for today's student.

ACTIVITY
4.8   Writing Appropriate Repetitions

Read the following paragraphs, and in the blanks, write appropriate repetitions for the term in bold type in the first sentence. Remember to use a mix of the actual word, synonyms, and pronouns.

1. At the corner of the alley was **Hong Sing's,** a four-table café with a recessed stairwell in front that led to a door marked "Tradesmen." My brothers and I believed that bad people emerged from this door at night. Tourists never went _____ since the menu was printed only in Chinese. A Caucasian man with a big camera once posed me and my playmates in front of _____. He had us move to the side of the picture window so the photo would capture the roasted duck with its head dangling from a juice-covered rope. When he took the picture, I told him we should go into _____ and eat dinner. Then he smiled and asked me what they served. I shouted, "Guts and duck's feet and octopus gizzards!" I ran off with my friends, shrieking with laughter, and we scampered across the alley and hid in the entryway grotto of the China Gem Company, my heart pounding with hope that he would chase us. [Amy Tan, *The Joy Luck Club*]

2. For a number of reasons, **bats** have fascinated people down through the ages. In the early days, people shared their homes with _____. Early in man's cultural evolution, _____ became the subject of myth and superstition. Misinformation about _____ continues to the present day, even among otherwise enlightened peoples. _____ are secretive and most are nocturnal. _____ have the ability to navigate precisely in dark places through the means of echolocation. The book by G. M. Allen, called simply *Bats,* remains the best single reference on _____ in folklore, and is fascinating reading. [David M. Armstrong, *Rocky Mountain Mammals*]

Demonstratives

Look at the following sentence.

1. INCORRECT: The tires on my car are worn, and the road was a little slippery. *This* made me worry all the way home.

What does *this* refer to? The worn tires? The slippery road? Both?

2. CORRECT: The tires on my car are worn, and the road was a little slippery. *This combination* made me worry all the way home.

Demonstratives, which are the words *this, that, these,* and *those,* should always serve as adjectives, not pronouns, when referring to something. In other words, a noun should always follow a demonstrative.

ACTIVITY

4.9   **Using Demonstratives**

Fill in each blank in the paragraph about the chest region of the human body with a demonstrative and noun.

There are twelve ribs connected to each side of the spinal column in the chest region. Ten of _____ are joined to the sternum in front by cartilage; the other two are called floating ribs. From the upper end of the sternum, the collarbone connects to join the scapula. All of _____ make up the rib cage.

If several ribs are fractured, breathing is impaired. Therefore, _____ may endanger a person's life. In addition, the lungs may be punctured if a rib is displaced from its normal position, allowing air and perhaps blood to escape into the chest cavity. _____ of air and blood between the chest wall may compress lung tissue. [American Red Cross, *Advanced First Aid and Emergency Care*]

ACTIVITY

4.10 Revising for Paragraph Coherence

Read and revise the following essay for paragraph coherence. Check the use of transitional expressions, repetitions of key words and phrases, and demonstratives, adding where necessary. Then write out the corrected essay on a separate sheet of paper.

> In Thailand, the biggest holiday is Songkran, or the Thai New Year. It is on April 13. It is the hottest month. The holiday is a water-throwing festival.
> Usually, early in the morning of April 13, we go to the temple to put food in the bowls of Buddhist priests. We go to visit our close relatives. We pour a special kind of water with rose and jasmine in their hands. After we pour it, they give us good words and money.
> Teenagers throw water at each other with bowls. Some children play with water guns. They don't get angry if they get wet. Some people use powder mixes with water. They wipe this on other people's faces. They look so funny because this makes their faces white.
> In the evening, we have a beauty contest in the national park. The one who wins is called "Miss Songkran." She wears a real Thai costume. She walks on the stage showing it to the people. They have fireworks. Most of the people celebrate this until the next day. [Rosarin Putipanpong, Thailand]

4e SENTENCE VARIETY

ACTIVITY

4.11 Identifying Tools for Sentence Variety

The following paragraph illustrates one kind of problem a writer can have with sentence variety. This paragraph, adapted from a book on contemporary American folk legends, relates a bizarre tale that is told in many parts of the country.

> A man was camping out in the wilds. He was in his pickup camper. He parked at the edge of a clearing. He ran across a wounded coyote. He hated coyotes anyway. He decided he'd create a little excitement. He had some dynamite in his truck. It was left over from blowing stumps on his farm. He tied a stick of dynamite to the coyote. He lit the fuse. He ran over behind some trees to watch the results. The man was horrified. The man watched the coyote summon his last bit of strength. The coyote dragged himself over to the camper. There was nothing the man could do. The coyote pulled himself under the camper. The coyote blew himself and much of the camper to bits.

This paragraph is unsuccessful for two reasons: it lacks variety both in the lengths of the sentences—they are all fairly short—and in sentence structure—they are all simple declarative sentences with a single subject and verb.

Now read a revised version of the story.

A man was camping out in the wilds with his pickup camper. At the edge of the clearing where he was camped, he ran across a wounded coyote. Hating coyotes anyway, he decided he'd create a little excitement. He had some dynamite in his truck, left over from blowing stumps on his farm. So he tied a stick of dynamite to the coyote, lit the fuse, and ran over behind some trees to watch the results. To his horror, the man watched the coyote summon his last bit of strength and drag himself over to the camper. There was nothing he could do as the coyote pulled himself under the camper and blew himself and much of the camper to bits. [Jan Harold Brunvand, *The Choking Doberman and Other "New" Urban Legends*]

What tools were used to make this paragraph more interesting and more effective? Study the list of tools for varying sentences in the box on the facing page. Then fill in the chart below by choosing from this list of techniques.

Tool	Example
Opening sentences with introductory phrases	*To his horror, the man watched . . .*

ACTIVITY

4.12   Achieving Sentence Variety

Rewrite the following paragraph to create more sentence variety. Use the tools for sentence variety listed in the box.

People complain how dark it is in the morning. But this is often the best time of the day. The dawn peers gray and silent into my pale windows. My bright little table lamp becomes a blazing spotlight. It floods over the big black shadow of my

TOOLS FOR SENTENCE VARIETY

Varying sentence openings:

1. Opening sentences with transitional expressions

   Nevertheless, my phone is now out of order.

   In fact, the entire argument was based on a misunderstanding.

2. Opening sentences with introductory phrases

   After a sleepless night, Susan anxiously called her psychologist.

   Laughing hard, Micah fell off his chair.

   To let my cat out, I had to get completely dressed.

   Defiant and angry, the mob marched into the administration building.

   Slowly and cautiously, Maxine lifted the cover off the ticking box.

   Gracefully, Gina danced her way off the stage.

   Our minds made up, we knocked on the boss's door.

3. Opening sentences with adverb clauses

   When Carla called, I was just finishing my assignment.

   Because Marc lives in the city, he pays much more than I do for car insurance.

Combining sentences:

1. Forming compound sentences

   A dark surface will absorb heat, *but* a light surface will reflect it.

   Sulfur dioxide comes from burning coal; methane comes from cattle.

   Jack did not like kimchi; *however,* his mother made him eat it.

2. Forming complex sentences

   The police officer asked the witness *when the accident occurred.*

   The coach *who is crying* is from the losing team.

   Because she ate ice cream every day, Maureen gained twenty pounds.

Using inverted word order:

   In a vase on the dining room table were a dozen stargazer lilies.

   Particularly impressive was Paul's performance on the parallel bars.

Using commands, questions, and quotations:

   Consider the environment.

   Unless the first generation created the society, how could it shelter any new generations?

   "Women can do everything; men can do the rest."

desk. Last week it really felt marvelous. I sat engrossed in *The Idiot.* I translated a few lines. I wrote them down in an exercise book. I made notes. Suddenly it was 10 o'clock. Then I felt: yes, that's how you should always work. You are so deeply immersed. You forget time. This morning I am wonderfully peaceful. [Etty Hillesum, *An Interrupted Life*]

4f PARAGRAPH LENGTH

Because the range for acceptable paragraph length is so great, the following guidelines may help you determine when to start a new paragraph:

- To signal that you are starting a new point
- In narration, to indicate a major shift in time
- In description, to indicate that you are focusing on a new section or portion of what you are describing
- To emphasize a major point by giving it a paragraph of its own
- To break up an overly long block of text

ACTIVITY

4.13 **Breaking Paragraphs Appropriately**

Read the following text, and decide where to break the paragraphs. Use the paragraph symbol (¶) to indicate these places.

Coca-Cola is one of the most famous beverages in the world. It is consumed in more than one hundred and seventy countries, and a Coca-Cola is drunk forty thousand times each minute, which is about sixty million times a day. Coca-Cola was first developed by Dr. Pemberton in 1886, in the backyard of his house in Atlanta, Georgia. It was originally intended as a headache remedy, by adding caffeine to the syrup blend. Additional improvements were made when the product was flavored with a relatively large variety of essential oils, which imparted a delicious aroma. The popularity of Coca-Cola abroad started in 1907 when the company set up shop in Hawaii. Two years later, another bottler was appointed in Panama. By 1956, there were four-hundred and forty-five Coca-Cola bottlers outside the United States. And in 1976, Coca-Cola was sold in more than four million shops and advertised in more than eighty languages. This popularity has certainly led to financial reward for the company. These rewards are reflected in the sales and profits of the product. The profit of Coca-Cola inside the United States is about four billion dollars, while the foreign business contributes about one quarter of the sales and profits of the company. Sales in 1991 totaled 11.5 billion, which is almost thirteen percent over 1990 sales. Coca-Cola has been in competition with other brands, both in and out of the United States. One of its greatest competitors is Pepsi Cola. Both of these companies dominate soda sales, sharing more than seventy percent of the domestic market. Although Pepsi is moving more aggressively into foreign markets, Coca-Cola still owns the world. Coca-Cola has to compete not only with Pepsi but also with other companies such as Fanta, which maintains an international presence today. Fanta is the second largest soft drink brand in the world, available in one hundred and twelve countries. The Coca-Cola Company is involved in activities other than the production of the beverage. For example, the company took a giant leap outside its familiar food and beverage domain in 1982 with the acquisition of Columbia Pictures, Inc. Moreover, Coca-Cola manufactures coin-operated electronic games through its Mistar Electronic Subsidiary. In the beginning, Coca-Cola was sold as a medicine for headaches. Today the company has evolved into a multinational conglomerate involved in much more than simply making a soft drink. [Ahmad al-Ghandi, Saudi Arabia]

4.14 Putting It All Together

Refer to the second draft of Mowli Kamal's paper on black mortality rates in Activity 3.4, part B. Revise it in response to the following questions:

- Does each paragraph have an appropriate topic sentence?
- Are the paragraphs unified, or is there irrelevant information that should be taken out?
- Is the paper coherent? Are transitions used appropriately and not excessively? Is there appropriate repetition of key nouns? Are demonstratives used appropriately?
- Is there enough sentence variety in the paragraphs?
- Are the paragraphs split appropriately?

Rewrite the paper, incorporating your revisions.

DEVELOPING IDEAS

5a TYPES OF SUPPORT

Paragraphs in English usually include a topic sentence and supporting details. There are several ways to support the main idea of a paragraph.

ACTIVITY
5.1 Recognizing Types of Support

Read this text. Then fill in the chart with examples of the various kinds of supporting details that are used.

Kerr-McGee's plutonium plant, built next to one of its uranium plants, opened in 1970, shortly before 8583 fish turned belly up in the river, following a big ammonia spill at the facility. Kerr-McGee had assured the Atomic Energy Commission (AEC) it could deal safely and circumspectly with the plutonium. But the AEC soon received numerous reports of irregularities and accidents at the Kerr-McGee plant.

In October 1970, two workers were contaminated when a radioactive storage container was left open for three days. Twenty-two more workers were exposed to plutonium in January, 1971, when defective equipment allowed plutonium oxide to escape into the air. The protective "glove boxes" the workers used often had holes. Sometimes the drums, specially designed to store the volatile liquid, unaccountably leaked. According to radioactive safety engineer Wes McGovern, "All of these incidents were minor incidents in the larger picture of safety."

One day a worker bent down to adjust a compressor unit; it exploded, ripping through his hand and tearing off the top of his face. He died instantly. "When I got down there," remembers a former lab technician, "they were washing the goo down the drain. Kerr-McGee didn't give a damn about the people who worked there—it didn't care whether its safety program was effective or not." [Howard Kohn, "Malignant Giant"]

Type of Support	Example
Facts or statistics	*opened in 1970, shortly before 8583 fish turned belly up . . .*
Examples	
Personal experiences	
Expert testimony	
Descriptive details	

The following activity is a tool to help you develop details in a paragraph.

Generating Details

Select a word or phrase related to a topic that you like. Then gradually expand your word or phrase by adding details, as in the following example.

Word or phrase: red bike

What: red bike

Who: My sister Laura had a red bike.

When: My sister Laura had a red bike when she was five years old.

Where: My sister Laura had a red bike when she was five years old in Minneapolis.

Why: My sister Laura got a red bike for her fifth birthday when we lived in Minneapolis.

Word or phrase:

What:

Who:

When:

Where:

Why:

Writing Supporting Details

Read the following topic sentences. Then, using the various types of support, write supporting statements.

1. The computer is perhaps the most important invention of the twentieth century.

2. Mass transportation is essential in every large city.

3. There are advantages and disadvantages to living in a big city.

ARRANGING SUPPORTING MATERIAL

In English, paragraphs are usually arranged according to one of four organizational patterns: space, time, emphasis, and patterns of development.

Space

In spatial organization, the writer's focus moves physically from one location to another. For example, if you were describing your room, you might start from the right side of the room and move toward the left.

5.4 Recognizing Language Used in Spatial Organization

A. Read the following paragraph, underlining all the language cues that indicate spatial patterns.

> Robert Jordan lay behind the trunk of a pine tree on the slope of the hill above the road and the bridge and watched it become daylight. He loved this hour of the day and now he watched it; feeling it gray within him, as though he were a part of the slow lightening that comes before the rising of the sun. . . . The pine trunks below him were hard and clear now, their trunks solid and brown, and the road was shiny with a wisp of mist over it. The dew had wet him and the forest floor was soft and he felt the give of the brown, dropped pine needles under his elbows. Below he saw through the light mist that rose from the stream bed, the steel of the bridge, straight and rigid across the gap, with the wooden sentry boxes at each end. [Ernest Hemingway, *For Whom the Bell Tolls*]

B. Write your underlined terms below. Can you think of any other words or phrases that might be used with this type of organization? Add them to the list.

5.5 Writing Paragraphs Using Spatial Organization

Choose one of the following situations and write a paragraph about it.

- Describe the view from your bedroom.
- Tell about the most beautiful city in your country.

Time

Another common organizational pattern is chronological or sequential: the writer reports events as they happen over time. For example, you might describe how to change the oil in a car by explaining the sequence of actions to take, step by step.

ACTIVITY 5.6 Organizing Paragraphs Chronologically

Write a paragraph by putting the following sentences in logical order. Pay close attention to transitional words and phrases. Indicate the appropriate chronological organization by numbering the sentences from 1 to 6.

_____ In spring a year later, gas workers at nearby Canning Town likewise successfully formed a union and won an eight-hour day.

_____ In November the following year, an angry crowd estimated at ten thousand marched on Trafalgar Square.

_____ First, in the spring of 1888, Annie Besant led the exploited girls at the Bow match factory to form their own union and strike successfully for better pay and protection from industrial disease.

_____ Violence alarmed the inhabitants of the West End of London in February 1886 when the country was in the grip of a severe depression. After a mass meeting in Trafalgar Square, a column of unemployed marched through St. James, smashing windows and looting shops.

_____ Finally, the most dramatic triumph came when sixty thousand protesters paralyzed shipping on the Thames, demanding a basic wage of sixpence an hour.

_____ Perhaps by highlighting so forcefully the futility of violent tactics, the failures of 1886–1887 unwittingly prepared the way for spectacular successes on the London industrial front soon afterward. [Adapted from Richard Tames, *A Traveller's History of London*]

ACTIVITY 5.7 Writing Paragraphs according to Time or Sequence

Choose one of the following situations and write a paragraph about it.

- Describe a vacation you have taken by telling your readers the order of events on your trip.
- Explain how to prepare a favorite recipe.

Emphasis

Most paragraphs in English are ordered from general to specific. Some writers, however, may choose to move from specific to general to build anticipation. Other related patterns include moving from the most familiar to the least familiar, and vice versa, or from simple to complex.

To understand the process of organizing paragraphs by emphasis, it is important first to distinguish between general and specific ideas.

General: While waiting to take the exam, she *became nervous.*

Specific: While waiting to take the exam, she *began to bite her nails, tap her foot, and perspire.*

General: The company expects to lose *a lot of money* this year.

Specific: The company expects to lose *between seven and eight million dollars* this year.

5.8 Recognizing General Ideas and Specific Details in Paragraphs

In each of the following paragraphs, underline the general idea once and the specific details twice.

1. The past four decades have not been kind to poor old Mount Everest. Since the first ascent on May 29, 1953, climbers have forged fourteen new routes up the mountain, leaving it, in the view of some, "climbed out." The South Col route, once a wilderness of rock and pristine slopes, is now marked out by the inevitable detritus of human endeavor. Each campsite is marked with the faded remains of flattened tents, and the South Col campsite is littered with hundreds of abandoned oxygen cylinders. [Adapted from "Queue at the Top of the World"]

2. The Civil War saw the first large-scale use of railroads and steam engines to transport and supply armies in the field. Metallic cartridges and breech-loading, multishot weapons were used in large numbers. Ironclad warships and submarines were introduced, and soldiers first suffered the horrors of extended trench warfare. This war was thus considered the first modern war. [Adapted from Christopher Nelson, *Mapping the Civil War*]

Patterns of Development

Writers in English use eight patterns of development. These patterns are defined in Activity 5.9.

5.9 Defining, Recognizing, and Using Patterns of Development

A. Match each pattern of development with its meaning.

a. Description   e. Narration
b. Comparison and contrast   f. Process
c. Division and analysis   g. Cause and effect
d. Definition   h. Classification

_____ 1. Used to recount something that happened, such as a story or an event

_____ 2. Used to tell how to do something or how something was done

_____ 3. Used to sketch a person, place, or thing

_____ 4. Used to discuss similarities or differences between two subjects

_____ 5. Used to clarify the meaning intended for a particular word or phrase

_____ 6. Used to group items according to a particular principle

_____ 7. Used to take a single item and break it down into its constituent parts

_____ 8. Used to describe why something happens and the ensuing result

B.   Using the same key, match the appropriate organizational form to each of the following paragraphs. As you read the paragraph, underline the language cues that helped you identify the organizational form. Not all patterns of development are represented, so read carefully.

_____ 1. Wash the beans and soak overnight in water to cover. The next day, prepare the chicken stock by simmering the chickens in two quarts of water to which the whole onion, celery, carrot, parsley, and bay leaves are added. Remove the chickens and take the meat and skin from the bones and dice the meat. Mix the beans, chicken broth, and one chopped onion. Cook until the beans are tender. Simmer the mixture for twenty minutes and add the chicken. Simmer for another fifteen minutes, and your white chili is ready to serve. [Neiman-Marcus, *Pure and Simple*]

_____ 2. Alcohol can be divided into five groups. First, distilled spirit is an alcoholic beverage obtained from the distillation of an alcohol-containing liquid. Wine is another type of alcohol, which is the naturally fermented juice of freshly gathered ripe grapes. Cider is similar to wine, but it is made from apples. The fourth type of alcohol is mead, the combination of honey and sugar. Finally, beer is a liquor fermented from corn sugar, malt, and yeast and is flavored with hops. [Rosarin Putipanpong, Thailand]

_____ 3. Gauguin went for a walk in the evening, and van Gogh, suspicious as ever, followed him. Gauguin, who heard the familiar steps approaching nearer and nearer, turned around and looked straight into van Gogh's disturbed face. Van Gogh was supposedly holding a razor blade in his hand. Gauguin spoke softly to Vincent, who then turned around and went back home. Gauguin, disturbed by the whole incident, spent the night at a hotel. When he returned to the "yellow house" the next morning, the whole of Arles was already up on its feet. Van Gogh, plagued by hallucination, had cut off one of his ears with the razor blade which Gauguin claimed to have seen earlier in van Gogh's hand. [Ingo F. Walther, *Vincent van Gogh*]

_____ 4. Over the past 160,000 years, whenever the amount of iron-rich dust falling into the Antarctic has gone up, the amount of carbon dioxide in the atmosphere has gone down, and vice versa. [Robert Kunzig, "Earth on Ice"]

_____ 5. The Amish have been the focus of government studies since the 1940's, precisely because they have remained highly energy efficient. Their cropland continues to produce abundant crops far more efficiently than "modern" operations. Without the benefit of chemical fertilizers and large amounts of plant herbicides, they continue to increase their output on older land and continue to upgrade the new farms they take over. Research has shown that since the 1950's average American farmers have been steadily increasing their energy consumption yet there has not been a corresponding increase in their production of yields per acre. The Amish, on the other hand, preside over a system which comes much closer to an ecological balance. This accounts for their success. [John M. Zielinski, *Amish Horsefarming across America*]

C. Using the passages in part B and your own knowledge, fill in the following chart. A few examples have been provided already.

Pattern of Development	Language	Topic
Description		
Comparison and contrast		*cultures*
Division and analysis		
Definition		
Narration		
Process	*First, then*	
Cause and effect		
Classification		

D. Choose one of the topics you listed in the chart, and, on a separate sheet of paper, write a paragraph using the appropriate pattern of development.

6 WRITING INTRODUCTIONS AND CONCLUSIONS

Beginning and ending a paper can sometimes be the most difficult part of the entire writing process. In this chapter you will learn several different methods for writing introductions and conclusions.

6a PURPOSE OF INTRODUCTIONS

First impressions count. Introductions—opening paragraphs—are where you make your first impression in writing, so they are worth some extra time and attention.

First, a word or two about writing an introduction. Many writers find them the hardest part of writing. If you are in this group, you might consider one of two strategies.

- *Postpone writing the opening.* Start on the body of the essay, and leave the introduction for later, perhaps after you've completed the entire first draft. The problem with this strategy is that sometimes it is difficult to write anything else until you have set the tone and defined the topic in the introduction. The benefit, however, is that this strategy allows you to write more freely and to discover your thesis as you write.
- *Write an extremely tentative introduction.* Get something down, but don't labor over it. Assume that whatever you write will be revised heavily, perhaps even discarded, later on. This attitude may allow you to get something on the page without slowing you down for hours while you struggle to find the perfect opening.

An effective introduction accomplishes one or more of the following three goals:

- Getting the reader's attention
- Letting the reader know the point of the writing
- Providing background information or context to help the reader get into the essay itself

ACTIVITY 6.1 Identifying the Parts of an Introduction

A. Read the following introductory paragraph. Write the sentences from the text that serves each purpose of the introduction.

The Middle East Crisis: President Bush's Crusade

Iraq's invasion of Kuwait on 2 August 1990 plunged the world into one of the most acute crises since World War II and provoked the largest military and political challenge since the Cold War. Saddam Hussein attempted to defy the established world order. . .3 In the past, the United States preferred to rely on diplomacy to defuse regional tensions and to avoid massive direct involvement.

Although the United States was not bound by any defense treaty, it assumed the leadership position of the international response to Iraq's seizure of Kuwait. The United States' stated rationale for the intervention was the defense of its long-standing interests in the Middle East and the desire to shape a new world order. However, beyond the conventional rationale, the American decision to intervene may also have been influenced by less ostensible, nonconventional factors. These factors can be assessed through an overview of the origins of the crisis, a survey of the conventional justifications, and the introduction of a hidden-hand explanation of American foreign policy. This analysis will demonstrate the pertinence of using two different approaches for establishing the role of different factors in shaping American foreign policy. [Amaury Aumond-Achard, "The Middle East Crisis: President Bush's Crusade"]

1. Getting the reader's attention

2. Letting the reader know the point of the writing

3. Providing background information or context

B.   Repeat the exercise for the following introductory paragraph.

The Death Threat against Rushdie: A Case Study in Political Scapegoatism

On February 14, 1989, Ayatollah Ruhollah Khomeini, the supreme religious guide of Iran, issued a death sentence against Salman Rushdie. He announced that the author of *The Satanic Verses* must be killed for the sin of insulting Islam, the prophet Mohammed, and the Holy Koran. The social, political, and economic conditions during three time periods—just before the cease-fire of the Gulf War; the period following the cease-fire until Khomeini's proclamation against Rushdie; and the period following Khomeini's death until the reaffirmation of the death threat—illustrate the inability of the Islamic Republic to live up to its original goal of freeing the oppressed people. Because the Iran-Iraq war broke out less than a year after the 1979 revolution, the Islamic Republic never had to prove its political and economic viability. With the end of the war, however, came the task of truly establishing the Republic as a political entity that could provide the basic necessities of life for its people. The motive for the threat against Rushdie was, on the surface, wholly religious. However, the analysis of these three time periods will show that the death threats against Salman Rushdie were politically and not religiously motivated. [Melina Turtle, "The Death Threat against Rushdie"]

1. Getting the reader's attention

2. Letting the reader know the point of the writing

3. Providing background information or context

6b THESIS STATEMENTS

The part of the introduction that lets the reader know the point of the writing is called the **thesis statement.** The **subject** is merely the topic that a paper focuses on; a **thesis** states a point about that subject.

SUBJECTS	THESES
Washington	Washington is an attractive place to visit.
credit cards	Credit cards charge too much interest.
libraries	Libraries can be intimidating.
motorcycles	Motorcycles are too dangerous.
jogging	Jogging does your body more harm than good.

Notice that each thesis includes both a subject and a point to be made about that subject. Here are some other guidelines for effective theses:

1. *A thesis must not be too broad.* A five-hundred-word essay that tries to prove that "the Supreme Court has a long record of protecting individual rights" is probably not going to succeed because the thesis is too broad for so short a piece of writing.
2. *A thesis must not be too narrow and factual.* A thesis that merely states a fact will not provide an opportunity for you to write an essay of any length at all. For example, after you've stated a thesis like "Lagos is the capital of Nigeria," there is nothing left for you to prove. If you start adding information about Lagos—the climate, living conditions, the school system, and the like—you will not be supporting the thesis; they don't help prove that it is the capital of Nigeria.
3. *A thesis cannot be a question.* A thesis has to make an assertion that you are going to prove in your paper; a question is not an assertion.

ACTIVITY

6.2 **Critiquing Thesis Statements**

Look at the following thesis statements for essays, and explain why they would be good or bad.

A.   Culture in Korea and the United States differs greatly.

1. What will this paper discuss?

2. Can you think of a few supporting ideas the paper might include?

3. Is this a good thesis statement? Why or why not?

B.   Saint Vitus's Cathedral in Prague was founded in 1344.

1. What will this paper discuss?

2. Can you think of a few supporting ideas the paper might include?

3. Is this a good thesis statement? Why or why not?

C.   Life in the twentieth century is challenging.

1. What will this paper discuss?

2. Can you think of a few supporting ideas the paper might include?

3. Is this a good thesis statement? Why or why not?

ACTIVITY
6.3 **Writing Thesis Statements**

Write an appropriate thesis statement for each of the following subjects.

1. Recycling

2. Retirement homes

3. Compact cars

4. Living off campus versus living on campus

5. Socialized medicine

6c TECHNIQUES FOR WRITING INTRODUCTIONS

A variety of techniques for writing introductions are presented in the accompanying box.

TECHNIQUES FOR WRITING PARAGRAPHS	
Technique	**Example**
Opening with a question	Do you know how much of each dollar that you donate to charity pays the salaries of administrators?
Opening with a rhetorical question	Would your life really change after winning the lottery?
Opening with a quotation	"No new taxes," promised George Bush.
Opening with a provocative statement	The new law requiring motorcyclists to wear helmets violates the basic principles of democracy.

(continued)

TECHNIQUES FOR WRITING PARAGRAPHS *(continued)*

Opening with a striking image or description	A shiny bright green frog stared up at me from the bathroom floor.
Opening with humor	It occurred to me . . . in the course of watching first the California primary and then the Democratic and Republican national conventions, that it had not been by accident that the people with whom I had preferred to spend time in high school had, on the whole, hung out in gas stations. [Joan Didion, "Insider Baseball"]
Opening with a startling fact	At least 60 million female adults and children in Asia are missing and feared dead. [Jonathan Power]
Opening with an interesting or emotional story	I was alone when I saw the light flicker. Then the lamp began to swing, and I could hear the roar in the background. Suddenly, everything was shaking, and I realized I had to run for the doorway. Just as my feet caught up with my brain, the bookshelf went crashing to the floor. Welcome to life in California, I thought.

ACTIVITY

6.4   **Recognizing Introduction Techniques**

Go back to Activity 6.1. What techniques were used in those introductions?

A. _____

B. _____

Some techniques for opening paragraphs are best avoided. Common mistakes are listed in the accompanying box.

THINGS TO AVOID IN OPENING PARAGRAPHS

- Avoid a discussion that is so general and abstract that it appears to be wasting time.
- Avoid saying, "The purpose of this paper is . . ."
- Avoid saying, "In this paper I will prove . . ."
- Avoid saying, "——— means different things to different people."
- Avoid saying, "Everyone is entitled to an opinion, but . . ."
- Avoid saying, "In this modern world of today . . ."
- Avoid saying, "According to Webster, . . ."
- Avoid apologizing with phrases such as "I really don't know much about this topic" or "I'm not an expert, but . . ."
- Avoid repeating the topic or question you may have been given by your instructor.
- Avoid restating your title, if you have one.

6d **TECHNIQUES FOR WRITING CONCLUSIONS**

The following list is a summary of techniques used in writing conclusions:

- Briefly summarize the main points of the paper.
- Emphasize the action you want the reader to take.

- Refer to an image or event from the opening of the writing.
- Use a question or quotation.

ACTIVITY

6.5 Recognizing Conclusion Techniques

Three techniques for writing conclusions are illustrated here. Study the examples provided, and answer the questions after each.

A. Since I possess both the experience you are looking for and the necessary educational background for the position you have advertised, I hope it will be possible for me to come in for an interview in the next few weeks.

1. Which technique was used in this conclusion?

_____

2. What do you think this piece of writing is about?

_____

B. But the Baltimore-Washington corridor is filling up. Washington and its Maryland suburbs already have the third-worst traffic congestion in the country. If you don't believe me, drive down Route 95 one morning. It's headed straight toward Los Angeles. [Tim Baker, "The Future: It Doesn't Work"]

1. Which technique was used in this conclusion?

_____

2. What do you think this piece of writing is about?

_____

C. Why stop? As Satchmo answered, when asked to define jazz, if you've gotta ask, you're never gonna know. [Mary Hood, "Why Stop?"]

1. Which technique was used in this conclusion?

_____

2. What do you think this piece of writing is about?

_____

As with introductions, certain approaches to writing conclusions should be avoided. Common ones are listed in the following box.

THINGS TO AVOID IN CLOSING PARAGRAPHS

- Avoid going on too long.
- Avoid introducing ideas that were not discussed earlier, even if they support your thesis. The conclusion is not the place to bring up new ideas.
- Avoid apologizing. Don't say, "Although I am no expert" or "This may not be convincing, but . . ."
- Avoid overstating your case.
- Avoid using *In conclusion* or *In summary*. These are too obvious. It should be clear from what you say that you are concluding or summarizing.

ACTIVITY

6.6   Identifying Introductions and Conclusions

Read the following stories about van Gogh, the famous Dutch painter, and Aunt Arie, a woman who makes white oak baskets. For each story, number the paragraphs in the proper order. To do this, you will need to identify the introductions and conclusions, as well as use the tools of paragraph coherence you learned about in Chapter 4. Notice the techniques that are used for the introductions and conclusions.

Gauguin and van Gogh

_____ But bliss was not eternal. When van Gogh saw the portrait Gauguin painted of him, he said, "Yes, it's me all right, but me mad." The words proved prophetic. Later, they argued at a cafe and van Gogh threatened Gauguin with a straight razor. Gauguin stared him down, until van Gogh slunk away. That night, van Gogh sliced off his left ear lobe, wrapped it in a handkerchief, and presented it to a prostitute.

_____ Van Gogh rented a small house, painted it bright yellow, and decorated a room with sunflowers for Gauguin. When the idolized Gauguin arrived in 1888, van Gogh was ecstatic. They painted, debated art passionately, drank, and caroused at brothels together.

_____ Gauguin sensed something special about their brief sojourn together. "Though the public had no idea of it," he wrote, "two men were doing a tremendous job there, useful to both. Perhaps to others too? Some things bear fruit."

_____ Gauguin took the first train north. Van Gogh was thoroughly ashamed of himself. They continued to communicate by letter, and shortly before committing suicide, van Gogh referred to Gauguin as his "dear master."

_____ Ever since they first met in Paris, van Gogh was positive he had found a kindred spirit in Gauguin. While Gauguin painted in Brittany surrounded by disciples, the Dutchman bombarded him with letters begging him to come to the South of France where they could work side by side. [Carol Strickland, *The Annotated Mona Lisa*]

Aunt Arie

_____ While we were making the basket, Aunt Arie talked of her childhood. Her eyes sparkled as she told us how she used to carry corn and eggs for miles in baskets like the one we were making.

_____ "I've been a'hopin' and a'hopin' I'd have company today. That just shows you if you wish and want somethin' bad enough, God'll usually bless y'with it." With a delighted look on her wrinkled face, Aunt Arie greeted us early one hot summer day.

_____ At noon, she cooked dinner for us. Mary and I tried to help, but with an old wooden stove, black iron kettles, water drawn from the well, and general inexperience, we could do little more than watch Aunt Arie hustle about, laughing gently at our mistakes.

_____ With people like Aunt Arie, making white oak baskets has been very rewarding for me. I've learned not only the skills, but the value of sincere friendliness, honesty, and hard work—and that may be the most important lesson of all.

_____ I first met Aunt Arie in June. My immediate reaction was one of shock. How could such a tiny, delicate woman, eighty-five years old, maintain her own garden, do all her cooking and cleaning, make quilts every winter for her family and friends, and still manage to survive without luxuries? I didn't wonder long. During the day, as Aunt Arie patiently taught us how to make white oak baskets, I realized why Mike and Paul spoke of her with such affection. She is, to put it simply, just plain good. She is full of vitality [and] determination, and she radiates a warmth that few people have. [Jan Brown, "Making a Basket out of White Oak Splits"]

ACTIVITY 6.7 Writing Introductions and Conclusions

Here is a new version of Mowli Kamal's paper on black mortality. The second draft has been revised and the grammar corrected, but the introduction and conclusion are missing. Read the paper; then write an appropriate introduction and conclusion.

```
     Infant mortality in the United States during 1989 was the
lowest it has ever been, but it is still higher than in other
developed countries.  In 1989, the infant mortality rate for
blacks was twice that of whites, and infant deaths among blacks
have decreased at a much slower rate than among whites.  Black
infants have over twice the risk of dying in their first year of
life compared to white infants.
```

Between 1988 and 1989, the main causes of infant death were premature birth and low birth weight, respiratory distress syndrome, and complications associated with pregnancy. Prematurity is the primary cause of newborn deaths and illness, and poverty and unplanned pregnancies are important causes of preterm births. Teenagers, unmarried black women, and women receiving Medicaid are at greatest risk for both poverty and unplanned pregnancy.

It seems that racism is a contributing factor to the high infant mortality rate. Poor black women who have no education and cannot get the same health care as whites are giving birth to these premature babies. Black women are often the victims of a national policy that prevents them from receiving information about family planning, including ready availability of contraceptives. Poverty, illiteracy, and unplanned pregnancy are responsible for premature births.

The United States has the best health care system in the world technologically, but it is lacking in measurements of good health care service. Services are not easily available, nor are health care resources used efficiently. The United States spends 40 percent more than Canada for health care and much more than England, though England's level of health care is equivalent to that of the United States. Distributional equity is lacking. A specific level of health care is not available to all citizens.

The differences in the quality of health care among people in the United States are persistent and often substantial, with considerable disparity between white and black people. Differences also exist in need for and access to health care. It appears that even when blacks are treated, they are less likely to receive certain kinds of treatment. Treatment of some conditions, such as pneumonia, was found to be more aggressive for white people. Differences in the rates of cesarean sections were noted, with more being performed for white women. Here racial prejudice is probably the factor.

In addition, blacks living in urban areas of the United States are generally more disadvantaged in economic, social, and

health care areas than whites. Blacks are more likely to be
sick and disabled and to have lower incomes and education
levels.

The leading cause of death among young black males is
homicide and "legal intervention"--in other words, being shot by
police officers. These two causes accounted for 98.9 per
100,000 deaths of black males aged 24 to 34 in 1987. For white
males of the same age, the rate was 13.2 per 100,000. The
probability of a black male being killed is 500 percent greater
than it is for his white counterpart.

In this case, racism is also a factor. In most of the
cases, blacks are being shot without any reason. Sometimes
police officers kill black people only under suspicion. As
blacks have little or no power against whites, police officers
are killing these people without any hesitation. They know that
they are not going to be charged.

PART III

REVISING FOR EFFECTIVE SENTENCES AND WORD USE

7 Avoiding Unnecessary Shifts

8 Forming Compound and Complex Sentences Using Coordination and Subordination

9 Using Parallel Structures for Parallel Ideas

10 Avoiding Mixed or Incomplete Constructions

11 Avoiding Misplaced and Dangling Modifiers

12 Choosing the Right Words

7 AVOIDING UNNECESSARY SHIFTS

Readers expect consistency. If you start writing in one way and shift to another without any apparent reason, your reader may be confused. In this chapter we will discuss five kinds of shifts that can cause trouble in your writing.

7a AVOIDING SHIFTS IN TENSE

In English, verb tenses must be used consistently (see Chapter 14 for a discussion of verb tenses). However, tense can and does change in a paragraph when there is a reason for the shift. Look at the following example.

> When I was young, I was afraid of the ocean, but now I love to swim in the waves.

> Notice that in this sentence, the verb tense changes from the past tense *(was)* to the present tense *(love)*. Is this incorrect? The answer is no; it is appropriate because of the shift from "when I was young" to "now."

Now let's look at a longer example in Activity 7.1.

ACTIVITY 7.1 **Explaining Shifts in Tense**

Read the following passage; then answer the questions that follow it.

> The Jensens' twin sisters, Rachel and Rebecca, are also excellent tennis players. Rachel is in her second year on the women's tour (she's ranked 287) and Rebecca is an All-American at Kansas. Luke and Murphey already know how the four of them will pair up if such a final ever takes place. On the way to the hospital to see their newborn sisters twenty years ago, the brothers picked their doubles partner. Luke chose Rebecca, and Murphey took Rachel. Always planning. [Kelli Anderson, "Luke and Murphey Jensen"]

1. There are two shifts in verb tense in this paragraph. The paragraph begins in the simple present tense. Write the sentence where the verb tense shifts to the future tense:

   _____

2. Why does this shift take place? What language cue in the sentence tells you there will be a shift to the future tense?

   _____

3. The second shift in this paragraph is from the future tense to the past tense. Write the sentence where this occurs:

_____

4. Why does this shift take place? What language cue in the sentence tells you there will be a shift to the past tense?

_____

ACTIVITY

7.2   **Revising Paragraphs for Tense Consistency**

Read the following paragraphs carefully. Look for the sentences where there is a shift in verb tense, and decide if that shift is correct. If the shift is not correct, rewrite the sentence so that the tense is consistent.

1. When I entered the classroom, I noticed immediately that something was wrong. One student is standing in the front of the room looking very disturbed, and everyone else is crowded against the back wall. Several chairs are turned over, and no one is saying anything. Then I notice that the student in the front of the room is pointing a large, shiny pistol at everyone else. As I walk in, he runs past me, out of the room, and down the hall. Everyone breathed deeply and started talking at once. I finally figured out that the student with the gun had robbed everyone else and then fled.

2. Anyone familiar with a large opera house would testify that it is an extraordinary labyrinth of people and passageways, but the Paris Opera House of the last quarter of the nineteenth century was remarkable by any standards. This opera house, which was the inspiration for the book *The Phantom of the Opera*, was built between 1861 and 1875. At the time in which the novel was set, the Opera House boasts over fifteen hundred employees and has its own stables. Even today it employs over a thousand people and contains two permanent ballet schools within the building. [Playbill, *The Phantom of the Opera*, Her Majesty's Theatre, London]

3. The Park Service, established by Congress in 1916, was directed not only to administer the parks but also to "provide for the enjoyment of same in such manner and by such means as will leave them unimpaired for the enjoyment of future generations." This appropriately ambiguous language, employed long

before the onslaught of the automobile, has been understood in various and often opposing ways ever since. Today, the Park Service, like any other big organization, included factions and factions. The Developers, the dominant faction, placed their emphasis on the words "provide for the enjoyment." The Preservers, a minority but also strong, emphasized the words "leave them unimpaired." It is apparent, then, that we cannot decide the question of development versus preservation by a simple referral to holy writ or an attempt to guess the intention of the founding fathers; we must make up our own minds and decide for ourselves what the national parks should be and what purpose they should serve. [Edward Abbey, *Desert Solitaire*]

7b AVOIDING SHIFTS IN PERSON AND NUMBER

English has three different **persons** (first, second, and third) and two **numbers** (singular and plural) expressed through pronouns, as the chart demonstrates.

NUMBER AND PERSON OF PERSONAL PRONOUNS

	Number	
Person	**Singular**	**Plural**
First person (the person or persons speaking)	*I, me, my, mine*	*we, us, our, ours*
Second person (the person or persons spoken to)	*you, your, yours*	*you, your, yours*
Third person (the person or persons spoken about)	*he, she, it, one* *him, her* *his, her, hers, its*	*they* *them* *their, theirs*

The following paragraph has coherence problems that stem from inconsistencies in person and number. Read the paragraph, and see if you can identify the problems.

If someone takes yoga classes, they do not have to do any meditation. They can just do the various positions, which are good for your posture and for reducing tension. If one practices the various positions about three times a week, you will experience considerable progress within six months. One will get out of yoga as much as he puts in.

The paragraph is incoherent because the writer couldn't decide which person or number to use. The paragraph starts with third-person singular (*someone*), then shifts to third-person plural (*they*), and then shifts to second person (*you*). Next the third-person singular appears again (*one*), followed by second person (*you*). Finally, in the last sentence, the writer switches back to third-person singular (*one, he*).

Inconsistency in person or number makes writing confusing to the reader. In fact, the writer of the paragraph about yoga could have used just about any *one* of the persons and numbers, as long as he or she used it consistently.

By the way, you may have been cautioned never to use the pronoun *you* in your writing. Teachers sometimes give this advice because using the pronoun *you* is less formal (more familiar) than using third person. They also warn against the use of *you* because it is the most frequent source of inconsistency of person and number. It seems almost natural to start with "If a student wants to get an A in biology," and then to continue, "you must be prepared to memorize a lot of terms." Because this shift occurs so easily, you must guard against it. However, the fact that second person is more personal can make it the most powerful person to use. So you need not avoid *you* completely; just use caution when you choose to use it.

ACTIVITY
7.3   **Revising Paragraphs for Consistency in Person and Number**

Rewrite the paragraph you just read about yoga, making it consistent in person and number in the two ways indicated.

1. If you take yoga classes, you do not have to do any meditation.

2. If people take yoga classes, they do not have to do any meditation.

Even the principle of consistency has some room for flexibility. The following sentence is perfectly correct, even though it shifts its point of view.

Although many students put off their English courses as long as possible, you should probably take an English course in your first semester.

The sentence begins in third-person plural (*students, they*). In the second half, however, it shifts to second person (*you*). In this case, the shift is not a mistake because it represents a genuine shift in whom the writer is speaking about. In the first half of the sentence, the writer is speaking about students in general and so uses third person; in the second half, the writer addresses the reader directly and so, correctly, shifts to the second-person pronoun, *you.*

ACTIVITY
7.4   **Editing Sentences for Consistency in Person and Number**

Read the following sentences, and edit them for consistency in person and number.

1. People should eat right and exercise if you want to live a long life.

2. A dog is a very loyal pet, and they love to play.

3. You must sign in when entering the pool area, or else we can't swim.

4. I went to see my teacher about my grades, but she wouldn't talk to us.

5. Last week we went to the ballpark. When we entered the stadium, you could hear the roar of the crowd.

7c AVOIDING SHIFTS IN MOOD

Three moods are possible for verbs in English:

- The **indicative mood**—the most common—is used to express facts and opinions.
- The **imperative mood** is used to express commands or advice.
- The **subjunctive mood**—fairly rare—is used to express wishes, proposals, or conditions that do not exist. (See Chapter 15 for further discussion on the subjunctive mood.)

In the following example, the mood shifts from indicative to imperative.

1. Use plenty of concrete examples in your writing and ~~you should~~ focus on one subject.

The first half of this sentence is in the imperative mood—it gives a command—and the second half is in the indicative. Either mood would work in this sentence but shifting from one to the other is confusing for the reader.

In sentence 2, the shift is from subjunctive to indicative.

were

2. I wish that my job were less stressful and that I ~~was~~ promoted to manager.

The first part of sentence 2 is in the subjunctive mood because it expresses a wish. The second half of the sentence was erroneously written in the indicative mood.

Once you start with one mood, do not shift to a different mood for no apparent reason.

ACTIVITY 7.5 Editing Sentences for Shifts in Mood

Edit the following sentences for consistency in mood.

1. Doctors advise against playing in the woods during tick season. Also, check your pets carefully.

2. If Ross Perot were elected, leave the country.

3. Don't walk on campus late at night, and you should carry mace with you at all times.

4. The principal asks that students come to class on time and sit in your seats during class.

5. If you want to learn how to sail, read the book *All about Sailing* and then you should take lessons.

7d AVOIDING SHIFTS IN VOICE

Two voices are possible for verbs in English: (See Chapter 14 for a discussion of passive voice.)

- In the **active voice,** the subject is the person or thing performing the action.
- In the **passive voice,** the subject is the person or thing receiving the action.

In the following example, the writer shifts from active to passive voice.

she asked me
My college roommate called me, and ~~I was asked~~ for a donation to the alumni fund.

This sentence begins with a clause in active voice—the subject *roommate* performs the action of calling—but the second half is a clause in passive voice—the subject *I* does not do the asking but is rather the receiver of the action of asking.

Passive voice is generally less direct and less clear than active voice; it is especially weak when it is the result of a shift like the one in the previous example. In general, if you begin a sentence in one voice, do not shift into the other.

ACTIVITY 7.6 **Editing Sentences for Shifts in Voice**

Edit the following sentences to avoid shifts in voice.

1. The students went to the library, and books were checked out by them.

2. Jack washed and cut the vegetables, and the salad was prepared.

3. The attorney elicited the information from the witness, and the details were documented.

4. The scientist identified the insect and concurred that many people have been hurt by it.

5. Many trees were blown down by the tornado, and it destroyed several houses.

7e AVOIDING SHIFTS BETWEEN DIRECT AND INDIRECT QUOTATION

In English, there are two ways to report someone's words:

Direct quotation: Juanita said, "I am going back to college."

Indirect quotation: Juanita said that she is going back to college.

In direct quotation, the writer reports the exact words of the speaker and places them in quotation marks. In indirect quotation, the writer accurately reports what a person said but not in the exact words the person used.

1. **INCORRECT:** Mr. Hernandez said that he is firing Jackie because she did not come to work yesterday and she did not call to tell me she was sick.

2. **CORRECT:** Mr. Hernandez said that he is firing Jackie because she did not come to work yesterday and she did not call to tell him she was sick.

3. **CORRECT:** Mr. Hernandez said, "I am firing Jackie because she did not come to work yesterday and she did not call to tell me she was sick."

In sentence 1, the writer mixed indirect quotation with direct quotation, and the result was a confusing sentence. In sentence 2, the writer has corrected the problem by making both parts of the sentence indirect quotations; in sentence 3, the writer has corrected the problem by making both parts direct quotations.

ACTIVITY

7.7   **Editing Sentences for Shifts in Discourse**

Edit the following sentences for consistency in direct and indirect quotation.

1. I wonder if the defense secretary knew of the attack and did he authorize it.

2. My doctor said that eating garlic will lower cholesterol and eat the garlic fresh.

3. The newscaster reported that the queen of Thailand looks lovely as she approaches the limousine.

4. My veterinarian said your puppy is healthy but that I should give him more exercise.

5. The dean recommended that each department trim its budget and I will expect to receive a statement by the end of the month.

FORMING COMPOUND AND COMPLEX SENTENCES USING COORDINATION AND SUBORDINATION

DIAGNOSTIC ACTIVITY: COORDINATION AND SUBORDINATION

ACTIVITY

8.1 **How Much Do You Know?**

Read each sentence, and determine if it contains an error in coordination or subordination. If there is an error, correct it. Not all sentences contain errors. An example is provided.

Example: Big cars are comfortable, however, they consume a lot of gas.

1. The train is convenient, in addition it is cheaper.
2. Summers near a lake are wonderful, but there are many mosquitoes.
3. The house was very clean, and Joe didn't make it to the restaurant.
4. Seth didn't like to go camping, and he went with his family over the holiday.
5. The swimming pool is located behind Building A, it is open from 9 to 5.
6. Sam is studying to be a doctor. He has three years left.
7. Betty's aunt runs a catering business will cook lunch for us.
8. The jacket in the closet is mine.
9. Since the game was on at seven o'clock we decided to eat early.
10. I went along with the plan even though I disagreed with it.
11. Mary wondered whether the windows are shut.
12. Helena decided Pan will begin preschool this year.
13. Because the river is so wide and the tremendous amount of rain in the last few days.
14. The periods Picasso went through were diverse. For example, his blue period, pink period, and Cubist period.

Determine which items you missed in this Diagnostic Activity. If you missed or had trouble with any of the items, please go to the appropriate section in *The*

HarperCollins Concise Handbook for Writers and this workbook for further practice and study.

It is important to know which items cause you difficulty. When revising your writing, you might want to go through your paper one time checking only for coordination or subordination. Concentrate on items that you had difficulty with in this activity.

8b UNDERSTANDING THE TERMINOLOGY

A **simple sentence** contains one independent clause:

I like fishing.

When coordination is used to join two *independent clauses,* the result is a **compound sentence:**

I like fishing, but I hate hunting.

When subordination is used to join an *independent clause* with a *dependent clause,* the result is a **complex sentence:**

I like fishing when the weather is good.

Coordination is used to link ideas that are of *equal importance.* These ideas may be independent clauses, phrases, or just single nouns:

My father lives in Tampa, and my mother has a condo in Clearwater.

Subordination is used to link ideas that are of *unequal importance.* The less important idea is subordinated to the main idea:

Give your form to the woman who is sitting at the information desk.

8c FORMING COMPOUND SENTENCES USING COORDINATION

Compound sentences—sentences combining two independent clauses—are formed in one of three ways:

- With a comma and a coordinating conjunction
- With a semicolon
- With a conjunctive adverb

Comma and Coordinating Conjunction

A dark surface will absorb heat, but a light surface will reflect it.

There are only seven coordinating conjunctions in English: *and, but, or, for, so, yet, nor.* Notice that each of them contains three or fewer letters. It may help to remember the nonsense word *fanboys,* which contains the first letter of each of the coordinating conjunctions.

Semicolon

Carbon dioxide comes from burning coal; methane comes from cattle digestion.

Conjunctive Adverb

Bird watching is not an expensive hobby; however, you do need to invest in a pair of binoculars.

Bird watching is not an expensive hobby; you do, however, need to invest in a pair of binoculars.

Bird watching is not an expensive hobby; you do need to invest, however, in a pair of binoculars.

Bird watching is not an expensive hobby; you do need to invest in a pair of binoculars, however.

Bird watching is not an expensive hobby. However, you do need to invest in a pair of binoculars.

Unlike coordinating conjunctions, conjunctive adverbs are movable in sentences. The most common conjunctive adverbs are listed in the accompanying box. The phrases on the list are sometimes called *transitional expressions,* but since the words and phrases are all used in the same way, we will refer to all of them as *conjunctive adverbs.*

CONJUNCTIVE ADVERBS

accordingly	for example	in other words	on the other hand
after all	for instance	instead	otherwise
also	further	likewise	similarly
anyway	furthermore	meanwhile	still
as a result	hence	moreover	subsequently
besides	however	nevertheless	then
certainly	in addition	next	thereafter
consequently	incidentally	nonetheless	therefore
even so	indeed	of course	thus
finally	in fact		

8d ABOUT COORDINATION

Three rules apply to coordination:

1. Coordinate only ideas that are logically equivalent.
2. Use conjunctions that reflect the logical relationship between the ideas.
3. Avoid excessive coordination.

Logical Equivalence

Tom is very selfish and young.

The movie we saw was offensive, and it was filmed in California.

The problem here is that the writer has used coordination (in this case using the conjunction *and*) to join ideas that are not logically equivalent.

Appropriate Conjunctions

Maxine hasn't read the book, and she saw the movie.

The problem here is that the conjunction *and* is normally used to join two ideas that are *equal* and *have compatible meanings.* In this case, the meanings are not compatible because they make opposite assertions.

Excessive Coordination

The following paragraph illustrates excessive coordination:

Marcy intended to graduate in four years, but she soon discovered that this was not going to be possible. In her first semester she had to drop one course, and she took an incomplete in another, and the next year she registered for only three courses, and she worked thirty hours per week, and then she learned that the anatomy course she needed would not be offered in the spring, so she had to take another incomplete in statistics, and now she will be lucky if she graduates in six years.

ACTIVITY
8.2 Identifying the Function of Coordinating Conjunctions and Conjunctive Adverbs

Place the coordinating conjunctions and conjunctive adverbs from 8c in the chart below according to the following categories:*

Additive: used to signal addition, introduction, exemplification, similarity

Adversative: used to signal conflict, contradiction, concession

Causal: used to signal cause and effect, reason and result

Sequential: used to signal a chronological or logical sequence and summation

Category	Coordinating Conjunctions	Conjunctive Adverbs
Additive	*and*	
Adversative		
Causal		*consequently*
Sequential		

ACTIVITY
8.3 Forming Compound Sentences

A. For each item, combine the two sentences using the option indicated.

Example: Pigs are intelligent animals.
They are dirty and smelly. (conjunctive adverb in mid position of second clause)

Pigs are intelligent animals; they are, however, dirty and smelly.

*Marianne Celce-Murcia and Diane Larsen-Freeman, *The Grammar Book* (City: Rowley House, 1983), p. 324.

1. I've been a flight instructor for ten years.
   I know that students tend to make easy things hard. (coordinating conjunction)

   _____

2. There are many different options to think about when buying a computer.
   You must choose the size of the hard drive, the type of monitor, and the amount
   of memory. (conjunctive adverb at beginning of second clause)

   _____

3. Garbage is a big problem in the United States.
   Every American produces 3.5 pounds of garbage a day. (semicolon)

   _____

4. André complained that he was very hungry.
   He said he was so hungry he could eat a horse. (conjunctive adverb at beginning of second clause)

   _____

5. Ramon has never visited Alcatraz.
   He doesn't ever want to. (coordinating conjunction)

   _____

B.   Rewrite the following story about a Native American legend by combining
some of the sentences. Use a combination of the three options for forming compound sentences.

A Garden of Eden

Old legends say that all Indian people lived as one in a big village. The Great
Spirit fulfilled all their needs. In the middle of the village grew a huge tree. It bore
all sorts of fruits and vegetables. The tree had apples, pears, peaches, potatoes,
beans, and carrots. The people depended on the tree for their food.

Soon the people began to argue. They grew angry with one another. One day
the Great Spirit told them to change their ways. He told them to get along. They
didn't listen. The Great Spirit sent a violent storm. The storm blew the tree over.

The people looked at the tree. It was lying on the ground. Their existence
depended on the tree. Now it was gone. They tried to exist on the fish and animals.
They went hungry. Many of them grew sick and weak.

They held a council. Many things were discussed. It all came back to the big
tree. They knew they must try to appease the Great Spirit. Perhaps they should
talk to Penaywog (Many Partridge). He was an old man who knew everything.

They went to Penaywog. They told him of their plight. Penaywog knew that
the Great Spirit destroyed the tree because they had careless ways of living. He told
them that this was their punishment. Now they must raise their own food. "How
do we do that?" they asked. Penaywog said, "Go to the tree, pick up the leaves and
branches, dig up the ground, and put them in. You will have to tend these plants
forever."

They went back to the village. They took the leaves from the trees. They planted them. They worked in the hot sun. They pulled weeds and hoed. Fruits and vegetables began to appear. They harvested the crops. They remembered that they should get along with one another. They should live in balance with the Earth Mother. [Simon Otto, *Walk in Peace*]

8e AVOIDING COMMA SPLICES AND FUSED SENTENCES

Two common problems that occur when forming compound sentences are comma splices and fused sentences:

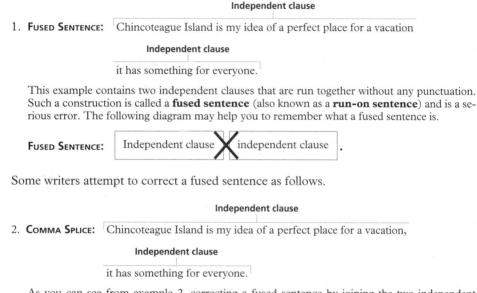

Independent clause

1. **FUSED SENTENCE:** Chincoteague Island is my idea of a perfect place for a vacation

Independent clause

it has something for everyone.

This example contains two independent clauses that are run together without any punctuation. Such a construction is called a **fused sentence** (also known as a **run-on sentence**) and is a serious error. The following diagram may help you to remember what a fused sentence is.

FUSED SENTENCE: Independent clause ✕ independent clause .

Some writers attempt to correct a fused sentence as follows.

Independent clause

2. **COMMA SPLICE:** Chincoteague Island is my idea of a perfect place for a vacation,

Independent clause

it has something for everyone.

As you can see from example 2, correcting a fused sentence by joining the two independent clauses with a comma creates another error, known as a **comma splice.** A comma splice, like a fused sentence, is a *serious* error.

COMMA SPLICE: Independent clause ✕ independent clause .

To correct fused sentences, you can choose from the three options discussed in 8c. You can also create two separate sentences, using a period and a capital letter. Be careful with this approach; if used too often, it results in a choppy, immature style of writing because of an excessive number of short, simple sentences.

ACTIVITY
8.4 **Revising Fused Sentences**

Revise the sentence about Chincoteague Island using the three options in 8c and the fourth option of creating two sentences.

1. _____

2. _____

3. _____

4. _____

ACTIVITY
8.5   **Identifying and Correcting Fused Sentences and Comma Splices**

Read the following sentences. Decide if there is a problem with a fused sentence or a comma splice. If there is an error, correct it. Not all of the sentences contain errors.

1. Diving in the Cayman Islands is spectacular, the fish are brightly colored.

2. Debates are very important for the candidates, so careful planning goes into each debate.

3. Music can be used to stimulate and help in a variety of situations there are two different kinds.

4. A dog was left in a car with the windows rolled up, the dog might die.

5. Shanghai is one of the most crowded cities in the world, its population density is five times that of Paris.

8f FORMING COMPLEX SENTENCES USING SUBORDINATION

The three types of subordinate clauses are italicized in the following examples:

1. The coach *who is crying* is from the losing team.
2. *When she quit smoking,* Maureen gained twenty pounds.
3. *Whoever stole my disk* is going to be surprised.

The subordinate clause in sentence 1 is an **adjective (adjectival, relative) clause.** The one in sentence 2 is an **adverb (adverbial) clause.** The one in sentence 3 is a **noun clause.** These three types of subordinate clauses are discussed in detail in 8g, 8h, and 8i, respectively.

Subordination is useful because it allows the writer to avoid a series of short simple sentences, to indicate which are main ideas and which are subordinate, and to convey the relationship between main ideas and subordinate ones.

We will look at these applications of subordination later in this chapter, but first let us look at how to form complex sentences.

8g FORMING ADJECTIVE CLAUSES

Relative Pronouns (*who, which,* and *that*)

The relative pronouns *who, whom, whose, which,* and *that* are used to begin adjective clauses. In each of the following sentences, two independent clauses are combined to form a single sentence. One clause remains an independent clause while the other is changed into an adjective clause. If your writing has too many short, choppy sentences, you may want to try combining some of them in this way.

To combine

Independent clause		Independent clause
The woman is my daughter.	**+**	The woman is wearing a purple dress.

first convert one independent clause to an adjective clause:

Independent clause		Adjective clause
The woman is my daughter	**+**	who is wearing a purple dress

Then insert it into the remaining independent clause so that it follows the noun that the relative pronoun (in this case *who*) stands for

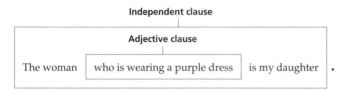

In adjective clauses, the relative pronoun can serve one of four different functions: subject, direct object, object of a preposition, or possessive.

Relative Pronouns as Subjects

The man is the detective. **+** The man smokes a cigar. **=**

The man *who* smokes a cigar is the detective.

The relative pronoun *who* is functioning as the subject of the dependent clause. In this case, the subject of the two sentences that were combined is the same: *man.*

Christopher went to Columbia University. **+** Columbia University is in New York. **=**

Christopher went to Columbia University, *which* is in New York.

Although the subjects of the two independent clauses, *Christopher* and *Columbia University,* are different, you can use a relative pronoun to introduce the adjective clause when the relative pronoun follows immediately after the noun it is standing for; in this case, *which* follows immediately after *Columbia University.*

Relative Pronouns as Direct Objects

The butterfly pin is very pretty. **+** Maria will wear the pin to the barbecue. **=**

The butterfly pin *that* Maria will wear to the barbecue is very pretty.

Relative pronouns can replace the direct object *(pin)* in a sentence that is changed into an adjective clause.

Relative Pronouns as Objects of Prepositions

Paco was my host in Spain. **+** I received a letter from Paco. **=**

Paco, from *whom* I received a letter, was my host in Spain.

The relative pronoun *whom* can be used as the object of a preposition.

Relative Pronouns Used as Possessives

The woman is taking me to court. **+** I hit the woman's car. **=**

The woman *whose* car I hit is taking me to court.

The relative pronoun *whose* can be used as a possessive in an adjective clause.

The chart summarizes the relative pronouns and their functions in a sentence.

RELATIVE PRONOUNS		
Function	**Human Being**	**Thing**
Subject	*who*	*which*
	that	*that*
Direct object	*whom*	*which*
	that	*that*
Object of preposition	*whom*	*which*
Possessive	*whose*	*whose*

Deciding Which Pronoun to Use in the Subject and Object Position

Choosing the correct relative pronoun in the subject and object position depends on whether the sentence is a restrictive adjective clause or a nonrestrictive adjective clause.

Restrictive: Sadako's cousin *who writes children's books* is coming for a visit.

Nonrestrictive: Theresa's cousin, *who writes children's books,* is coming for a visit.

A restrictive clause contains information essential to understanding the sentence. Sadako has more than one cousin, and this clause identifies exactly which cousin she will visit—the one who writes children's books. A nonrestrictive clause contains extra information that is not necessary to understanding the sentence because it *does not* restrict the word it modifies (in the example, *cousin*) to a particular one. Notice that restrictive clauses are *not* set off by commas; nonrestrictive clauses are.

Correct: The woman *who is wearing a blue hat* is angry.

Correct: The woman *who is wearing a blue hat* is angry.

Correct: Stefan Martin, *who is wearing a blue hat,* is angry.

Incorrect: Stefan Martin, *wearing a blue hat,* is angry.

In the subject and object position, the pronoun *that* cannot be used in nonrestrictive adjective clauses.

Correct: My sister, *who is older than me,* is coming next week.

Incorrect: My sister, *that is older than me,* is coming next week.

When you use the relative pronoun *that*, it automatically makes the clause restrictive. In the first example, the writer is simply providing extra information about her sister. In the second example, the writer is restricting the visiting sister to the one that is older.

Omitting the Relative Pronoun and the Verb *Be* in Adjective Clauses

The rules for when one can and cannot omit a relative pronoun also depend on the distinction between restrictive and nonrestrictive adjective clauses.

It is sometimes permissible to omit the relative pronoun and the verb in a restrictive adjective clause. You can *never* omit a relative pronoun in a nonrestrictive clause.

You *can* omit a pronoun and a form of the verb *be* in a restrictive adjective clause in the following instances:

1. When a participle follows the verb:

    CORRECT: The woman *who is wearing a blue hat* is angry.

    CORRECT: The woman *wearing a blue hat* is angry.

2. When the verb is followed by a prepositional phrase:

    CORRECT: The woman *who is in the pool* is a champion swimmer.

    CORRECT: The woman *in the pool* is a champion swimmer.

You *cannot* omit relative pronouns and verbs in restrictive adjective clauses in the following instances:

1. When the verb is an action verb and does not include a form of the verb *be* in front of it:

    CORRECT: The woman *who bought a blue hat* is angry.

    INCORRECT: The woman *a blue hat* is angry.

2. When the verb *be* is in the past tense:

    CORRECT: The cat *that was under the table* is gone now.

    INCORRECT: The cat *under the table* is gone now. (The situation no longer exists.)

3. When the verb is followed by an adjective:

    CORRECT: The woman *who is angry* is my sister.

    INCORRECT: The woman *angry* is my sister.

SUMMARY OF RULES FOR OMITTING RELATIVE PRONOUNS AND VERBS IN ADJECTIVE CLAUSES

The relative pronoun and the verb *be* in an adjective clause may be omitted if the following conditions are met:

- The adjective clause is restrictive.
- The verb *be* is in the present tense.
- The verb *be* is followed by a participle or a prepositional phrase.

Omitting the Relative Pronoun in Adjective Clauses

Another option is omitting just the relative pronoun. As before, relative pronouns cannot be omitted from nonrestrictive clauses. But a relative pronoun *can* be omitted when the pronoun is *not* the subject of the adjective clause (in this example, it is the direct object):

CORRECT: A woman *whom I respect* was elected president.

CORRECT: A woman *I respect* was elected president.

You should *not* omit the relative pronoun when it is used in a prepositional phrase and both the preposition and the relative pronoun appear at the beginning of the adjective clause:

CORRECT: Here is a bowl *in which* you can put those beans.

INCORRECT: Here is a bowl *in* you can put those beans.

You may *not* omit the relative pronoun when it is used as a possessive in the adjective clause:

CORRECT: When I moved to Lansing, I met the Bordens, *whose* dog is a German shepherd.

INCORRECT: When I moved to Lansing, I met the Bordens, dog is a German shepherd.

SUMMARY OF RULES FOR OMITTING RELATIVE PRONOUNS IN ADJECTIVE CLAUSES

The relative pronoun at the beginning of an adjective clause may be omitted if the following conditions are met:

- The adjective clause is restrictive.
- The relative pronoun is not the subject of the adjective clause.
- The relative pronoun is in a prepositional phrase in the adjective clause, and the preposition is moved to the end of the clause.
- The relative pronoun is not a possessive in the adjective clause.

ACTIVITY

8.6   **Forming Adjective Clauses**

Combine the following sentences using an appropriate relative pronoun. If a pronoun and/or the verb *be* is not necessary, omit it.

> *Example:*   The hammer is in the garage.
> The hammer is Fred's.
>
> *The hammer in the garage is Fred's.*

1. Mr. Jensen works for a computer company.
   Mr. Jensen's car is a Mercedes-Benz.

   _____

2. There is a great restaurant on Grant Street.
   The restaurant serves *tapas*.

   _____

3. You can see an eclipse.
   The best time is in winter.

   _____

4. The woman cuts my hair.
   The woman is from Argentina.

   _____

5. Garlic is a great flavor enhancer.
   Garlic can lower your cholesterol.

   _____

6. The house is on the corner.
   The house is for sale.

   _____

7. Geraldo is a member of the committee.
   The committee will not meet on Saturday.

   _____

ACTIVITY
8.7 **Omitting Relative Pronouns**

Read the following passage, and decide if the relative pronoun and/or the verb *be* can be omitted. If it can, cross the word out.

> When Erfan first came to the United States, he stayed with a family that lived on a lake. The Ripples had three children. Mike, who was the oldest, was interested in water-skiing and playing the guitar. The sister that Erfan liked best was the second oldest. She was very outgoing and had a boyfriend who owned a speedboat that Erfan loved to ride in. Sarah, who was the youngest daughter, was constantly getting into trouble when she played near the lake. She had a shovel that she loved to use to throw sand at people. One time, a neighbor who was sitting in a boat next to the dock was thrown into the lake by Sarah, who had tipped the boat over. Erfan was really surprised that her parents didn't scold her more. The Ripples also had a dog that was named Max. The ball that Max loved to chase after was a dirty, soggy tennis ball. Erfan was never very happy to throw it, but he loved Max, so he would make the sacrifice.
>
> Although life was very different for Erfan in the Ripples' house, he had a wonderful time staying with a family that treated him so well. He also learned a great deal about American culture. Still, he was happy when he finally got an apartment that was near campus so that he could live alone again.

ACTIVITY
8.8 **Using Adjective Clauses**

Write a sentence that defines each of the following words.

   Example: a Brazilian: *A Brazilian is a person who lives in Brazil.*_____

1. coffeemaker: _____

2. bicycle: _____

3. monkey: _____

4. library: _____

5. butcher: _____

8h FORMING ADVERB CLAUSES

Adverb clauses modify a verb, an adjective, or an adverb in a sentence. Like adverbs, they often answer the questions *why? when?* or *in what manner?*

Because his dog had died, Larry did not enjoy the party.

Larry did not enjoy the party *because his dog had died.*

In the first example, the adverb clause precedes the independent clause and emphasizes the fact that Larry's dog has died. Notice that a comma must be used after the clause. In the second example, the adverb clause follows the independent clause, emphasizing the idea that Larry can't enjoy the party. No comma is needed when the adverb clause follows the main clause.

The accompanying box lists subordinating conjunctions that introduce adverb clauses.

SUBORDINATING CONJUNCTIONS

Conjunction	Meaning
after	following in place or time
although	regardless of the fact that
as	because, for the reason that
as if	in the same way that it would be if
as long as	for the period of time during which
as soon as	at the time when
as though	in the manner as if
because	for the reason that, as a result of the fact that
before	in advance of the time when
even if	regardless of the possibility that
even though	regardless of the fact that
how	by what means, in what manner
if	in the event that
if only	only in the event that
in case	because of the unlikely event that
in order that	to make possible that
insofar as	to the extent that
in that	inasmuch as
lest	so as to prevent the possibility that
no matter how	regardless of the manner in which
now that	at this time, in consequence of the fact that
once	as soon as

(continued)

SUBORDINATING CONJUNCTIONS *(continued)*	
provided (that)	on the condition that
since	from the time when, as a result of the fact that
so that	in order that
supposing (that)	in the unlikely case that
than	(used to introduce the second half of a comparison)
that	(used to introduce a subordinate clause that states a fact, wish, consequence, or reason)
though	despite the fact that, conceding the fact that
till	up to the time that
unless	except under the condition that
until	up to the time that
when	at the time(s) that
whenever	at whatever time that
where	at or in the place that
whereas	it being the fact that
wherever	in or to whatever place
whether	should it be the case that
while	as long as, during the time that
why	for what purpose, for what reason

Note: Many of these conjunctions can also be used as prepositions, sometimes with slightly different meanings.

ACTIVITY
8.9 Using Subordinating Conjunctions

The following passage tells the story of the Donner party, heading west from Illinois, who foolishly took the advice from a book to take a cutoff that led them over the Wasatch Mountains in Utah. For each blank in the passage, choose an appropriate subordinating conjunction from the list in the box (more than one choice may be appropriate), and write it in.

_____ a harrowing trip across the fiery desert, the party was rife with dissension and ill feeling. _____ the Donners reached the Truckee River at the foot of the Sierra [in late October], they were far behind schedule. _____ they prepared to climb the 2,000-foot granite ridge of the Sierra, the first winter storm came whistling out of the north. _____ long the mountains were buried under snow, stalling [the travelers] completely; by December the emigrants were reduced to eating twigs and bark. _____ four men died and one went insane, a party of fifteen of the strongest started for help. Thirty-two days later, seven of them arrived at an Indian village _____ they were more dead than alive. The seven told of having been forced to eat the bodies of companions who died along the way.

The first of several relief parties reached Donner Lake on February 18, 1847, _____ those who had stayed behind had suffered unimaginably. Of the 89 men, women, and children who set out from Fort Bridger, only 45 had survived the awful winter. [Richard M. Ketchums, *Great Historic Places*]

ACTIVITY 8.10   Writing Sentences with Adverb Clauses

Write a sentence using each subordinating conjunction provided.

1. meanwhile: _____

2. although: _____

3. when: _____

4. once: _____

5. since: _____

8i   FORMING NOUN CLAUSES

There are three types of noun clauses:

- Answers to information questions
- Answers to yes-or-no questions
- Concepts introduced by *that*

Answers to Information Questions

Why she ever dated Jim is a mystery to me.

I do not know *where the emergency exits are.*

The noun clauses in these sentences are derived from questions that ask for information. Such noun clauses can be introduced by any of the following words:

what	where	who
whatever	wherever	whom
when	which	whose
whenever	whichever	why

Answers to Yes-or-No Questions

My daughter asked *if she could go to the movies.*

I wonder *whether the presidential candidates will debate in my hometown.*

This kind of noun clause is derived from a question that can be answered with *yes* or *no*. Such a noun clause is introduced by the word *if* or *whether*.

Concepts Introduced by *that*

That she was embarrassed was clear by the color of her face.

We decided *that Leonie will go to Eastern Europe.*

Noun clauses of this type are introduced by *that*. The relative pronoun *that* can be omitted, however, if such a clause is used as the direct object:

CORRECT: I am happy *that you are coming to dinner.*

CORRECT: I am happy *you are coming to dinner.*

When a noun clause beginning with *that* is the subject of the sentence, *that* cannot be omitted:

CORRECT: *That you are coming to dinner* is a great surprise.

INCORRECT: *You are coming to dinner* is a great surprise.

USE OF NOUN CLAUSES

Type of Noun Clause	Introductory Pronoun	Omission of Pronoun
Answer to information question	*what, whatever, when, whenever, where, wherever, which, whichever, who, whom, whose, why*	Not permitted
Answer to yes-or-no question	*if, whether*	Not permitted
that clause	*that*	Permitted only if direct object

ACTIVITY

 8.11   **Writing Sentences Using Noun Clauses**

A.   Rephrase each sentence into a statement using a noun clause.

Example: Where was the treaty signed?

I don't know <u>*where the treaty was signed.*</u>

1. Whose shoes are in the hall?

   My mother wanted to know _____

2. When will there be peace in the Middle East?

   I wonder_____

3. Do you vote Republican?

   Amy asked Tom _____

4. Are you happy with your test results?

   Astrid replied _____

   5. Would adopting a baby be a smart idea?

      Katarina wondered_____

   6. Will two loaves of bread be enough for the party?

      The caterer decided _____

   B.   Now write four questions of your own and rephrase them into statements with noun clauses as in part A.

   7. Question: _____

      Statement: _____

   8. Question: _____

      Statement: _____

   9. Question: _____

      Statement: _____

   10. Question: _____

      Statement: _____

8j FINDING AND REVISING FRAGMENTS

The grammatical problem of fragments commonly occurs when forming complex sentences.

Defining Fragments

   Matisse's painting of a pink nude woman against a checked background.

This example begins with a capital letter and ends with a period—the conventions for indicating a sentence in Standard Written English—but it is not a sentence because it does not contain an independent clause; specifically; it does not contain a verb. This violation is called a **fragment,** and it is considered a serious error.

   The stages or periods Picasso went through were quite diverse. For example, his blue period, pink period, classical period, and Cubist period.

The fragment here is in the second clause.

   A dog sitting under a table.

   To look at this painting for more than thirty seconds.

These examples are a little more confusing because they include verbals. A **verbal** is a word that would normally be a verb but is being used as an adjective or a noun. There are two kinds of verbals: gerunds (and participles) and infinitives. **Gerunds** and **participles** are forms of the verb that end in -*ing* and do not have helping verbs. **Infinitives** are verbs with the word *to* in front of them. Verbals are *never* verbs.

Many people would recognize a painting by Matisse. Who is one of the great painters of the twentieth century.

The best-known twentieth-century paintings are by Pablo Picasso. The artist who defined modern painting.

These examples contain fragments in the second clause with the use of a relative clause.

Correcting Fragments

Picasso painted *Guernica*, $\overset{a}{\cancel{A}}$ representation of the horrors of war.

Here the writer corrected the fragment by joining it to the preceding sentence.

Although Matisse was not a religious man, $\overset{t}{\cancel{T}}$he Catholic chapel he designed at Vence, France, is one of his masterpieces.

The writer corrected this fragment by joining it to the following sentence.

In the 1940s, Matisse was confined to bed with a serious illness. As a result, $\overset{he\ began}{\wedge}$ making paintings out of cut-out pieces of colored paper.

A final method for fixing a fragment is to revise the fragment by adding, deleting, or changing a few words to turn the fragment into an independent clause. In this case, the writer added the words *he began*.

Intentional Fragments

Take a look at the following paragraph from the J. Crew clothing company's Fall 1992 catalog. We have italicized the fragments.

The relaxed flannel jacket. The silhouette is overscaled: cut very generously through the shoulders and back. See p. 4 for coordinating shorts. *Wool and cashmere, with just a touch of nylon. Fully lined. Import.* Dry clean. *Sizes 2 –14.*

Look at all those fragments! Can't the people at J. Crew write? Of course they can. Good writers, especially writers of advertising copy, frequently and consciously use fragments, but they use them only when they want to create a certain informal, telegraphic style. Novelists and poets use intentional fragments too, for the same reasons. In general, however, fragments are not acceptable in academic writing.

ACTIVITY

8.12 Identifying and Correcting Fragments

Identify the fragments in the following paragraphs. Rewrite the corrected paragraphs on a separate sheet of paper.

Budget Meals for New Homeowners

Dixie Cups Filled with Sugar

This easy-to-prepare meal is not only economical. It is extremely popular with children, who find it gives them that extra energy boost they sometimes need. To stay awake for six days in a row.

Wedding Reception Food

If you go to any major hotel or country club on a weekend. A large formal wedding reception going on, featuring people walking around. Who actually give away teeny little sandwiches with the crust cut off. This is an excellent source of food for you, the new homeowner. Looking like you are a close personal friend of either the bride or groom. Help yourself to as many trays as you feel you will need during this particular mortgage payment period. To keep people from getting suspicious. Stop from time to time and remark aloud, in a natural tone of voice: "I am a close personal friend of the bride! Or the groom!" [Dave Barry, *Homes and Other Black Holes*]

8k ABOUT SUBORDINATION

Four rules apply to subordination:

1. Use subordination to emphasize the main idea.
2. Avoid subordinating the main idea.
3. Use subordinating conjunctions that express your meaning.
4. Avoid excessive subordination.

Emphasizing the Main Idea

After Frances was promoted, she got a much bigger office.

Subordination is used to give unequal emphasis to two or more ideas. Usually, the major idea is expressed in the independent clause, and minor ideas are placed in the subordinate clause. In this example, the idea that Frances got a much bigger office is emphasized.

Not Subordinating the Main Idea

Be certain that you do not subordinate the main idea that you wish to express.

INCORRECT: My dog, which was hit by a car last night, was a dachshund.

CORRECT: My dog, which was a dachshund, was hit by a car last night.

Appropriate Conjunctions

It is important to select the subordinating conjunction that expresses exactly the meaning you intend.

INCORRECT: Because Mark took his eyes off the road, a young child ran in front of his car.

CORRECT: When Mark took his eyes off the road, a young child ran in front of his car.

Excessive Subordination

Subordination can be overused, as the following example illustrates.

INCORRECT: My cat, whose name is Jimmy and who was sleeping on the front porch, was dive-bombed by a mockingbird that had a nest in a large holly tree that was planted by my ex-husband when he first came back from the army.

CORRECT: Sleeping on the front porch, my cat, Jimmy, was dive-bombed by a mockingbird whose nest sat in a large holly tree. My ex-husband planted that tree when he first came back from the army.

Emphasizing Important Ideas through Subordination

Combine the following sentence pairs using a subordinate clause. The sentence marked with the asterisk expresses the idea you should emphasize.

> *Example:*   The dog got wet.*
>   She went swimming in the pool.

> *Because she went swimming in the pool, the dog got wet.*

1. The Sears Tower is in Chicago.
   The Sears Tower is the tallest building in the United States.*

   _____

2. Kathy went roller-blading.
   She had a lot of work to do.*

   _____

3. Maria is an aerobics instructor.
   Maria has seven children.*

   _____

 FORMING COMPOUND AND COMPLEX SENTENCES USING COORDINATION AND SUBORDINATION: COMPREHENSIVE CHECK

Diagnostic Retest

Complete Activity 8.1 again. If you still miss or have difficulty with any items, review the relevant sections of the workbook.

Putting It All Together

Rewrite the following passage about the Tasaday tribe of the Philippines, combining sentences using the tools for coordination and subordination.

> The name *Tasaday* means "people of the caves" in the language of the neighboring Filipino tribes. There are twenty-seven people. They live in three big

limestone caves in the rainforest of Mindanao. The caves are in a cliff. The cliff overlooks a rushing stream.

The Tasaday settlement is invisible from the air. It is invisible sometimes from a few yards away. Dense forest growth hides the settlement. There are no roads in this part of the forest. There is no way to reach the settlement except by helicopter. The Tasaday have been living in the caves for possibly a thousand years. The Tasaday are certainly native Filipinos. They have brown skin and high cheekbones. They have dark curly hair. They are of slight build.

The Tasaday have no chief or leader. They need none. They share their food. They share their tools. They compete with no one. They live in peace and harmony with one another. They are gentle, nonaggressive people. They have no words in their language for anger, war, weapons, or hostility.

A family is made up of a man, his wife, and their children. In some families, a widowed mother or father stays with a son or daughter. There are three generations living together in their part of a cave. Each family collects its own firewood. Each family does its own cooking. A child feels free to wander over to another family and eat with them. He is hungry, and his own meal is not ready.

The Tasaday have one serious problem. They may not marry anyone from their group. They must find mates elsewhere. They are so isolated. They do have occasional contact with groups deeper in the forest. They get mates from these groups and probably give their own girls to these groups as wives. [Adapted from Rebecca B. Marcus, *Survivors of the Stone Age*]

 **USING PARALLEL STRUCTURES FOR PARALLEL IDEAS**

Parallelism is simply placing two or more related elements in the same grammatical form, which helps make reading more coherent. Parallelism gives writing a rhythm that appeals to readers' ears.

Parallel thoughts must be expressed in grammatically parallel sentences. Think of parallel lines, which run in the same direction and never cross. In English, words that express parallel ideas must be in agreement as well. By using parallel forms, the reader can more easily recognize the content and meaning of your sentences. In this chapter we will consider the concept of parallelism and will learn several techniques for using it effectively. Before we begin, let's determine how much you already know about parallelism.

9a DIAGNOSTIC ACTIVITY: PARALLELISM

ACTIVITY
9.1 **How Much Do You Know?**

Read each sentence, and determine if it contains an error in parallelism. If there is an error, correct it. Not all the sentences contain errors. An example is provided.

Example: My sister Nadine is pretty, ambitious, and ~~has talent~~. *talented*

1. I swam and canoed in the river and hiking in the forest.

2. Eating vegetables, drinking water, and to exercise regularly are necessary for good health.

3. Louis XVI was king of France in the eighteenth century and who was married to Marie-Antoinette.

4. Dogs and to live in the wild are common subjects in Jack London's short stories and novels.

5. When Ed was in college, he was involved in karate, student government, and he played tennis.

6. Mr. Bray is known to be an honest man and an intellectual.

7. It's amazing that cats can walk on thin fences and looking down without falling off.

Chapter cowritten with Cheryl Delk, Michigan State University.

8. In tennis class, I improved my backhand and serving.

9. Driving in Europe is just as expensive as to take a plane.

10. Buying a car and to move into a new apartment are her goals for next year.

11. I like both his energy and enthusiasm.

12. Salespeople need to be both friendly and persuade you to buy their products.

13. The hotel was not only dirty but also we didn't feel comfortable there.

14. Arthur neither works nor studies.

15. No food, drink, or smoking is allowed in the theater.

16. Hawks can catch mice as easily as lions.

17. I would rather eat cake than to eat ice cream.

18. I am excited to go to Paris, to go to Brussels, and to go to Barcelona.

19. I planned to buy a backpack, a map, to purchase my plane ticket, and leave for Maine.

20. My aunt's cat likes to hide behind the TV, to hide under the bed, and under the stairs.

Determine which items you missed in this Diagnostic Activity. If you missed or had trouble with any of the items, please go to the appropriate section in *The Harper-Collins Concise Handbook for Writers* and this workbook for further practice and study.

It is important to know which items cause you difficulty. When revising your writing, you might want to go through your paper one time checking only for parallelism. Concentrate on items that you had difficulty with in this activity.

9b   PARALLELISM WITH COORDINATING CONJUNCTIONS

The following sentences illustrate one situation in which items must be parallel:

swimming
Jogging and ~~to swim~~ are two good forms of exercise.
placed
We set the table and/a bowl of fruit on it.

Items joined by a coordinating conjunction must be parallel—that is, in the same grammatical form.

Nouns

NOT PARALLEL: The new plan has value *and* is appealing. (noun + adjective)

PARALLEL: The new plan has value *and* appeal. (noun + noun)

Adjectives

NOT PARALLEL: My dog is small *but* snarls a lot. (adjective + verb phrase)

PARALLEL: My dog is small *but* ferocious. (adjective + adjective)

Verb Phrases

NOT PARALLEL: Kathy watered my plants *and* feeding my dog. (verb phrase + gerund)

PARALLEL: Kathy watered my plants *and* fed my dog. (verb phrase + verb phrase)

Adverbs

NOT PARALLEL: Giraffes walk slowly *yet* with grace. (adverb + noun)

PARALLEL: Giraffes walk slowly *yet* gracefully. (adverb + adverb)

Prepositional Phrases

NOT PARALLEL: My keys are either in the drawer *or* the table. (prepositional phrase + noun)

PARALLEL: My keys are either in the drawer *or* on the table. (prepositional phrase + prepositional phrase)

Remember that *and* is used to combine sentences containing matching ideas and that *but, yet,* and *or* are used to combine sentences containing opposite ideas.

ACTIVITY

9.2 Creating Parallel Sentences Using Coordinating Conjunctions

Use the coordinating conjunction in parentheses to expand each sentence into one containing a parallel structure.

Example: France has many cathedrals. (and)

France has many cathedrals and castles.

1. My mathematics class is interesting. (but)

2. During my three-week vacation, I'll go to Niagara Falls. (or)

3. Jason hasn't come to class. (and)

4. Anita was born in Iran. (yet)

5. When I was a child, I used to play in the park. (and)

ACTIVITY
9.3 Combining Sentences Using Coordinating Conjunctions

Combine the following sentences using a coordinating conjunction. You will have to omit words in some sentences.

Example: I like carrots.
I don't like peas.

I like carrots, but I don't like peas.

1. I've taken algebra and geometry.
I haven't taken calculus.

2. I can't wait to go to France.
I can't wait to eat the delicious pastries.

3. My brother would enjoy a career in editing.
My brother would also enjoy a career in publishing.

4. In 1990, I graduated from college.
In 1990, I moved to Chicago.
In 1990, I got married.

5. I was very tired after my trip to Japan.
I was happy to be back home.

9c PARALLELISM WITH CORRELATIVE CONJUNCTIONS

Certain paired conjunctions in English sometimes cause problems and lead to faulty parallelism. Some of these **correlative conjunctions** are *either . . . or, neither . . . nor, both . . . and, as . . . as,* and *not only . . . but also.*

Not Parallel:	My friend Jim neither drinks nor is a smoker. (verb paired with noun)
Parallel:	My friend Jim neither drinks nor smokes. (verb paired with verb)
Not Parallel:	It was both a long speech and boring. (noun paired with adjective)
Parallel:	The speech was both long and boring. (adjective paired with adjective)

NOT PARALLEL: Walking near the ocean is not only enjoyable but it is healthful. (adjective paired with phrase)

PARALLEL: Walking near the ocean is not only enjoyable but also healthful. (adjective paired with adjective)

ACTIVITY

9.4 Writing Parallel Sentences with Correlative Conjunctions

Combine each pair of sentences into a single sentence using the correlative conjunction in parentheses.

Example: John doesn't have time to go fishing tomorrow morning.
He doesn't have the energy to go. (neither . . . nor)

John has neither the time nor the energy to go fishing tomorrow morning.

1. Nadine could study at Northern Illinois University.
She could study at Columbia University. (either . . . or)

2. Most lawyers are hardworking.
They are dedicated to their clients. (both . . . and)

3. He didn't have the courage to join the navy.
He didn't have the stamina to join the navy. (neither . . . nor)

4. Larry loved studying in a foreign country.
He liked meeting new people. (not only . . . but also)

5. Professor O'Gorman is very patient with students.
Her secretary is also very patient with students. (both . . . and)

ACTIVITY

9.5 Writing Parallel Sentences Using Both Coordinating and Correlative Conjunctions

Combine the following pairs of sentences using the following conjunctions. Use each conjunction at least once.

and	but	not only . . . but also	neither . . . nor
or	yet	either . . . or	both . . . and

1. They wanted to go to a movie. They wanted to see a play.

_____

2. My mother worked in a supermarket. My father worked in a supermarket.

_____

3. You can buy a new car. You can lease a new car.

_____

4. John didn't study for his statistics exam. He passed the exam.

_____

5. I didn't hear the explosion. I didn't smell the smoke.

_____

6. Work productivity at Hutton Computers, Inc., has increased. Sales have dropped.

_____

7. He should have quit his job a long time ago. He should have worked in Japan instead.

_____

8. I'm taking a physics exam tomorrow. I'm taking a statistics exam also.

_____

9d   PARALLELISM WITH ITEMS IN A SERIES

The following examples illustrate another situation in which items must be parallel:

> I bought a loaf of bread, a jar of peanut butter, and ~~I bought~~ a Diet Coke.
>
>   *eating*
> Smoking, drinking, and ~~food~~ are not allowed in this auditorium.

Items in a series must be parallel.

ACTIVITY

9.6   Completing Series with Parallel Items

Complete each sentence, making sure that the item you add is parallel with the other items in the sentence.

Example: Activities offered at the ski resort include skiing, ice-skating, and *sledding* .

1. The president is dedicated, thoughtful, and _____.

2. Before leaving the house, you should close the windows, turn off the lights, and _____.

3. I enjoy reading novels, swimming, and _____ during the summer months.

4. My parents' home makes me feel secure, warm, and _____.

5. The local art institute offers courses in sculpture, drawing, and _____.

6. The weather in August is usually bright, humid, and _____.

7. Entering a university, starting a new job, and _____ are all significant events.

8. Students must come to class attentive, prepared, and _____.

9. During my first week at college, I met four people, saw two plays, and _____.

10. The soldiers were praised for their courage, endurance, and _____.

9e   PARALLELISM WITH COMPARISONS

The following sentences illustrate yet another situation in which items must be parallel:

> *give*
> Jamie would rather take a test than ∧give an oral report.
> *baking*
> Buying a cake from Deli-Desserts is as cheap as ~~to bake~~ one yourself.

Items compared with *than* or *as* must be parallel.

ACTIVITY
9.7   Parallelism with Comparisons Using *than* or *as*

Edit the following sentences so that the items are parallel.

> *visiting*
> *Example:*   Taking the whole family to a museum is as expensive as ~~to visit~~ the zoo.

1. Swimming no longer interests me as much as to lie on the beach.

2. European cities have many more outdoor cafés than American cities.

3. Riding in an airplane is not more comfortable than to take a train.

4. Janine finds volleyball as interesting as Jim does.

5. Money is harder to earn than spending it.

6. I would rather travel than to stay at home all summer long.

7. Running is as important as to eat well for good health.

9f PARALLELISM IN LISTS AND OUTLINES

The following outline shows another instance in which items must be parallel:

I. Types of African Art

    A. Figure sculpture

    B. Masks

    C. Gold pendants

    D. Bronze plaques

    E. ~~Casting~~ *Bronze* figures ~~in bronze~~

Items at each level in outlines must be parallel.

The following is a list from an office memo.

In response to the company's recent losses in the small appliance division, the following changes will be implemented:

- Offices will not fill vacant positions.
- Employees will not travel out of state at the company's expense.
- No equipment purchase over $2,000 ⌃*will be permitted.*

Items in a list must be parallel.

ACTIVITY

9.8 Parallelism in Outlines

Edit the following outlines to make all supporting items parallel.

1. I. Weekend Activities in Chicago

    A. Visiting the Art Institute

    B. Going to Lincoln Park Zoo

    C. Restaurants in Chinatown

2. I. Reasons to Buy a Compact Car

    A. Costs under $15,000

    B. Fuel-efficient

    C. Easy to park

3. I. Disadvantages of Living in Dormitories

    A. Noisy rooms

    B. Sharing the bathrooms

    C. Bad food

II. Advantages of Living in Dormitories

    A. Getting to class on time

    B. Meeting a lot of people

    C. Economical

ACTIVITY

9.9 Parallelism in Lists

Edit the following lists to make them parallel.

1. **OFFICE OF THE REGISTRAR**
   Registration Process

   - Pick up your Registration Billing Statement (RBS).

   - Make payment of at least the "minimum amount due" on your RBS.

   - You can take action on your pending financial aid.

   - Obtain a refund of your excess financial aid.

2. **SCHELLER HEALTH CENTER**
   Health Tips for the Winter Months

   - Getting a good night's sleep.

   - Engage in relaxation exercises before bed.

   - Arrange a quiet time each day.

9g REPEATING KEY WORDS IN PARALLEL STRUCTURES

Notice the effect of the words added in the following sentence.

> My parents decided to request a meeting with the lawyer who had drawn up my grandmother's will,
> *to*
>   hire an investigator to look into the circumstances of my grandmother's death, and talk to the di-
> rector of the nursing home where she died.

The added words—that is, the repetition of the word *to*—make the sentence easier to read because they clearly mark the beginning of each item in the series.

In the following sentence, why do you think the word *to* has been removed?

> My parents decided to sell their house, ~~to~~ retire from their jobs, and ~~to~~ move to Florida.

This sentence is clearer with the *to*'s removed because the items in the series are relatively short and simple. The repetition of *to* only clutters up a perfectly clear sentence.

In most cases, repetition of the same word or two at the beginning of every item in a series is not advisable. Such repetition is justified only when it makes the sentence clearer.

9.10   Repetition of Key Words in Parallel Structures

Combine the following sentences into one sentence. Decide if the key structures need to be repeated.

1. Before I left on vacation, I talked to the landlord of my apartment building. Before I left on vacation, I talked to the superintendent of my apartment building.

   _____

2. I believe that she is confident.
   I believe that she will find a job.
   I believe that she will be successful.

   _____

3. She chose to stay in Bloomington.
   She chose to find a new job.
   She chose to sign up for an art class.

   _____

9h PARALLELISM: COMPREHENSIVE CHECK

9.11   Diagnostic Retest

Complete Activity 9.1 again. If you still miss or have difficulty with any items, review the relevant sections of the workbook.

9.12   Putting It All Together

Read the following passage, and note the errors in parallelism. Rewrite the passage with your corrections.

The United States is a consumer society. The range in price, amount of goods available, and choosing from the large selection make us the envy of the world. Appealing to the consumers is more important now than to meet their basic needs. The term *selling* suggests that the desire to buy must be created in the consumer, reinforced by values and what social norms exist.

In the colonial era, there was little effort at selling and to advertise because there was little need. Signs outside shops indicated both type of merchandise and how much it would cost. Basic commodities were sold in bulk. More exotic goods arrived by ship, but their availability was made known primarily through a newspaper notice of the ship's arrival. Sometimes not only when the products would arrive but also the quantity was printed in the newspapers.

Early retail selling was done both in shops and peddlers too. Peddlers sold a variety of items and who traveled all over the countryside. Sales were governed by *caveat emptor*—let the buyer beware. A typical transaction might involve cash, credit, or involving bartering. There was no guarantee of quality, and price was subject to bargaining between seller and buyer. Through the years, it was found that many Americans would rather visit one store to buy everything necessary than going to several different shops. [Adapted from Arthur Johnson, *American Issues*]

 # AVOIDING MIXED OR INCOMPLETE CONSTRUCTIONS

Have you ever written a sentence that just didn't "sound right"? It happens to all of us. In this chapter we will consider several causes of awkward-sounding sentences. You will also identify and correct awkward and ungrammatical sentences.

10a DIAGNOSTIC ACTIVITY: AVOIDING MIXED CONSTRUCTIONS

ACTIVITY 10.1 **How Much Do You Know?**

Read each sentence and decide if it sounds awkward or is ungrammatical and, if so, correct the error. Not all sentences require revision. An example is provided.

Example: By acting quickly and calling the ambulance, ~~meant~~ Paul saved the young boy's life.

1. The purchasing error that Julie made at work which cost the company thousands of dollars.

2. By working overtime last summer, Cathy was able to buy herself a new bicycle.

3. The people in the dorm next to ours, they are having a party tonight.

4. Dedication is when you refuse to give up your hopes and dreams.

5. The best time of my life was when I was a young girl growing up in Minnesota.

6. Renting a car for the week is cheaper than flying to Chicago.

7. My most interesting dream was where I was flying in the air like a bird.

8. The city in which I was raised recently renovated its capitol building.

9. The reason I didn't return your phone call yesterday was because I didn't get home until after midnight.

10. Sabine's explanation for going to Florida was because she greatly needed a vacation.

Chapter cowritten with Sharon Cavusgil, Georgia State University.

11. All of the stores in Township Plaza are having a huge sidewalk sale.

12. The movie in which I rented last night was full of mystery and suspense.

13. My uncle studied for one year in Spain and two years in France.

14. The performer's jokes were distasteful and songs off-key.

15. This strawberry pie is better than any other pie I have eaten in the United States.

16. Amtrak is faster.

17. In college, I lived with six other women in a three-bedroom apartment.

18. After I graduate, will return to my native country.

Determine which items you missed in this Diagnostic Activity. If you missed or had trouble with any of the items, please go to the appropriate section in *The HarperCollins Concise Handbook for Writers* and this workbook for further practice and study.

It is important to know which items cause you difficulty. When revising your writing, you might want to go through your paper one time checking only for mixed constructions and awkward-sounding sentences. Concentrate on items that you had difficulty with in this activity.

10b REVISING MIXED GRAMMATICAL CONSTRUCTIONS

The following fragment illustrates a problem known as a **mixed grammatical construction.**

Subject	Dependent clause	Dependent clause

INCORRECT: The fact that Jacqueline was late for work which made the manager furious.

This fragment starts with a subject, *The fact,* which is followed by the dependent clause *that Jacqueline was late for work.* One would expect the next part of the sentence to be a verb that goes with the subject, *The fact.* Instead, the sentence concludes with another dependent clause, *which made the manager furious.* This unexpected ending causes the sentence to sound odd, to confuse the reader, and therefore to be ineffective—in fact, it isn't even a sentence; it is a fragment. One way to correct the problem is to provide an ending for the sentence that fits the beginning with a verb to go with the subject, *The fact.*

CORRECT: The fact that Jacqueline was late for work *made the manager furious.*

The following sentence illustrates another mixed grammatical construction.

INCORRECT: By going to the movie last night meant I did not finish my algebra homework.

When *By* is removed, this mixed construction is transformed into an effective sentence:

CORRECT: *Going* to the movie last night meant *I* did not finish my algebra homework.

A second way to correct the mixed construction is as follows:

CORRECT: By going to the movie last *night, I* did not finish my algebra homework.

In summary, mixed constructions occur when a sentence starts out with one kind of grammatical structure and shifts to a different one someplace in the middle. Mixed constructions must be revised to eliminate the problem.

ACTIVITY

10.2 **Revising Mixed Grammatical Constructions**

Read each of the following sentences, and determine if it contains a mixed grammatical construction. If so, revise the sentence to make it grammatically correct. Not all sentences need revision.

> *Example:* The student who receives the highest grade point average ~~who~~ becomes valedictorian.

1. Working on my paper until 3 A.M., and I was tired this morning.

2. Having studied French in high school, I was able to read the menu at L'Auberge Française.

3. The computer that I bought last week was a Macintosh.

4. My sister who attended Johnsley College, which is a local community college.

5. By working overtime last week meant I made an extra $75.

6. The book that you recommended which is now a best seller.

7. Looking out the window, I saw a squirrel in my birdbath!

8. Having completed her research paper early; thus, she could relax for the weekend.

9. My husband who drives eighty-five miles to work each day, which is a long way to commute.

10. By eating more vegetables and fewer sweets, I lost ten pounds.

10c REVISING MIXED MEANING

A slightly different problem with mixed sentences occurs when the subject and the verb don't fit together or don't make sense together. This problem is known as **mixed meaning** or **faulty predication.**

INCORRECT: The purpose of this course is designed to improve your writing skills.

This sentence says that *the purpose . . . is designed,* but surely the writer intended to say that *this course is designed* or that *the purpose is to improve your writing skills.* To eliminate the mixed meaning, the sentence could be revised in either of two ways:

CORRECT: This course is designed to improve your writing skills.

CORRECT: The purpose of this course is to improve your writing skills.

The following examples represent three common constructions that often result in mixed meanings or faulty predication.

INCORRECT: Success in this course is when you get a C.

CORRECT: Success in this course is getting a C.

Success is not a *when;* it is a *what. Success* is something you achieve, not a *time* when you achieve it. So be careful when you write that anything "is when." Make sure that the thing you are talking about actually is a time.

INCORRECT: The best kind of revenge is where you get even with someone who isn't even aware of it.

CORRECT: The best kind of revenge is getting even with someone who isn't even aware of it.

A *kind of revenge* cannot be a *where* because it is not a place. Use *where* only with reference to places.

INCORRECT: The reason for the breakup of our relationship is because Laura can't ever make a commitment.

CORRECT: The reason for the breakup of our relationship is that Laura can't ever make a commitment.

CORRECT: Laura and I broke up because Laura can't ever make a commitment.

The reason is and *because* mean the same thing, so there is never any need to use both expressions together. One or the other will suffice.

In summary, mixed meaning or faulty predication occurs when the subject and the verb are mismatched—when they don't make sense together. Such problems require revision to eliminate the awkwardness. Be especially careful with sentences that fall into the patterns *something is when, something is where,* and *the reason is because.*

ACTIVITY

10.3   ### Revising Sentences with Mixed Meaning

Read each of the following sentences, and determine if it contains a mixed meaning. If it does, revise the sentence to make it grammatically correct. Not all sentences need revision.

> *Example:*   The husband's promise to his new wife was ~~that he wanted~~ to stay faithful.

1. It is imperative that Joan should call the office by 5:00 P.M.

2. The supermarket where I used to shop went out of business.

3. The reason why I was late for class this morning is because my car broke down.

4. Alper's biggest dream is when he wins the lottery.

5. I recommend that your daughter should take the chemistry class again.

6. The winning candidate promised to improve the welfare of children in our city.

7. My plan is I wish to become a teacher after I graduate.

8. The biggest reason my sister won't swim in the ocean is because she is afraid of sharks.

9. My favorite childhood memory is when I visited my grandparents' farm.

10. The best romance novels are where the two main characters fall in love.

10d ## REVISING SENTENCES OF THE PATTERN "MY BROTHER, HE . . ."

In English, awkwardness results from adding a pronoun subject that repeats the noun subject.

> My brother, ~~he~~ enlisted in the army.

> The essay question on the final exam, ~~it~~ caused me a lot of problems.

Study these sentences and note how they have been corrected. The rule in English is straightforward and clear: Do not use a pronoun with the subject if the pronoun merely repeats the meaning of the noun subject of the sentence.

ACTIVITY

10.4   **Revising Sentences of the Pattern "My brother, he . . . "**

Read each of the following sentences, and determine if it is grammatically correct. If the sentence is not correct, revise it. Not all sentences need revision.*

> *Example:* The first people of North and South America, ~~they~~ traveled across the Bering Strait more than 25,000 years ago.

1. The people who remained in the Canadian Arctic, Alaskan, and Aleutian areas, they were the Eskimos.

2. The Eskimos invented skin boats, harpoons, stone oil lamps, and dog sleds.

3. Some of the Asian immigrants, they traveled farther south than the Eskimos did.

4. The Indians who settled along the Pacific Coast were skilled woodcarvers and made wooden tools, houses, canoes, and dishes.

5. The Indians who migrated to the Central Plains, they were similar in some ways to the Pacific Coast settlers.

6. The people of the Central Plains were hunters, but they were also farmers.

7. They surrounded their round straw houses or clay huts with bean, corn, and melon gardens.

8. Native American Indians who settled in the southwestern United States and northern Mexico, they were stable and skilled.

9. Some of their stone apartment houses are still occupied by Pueblo Indians today.

10. The American Indian culture, it was highly developed.

10e REVISING ERRORS WITH *IN WHICH*

The phrase *in which* has many perfectly good uses in English, but it is frequently used in a way that doesn't make sense and is grammatically incorrect, as the following sentence illustrates.

> The novel ~~in~~ which I read over the weekend had a disappointing ending.

In which in this sentence did not make sense because you don't read *in* a novel. Grammatically, you should only use the phrase *in which* when there is a prepositional phrase in one of the two original sentences.

---

*Activity adapted from Jewell A. Friend, *Writing English as a Second Language* (Glenview, Ill.: Scott, Foresman, 1971), pp. 119–120.

I read a novel over the weekend.

The novel had a disappointing ending.

When we break this sentence into the two original sentences, you can see there is no prepositional phrase. But notice that *in which* in the following sentence is fine.

One movie in which Meryl Streep starred was *The French Lieutenant's Woman.*

In which makes sense here because a person can star *in* a movie. You can also find a prepositional phrase when you break this sentence into the two original sentences.

Meryl Streep starred *in many movies.*

One of these movies was *The French Lieutenant's Woman.*

In summary, be careful to use *in which* to refer only to nouns that something can be put in, and when one of the original sentences contains a prepositional phrase.

ACTIVITY
10.5 Revising Errors with *in which*

Read the following sentences, each containing the phrase *in which*. Determine if each sentence is grammatically correct. (If you are not sure, determine what the two original sentences were.) If it is not correct, revise it. Not all sentences need revision.

Example: *Basic Instinct* was the movie ~~in~~ which I saw last night.

1. That was the newspaper in which the article was printed.

2. The cake in which you baked was delicious!

3. Those were the trees in which we planted last spring.

4. I visited the town in which my grandmother was born.

5. That Saab is the car in which I was telling you about.

6. The house in which I lived as a child burned down.

7. This is the store in which I bought my new dress.

8. The book in which you bought for $42 is on sale now.

9. We are studying sentences in which contain grammatical errors.

10. I am impressed with the essay in which you wrote.

10f REVISING INCOMPLETE SENTENCES

Elliptical Constructions

Writers can sometimes make their sentences more concise by omitting certain words in compound constructions rather than repeating them. For example, the following sentences could be effectively revised by removing the words that would otherwise be repeated.

The first test in my math course was difficult, and the second ~~test was~~ even harder.

I spent two hours in the library, and then ~~I spent~~ three hours at my computer.

However, words may not be omitted if the omitted words are different from those at the beginning of the sentence.

That movie's characters are unconvincing, and the plot _{is} predictable.

The verb cannot be omitted in the second half of this sentence because it must be *is,* which is not the same as *are* in the first half.

Here are two more instances in which words essential to the meaning must not be omitted.

Houng was afraid _{of} and mad at his landlord.

Of must follow *afraid* because without it, the sentence would say that Houng was *afraid at* his landlord. *Afraid at* is not acceptable English.

My husband and _{my} accountant will be arriving at seven.

My must be repeated to indicate that the writer's husband and her accountant are two different people. If they were the same person, the second *my* should be omitted.

Ambiguous Comparisons

Comparisons should be stated fully enough so that no ambiguity is created.

AMBIGUOUS: My mother always liked me more than my sister.

This sentence is ambiguous. It may mean that my mother liked me more than she liked my sister, or it may mean that my mother liked me more than my sister liked me. To clear up this ambiguity, the sentence should be revised as either of these:

CLEAR: My mother always liked me more than she liked my sister.

CLEAR: My mother always liked me more than my sister did.

When comparing an item with all the others in the same class, use the word *other.*

The ginkgo tree is older than any _{other} tree that still exists.

The word *other* must be inserted to indicate that the ginkgo is older than any tree *other than a ginkgo.* Otherwise, you are asserting that the ginkgo is older than itself—clearly an impossibility.

Comparisons must always be made with something. It is confusing or even deceptive to say that something is cheaper or larger or more nutritious without specifying what it is cheaper or larger or more nutritious than.

INCORRECT: The new Parcel is safer and more economical.

CORRECT: The new Parcel is safe and economical.

CORRECT: The new Parcel is safer and more economical than other cars of its size.

Omitting *that*

The subordinating conjunction *that* can often be omitted, but not if omitting it makes the sentence hard to read.

Zamir has discovered _{that} a car is necessary in America.

In this sentence, *that* must be inserted to prevent the reader from misreading the sentence and thinking that Zamir "has discovered a car."

I am afraid Mikelle has missed the bus.

By contrast, here it is not necessary to insert *that* because there is no possibility of misreading the sentence.

Adding Missing Subjects

In certain languages, including Spanish and Italian, the subject of a sentence or clause may be omitted. English, however, allows you to omit the subject only if the sentence is imperative—if it gives a command.

Imperative: Go to the dean's office!

Declarative: *I w* Went to the dean's office to interview her for the school paper.

Imperative: Pay for your purchases at the register.

Declarative: If a country uses raw materials from another country, *it* has to pay for them.

Adding Missing Expletives

Whenever you place your subject after a linking verb, you must put either *there* or *it* in front of the verb to make the sentence complete.

There a Are a large number of books about the Vietnam War.

It i Is widely known that cats are fierce predators.

ACTIVITY
10.6   Recognizing and Correcting Incomplete Sentences

Study each of the following sentences. If the sentence contains an error, indicate the type of error in the blank after the sentence, using the following key:

     a. elliptical construction
     b. ambiguous comparison
     c. omission of *that*
     d. missing subject
     e. missing expletive

Then revise the sentence. Not all sentences need revision; if a sentence is correct as written, write "OK" in the blank.

Examples: My sister is very shy, but my brothers *are* outgoing and gregarious. __*a*__

          This school year, my sister wrote me more than *she wrote* my brother. __*b*__

1. Your class is better than any class I have taken at the university. _____

2. I can talk more openly with my mother than my father. _____

3. When I finish this book report, will go to the movies with you. _____

4. Are 1,200 employees working at my father's company. _____

5. My sister, Sharla, is more intelligent. _____

6. Our physics and biology professor should be at the graduation party this Saturday. _____

7. It is a myth that Elvis is still alive. _____

8. Walter realizes he should have taken a vacation when he had the money. _____

9. In the small northern town, winter temperatures were cold and the wind strong. _____

10. My wife found a puppy requires a lot of patience and energy. _____

11. Called the telephone company to inquire about my outrageous phone bill. _____

12. Since my car broke down, I have been taking the bus to school. _____

13. In Boston are many interesting historical tourist attractions. _____

14. I am disappointed in and angry at the accusations you have made. _____

15. In my English class are people from eleven different countries! _____

16. Unfortunately, at my first dinner party, my guests were late and the meal cold. _____

17. I love Korean food but dislike Japanese. _____

18. I think the course helped Paco more than Donna. _____

19. Erin's best friend and neighbor will both be coming to her birthday party. _____

20. Is interesting to watch how mother birds care for their young. _____

21. I recently moved to a new city, but my job is interesting and my neighbors friendly. _____

22. I am aware and ashamed of the lies my son told. _____

23. This chicken is spicier than any other I have tasted. _____

24. The winter season in Wisconsin is colder. _____

25. Judy was proud but surprised by the announcement of her scholarship. _____

26. I enjoy studying English more than my roommate. _____

27. I understand a second language is needed for a person to advance to a management position. _____

28. Hopes to complete his degree in hotel management by December of next year. _____

29. My mother has taught linguistics at the local college since 1985. _____

30. In my family, it is an honor to sit at the head of the table. _____

10g MIXED CONSTRUCTIONS: COMPREHENSIVE CHECK

ACTIVITY 10.7 Diagnostic Retest

Complete Activity 10.1 again. If you still miss or have difficulty with any items, review the relevant sections of the workbook.

ACTIVITY 10.8 Putting It All Together

Read the following passage, and find the sentences with mixed constructions. Rewrite the passage, incorporating corrections.

> A painful experience at the dentist's office for many people is when they get their wisdom teeth pulled. What purpose do wisdom teeth serve? These teeth serve a powerful purpose for dentists, they are paid to extract them. Otherwise, are commonly regarded as useless to modern humans. However, a little investigation is necessary because nature, it rarely provides us with useless body parts.
>
> Primitive people, they ate meals so tough that eating beef jerky feels like mashed potatoes in comparison. The reason for the extra molars in the back of the mouth, now known as wisdom teeth, is because they undoubtedly aided in our ancestors' chewing.
>
> Modern human brains are larger. In addition, the face position has moved farther downward and inward. About the time that primitive people started walking in an upright position, other changes in the facial structure occurred. The fact that the protruding jawbones of early humans gradually moved backward, which made the jaw itself shorter. By leaving no room for wisdom teeth meant that most people's jaws no longer had the capacity to accommodate these now superfluous teeth—teeth in which cause many modern humans pain. [Adapted from David Feldman, *Why Do Clocks Run Clockwise? and Other Imponderables*]

11 AVOIDING MISPLACED AND DANGLING MODIFIERS

A **modifier** is a word, phrase, or clause that describes or provides extra information about another word or phrase. Adjectives and adverbs are the simplest modifiers, but prepositional phrases, infinitive phrases, participial phrases, appositive phrases, adjective clauses, and adverb clauses are other types of common modifiers. Examples of each are given below. The arrows indicate what the modifiers are modifying or describing. Look these over to make sure you understand what a modifier does in a sentence.

Adjective:	We had our picnic under a beautiful dogwood tree.
Adverb:	Leslie danced effortlessly even though her toe was injured.
Prepositional phrase:	The little boy in the sandbox is my son Kent.
Infinitive phrase:	Mollie's graduation was an event to remember the rest of our lives.
Participial phrase:	The man wearing sunglasses is my economics professor.
Appositive or appositive phrase:	Austin Brightman, my college roommate, is getting married next week.
Adjective clause:	*The Scarlet Letter*, which is set in Salem, Massachusetts, is a novel about adultery.
Adverb clause:	I have to finish writing my English paper before I can go anywhere.

ACTIVITY

11.1 **Recognizing Modifiers in a Sentence**

Underline each modifier in the following sentences. Decide which type of modifier it is, and write that type on the blank line.

> *Example:* The new boss, Mr. Bingham, went to the bank.
>
> *Appositive* _____

1. The students read a book about the life of Thomas Sawyer.

_____

122

2. Valdez, which is in the southern part of Alaska, is very beautiful.

_____

3. The fireworks last night were something to see.

_____

4. Eponine sang beautifully in _Les Miserables._

_____

5. The chimp eating the banana is the biggest.

_____

6. The lonely howl of the coyote scared the children.

_____

7. I am going to the doctor after lunch.

_____

11a   **DIAGNOSTIC ACTIVITY: MISPLACED AND
DANGLING MODIFIERS**

ACTIVITY
11.2   **How Much Do You Know?**

Each sentence contains an error with either a misplaced modifier or a dangling modifier. See if you can correct the error. An example is provided.

   Example: In the washer Bruce added the detergent.

1. Corado only ate breakfast yesterday.

2. Sharon told Cheryl quietly to sneak into the office.

3. On the table, Kwo arranged the flowers.

4. Mick almost sat in the sun for five hours!

5. Driving quickly into the driveway, my car nearly hit the house.

6. To avoid being drenched in the rainstorm, umbrellas were put up.

7. Sheila decided to quickly go to the doctor.

8. I always try to, if possible, eat lots of fruits and vegetables.

Determine which items you missed in this Diagnostic Activity. If you missed or had trouble with any of the items, please go to the appropriate section in *The Harper-Collins Concise Handbook for Writers* and this workbook for further practice and study.

It is important to know which items cause you difficulty. When revising your writing, you might want to go through your paper one time checking only for misplaced or dangling modifiers. Concentrate on items that you had difficulty with in this activity.

11b PLACING MODIFIERS NEAR THE WORDS MODIFIED

The following sentences illustrate the problem known as the **misplaced modifier.** To avoid confusion in these sentences, the modifier must be placed near the word it is modifying.

INCORRECT: The police officer told Eileen carefully to drive across the bridge.

Did the police officer *speak* carefully, or did the officer tell Eileen that she should *drive* carefully?

This mistake is often called a **squinting modifier** because the modifier "squints" in two directions.

CORRECT: The police officer carefully told Ellen to drive across the bridge.

CORRECT: The police officer told Ellen to drive carefully across the bridge.

Here are two more examples.

INCORRECT: I saw a man pushing a baby carriage in my rearview mirror.

Were the man and the baby carriage in the rearview mirror?

CORRECT: In my rearview mirror, I saw a man pushing a baby carriage.

INCORRECT: Hanging over the fireplace, Jackie saw a portrait of her grandmother.

Participial clauses at the beginning of a sentence always modify the first noun or pronoun after the phrase—in this case, *Jackie.* However, common sense tells us that Jackie wasn't hanging over the fireplace; the portrait of her grandmother was.

CORRECT: Jackie saw a portrait of her grandmother hanging over the fireplace.

In summary, a misplaced modifier is any modifier placed so that it could be interpreted as modifying more than one word. Misplaced modifiers make sentences unclear and should be avoided.

ACTIVITY

11.3 **Recognizing and Correcting Misplaced Modifiers**

Read the following sentences, and identify the misplaced modifiers. Revise each sentence, writing the improved version on the line provided.

1. The teacher told us about the sinking of the *Titanic* in the afternoon.

_____

2. Screaming and crying, the doctor attended to the little girl.

_____

3. Dangling in midair, Roberta batted the spider away.

_____

4. Val asked Dino quickly to go to the store.

_____

5. The lawyer gave us advice about suing people in his office.

_____

11c LOCATING LIMITING MODIFIERS

One class of modifiers often causes problems.

> **INCORRECT:** The baby almost cried for two hours.

This sentence says that the baby was close to crying and remained in that state of near-crying for two hours. It is unlikely that this was the intended meaning, however.

> **CORRECT:** The baby cried for almost two hours.

Certain modifiers should be placed in front of the verb only when they actually modify the verb. If they modify some other word in the sentence, they must precede that word directly. Modifiers of this type are sometimes known as **limiting modifiers** because they limit the meaning of the word immediately following them. *Almost, even, exactly, hardly, just, merely, nearly, only, scarcely,* and *simply* are limiting modifiers. *Almost* and *only* are the two that are misused most often.

ACTIVITY 11.4 **Placing Limiting Modifiers Appropriately in a Sentence**

Rewrite each sentence with the limiting modifier in parentheses in the correct position.

1. Rob had eaten his dinner when the phone rang. (scarcely)

_____

2. Stephanie paid $20,000, but decided it wasn't worth it. (nearly)

_____

3. John worked in the garden for six hours. (almost)

_____

4. Sugu had eaten two meals a day for a week, but she still gained weight. (just)

_____

5. The little boy touched the crystal vase, yet it shattered. (hardly)

_____

11d AVOIDING DANGLING MODIFIERS

In English, a phrase that opens a sentence must relate to the first noun or pronoun that follows the phrase. That is why constructions such as this are so confusing and even comical:

INCORRECT: Running after the bus, my nose got cold.

Was the nose running after the bus?

Mistakes like this are called **dangling modifiers** because the modifier is not connected to any word in the sentence; it dangles all by itself, usually at the beginning of the sentence.
Dangling modifiers can be corrected in either of two ways:

CORRECT: Running after the bus, I got a cold nose.

CORRECT: While I was running after the bus, my nose got cold.

In summary, a dangling modifier occurs when a phrase at the beginning of a sentence is not followed by the noun or pronoun it modifies.

ACTIVITY 11.5 Revising Sentences with Dangling Modifiers

Revise the following sentences with dangling modifiers in both ways shown in 11d. If a subject is missing, supply a relevant one of your own.

1. Chewing the cereal loudly, my mother told me I sounded like a pig.

_____

_____

2. When driving, the baby should be in a car seat at all times.

_____

_____

3. Turning circles in midair, the children were amazed at the Flying Blue Angels.

_____

_____

4. Delighted about the snowfall, snowmobiles were everywhere.

_____

_____

5. Before registering for classes, tuition must be paid.

_____

_____

11e AVOIDING SPLIT INFINITIVES

The infinitive in English consists of the word *to* and a verb. Ordinarily, no word should come between them.

Incorrect: Uschi decided to daily jog several miles.

This is known as a **split infinitive** because a modifier, in this case *daily*, has been placed between the two parts of the infinitive, *to* and the verb *jog*. Moving the modifier usually solves the problem:

Correct: Uschi decided to jog several miles daily.

However, sometimes a split infinitive is not particularly awkward.

My parents decided to legally dissolve their marriage.

Here the infinitive is split, but no awkwardness results. People disagree about whether there is any problem with a split infinitive like this in the above example. Perhaps they disagree because the usual ways of revising a split infinitive in this case make the sentence worse:

Awkward: My parents legally decided to dissolve their marriage.

This revision makes the sentence sound like they *decided* legally rather than to *dissolve* legally and so distorts the intended meaning.

Awkward: My parents decided to dissolve legally their marriage.

This revision is even worse than the original.

Awkward: My parents decided to dissolve their marriage legally.

This revision also changes the meaning somewhat. It sounds as if the parents were considering some kind of illegal divorce but finally decided instead to do it legally.

One solution to this dilemma is to leave the sentence in its original form; however, because a split infinitive is offensive to some readers, a writer might want to recast the sentence completely and thereby avoid the problem:

Clearer: My parents have decided to file for divorce.

In summary, a split infinitive occurs when a modifier appears in between the word *to* and the verb that follows it in an infinitive. Split infinitives that cause awkwardness should always be revised; those that are not awkward should also be revised if there is any chance that your audience will find them problematic.

ACTIVITY

11.6 **Recognizing and Revising Sentences with Split Infinitives**

All of the following sentences have split infinitives. Decide if each sentence sounds awkward enough to be revised. If it does, revise the sentence.

1. The students decided to actually read the articles for class.

   _____

2. They tried to with all their might prevent the accident, to no avail.

   _____

3. Luiz decided to always eat before eight o'clock.

   _____

4. Wayne wanted to quickly go to the store before the game started.

   _____

5. I am always forgetting to, it seems, lock the door.

   _____

11f MISPLACED AND DANGLING MODIFIERS: COMPREHENSIVE CHECK

ACTIVITY

11.7 **Diagnostic Retest**

Complete Activity 11.2 again. If you still miss or have difficulty with any items, review the relevant sections of the workbook.

ACTIVITY

11.8 **Putting It All Together**

Read the following news briefs. Edit them for misplaced or dangling modifiers. Write the corrected versions after the examples.

News around Town

1. **Fun, Fun, Fun**
   The corner of Main Street and Emerson Avenue will be the site of Bloomington's annual Town Parade and Festival. Workers have almost been setting up

12b **CONFUSING WORD CHOICES**

Do and *make*

The verbs *do* and *make* have similar meanings, but in most cases you cannot use one in place of the other.

> *Did* you go to the party last night?
>
> I *do* not like cranberries with my Thanksgiving dinner.
>
> Peter tends to procrastinate, and so *does* Amy.

In these sentences, the verb *do* is acting as an **operator,** sometimes called a **helping verb** or an **auxiliary verb.** Helping verbs are used in questions, negatives, and sentences with repeating verbs. The verb *make* cannot be used as an operator.

> The thunderstorm *made* Shane very nervous.

In this example, make is a **causative verb.** The verb *do* is usually not used as a causative verb.

Aside from these distinctions, there are only general guidelines you can use to decide whether to use *make* or *do;* be aware, however, that many exceptions exist.

> Rick *does* the laundry and the cooking.
>
> Gloria *makes* a turkey dinner every Sunday.

The verb *do* is used for situations related to actions or routine tasks performed primarily around the house. However, *make* is usually used with reference to meals or food.

> You will *do* harm to your body if you smoke.
>
> It is important to *do* the best you can.

The verb *do* is usually used with words or phrases expressing abstract ideas such as *harm* and *the best you can.*

> President Kennedy *made* a very famous inaugural speech.
>
> Alice *makes* her breakfast every morning before leaving school.

The verb *make* often means to create or produce something that wasn't there before. In the first example, the speech by President Kennedy was created. In the second example, the food was already there, but Alice has prepared the meal.

ACTIVITY
12.2   **Using *do* and *make***

Complete the sentences with the correct form of *do* or *make*.

1. Would you _____ me a favor and cut up some vegetables? I want to _____ a salad.

2. Cats don't _____ as much noise as dogs do.

3. My grandmother enjoys _____ the crossword puzzles in the daily newspaper.

4. I never have enough time in the morning to _____ my bed.

5. My family goes to New York every November to _____ our Christmas shopping.

USES OF *DO* AND *MAKE*

Do	*Make*
Routine Tasks or Activities:	*Food or Meals:*
do a job	make breakfast, lunch, dinner
do the dishes	make a cake
do housework	make spaghetti
do laundry	make a snack
do cleaning	make a sauce
Abstract Ideas:	*Creating or Producing Something:*
do business	make a mistake
do one's best	make peace
do one's duty	make noise
do a favor	make a statement
do well	make friends
do justice	make a mess

6. I _____ a lot of new friends when I studied abroad in England.

7. My father still _____ business with supermarket chains in Illinois and Indiana.

8. If you _____ the best you can, nobody can complain.

9. I have to _____ one more errand and _____ a phone call.

10. Students sometimes think that teachers _____ them _____ useless exercises.

Another and *other*

Another and *other* are used as either adjectives or pronouns. The type of noun you are using in a sentence will help you decide whether to use *another* or *other.*

The losing candidate might want *another* chance at becoming mayor.

Other houses on the block have bigger yards.

The judge needed *other* information to reach a decision.

Another means "one more" in addition to what is mentioned. *Other* means "several more" or "much more." As an adjective, *another* is used with singular countable nouns *(chance); other,* with plural countable nouns *(houses)* and noncountable nouns *(information).*

I need *another* twenty dollars to buy a stereo.

It's *another* fifty miles to Detroit.

It will take Bill *another* ten minutes to wash the car.

These examples are exceptions to the rule. *Another* is always used with money, distance, or time, even if the noun is a plural countable noun.

An avalanche occurred in Colorado. *Another* is expected soon.

Avalanches have occurred in Colorado. *Others* have occurred in California.

When *another* and *other* are used as pronouns, *another* is used to replace singular countable nouns, and *others* replaces plural countable nouns.

Another one of my accounts is overdue.

All *others* are balanced accurately.

The *other* account that isn't balanced is my cousin's.

Certain determiners in a sentence will also help you decide when to use *another* or *other*. *Another* is used before the word *one* when the meaning is "one more." *Other* is used following *the, all,* and *every. The other* means "the second of two" or "all remaining items" in a larger group.

Dina and I telephone *each other* every month.

Dina and I telephone *one another* every month.

In these examples, *each other* and *one another* convey a reciprocal relationship: sometimes I call Dina; sometimes Dina calls me.

ACTIVITY

12.3   **Using *another, other, the other, each other,* and *one another***

Fill in each blank with *other, another, the other, each other,* or *one another,* as appropriate.

Yesterday, I received two letters. One was from my old roommate Laura. _____ letter was from my good friend Tanya. Both of them had some important news to share with me.

Laura just bought _____ puppy. She now has two. Both dogs are going to be big when they get older, so she'll have to get _____ doghouse. She said that both puppies play with _____ all day long, and they're very happy.

Tanya has a problem. She's been dating John for five years, but now she's in love with _____ man. She said that they talk to _____ almost every day at work. She explained that she loves John, but this _____ love is very strong. She's talked to _____ friends about it, but nobody really knows what to say.

I'm going to sit down right now and write Tanya a letter. I don't think she needs _____ man in her life if she really loves John. One man is enough, and she'll have _____ problems if she continues working and talking with this _____ man.

Already, yet, still

The ice cream has *already* melted.

Has the ice cream *already* melted?

Already implies that something has happened by this time, perhaps sooner than expected. In these examples, the person is surprised that the ice cream has melted, as it was probably just taken out of the freezer. *Already* is used with positive statements and questions.

The ice cream hasn't melted *yet,* even though I took it out of the freezer fifteen minutes ago.

Has the ice cream melted *yet?*

Yet implies that something hasn't happened but will happen. In this example, the writer expects the ice cream to melt because it isn't in the freezer. *Yet* is used with negative statements and questions.

Is the ice cream *still* frozen?

The chef is *still* waiting for the ice cream to melt, so that she can use it in a recipe.

Still implies that something continues longer than expected. In the first example, the person is asking in surprise whether the ice cream is *still* frozen, even though it has been out of the freezer a long time. In the second example, the chef is waiting longer than she expected for the ice cream to melt.

ACTIVITY 12.4 Using *yet* and *still*

Read the following situations. Respond to each question using the adverb in parentheses and the other words provided.

> *Example:*   You look really tired. What's the matter?
> (yet) not I recover from jet lag
>
> *I haven't recovered from jet lag yet.*

1. Cameron wants to borrow his parents' car again. Why?
   (yet) not take his car to the mechanic

   _____

2. Larry had to lend Anita money this week. Why?
   (still) wait for her paycheck

   _____

3. Vicky looks really worried. Is something wrong?
   (yet) not pay the rent

   _____

4. Karen studied for seven hours today. Why?
   (still) have two exams this week

   _____

ACTIVITY 12.5 Using *already, yet,* and *still*

Repeat each of the following statements and include *already, yet,* or *still,* as appropriate.

> *Example:*   It's only nine o'clock, and Rick is here.
>
> *It's only nine o'clock, and Rick is here already.*

1. John didn't like to play tennis before, and he doesn't like to play tennis now.

_____

2. My students began to study English just a few months ago, but they speak very well.

_____

3. The class should begin at one o'clock, but Dr. Matthews isn't here.

_____

4. People were complaining about the heat last week, and they are complaining now.

_____

5. We have just started cleaning up the patio, but Tom is tired.

_____

6. Pam is waiting for Jeff, but he hasn't come.

_____

7. We didn't expect the train to arrive early, but it's here.

_____

8. Jim was looking for a job a month ago, and he is looking for a job now.

_____

ACTIVITY
12.6   **Where Have You Been?**

What cities in the world have you already visited? What did you see there? What didn't you see there? What cities have you not yet visited but would still like to visit? On a separate piece of paper, write sentences or a short paragraph describing your past voyages and possible voyages in the future.

> *Example:* I've already visited New York and Chicago, but I haven't been to San Francisco yet. In New York, I've already seen the Statue of Liberty and the World Trade Center, but I haven't been to the Museum of Modern Art yet. . . .

12c AVOIDING MISTAKES IN USAGE

Study the accompanying box explaining the correct uses of words that are frequently confused. Then complete Activity 12.7.

WORDS COMMONLY CONFUSED

accept	**except**
(v) to take or receive	(v) to leave out
	(prep) excluding
I *accepted* the job offer.	Everyone agreed with my mother *except* me.
advice	**advise**
(n) opinion given to a person on how to act or behave	(v) to give advice
My counselor gave me some good *advice*.	My doctor *advised* me not to smoke.
affect	**effect**
(v) to influence, to produce an effect	(n) result
Rain *affects* my moods.	One of the *effects* of the dry weather is erosion.
amount	**number**
(Use with noncountable nouns.)	(Use with countable nouns.)
The fire produced a large *amount* of smoke.	A large *number* of people arrived early.
clothes	**cloths**
garments worn on the body	pieces of material made from fibers
Famous people wear interesting *clothes*.	I purchased several *cloths* when I was in Turkey.
compare to	**compare with**
to say that one thing is like another	to examine similarities and differences
Shakespeare often *compared* his lovers *to* flowers.	We *compared* modern English poets *with* modern American poets.
either	**neither**
one or the other of two	not one and not the other of two
I'll eat *either* pizza or ravioli.	*Neither* my mom nor my dad went to college.
fewer	**less**
(Use with countable nouns.)	(Use with noncountable nouns.)
Fewer children play in the park on weekdays.	I have *less* vacation time with my new job.
good	**well**
(adj)	(adv)
She does *good* work.	She does her work *well*.
its	**it's**
(possessive form of *it*)	(contraction of *it is* or *it has*)
Sabine's dog likes to chase *its* tail.	*It's* been four years since I've seen you.
kind of	**sort of**
(Do not use to mean "somewhat" in formal writing.)	(Do not use to mean "somewhat" in formal writing.)
lay	**lie**
(v tr) to place or put something	(v intr) to recline
(lay, laid, laid)	(lie, lay, lain)
I *laid* my clothes on the bed.	Pam likes to *lie* on the beach.
like	**as**
(prep)	(conj)
He looks *like* his dad.	He acts *as* if he were drunk.

(continued)

WORDS COMMONLY CONFUSED *(continued)*	
live *(v)* to reside; to dwell We don't *live* in Houston anymore.	**leave** *(v)* to go away He *leaves* for work at 7 A.M.
may (Use to express permission or possibility.) Some people *may* find him annoying.	**can** (Use to express ability.) I *can* play the piano.
past *(n) (adj) (prep)* In the *past,* he used to drink a lot.	**passed** *(v)* past tense of *pass* Time *passed* so quickly at the park.
rise *(v intr)* to get up *(rise, rose, risen)* I *rose* at 6 A.M. to go to school.	**raise** *(v tr)* to lift up *(raise, raised, raised)* My dad *raised* the baby to his shoulders.
say (Can have only words as its object.) Tom *said,* "I'm going home now."	**tell** (Cannot have words as its object.) He *told* us that he was going home.
than *(conj)* Cats are smarter *than* dogs.	**then** *(adv)* We watched the game; *then* we went home.

their (Possessive form of *they*) Teenagers find *their* own jobs.	**there** *(adv)* in that place Put the boxes *there*.	**they're** (Contraction of *they are*) *They're* going to Moscow.
to *(prep)* Give the money *to* Charles.	**too** *(adv)* It's *too* late to go now.	**two** a number The bus costs *two* dollars.

were *(v)* past tense of *be* Where *were* you yesterday?	**where** *(adv)* at or to what place I don't know *where* my friends are.
who's (contraction of *who is*) *Who's* going to Montana with us?	**whose** (Possessive form of *who*) The boy *whose* name was just called left the room.

Key: *(adj)* adjective, *(adv)* adverb, *(conj)* conjunction, *(n)* noun, *(prep)* preposition, *(v)* verb, *(v intr)* intransitive verb, *(v tr)* transitive verb.

ACTIVITY

12.7 **Avoiding Mistakes in Usage**

Read each of the following sentences, circling the correct word of the choices in parentheses.

1. Every state in the Union has (it's, its) own Supreme Court.

2. No one knows (who's, whose) name had just been called.

3. This year's budget at the elementary school will be larger (than, then) last year's.

4. The linguistics exam was (to, too) difficult for Charles.

5. I wanted to go camping (to, too, two).

6. As soon as (they're, their, there) finished, the students will be allowed to leave.

7. Kathy doesn't want to (live, leave) at home with her parents anymore.

8. The boy's mother didn't want him to play outside in his school (cloths, clothes).

9. I hope (its, it's) not too late to send in my refund notice.

10. When the car (passed, past) us, we were probably driving about fifty-five miles per hour.

11. (Whose, Who's) coming to the party on Friday?

12. Do you know (there, their, they're) new phone number in Seattle?

13. Did they (rise, raise) the prices again?

14. Everyone came to the meeting (accept, except) Dave.

15. I'd better not have any coffee because it really (affects, effects) me.

16. We couldn't believe the (amount, number) of people who marched in the parade.

17. Jim did really (good, well) on his driving test.

18. (Neither, Either) guest showed up at the restaurant.

19. There are (less, fewer) squirrels in the forest this summer.

20. How many people (where, were) in class this morning?

12d CONCISENESS

Wordiness is a result of using unnecessary words that mean the same thing, and the overuse of intensifiers and expletive constructions.

Redundancy

She had no idea of the ~~boundaries and~~ limitations on behavior at a dinner party.

My sister's perception of men changed as she entered ~~into~~ college.

~~Often~~ *M*any marriages break up as a result of the financial pressure when one spouse becomes unemployed.

When a sentence says the same thing twice, it is redundant. In the first example, *boundaries* and *limitations* mean the same thing. In the second example, *entered* means "went into," so *into* is redundant. In the third sentence, *often* and *many* convey the same meaning, so one or the other suffices.

ELIMINATING REDUNDANCY

Wordy	Concise
many different ways	many ways
at an early date	soon
run quickly	run
each separate course	each course
a number of	some, many
are made up of	make up
at this point in time	now
at the present time	now
so as to	to
based on the fact that	because
at the conclusion of	after, following
in connection with	about, concerning
take into consideration	consider
subsequent to	before
it is often the case that	often
it is our understanding that	we understand that
until such time as	until
in connection with	with
in order to	to
by means of	by
in relation to	with
of great importance	important
appears to be	is

ACTIVITY 12.8 Avoiding Redundancy

Revise the following paragraph, eliminating redundancy.

Henry David Thoreau was a writer and naturalist of great importance who once lived in the past, during the nineteenth century. He believed in the freedom of each separate individual and did not support a strong government based on the fact that he thought it was often the case that overpowering governments destroy people's freedom. In addition, he was a naturalist in many different ways. He believed that individuals should live in connection with nature and provide for themselves from nature in order to be happier. He even built a simple cabin for himself in the middle of the woods near Walden Pond in which to write about what he believed. Many people were impressed with a number of Thoreau's ideas at that point in time, and he remained the ideal of many Americans for many years after his death.

Intensifiers

It was *extremely* cold in January last year.

The waitress was *exceedingly* polite to the young couple.

I was *very* tired by three o'clock.

The italicized words, which increase the intensity of the adjectives or adverbs they modify, are called intensifiers. Many writers would think that these words contribute nothing to the sentences and would therefore remove them. Other writers might disagree. If the normal temperature in January for the area where the writer lives is in the low thirties but the temperature never got out of the single digits, the use of *extremely* is appropriate. However, always be careful not to overuse intensifiers. Be sure that each one you use adds real meaning.

ACTIVITY

12.9   **Avoiding Excessive Intensifiers**

Read the following sentences, and cross out all unnecessary intensifiers.

1. Young Americans definitely need to become aware about current affairs.

2. Students must take a rather difficult exam before entering college.

3. She was absolutely quite sure that it was going to snow yesterday.

4. Jim was somewhat relatively upset when his son's little league team lost the championship.

Expletive Constructions

~~There were~~ three police officers at the site.

~~It is required that~~ students pay their bills before the first day of classes.

There and *it* are used as expletives in these sentences, and they add no meaning to them. They simply hold the normal subject position so that the subject can be moved to a position following the verb.

ACTIVITY

12.10   **Avoiding *there* and *it***

Read the following paragraph. Then rewrite the paragraph to eliminate the wordiness resulting from an overuse of expletives.

> Oak Bridge police are deciding whether loud music from car stereos should be included under the city's current ordinance, which is used to stop noise from homes. There are police officers required to fine car owners driving vehicles with loud exhausts and squealing tires. However, there is no existing ordinance to prosecute those with massive speakers and amplifiers in their cars. It is amazing how many people have complained about the noise from these cars. There were forty-two complaints filed in the past two weeks. There have been several guidelines established by the council's transportation board members, and it is their intention to research the present ordinance and the complaints for next month's meeting. Of course, there are many car owners who believe there is nothing wrong with the stereo systems, and there were several options that were suggested.

12e USING LANGUAGE APPROPRIATELY

Humility

~~It is only my opinion, but I think that perhaps~~ this course requires too much work.

In three different ways, the writer of the original sentence revealed a lack of confidence. When you write an opinion about something, it is usually quite clear that you are stating your opinion, and to say so merely belabors the obvious. To do so three times is excessive.

T
~~In my opinion,~~ the Orioles will win the pennant next year.

Here the phrase *in my opinion* is more debatable, but if you think about it, there is no way you could know who is going to win the pennant. To point out that you are giving your opinion is to state the obvious and makes you sound less sure of yourself.

w
~~I feel that~~ we should hold an election within the next six months.

I feel should not be used to mean *I think,* and here either expression is probably unnecessary since it is perfectly clear without it that the writer is stating an opinion.

In some cultures, expressions of humility are expected of a writer, but in English they should be used sparingly. If it won't be clear to your reader that a statement is just your opinion, say so. But when it is clear, don't use these qualifying phrases to point out the obvious.

ACTIVITY

12.11 Avoiding Excessive Humility

Rewrite the following paragraphs from a student's answer to an essay question, paying special attention to avoid excessive humility.

> *Question:* What are some problems faced by foreign students studying abroad?
>
> Foreign students studying abroad face many problems, due, I feel, primarily to language and cultural barriers.
> In my opinion, English is one of the most difficult languages to learn because there are so many exceptions. Also, English has a very different word order from my native language, and there is so much slang!
> Cultural barriers are a second problem. I think this problem is the biggest, but it is only my opinion. The cultural barrier between Korea and the United States is maybe very wide. It's only my opinion, but I think we Asians respect our elders, whereas relationships in the United States are a lot different. I think this may really shock foreign students. Finally, loneliness can be a problem for foreign students. I feel that loneliness can cause homesickness and make it difficult to study. In my opinion, I think these are only some of the problems faced by foreign students, but in my point of view, they are the biggest problems.

Sexism

OFFENSIVE LANGUAGE
women
Those ~~broads~~ sure know how to bowl!
secretary
Please call my ~~girl~~ and make an appointment to meet with me.

Demeaning terms such as *broads* are so offensive as to be unacceptable to almost all readers, even those who do not agree with other aspects of feminism. *Girl* is unacceptable when applied to an adult.

NONINCLUSIVENESS
People
~~Men~~ have struggled to end injustice throughout history.

Referring to the entire human race with words that recognize only the male half is sexist.

JOB TITLES
letter carrier
The ~~mailman~~ delivered a package to our neighbors.

Most job titles now avoid the word *man: police officer, firefighter, chair* or *chairperson, diplomat* (for *statesman*), *member of Congress* (for *Congressman* or *Congresswoman*), *attendant* (for *doorman*).

PRONOUNS

INCORRECT: A doctor should put his instructions in writing.

CORRECT: A doctor should put his or her instructions in writing.

CORRECT: Doctors should put their instructions in writing.

CORRECT: A doctor should put all instructions in writing.

Some people find *his or her* awkward, so it is usually better to recast the sentence in the plural or in a form that requires no personal pronouns.

PARALLELISM

Mr. and Mrs. Hiroshige
~~Mr. Hiroshige and his wife Margaret~~ are meeting us at the movie.

When referring to men and women, identify them both in the same way.

AUDIENCE

a guest
At the end of this course, we will all go to the National Gallery; you may bring ~~your wives~~ if you wish.

The writer of the original sentence made the unwarranted assumption that everyone in the class was male and married.

ACTIVITY

12.12 Avoiding Sexist Language

Read the following sentences. If you recognize a problem with sexist language, write the letter of the corresponding problem from the list. Make all necessary changes to avoid sexist language in these sentences.

    a. Offensive language
    b. Noninclusiveness
    c. Job titles
    d. Pronouns
    e. Parallelism
    f. Audience

_____ 1. Man has inhabited the earth for thousands of years.

_____ 2. Mrs. Sneeden and her husband Mike are moving to Hoopestown, Illinois.

_____ 3. The milkman drops off the milk and butter every Monday at 1:00.

_____ 4. Most people never forget the language of their motherland.

_____ 5. A minister must be constantly aware of current events around him.

_____ 6. Every truck driver ought to know how to change his own oil.

_____ 7. The old bag who lives on the corner just got a puppy.

_____ 8. Everyone is required to carry his identification at all times.

_____ 9. "Be a cowboy for a day! You and your wives are invited to the annual rodeo and square dance."

_____10. All men are created equal.

12f BEING AWARE OF CONNOTATION

The explicit meaning of a word, the meaning you find if you look up the word in a dictionary, is referred to as the *denotative meaning*, or **denotation.** But words also have emotional colorings or associations that contribute to their meanings; these emotional colorings are called **connotations.** The denotative meanings of *lasting* and *endless* are nearly identical, but their connotations are quite different. *Lasting* has positive connotations; you would use it to describe something that you want to last. *Endless* has a negative connotation and would be used to describe something you wish would be over.

The accompanying chart compares the denotations and connotations of words meaning "not giving way to pressure or persuasion." Notice how different the connotations can be.

DENOTATIONS AND CONNOTATIONS

Word	Denotation	Connotation
firm	constant; steadfast; unyielding	neutral to positive
determined	marked by or showing fixed purpose; resolute; unwavering	positive, especially when applied to the pursuit of a goal
faithful	adhering strictly to a person or cause; dutiful; loyal	positive
single-minded	having one overriding purpose; steadfast	slightly negative, especially in connection with a particular goal
unyielding	not giving way; steadfast	neutral to negative
stubborn	not easily persuaded; persistent; unduly determined	negative

When you write, it is important to use words with appropriate denotative meanings, but you must also think about connotations. A number of reference books are available to assist you in choosing words with just the right connotations.

12.13 Recognizing Positive and Negative Connotations

Compare the words in each pair and indicate in the blanks which one has a negative connotation ("N") and which one has a positive connotation ("P").

1. broad _____   2. drunk _____

    woman _____   tipsy _____

3. cheap _____   4. aging _____

   bargain _____   mature _____

5. unmarried _____ 6. skinny _____

   single _____   slender _____

ACTIVITY

12.14 **Making Sentences More Neutral**

Rewrite the following sentences, replacing the italicized word with a more appropriate one. Your new sentence should be more neutral than the original.

> *Example:* The *fat* boy had trouble getting up the pool ladder.
>
> *The stocky boy had trouble getting up the pool ladder.*

1. The *mob* of protesters gathered outside the capitol.

_____

2. The chairperson's *stubbornness* surprised all the members of the board.

_____

3. She used to be tall and *scrawny* when she was in junior high school.

_____

4. The workers *begged* their boss for a longer lunch period.

_____

5. The schoolchildren *banished* the new child from their kickball game.

_____

12g **WORD CHOICE: COMPREHENSIVE CHECK**

ACTIVITY

12.15 **Diagnostic Retest**

Complete Activity 12.1 again. If you still miss or have difficulty with any items, review the relevant sections of the workbook.

Putting It All Together

Read the following passage, and determine if there are problems in word choice or appropriate language. Rewrite the passage, making any necessary changes.

Verbal communication is definitely one of the most studied human activities. At each and every level of schooling, from first grade through college, it is required that a student learn the structure of his written and spoken language. Nonverbal communication, on the other hand, is one of the least studied human activities. It is not considered important enough already to be included in the public school curriculum. However, when we communicate, as much as eighty percent of the meaning of our messages is derived from nonverbal language.

Human communication cannot be reduced to words alone. If it could, we would have less communication problems with other people. Telephone, radio, and television carry the voice of man to the most remote corners of the earth; yet in this age of instant communication, the term *communication gap* has become commonplace. Why? In my opinion, I think perhaps we are basically nonverbal creatures who have learned to speak, but we do not trust words that we use during speech.

A sort of conflict arises when people believe that their verbalizations should be excepted at face value by other people. Of all the channels of communication available to us, however, it is often the case that verbalization of words carries the least weight. We communicate with our entire bodies, and in situations of deep personal meaning and of great importance, body language is trusted more then words. Words count for very little when they combat with the silent language of the body. Thus we may talk and talk, but until our nonverbal behavior agrees with our words, a huge credibility gap, not a communication gap, will always and forever exist. [Adapted from James J. Thompson, *Beyond Words*]

PART IV

EDITING FOR GRAMMAR AND USAGE

13 Finding and Revising Errors with Verb Form

14 Finding and Revising Errors with Verb Tense and Voice

15 Finding and Revising Errors with Conditionals, Hypotheticals, and the Subjunctive

16 Finding and Revising Errors with Verbals

17 Finding and Revising Subject-Verb Agreement Errors

18 Finding and Revising Pronoun Agreement and Reference Errors

19 Finding and Revising Pronoun Case Errors

20 Finding and Revising Adjective and Adverb Errors

21 Finding and Revising Errors with Articles

22 Finding and Revising Errors with Prepositions

FINDING AND REVISING ERRORS WITH VERB FORM

Verbs are the most changeable words in the English language. They change their endings. They change their form. They add or change helping verbs. And all these changes indicate variations in the meaning they communicate.

In this chapter we will look at regular and irregular verb forms, phrasal verbs, and modals, all areas of difficulty for ESL students.

13a DIAGNOSTIC ACTIVITY: VERB FORMS

ACTIVITY 13.1 **How Much Do You Know?**

Read each sentence, and determine if it contains an error in the form of an irregular verb, a phrasal verb, or a modal. If there is an error, correct it. Not all sentences contain errors. An example is provided.

Example: You had better ~~to~~ ask if you want to use the copier.

1. The force of the storm bended the tree right in half.
2. The burglar creeped up behind the unsuspecting woman.
3. Samantha ran a business selling potholders.
4. You won't believe what I *have* seen!
5. The professor pointed *out* to Maryanne out that light travels faster than sound.
6. The chairperson said it was time to get back *to* business.
7. It was almost time to pick up *her* ~~her~~ at the airport.
8. We were expected to hand the reports *in* by Friday.
9. When my father was younger, he ~~would~~ *could* run ten miles a day.
10. I ~~would~~ like spinach when I was little.
11. You may have told me *that* you were coming to visit!
12. You should have ~~went~~ *gone* to the doctor last week.

Determine which items you missed in this Diagnostic Activity. If you missed or had trouble with any of the items, please go to the appropriate section in *The*

149

HarperCollins Concise Handbook for Writers and this workbook for further practice and study.

It is important to know which items cause you difficulty. When revising your writing, you might want to go through your paper one time checking only for the use of irregular verbs, phrasal verbs, and modals. Concentrate on items that you had difficulty with in this activity.

13b REGULAR AND IRREGULAR VERB FORMS

FORMS OF REGULAR VERBS

Base Form	Past Tense	Past Participle	Present Participle	-s Form
infinitive without *to*	base + *-ed* (or + *-d*)	base + *-ed* (or + *-d*)	base + *-ing*	base + *-s* (or + *-es*)
jump	jumped	jumped	jumping	jumps
love	loved	loved	loving	loves
pass	passed	passed	passing	passes

FORMS OF IRREGULAR VERBS

Base Form	Past Tense	Past Participle
are	were	been
arise	arose	arisen
awake	awoke, awaked	awaked, awoke
bear	bore	borne, born
beat	beat	beaten
become	became	become
begin	began	begun
bend	bent	bent
bet	bet	bet
bind	bound	bound
bite	bit	bitten, bit
blow	blew	blown
break	broke	broken
bring	brought	brought
build	built	built
burst	burst	burst
buy	bought	bought
cast	cast	cast
catch	caught	caught
choose	chose	chosen
cling	clung	clung
come	came	come
cost	cost	cost
creep	crept	crept
cut	cut	cut

(continued)

FORMS OF IRREGULAR VERBS *(continued)*

Base Form	Past Tense	Past Participle
deal	dealt	dealt
dig	dug	dug
dive	dived, dove	dived
do	did	done
draw	drew	drawn
drink	drank	drunk
drive	drove	driven
dwell	dwelt	dwelt
eat	ate	eaten
fall	fell	fallen
feed	fed	fed
feel	felt	felt
fight	fought	fought
find	found	found
flee	fled	fled
fling	flung	flung
fly	flew	flown
forbid	forbade, forbad	forbidden
forget	forgot	forgotten
forgive	forgave	forgiven
freeze	froze	frozen
get	got	got, gotten
give	gave	given
go	went	gone
grow	grew	grown
hang (an object)*	hung	hung
have	had	had
hear	heard	heard
hide	hid	hidden
hit	hit	hit
hold	held	held
hurt	hurt	hurt
is	was	been
keep	kept	kept
know	knew	known
lay (an object)	laid	laid
lead	led	led
leave	left	left
let	let	let
lie (recline)	lay	lain
light	lighted, lit	lighted, lit
lose	lost	lost
make	made	made
mean	meant	meant
meet	met	met
pay	paid	paid
prove	proved	proved, proven
put	put	put
quit	quit	quit
read	read	read
rid	rid	rid
ride	rode	ridden

Hang (a person) is a regular verb.

(continued)

FORMS OF IRREGULAR VERBS (continued)

Base Form	Past Tense	Past Participle
ring	rang	rung
rise	rose	risen
run	ran	run
say	said	said
see	saw	seen
seek	sought	sought
sell	sold	sold
send	sent	sent
set	set	set
shake	shook	shaken
shine (cast light)*	shone	shone
shoot	shot	shot
shrink	shrank	shrunk
sing	sang	sung
sink	sank	sunk
sit	sat	sat
slay	slew	slain
sleep	slept	slept
slide	slid	slid
speak	spoke	spoken
spend	spent	spent
spin	spun	spun
spring	sprang	sprung
stand	stood	stood
steal	stole	stolen
sting	stung	stung
stink	stank, stunk	stunk
stride	strode	stridden
strike	struck	struck, stricken
swear	swore	sworn
sweep	swept	swept
swim	swam	swum
swing	swung	swung
take	took	taken
teach	taught	taught
tear	tore	torn
tell	told	told
think	thought	thought
throw	threw	thrown
understand	understood	understood
wake	woke, waked	waked, woken
wear	wore	worn
win	won	won
wring	wrung	wrung
write	wrote	written

Shine (polish) is a regular verb.

ACTIVITY

13.2 **Using Regular and Irregular Verbs**

Write the past-tense form of the verb in parentheses in each blank in the following passage.

Yesterday, when the sun _rose_ (rise), Alper _woke_ (wake) up. He _got_ (get) out of bed and _thought_ (think) to himself, "This is the big day!" The lottery _was_ (is) at two million, and Alper _was_ (is) sure his ticket _was_ (is) the winning ticket. He had _lost_ (lose) many times in the past, but today he _felt_ (feel) lucky. As he was getting dressed, he _remembered_ (remember) the man who _sold_ (sell) him the ticket in the grocery. Sam had _worked_ (work) there for several years, and many people had _bought_ (buy) winning tickets from him. He _said_ (say) he had a "sixth sense" about the tickets, and he _told_ (tell) Alper that he was sure his ticket _was_ (is) the "big one." That night Alper _dreamed_ (dream) about his new home, new car, and all the money he _could_ (can) send to his family in Turkey.

The drawing _was_ (is) at 7:00 P.M. His friends _came_ (come) over to watch the big event. Unbelievably, when they _called_ (call) the winning number, Alper's ticket _was_ (is) only one number off. It _was_ (is) so close. The room _fell_ (fall) silent. Alper _looked_ (look) as if he was going to cry. But suddenly, a smile _crossed_ (cross) his face. He _said_ (say), "Don't worry, there's a lottery in Wisconsin that's worth a million. I'll go there tomorrow and get a ticket."

13c PHRASAL VERBS

Phrasal verbs are two- and three-word combinations that contain a verb and a **particle** (a preposition or an adverb). Because phrasal verbs are usually idiomatic, it is almost impossible to determine the meaning by looking at the verb and particle separately. Also, a phrasal verb can have several meanings. For example, the phrasal verb *put down* can mean, among other things, "to write down," "to criticize," "to assign to a category," or "to consume." The best way to learn these verbs is to pay attention when reading or listening to English. When you hear or read a phrasal verb, note it in your journal and look up the meaning in a dictionary. Then try using these phrasal verbs when you write or speak in English to reinforce your comprehension.

Phrasal verbs can also cause problems because they can be placed in different locations in a sentence. Look at the following examples.

INCORRECT: She was slow to *catch* to the game *on*.

CORRECT: She was slow to *catch on* to the game.

In this case, the phrasal verb *catch on* is intransitive (it cannot take a direct object), so the verb and particle cannot be separated in a sentence. See the accompanying chart for a list of intransitive phrasal verbs.

Some transitive phrasal verbs (those that can take a direct object) can be either separated or used together, some *must* be separated, and some *must* be used together. Unfortunately, there is no rule for determining this. The only solution is to check a grammar book or dictionary.

INCORRECT: I decided to *break* with my boyfriend *up*.

CORRECT: I decided to *break up* with my boyfriend.

Here the phrasal verb *break up* cannot be separated, and it also requires the preposition *with* to mean "end a romantic relationship." See the chart for a list of phrasal verbs that cannot be separated and require prepositions.

INCORRECT: Yesterday, I *called* my neighbor *on*.

CORRECT: Yesterday, I *called on* my neighbor.

The transitive phrasal verb *call on* cannot be separated in a sentence, but it does not require a preposition. The chart lists these types of phrasal verbs.

CORRECT: We *called* the baseball game *off* because of rain.

CORRECT: We *called off* the baseball game because of rain.

In these sentences, the direct object of the transitive verb *call off* is a noun *(baseball game)*. When this is the case, the parts of the phrasal verb can be separated or used together.

INCORRECT: I decided to *call off* it.

CORRECT: I decided to *call it off*.

In this case, the direct object for the transitive phrasal verb *call off* is a pronoun *(it)*. When this is the case, the phrasal verb must *always* be separated. See the chart for a list of phrasal verbs that can or cannot be separated, depending on whether the direct object is a noun or a pronoun.

PHRASAL VERBS

Intransitive Phrasal Verbs (cannot be separated)

*blow up (lose control)	drop by	pass away
boil over	get by	pass out (lose consciousness)
*break down (fall apart)	get up	play around
*break in (burglarize)	give in	*pull up (drive up)
break into	*give out (exhaust)	*show up (arrive)
break out	go ahead	stay up
catch on	go back	talk back
come away	grow up	*take off (leave the ground)
come in	look ahead	*turn up (appear)
come out	look away	wear away

*These phrasal verbs cannot be separated when used with the meaning in parentheses. They can, however, be separated with a different meaning.

Transitive Phrasal Verbs (cannot be separated)

Requiring prepositions:

break up with	end up with	look down on
catch up with	get along with	look in on
check out of	get away with	look up to
check up on	get back to	make away with
close in on	get down to	pick up on
come up with	get out of	put up with
cut down on	give in to	run out of
drop in on	go in for	stand up for
drop out of	keep up with	walk out on

Not requiring prepositions:

call on	cover for	go over
check into	decide on	hear about
come across	get into	insist on
come from	get off	keep on

(continued)

PHRASAL VERBS *(continued)*

count on	get over	let up
look after	run into	wait for
look at	take after	wait on
look into		

Transitive Phrasal Verbs (can be separated; must be separated if direct object is a pronoun)

ask out	find out	put on
blow up	give back	put out
break down	give out	show off
break in	give up	show up
bring about	hand in	shut off
bring on	hang up	take back
bring up	have on	take off
call back	hold up	take out
call in	leave out	take over
call off	look over	take up
call up	look up	tear down
carry out	make up	tear up
check out	name after	think over
cheer up	name for	throw away
clean up	pass out	throw out
cross out	pick out	throw up
cut out	pick up	try on
do over	point out	turn down
drop by	pull up	turn on
drop off	put away	turn out
figure out	put back	turn up
fill out	put off	

13.3 Understanding Common Intransitive Phrasal Verbs

A. Match the intransitive phrasal verb to its definition. Write the matching letter in the blank.

a. to occur suddenly	f. to speak disrespectfully
b. to consider the future	g. to understand
c. to appear	h. to concede
d. to proceed	i. to return
e. to arrive	j. to become exhausted

_____ 1. show up _____ 6. go back

_____ 2. talk back _____ 7. go ahead

_____ 3. break out _____ 8. look ahead

_____ 4. catch on _____ 9. turn up

_____ 5. give out _____10. give in

B. Substitute for the words in italics an intransitive phrasal verb from the chart on pages 154–155. Be sure to use the appropriate tense. (More than one phrasal verb may be appropriate.)

1. The Sandersons thought they could *manage* on only the husband's salary.

   _____

2. My car *stopped running* on the highway last week.

   _____

3. The paint on the house began to *fade.*

   _____

4. After the meeting, Lon *left* with a feeling of accomplishment.

   _____

5. Mario ran ten miles this morning without eating anything. Later, he *lost consciousness.*

   _____

6. Someone *burglarized* my car last week and stole my stereo.

   _____

7. Sometimes my younger brother Rob is permitted *not to go to bed* until three in the morning!

   _____

8. People were saddened to learn that the actress had *died.*

   _____

9. Sabine *was raised* in the Philippines, but she considers herself German.

   _____

10. The argument *got out of control* when Ms. Bunson called the president an ugly name.

   _____

ACTIVITY
13.4 **Understanding Common Transitive Phrasal Verbs**

A. Match the transitive phrasal verb to its definition. Write the matching letter in the blank.

a. to return to storage
b. to take charge
c. to tolerate
d. to serve people in a restaurant
e. to choose
f. to see if someone or something is okay

g. to discuss
h. to end an argument
i. to reduce use of
j. to escape without punishment for
k. to put into smaller pieces
l. to soften through use

_____ 1. check up on   _____ 7. break in

_____ 2. break down   _____ 8. pick out

_____ 3. make up   _____ 9. put up with

_____ 4. take over   _____10. wait on

_____ 5. put away   _____11. cut down on

_____ 6. go over   _____12. get away with

B. Substitute for the words in italics a transitive phrasal verb from the chart on pages 154–155. Be sure to use the appropriate tense. (More than one phrasal verb may be appropriate.)

1. Melissa always *removes* her makeup before she goes to bed.

_____

2. When Greg was looking through his closet, he *found* a picture of his old girl-friend and decided to *discard it*.

_____

3. People who *stop going to* high school have difficulty finding jobs.

_____

4. Rose *studied* the rental agreement carefully before she signed it.

_____

5. Chandra *left the train* at the wrong stop.

_____

6. Even though everyone is against him, I am going to *support* my congressman.

_____

7. We decided to *delay* building the deck because of the expense.

_____

8. Mr. Plough *returned* the quizzes to the students.

_____

9. Cheryl is *researching* buying a new car.

_____

10. The terrorists decided to *explode* the dam.

_____

ACTIVITY

13.5 **Using the Correct Particle with Phrasal Verbs**

In the blanks in the following sentences, write the correct particle for intransitive and transitive phrasal verbs.

1. Karin decided to give _____ her daytime job so she could devote her time to studying.

2. People running for city council are constantly dropping _____ my house.

3. Journalists are having a difficult time keeping _____ _____ the changes in Eastern Europe.

4. Yesterday I ran _____ an old high school friend.

5. Byron decided to take _____ golf so he could spend more time with his clients.

6. You cannot take _____ sale items purchased at the Wooden Skate antique shop.

7. The mall stores were giving _____ free popcorn during the sale.

8. In the current economic situation, it is wise to look _____ to better times.

9. Rob tries to look _____ _____ his grandmother at least once a month to make sure she is well.

10. Chris takes _____ her mother more than Katie does.

ACTIVITY

13.6 **Writing Sentences Using Transitive Phrasal Verbs**

Write a sentence using the word and phrasal verb provided. If the phrasal verb can be separated, write two sentences, one in which the phrasal verb is separated and one in which it is not.

> *Example:* room (clean up)
> *I always clean up my room.*
> *I always clean my room up.*

1. her (take out)

2. sister (look up to)

3. garbage (take out)

4. it (look up)

5. paper (run out of)

6. radio (turn on)

7. golf (take up)

8. building (tear down)

9. them (cheer up)

10. book (check out)

ACTIVITY

13.7 **Editing for Usage of Phrasal Verbs**

Edit the following sentences for errors with phrasal verbs, such as incorrect particles or the separation of phrasal verbs that cannot be separated. Not all sentences contain errors.

1. My boss wanted to think up my proposal to start a textbook series.

2. The plan was to pick up her at the bus station and then go have dinner.

3. Gary is always trying to get out of work in our office.

4. The robber broke the house into next door and stole practically everything.

5. Certain religions look down to living together as a couple before marriage.

13d **MODALS**

Modals are a type of verb called **helping verbs** or **auxiliary verbs.** The accompanying chart lists the twenty-three helping verbs in English.

HELPING VERBS					
Always Helping Verbs			**Helping Verbs or Main Verbs**		
can	might	should	am	did	have
could	must	will	are	do	is
may	shall	would	be	does	was
			been	had	were
			being	has	

Modals include all the verbs in the left half of the chart (true modals) and another group composed of two or more words called **periphrastic modals,** which include *be able to, be about to, be allowed to, be going to, be supposed to, had better, have got to, have to, ought to,* and *used to.*

Modals differ from the other helping verbs in two ways:

TRUE MODALS	OTHER HELPING VERBS
He *can* fly a kite.	He *does* the laundry.
They *can* fly a kite.	They *do* the laundry.

1. Modals do not have verb endings *(-s, -ed, -ing),* and they do not follow subject-verb agreement rules.

    He *must* prepare the meal.

2. Modals are followed immediately by the base form of the verb. If an infinitive follows a modal, *to* is omitted.

    They *are able to* leave in the morning.

    He *is allowed to* leave with them.

Periphrastic modals, however, follow the subject-verb agreement rule and require that an infinitive with *to* precede the main verb. One periphrastic modal, *had better,* acts like a true modal in that it does not take verb endings or the infinitive *to:*

    You *had better go* to the store.

The accompanying chart will help you understand the meaning of various modals in English when they are used with the simple tenses. The perfective modals *(should have, would have,* etc.) will be discussed later in the chapter. For a discussion of modals used to signal tense, see Chapter 14.

MODAL VERBS

		Examples	
Modal	**Function**	**Present and Future**	**Past**
True modals			
can	Ability	I can bowl well.	I could sing well when I was young.
	Permission	Can I have some ice cream?	Maggie said I could go.
could	Polite question	Could you wash my car now?	
	Advisability	You could get a new haircut.	
	Possibility	I could buy a new car.	
may	Permission	May I go to the party?	
	Possibility	I may go to the Bahamas.	
might	Possibility	I might go to the Bahamas.	
	Advisability	You might want to sweep the floor.	
must	Certainty	She must be sick.	
shall	Polite offer	Shall I open a window?	

(continued)

MODAL VERBS *(continued)*

		Examples	
Modal	**Sense**	**Present and Future**	**Past**
should	Advisability Probability Expectation	You should clean your house. I should buy some groceries. He should be here soon.	
will	Certainty Polite request	I will go to work next week. Will you baby-sit tomorrow?	
would	Polite offer Preference Probability Polite request	Would you like some coffee? I would rather have tea. I would go to the movie. I would like a cup of coffee.	
	Repeated action in past		When I was little, I would always go to the park.
Periphrastic modals			
be able to	Ability	I am able to bowl.	I was able to sing well when I was young.
be about to	Probability	I am about to leave for work.	I was about to leave for work when the phone rang.
be allowed to	Permission	Am I allowed to go to the party? I am allowed to go to the party.	I was allowed to go to the party
be going to	Certainty	I am going to work today.	
be supposed to	Expectation	I am supposed to begin work at eight o'clock.	I was supposed to wash my car tomorrow.
had better	Advisability	You had better go to the doctor.	
	Probability	I had better wash my car.	
have got to	Advisability Probability	You have got to go to class. I have got to clean my house.	
have to	Command Certainty	You have to see the dean. I have to go to class.	I had to go to class.
ought to	Advisability	You ought to wear a raincoat.	
used to	Condition or state in the past		I used to like spinach.

In order to better understand the meaning and use of modals, this chart will be split into three categories for discussion: Modals for Social Interaction, Modals to Express Logical Meaning, and Other Uses of Modals.

Modals for Social Interaction

Modals can be used in social interactions to ask for or state permission, make requests, make offers, make polite statements, state preferences, and give advice.

MODALS FOR SOCIAL INTERACTION

Social Interaction	Modal	Examples	
Permission	can	Can I go to the party?	I can go to the party.
	could	Could I go to the party?	I could go to the party.
	may	May I go to the party?	
	be allowed to	Am I allowed to go to the party?	I am allowed to go to the party.
Polite request	will	Will you baby-sit tomorrow?	
	would	Would you help me with my math?	I would like a cup of coffee.
	could	Could you wash my car?	
Polite offer	would	Would you like a cup of coffee?	
	shall	Shall I shut the window for you?	
Preference	would	I would rather have tea than coffee.	
Advisability*	might	You might wash it before putting it away.	
	ought to	You ought to wash it before putting it away.	
	should	You should wash it before putting it away.	
	had better	You had better wash it before putting it away.	
	could	You could wash it before putting it away.	
Command	have got to	You have got to wash it before putting it away.	
	have to	You have to wash it before putting it away.	
	must	You must wash it before putting it away.	

*When the pronoun is changed to *I* in these sentences, they no longer express advisability; instead, they become simple statements that go from possibility to probability to certainty. These meanings of modals are discussed later in the text.

ACTIVITY

13.8 **Using Modals for Giving Advice**

Look at this sequence of statements giving advice, arranged from weakest to strongest:

> You *might* wash it before putting it away.
> You *could* wash it before putting it away.
> You *ought* to wash it before putting it away.
> You *should* wash it before putting it away.
> You *had better* wash it before putting it away.
> You *have got to* wash it before putting it away.
> You *have to* wash it before putting it away.
> You *must* wash it before putting it away.

Write one or two statements of advice based on the following prompts. An example is provided.

> *Example:* Mitsuko fell and broke her leg.
> *She must go to the hospital.*

1. Kyle is very tired. He keeps falling asleep in class.

2. It is raining and Xavier is going outside.

3. Dan has an exam tomorrow. It is worth twenty percent of his grade.

4. Becky thinks her life is dull.

5. Lois is inside a burning building.

ACTIVITY

13.9   **Using Modals with Permission and Requests**

A.   Read the following sentences. In the blank, write "F" if you think the statement is generally appropriate for *formal* situations and "I" if the statement is generally appropriate for *informal* situations.

PERMISSION   REQUEST

1. *Can* I go to the party? _____   3. *May* I go to the party? _____

2. *Could* I go to the party? _____   4. *Am I allowed to* go to the party? _____

5. *Will* you baby-sit tomorrow? _____   7. *Could* you wash my car? _____

6. *Would* you help me with my   8. *Can* you give me a ride home? _____
   math? _____

B.   Using this information, write letters to the following people. When you are finished, underline the modals you used in the letter. Did you use them appropriately?

1. Write a letter to your best friend in your hometown asking to borrow some money to buy a car.
2. Write a letter to your bank requesting a loan to buy a car.

Perfective Modals of Advice

The forms for the perfective modals are as follows:

modal + *have* + past participle

Active: You should have gone to school today.

modal + *have been* + past participle

Passive: The lawn should have been mowed days ago.

ACTIVITY

13.10 **Using Perfective Modals of Advice**

A. When the modals of advice are in the perfective form, they convey a judgment of a situation in the past. Look at the following sentences, and indicate in the blank if the sentence is expressing *anger, regret, criticism, desire,* or *irritation.*

1. The driver should have watched where he was going when he sped through the stop sign. _____

2. You could have asked me if it was all right to take my wallet! _____

3. You should have seen the concert at Orchestra Hall last night—it was wonderful! _____

4. The teacher might have told us about class being canceled. _____

5. You should have called when you got into town; I would have picked you up. _____

B. Now write sentences with perfective modals that respond to the following situations. An example is provided.

Example: Your friend Linda didn't tell you about a party.

She might have told me about the party.
_____

1. You saw an incredible exhibit of the art of Marc Chagall at the museum.

_____

2. Your friend was having problems with her boss at work. You are sorry she didn't tell you.

_____

3. Your spouse took the car without telling you, and you had plans to meet a friend.

_____

4. Your daughter went to a formal wedding dressed in shorts.

_____

5. You are annoyed at your son for not closing the garage door.

_____

Logical Meaning of Modals

Modals are used to infer something or make a prediction about something that can range from possibility to certainty. Perfective modals have the same meaning in this category.

LOGICAL MEANING OF MODALS

Logical Meaning	Modal	Examples	
		Present and Future	**Past**
Possibility	*may*	I may go to the Bahamas.	I may have gone to the Bahamas.
	might	I might go to the Bahamas.	I might have gone to the Bahamas.
	could	I could go to the Bahamas.	I could have gone to the Bahamas.
Probability	*should*	I should go to the Bahamas.	I should have gone to the Bahamas.
	supposed to	I am supposed to go to the Bahamas.	I am supposed to have gone to the Bahamas.
	ought to*	I ought to go to the Bahamas.	I ought to have gone to the Bahamas.
	had better*	I had better go to the Bahamas.	
	would	I would go to the Bahamas.	I would have gone to the Bahamas.
	have got to†	I have got to go to the Bahamas.	
	have to†	I have to go to the Bahamas.	
	must†	I must go to the Bahamas.	
	be about to	I am about to go to the Bahamas.	
Certainty	will	I will go to the Bahamas.	I will have gone to the Bahamas.
	be going to	I am going to the Bahamas.	

*These examples in the present and future tense also express obligation.
†These examples in the present and future tense also express necessity.

13.11 **Using Modals Expressing Degrees of Certainty**

Read the following passage, writing an appropriate modal in the blank based on the degree of certainty stated in parentheses.

> "If you have time, Morgan," said Mr. Bridge, "I'd like to see some of this Bohemian life we hear so much about."
>
> Hager looked at him doubtfully, for the request posed a problem. There were many things he _____ *(possibility)* shown them, but, even as certain murals in Pompeii are not open to casual tourists, so there were various Parisian experiences not listed in the guidebook.
>
> "Well," said Hager modestly, "I really don't know of anything very Bohemian, but you _____ *(possibility)* like to have dinner at a place on Montparnasse where a lot of art students eat. It's sort of dirty," he added thoughtfully.
>
> Mrs. Bridge thought this sounded exciting. "Perhaps we _____ *(probability)* go back to the hotel and change," she said.
>
> Hager did not know whether she meant to get more dressed up or less dressed up, so finally he said, "I don't think anybody _____ *(certainty)* notice you." [Evan S. Connel, *Mrs. Bridge*]

13.12 **Writing Sentences Using Modals Expressing Degrees of Certainty**

Write a sentence based on each of the following situations. An example is provided.

Example: The weather forecast calls for a thirty percent chance of rain tomorrow.

It could rain tomorrow.

1. Your employment contract provides for a five percent pay raise yearly.

   _____

2. You are thinking about taking a trip to Costa Rica, but you don't know if you have the money.

   _____

3. Your hair hangs down below your eyes. You can see things only some of the time.

   _____

4. You forgot your purse at the store.

   _____

Modals for Other Uses

Modals are used to express ability and to make statements about events that occurred in the past.

MODALS FOR OTHER USES

		Examples	
Meaning	**Modal**	**Present**	**Past**
Ability	*can* *be able to*	I can bowl well I am able to swim.	I could bowl well. I was not able to swim.
Condition or state in the past	*used to*		I used to eat spinach.
Repeated action in the past	*would*		I would go to the park every Saturday.

Note that *would* can only be used with action verbs, whereas *used to* can be used with both actions and conditions or states. When *would* is used to express a repeated action in the past, language that signals past time is needed. Without this language, the sentence has a conditional meaning. Sentences with *used to* that express a repeated action, however, do not need this additional language.

> CONDITIONAL: I *would* live in San Francisco.
>
> CORRECT: I *used to* live in San Francisco.

> CONDITIONAL: I *would* eat candy.
>
> CORRECT: I *would* eat candy when I was little.
>
> CORRECT: I *used to* eat candy.
>
> CORRECT: I *used to* eat candy when I was little.

ACTIVITY 13.13   Using Modals of Ability and Events in the Past

Fill in the blanks in the following passage with *can, be able to, could, would,* and *used to,* as appropriate.

When we were little, my sister Laura and I ___use to___ go to Margaret Fink's, Dyan Ripple's, and Maggie Cashman's houses to play. They _____ live down the street from us. Margaret had an incredible imagination. She ___waved___ think of a game to play at a moment's notice. The game we liked best was called "Family." We ___waved___ build a leaf house and then each take a role in a family. Laura _____ always play the mom—I guess she liked to yell at us. Dyan was also good at creating games. Our favorite was called "Broom." One person ___used to___ take the large push broom from Dyan's garage and had to chase the other people. When you were tagged with the broom, you were "it." Maggie didn't have to think of any games—she had a trampoline in her yard. Margaret

_____ jump on the trampoline the best, but Maggie _____ do a flip off of the trampoline, which was incredible. We _____ jump on the trampoline for hours, and there was always an argument about whose turn it was to jump. Laura _____ always manage to convince us it was her turn—maybe that's because she was the oldest. I _can_ still remember those days as if they were yesterday. I am lucky to have had such great childhood friends.

13e VERB FORMS: COMPREHENSIVE CHECK

Diagnostic Retest

Complete Activity 13.1 again. If you still miss or have difficulty with any items, review the relevant sections of the workbook.

Recognizing the Meaning of Modals and Periphrastic Modals

Read the following passage about two friends of author Isak Dinesen, who lived in Africa. Find and underline the eleven modals and periphrastic modals. Then try to determine the function or meaning of the modal, and write this meaning above the underlined word. Possible meanings of modals: ability, permission, polite questions, polite statements, advisability, prohibition, expectation, preference, possibility, probability, certainty, condition or state in the past, repeated action in the past.

As far as Berkeley Cole and Denys Finch-Hatton were concerned, my house was a communist establishment. Everything in it was theirs, and they took a pride in it and brought home the things they thought ought to be provided. They kept the house up to a high standard in wine and tobacco and got books and phonograph records out from Europe for me.

Berkeley was an early settler, intimate with the Masai, who in those days were the domineering nation of the land. He had known them before the European civilization cut through their roots, before they were moved from their fair north country. He could speak with them of the old days in their own tongue. Whenever Berkeley was staying on the farm, the Masai used to come over the river to see him. The old chiefs sat and discussed their troubles of the present time with him, and his jokes would make them laugh.

If Berkeley were a cavalier of the Stuarts' day, Denys should be set in an earlier English landscape, in the days of Queen Elizabeth. He could have walked arm in arm, there, with Sir Philip, or Francis Drake. And the people of Elizabeth's time might have held him dear because to them he would have suggested that Antiquity, the Athens of which they dreamed and wrote. Denys could indeed have been placed harmoniously in any period of our civilization, all up till the opening of the nineteenth century. His friends in England always wanted him to come back, but Africa was keeping him.

The particular, instinctive attachment that all natives of Africa felt toward Berkeley and Denys made me reflect that perhaps the white people of the past would have been better in understanding and sympathy with the colored races than we, of our industrial age, will ever be. When the first steam engine was constructed, the roads of the races of the world parted, and we have never found one another since. [Adapted from Judith Thurman, *Isak Dinesen's Africa.*]

ACTIVITY

13.16   **Editing Sentences for Modals**

Read each of the following sentences, and determine the error in form or meaning of the modal. Then write the corrected sentence below it.

1. I should have went to the store for Mom.

   _____

2. I would be a farmer when I lived in Minnesota in 1976.

   I should have been a farmer when I lived in M. in 1976

3. Anastasia might want to see a doctor for the headaches and weight loss she has experienced.

   m
   _____

4. I could like some french fries with my hamburger.

   Would

5. You can makes the trip from San Francisco to Sausalito by ferry in about thirty minutes.

   make

FINDING AND REVISING ERRORS WITH VERB TENSE AND VOICE

Verbs take different forms to indicate when the action or state of being of the verb is taking place. We call this quality of verbs their **tense.** English verbs have three simple tenses (present, past, and future) and three perfect tenses (present perfect, past perfect, and future perfect). In addition, there are progressive forms of each tense and active and passive voice forms. This chapter explains the meaning of each of the tenses and voices and how they are used.

14a DIAGNOSTIC ACTIVITY: VERB TENSE AND VOICE

ACTIVITY 14.1 **How Much Do You Know?**

Read the following passage about adoption. Fill in each blank with the appropriate tense or voice of the verb in parentheses.

How Adoption Works Today

It _____ (work) like this: A woman _____ (agree), for a fee, to bear a child for a couple who _____ (want) to adopt. She and the couple _____ (sign) a contract to this effect. In the past ten years or so, there _____ (be) somewhere between 1,200 and 2,000 such adoptions in the United States.

In theory, surrogate parenting _____ (be) a good way for both parties to _____ (get) what they need. The deal doesn't always _____ (go) smoothly, however. In one famous instance, it _____ (result) in a court case that _____ (catch) the attention of the entire country.

A young woman named Mary Beth Whitehead _____ (agree) to bear a child for a New Jersey couple, Bill and Betsy Stern. Whitehead _____ (sign) a contract for $10,000. But when the baby _____ (arrive), the new mother _____ (realize) she could not give it up. When authorities _____ (come) to pick up the baby to deliver it to the Sterns, she _____ (hand) the baby through a window to her husband and then _____ (drive) with him out of the state.

The court case that followed _____ (give) tremendous media attention. It _____ (know) as the "Baby M" case. Newspapers and television commentators _____ (debate) the questions endlessly. Should Whitehead be forced to give the baby to the Sterns in accordance with the contract she had signed? Or _____ (do) the natural rights of motherhood take precedence over a legal arrangement? The judge _____ (award) custody of the child to the Sterns. But not long afterward, surrogate parenting _____ (declare) illegal in New Jersey, and another judge _____ (decide) that Whitehead, as the birth mother, had the right to be with her daughter at least some of the time. The child now _____ (spend) a couple of nights a week with her birth mother, as well as alternate holidays.

Determine which items you missed in this passage. If you missed or had trouble with any of the items, please go to the appropriate section in *The Harper-Collins Concise Handbook for Writers* and this workbook for further practice and study.

It is important to know which items cause you difficulty. When revising your writing, you might want to go through your paper one time checking only for verb tense and voice. Concentrate on items that you had difficulty with in this activity.

14b THE ENGLISH TENSE SYSTEM

The English tense system is used to describe three different time frames: past, present, and future. The tenses indicate the time when an activity or state occurs. The progressive form indicates that the activity or state is in progress. (Note that the simple present tense can be used to discuss future time.)

TENSE IN ENGLISH

Tense	Example
Present time	
Simple present tense:	I *brush* my teeth every day.
Simple future tense:	Oil *will float* on water.
Present progressive tense:	I *am reading* a good book.
Past time	
Simple past tense:	I *ate* dinner at five.
Past progressive tense:	I *was eating* dinner at five.
Present perfect tense:	I *have been* to New York.
Present perfect progressive tense:	I *have been running* for two hours.
Past perfect tense:	I *had been* to New York.
Past perfect progressive tense:	I *had been living* in California until the earthquake.
Future time	
Simple future tense:	I *will go* to the dentist.
Future progressive tense:	They *will be arriving* at six.
Simple present tense:	I *have* a date next week.
Present progressive tense:	They *are coming* for dinner later.
Future perfect tense:	I *will have finished* by noon.
Future perfect progressive tense:	I *will have been working* exactly ten years next July.

This chapter will discuss the tense system from the viewpoint of the present, past, and future times. At the end of each section, we will briefly discuss modals that can be used to express the same time frame. (See 13d for discussion of modals and 7a for discussion of shifts in tense.)

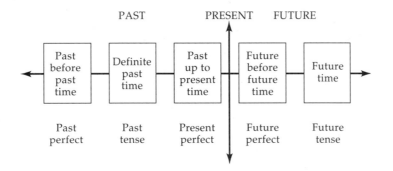

14c PRESENT TIME

The verb forms used to express present time are the simple present and present progressive.

Simple Present

The **simple present** tense is usually used to describe actions that are taking place at the time of speaking or writing, but it has many other uses as well.

ACTIVITY

14.2   **Identifying the Uses of the Simple Present Tense**

In the following statements, match the purpose to the corresponding sentence in the simple present tense by writing the letter in the blank.

a. to discuss literary or artistic works or the actions of the characters in them
b. to make statements about events scheduled to happen in the future
c. in research that quotes or paraphrases what other people have said or written in the past
d. to express a current condition
e. in narration of past event
f. to state general truths
g. to describe events as they are unfolding, as with sporting events
h. to describe habitual actions

_____ 1. I live in Santa Fe.

_____ 2. I go to class every day at 8:30.

_____ 3. The earth revolves around the sun.

_____ 4. Hester Prynne reminds us that strong women are often condemned by their communities.

_____ 5. Elway passes to Johnson. He catches the ball and runs twenty yards.

_____ 6. Classes begin on September 6.

_____ 7. In the book *Out of Africa,* Isak Dinesen talks about her life in Kenya in the early twentieth century.

_____ 8. Yesterday was terrible. First, I go to the bank and find I'm overdrawn. . . .

MODALS USED WITH PRESENT TIME TO EXPRESS GENERAL TRUTHS

Oil *will* float on water.

Carla *can* sing beautifully.

Present Progressive

The **present progressive** expresses ongoing action.

I *am typing* on my computer.

Lynn *is studying* advertising at Michigan State University.

Am typing and *is studying* express action that is occurring right now. The verb consists of a present-tense form of the verb *be* followed by the present participle of the main verb.

INCORRECT: She *is believing* that the test will be difficult.

INCORRECT: Even though she *is understanding* accounting quite well, she *is thinking* she might fail the test.

A small group of verbs, called **stative verbs,** are not normally used in the progressive form; they are listed in the accompanying box. These verbs express either a state of being or a mental activity rather than an action.

Some of these words, however, can express an action, depending on the context of the situation.

INCORRECT: She *is smelling* badly now.

CORRECT: The cook *is smelling* the soup.

In the first sentence, the verb *smell* is a state of being; therefore, it cannot be used in the progressive. In the second example, however, *smell* is an action.

STATIVE VERBS

Senses			
appear	hear	see	taste
feel	look (appear)	smell	

Mental states			
believe	know	remember	understand
doubt	mean	suppose	wonder
imagine	recognize	think	

Emotions			
appreciate	dislike	like	need
desire	hate	love	prefer
			want

(continued)

STATIVE VERBS *(continued)*			
Ownership, possession, or relationship			
belong	contain	have	own
Measuring			
cost	equal	measure	weigh
Conditions			
appear	be	resemble	seem

14.3 Using the Simple Present and the Present Progressive

Complete the following sentence pairs using the verb given in parentheses. Be sure to use the correct present form: simple present or present progressive.

1. (take)   Betty _____ a picture of the Lincoln Memorial.

    Rhonda _____ the train to work every day.

2. (have)   Edith _____ trouble convincing Gloria to go shopping with her.

    Georgia _____ a collection of rare Micronesian stamps.

3. (look)   Jacob is at the library. He _____ at the new copy of *Wicker Today*.

    Did you ever notice that Bob _____ almost exactly like John Wayne?

4. (speak)   Milton _____ with a strong New York accent.

    Violetta can't come to the phone right now; she _____ with some clients.

5. (read)   Though he can't write it, Kevin _____ Chinese very well.

    I _____ a novel by Emile Zola this semester.

6. (see)   Ji-Fen _____ her grandmother tomorrow for the first time in ten years.

    An eagle _____ its prey from an incredible distance.

14.4 More Simple Present and Present Progressive

Fill in the blanks in the following passage using the verbs provided at the beginning of the activity. Be sure to use either the present progressive or the simple present, as appropriate to the context.

be	give	prepare	have	end
rise	demand	face	hold	elect

The UN Security Council is the United Nations organ to which the charter _____ primary responsibility for maintaining peace and security. The council _____ fifteen members. Five of the members _____ permanent: China, France, Russia, the United Kingdom, and the United States. The General Assembly _____ the other ten members.

Currently, the members of this council _____ a large number of grave obstacles. In the Middle East, countries _____ for war, and peace talks _____ prematurely. In Eastern Europe, ethnic tensions _____ daily. These problems, along with enduring troubles in other regions of the world, _____ the undivided attention of the Security Council, which _____ session an average of seventy-five hours per week this year.

14d PAST TIME

The verb forms used to indicate past time are the simple past, the present perfect, the past progressive, the present perfect progressive, the past perfect, and the past perfect progressive.

Simple Past and Present Perfect

The **simple past** tense is used to indicate an action or state that occurred in the past, in three different ways:

1. To express an action that occurred habitually or repeatedly but not continually:

   Susanna *walked* to work when she first *moved* to Cleveland.

2. To express a state of affairs that existed conditionally in the past:

   Mr. Ochoa *liked* to work in his garden.

3. To express a single event that happened at a particular time in the past:

   My car *blew up* on the way home last night.

The **present perfect** also expresses three different kinds of actions or states but implies that the action or state continues up to (and perhaps beyond) the present. The present perfect is used in the following situations:

1. To express a habitual action that started in the past and continues to the present:

   My committee *has met* every Thursday evening this semester.

2. To express a state of affairs that existed continually in the past and continues to the present:

   Chinua *has lived* in America for three years.

3. To express a single event that may still occur again:

   My math professor *has given* only one quiz so far.

Choosing between the Simple Past and the Present Perfect

INCORRECT: Stefan *has visited* the company in Philadelphia last week.

CORRECT: Stefan *visited* the company in Philadelphia last week.

The first sentence is incorrect because the event does not continue up to the present—it ended last week—so the present perfect is inappropriate. This is one of the two situations where the simple past CANNOT be substituted for the present perfect.

CORRECT: I *have lived* in Michigan since 1991.

CORRECT: I *have lived* in Michigan for two years.

When the present perfect is used with *since* or *for*, it expresses an action, emotion, or event that started in the past and continues into the present. Notice the difference between *since* and *for* in these sentences. *Since* is used with a specific time, whereas *for* is used with an expression for a span of time—in this case, *two years*.

INCORRECT: I *lived* in Michigan since 1991.

CORRECT: I *have lived* in Michigan since 1991.

The simple past can never be used with *since,* as this word implies that the action or event started in the past and continues up to the present.

CORRECT: I *lived* in Michigan for two years.

The simple past tense can be used with *for,* but doing so changes the meaning. This sentence means that the writer lived in Michigan for two years at some period in the past but is no longer living there today.

ACCEPTABLE: I *already mailed* the letter.

BETTER: I *have already mailed* the letter.

With the words *just, already,* and *recently,* the present perfect tense expresses an action that occurred in the past and finished recently—close to the moment of speaking. You can also use the simple past without a change in meaning, but the present perfect is slightly clearer.

Divorce rates *have increased* dramatically.

Divorce rates *increased* dramatically in 1968.

The present perfect tense is also used to express an action that happened at an *indefinite* time in the past. When the tense is the simple past, as in the second sentence, the reader would expect to be told when the event happened.

I *haven't done* my homework *yet.*

I *didn't do* my homework *yet.*

Use *yet* and *still* negative sentences with the present perfect tense when you want to emphasize that an action has not yet happened up to the present moment, but you expect the action to occur at some time in the future. If you use the simple past tense, the sentence does not imply as strongly that you *do* expect to complete the action in the future.

Eduardo *has always been* good at fixing cars.

Eduardo *was always* good at fixing cars.

Use the present perfect tense of the verb *be* with adverbs, such as *always, often,* and *sometimes.* If you use the simple past tense, you imply that the meaning expressed by the verb is no longer true—Eduardo may have once been good at fixing cars, but he is no longer.

The Batistas *haven't been skiing* this year.

The Batistas *didn't ski* this year.

Use the present perfect tense with time expressions using *this* (*this morning, this year*) when the time frame is still possible. In the first example, the writer is saying that it is still possible to go skiing this year. Using the simple past tense, as in the second sentence, communicates that skiing is no longer possible, perhaps because it is now summer.

ACTIVITY
14.5 **Choosing between the Simple Past and the Present Perfect**

Use the verbs on the list to complete the following sentences. Be sure to make the right choice between the simple past and the present perfect.

> increase   vote   take   see   work   be   study   live

1. Before moving to London, Bernie _____ in Birmingham, Alabama, for two years.

2. Brenda _____ in a presidential election yet because she is only seventeen.

3. Raymond _____ at that company since 1966.

4. Phil graduates from Eastern Kentucky University this spring. He _____ there for four years.

5. During his job at the Mexican restaurant, Joe _____ excellent at making fajitas, but now he's forgotten how.

6. Larry _____ a ball game this year, but he's still got time—it's only July, and the season ends in October.

7. Prices _____ a lot lately, especially for food.

8. For lack of time, the Denbrabers _____ a vacation this year. Now they can't because the kids are back in school.

Past Progressive

The **past progressive** tense expresses an action or activity that was in progress at a specific point in time in the past. You could use the simple past, but it would not give the same emphasis on the duration of the activity.

Rajani *was reading* yesterday about the latest events in Sri Lanka.

Often the past progressive is used for an event that was in progress when another event happened:

Ms. Acosta *was washing* her car this morning when the real estate agent arrived.

In these kinds of sentences you cannot use simple past; only the past progressive will suffice.

Present Perfect Progressive

The **present perfect progressive** tense is used for an activity that began in the past and continues up to the present.

It *has been snowing* since yesterday.

The snowing started at some time in the past and continues up to the time when these words were spoken or written. The present perfect progressive tense is often used with words expressing a period of time such as *for* so many *minutes, hours,* or *days; since* some time in the past; or *all morning, all day,* or *all week.*

Andrea's boss *has been giving* her too much work.

This sentence has no specific mention of time; when that is the case, the sentence expresses a general activity in progress up to the present and still continuing.

Tom *has been working* at Leigh's for seven years.

Tom *has worked* at Leigh's for seven years.

With certain verbs, including *live, work,* and *teach,* there is no difference between the present perfect and the present perfect progressive when *since* or *for* is used.

Past Perfect

The **past perfect** tense describes an action or activity that has been completed in the past prior to some event that also occurred in the past.

The movie *had started* when we arrived.

Two events are being discussed in this sentence: the movie's starting and our arriving. Both events happened in the past, but the movie's starting happened first. Notice that the past perfect form consists of *had* plus the past participle *started.*

Wayne *had shaved off* his beard before he went to Chicago.

Wayne *shaved off* his beard before he went to Chicago.

Either the simple past or the past perfect is correct in sentences with *before.*

Past Perfect Progressive

The **past perfect progressive** indicates an action or activity that took place for a period of time in the past prior to some action or activity also in the past.

I *had been living* in California before I got a job in Michigan.

In this example, the simple past could be substituted. As with the past progressive, however, you must use past perfect progressive when referring to an action or activity that was in progress for a period of time in the past when another event happened:

I *had been gardening* for three hours when I noticed it was getting dark.

MODALS THAT EXPRESS PAST TIME

My dog *could climb* through the fence when he was a puppy.

Use *could* + verb to indicate something that the subject could do in the past.

Mary *would jump* off the fence when the children gave her money.

Would + verb represents an action or event that happened habitually or regularly.

Rafael *would have gone* to the store, but his car was stolen.

Would have + past participle represents an action or event that was not completed in the past because of some condition.

The Acostas *must have gone* on vacation because their house is totally dark.

Must have + past participle can be used to express guesses or assumptions about the past.

ACTIVITY

14.6 **Using Past Time Tenses**

Complete the following passages by writing each verb in parentheses in the past time tense appropriate to the context.

1. Before moving to Missouri in 1984, Marvin _____ (spend) more than one year living in each of the following places: China, Australia, Tanzania, Moldova, and the Falkland Islands. During that time, he _____ (work) for the United Nations Economic and Social Council (UNESCO). For instance, while he was in Moldova, he _____ (organize) a system of low-interest bank loans for new housing. Since 1984, however, he _____ (hold) jobs with various international famine relief organizations. For these organizations, he _____ (do) special projects in impoverished regions of the southern and central United States. Up until his current project in Arkansas, he _____ (direct) a retraining and adult education program in West Virginia.

2. Isabella _____ (travel) to Ukraine six times in the past three years. The first few times, she _____ (visit) just to see some family. But two years ago, those family members _____ (move) back to Spain. She must have been so intrigued by those first trips that she _____ (decide) to get to know Ukrainian culture better. At her university, she _____ (study) the language and culture of that land since last year, and she (plan) _____ another trip for next year.

ACTIVITY

14.7 **Using Present and Past Time Tenses**

All of the verbs have been left out of the following paragraphs. Fill in the blanks using the verbs in parentheses, paying special attention to the proper use of the present and past tenses.

   The United Nations _____ (establish) the Trusteeship Council in 1946 with the goal of achieving independence for non-self-governing territories or colonies. Originally, it _____ (be) responsible for the eleven trust territories voluntarily placed under its supervision by the seven member states who _____ (own) them before World War II.

   This organ _____ (be) the only one in the UN whose work _____ (diminish) rather than _____ (expand) over the years. Of the original eleven, only one trust territory _____ (remain)—the Pacific islands of Micronesia. The others, mostly in Africa, _____ (attain) independence, either as separate states or by joining neighboring countries.

In addition to efforts on behalf of trust territories, the United Nations _____ (be) instrumental in promoting self-determination or decolonization throughout the world—in Africa, the Caribbean, Southeast Asia, and the South Pacific. Since 1945, more than eighty colonial territories _____ (achieve) independence or self-government, and the number of people living in dependent territories _____ (go) down from about 750 million to under 3 million. What's more, that number _____ (decrease) every year for the past ten years. It _____ (diminish) this year as well.

ACTIVITY

14.8 Writing Situation

Write a few paragraphs describing the best vacation you've taken in your life. Be as descriptive and as creative as possible, and try to experiment using the different tenses of present and past time. When you are finished, edit your paper for the use of tenses.

14e FUTURE TIME

The verb forms that can be used to represent future time are the simple future, the simple present, the present progressive, the future perfect, the future progressive, and the future perfect progressive. Although all the modal auxiliaries can be used to express actions or events occurring in the future, the most common modals used with future time are *will* and *be going to*.

Simple Future

The **simple future** tense represents an action that takes place at some definite time in the future:

Kelly *will be* back home on Sunday.

The simple future can also be used to express an action that will happen habitually or regularly:

I *am going to ride* my bike to work from my new house every day.

The simple present tense can be used to indicate future events that are considered certain to happen, or events that are planned or scheduled. Verbs often used in this way include *arrive, be, begin, close, end, leave, open,* and *start:*

The plane *leaves* at 6:45.

Verbs in the simple present tense are also used in a subordinate clause to express actions or events that will happen in the future:

When Ms. Esenbel graduates, she *will move* to Turkey.

The present progressive can be used to represent scheduled or planned events in the future. Usually these sentences have some type of time marker such as *next week:*

My parents *are coming* next week.

Future Progressive

The **future progressive** is used to express an action that will be in progress at a specific time in the near future:

I *will be eating* a delicious meal at this time tomorrow.

The future progressive can also be used to indicate the duration of some specific future action:

Don *will be working* on his doctorate for the next three years.

You can use the simple future here, but it does not stress the duration of the event as well as the future progressive.

Future Perfect

The **future perfect** tense expresses an action that will be completed prior to a specific time in the future:

I *will have finished* my research paper by tomorrow.

In this sentence, the paper will be finished before tomorrow.

The future perfect can also represent a state or an action that will be completed in the future prior to some other future time or event:

Rob *will have run* ten kilometers before Laura gets out of bed.

Rob's running will be completed before Laura gets out of bed.

Future Perfect Progressive

The **future perfect progressive** indicates a habitual or regular action taking place in the future that will continue up to or through a specific future time:

Jim *will have been training* for six months by the time the race begins next May in Boston.

Jim's training will be taking place in the future and will continue up to (and perhaps through) the race next May.

Note that when the independent clause is in the future tense, it is not correct to use the future tense for dependent clauses:

remains

She will do well on the test if she ~~will remain~~ calm.

ACTIVITY

14.9 Using Future Tenses

Choose the best possible form of the future tense to complete the following sentences.

1. When the restaurant _____ (close) tonight, all the workers _____ (go) to the neighboring restaurant for a late dinner.

2. By the end of next year, Anton _____ (give) his professor all the work necessary for the Ph.D.

3. For the next ten years, Larry _____ (pay off) his student loans.

4. Mr. Sears _____ (teach) math for forty years by the time he retires next June.

5. My niece _____ (come) to Kansas next September.

6. Class _____ (begin) tomorrow morning at 9:00 and _____ (end) at 11:30.

7. John _____ (eat) less fat on his new diet that he starts today.

8. When you _____ (take) the Chicago-Detroit train next Wednesday, be patient. It may be running late.

14.10 Editing Sentences for Tense

Edit the following sentences for the correct use of all tenses. Not all sentences require revision.

1. André worked at the department store since 1985.

2. Naoki is needing to buy books for the fall semester.

3. The car engine will cool down if the radiator will work.

4. Park has been skiing in Colorado every winter before he broke his leg.

5. Alessandro will have been studying ten hours by daybreak.

6. Water could turn to ice at the freezing point.

7. Kari has been to Paris last year.

14.11 Using Tenses Correctly

Complete the passage by writing the correct tense of each verb in parentheses.

The United Nations General Assembly _____ (be) formed as the main deliberative organ of the UN. Each member state _____ (have) a single vote. During the assembly's first regular session in 1945, held from mid-September to mid-December, its main committees _____ (discuss) and _____ (make) recommendations on virtually every issue that _____ (affect) life on this planet. By 1960, the assembly _____ (pass) major laws, and its role in the world _____ (continue) to grow for almost fifty years since its conception. Today, it _____ (become) perhaps the single most important legislative body in the world. Between now and the year 2000, the assembly _____ (double) the number of major decisions it _____ (make) since 1945. The world situation today _____ (continue) to command more measures of control and security than it _____ (need) even twenty years ago. The world's capacity for change _____ (grow) at an accelerated pace. Let us hope that the General Assembly's capacity to keep a controlling hand over the world's chaos _____ (adapt) to this change in the years to come.

14f ACTIVE AND PASSIVE VOICE

Verbs that take objects (transitive verbs) can appear in two voices in English: active and passive.

 Active: Eve *ate* the apple.

 Passive: The apple *was eaten by* Eve.

In an active-voice sentence, the subject performs the action of the verb, and that action is received by another noun or pronoun, the direct object. In a passive-voice sentence, the subject receives rather than performs the action of the verb. The performer of the action, sometimes referred to as the agent, is identified in a prepositional phrase starting with *by.*

 When using the passive voice, it is even possible to omit the performer of the action altogether:

 The apple was eaten.

FORMS OF THE PASSIVE

The passive voice is formed from the active voice by making the direct object into the subject, using the past participle of the verb, and adding the appropriate form of the verb *be* as a helping verb.

Simple present:	The petition *is supported* by the students.
Simple past:	The petition *was supported* by the students.
Simple future:	The petition *will be supported* by the students.
Present progressive:	The petition *is being supported* by the students.
Past progressive:	The petition *was being supported* by the students.
Future progressive:	The petition *is going to be supported* by the students.
Present perfect:	The petition *has been supported* by the students.
Past perfect:	The petition *had been supported* by the students.
Future perfect:	The petition *will have been supported* by the students.

In general, your writing will be stronger and more readable if you write most sentences in the active voice. However, **the passive is useful in the following situations:**

1. When the agent is obvious, unknown, or unimportant:

 Oranges are grown in California.

 The house was built in 1934.

2. When the writer wants to avoid mentioning the agent:

 I was given bad advice about my car.

 Two computers were stolen over the weekend.

3. When the agent is an inanimate object:

The engine is powered by steam.

4. When the writer wants to emphasize the receiver or result of the action:

Four people were killed by the hurricane.

5. When the writer wishes to retain the same grammatical subject in successive clauses, even though the function of the noun phrase changes from agent to theme:

Sydney was in a terrible accident. She was hit by a drunk driver.

 Use of the Passive Voice

Decide if the following statements are true or false by writing "T" or "F" in the blank.

___F___ 1. The passive voice is used more in speaking than in writing.

___F___ 2. The passive voice is found more often in scientific writing than in fiction.

_____ 3. There are more passive sentences without agents than those with agents.

___F___ 4. Some verbs can only be used in the passive voice.

___T___ 5. Some verbs can only be used in the active voice.

 Editing Sentences for Use of the Passive Voice

Read each of the following sentences and determine if there is an error in voice. If there is, mark an X in the blank and rewrite the corrected sentence below the original. If the sentence is correct, write a C in the blank.

___X___ 1. By the time Jan arrived, all of the food had been ate. *eaten*

_____ 2. Having stolen the money, the thief ran away.

___X___ 3. Wrote in 1847, the opera has never had success.

___X___ 4. Betty began to cry when she realized her dress was torn.

___X___ 5. The railroad station *was* built during the eighteenth century.

___X___ 6. Champagne is used for celebrating on New Year's Eve.

_____ 7. The "b" in thumb is not pronounced.

✗ 8. The United Nations was found^ed in 1945.

_____ 9. Extra food will be distributed to the victims.

✗ 10. The schoolchildren were ~~took~~ taken to the zoo yesterday.

ACTIVITY

14.14 **Further Practice with Forming the Passive**

Rewrite the following paragraph by converting each active construction into the passive. You may have to change some other words or add transitional expressions. You may also omit the agent when it is not necessary.

> In the early 1980s, the Ford Motor Company was in trouble. People were saying that the Ford name stood for "Fix or Repair Daily." The company recognized the need for dramatic changes, which were incorporated in the project "Team Taurus." Rather than have each unit do the various tasks sequentially, Ford established a team consisting of planners, designers, engineers, manufacturing people, and even suppliers. It also involved assembly-line workers in development: management asked them to describe difficulties they had in assembling the parts and to make recommendations for improvements.
>
> Instead of adopting a know-it-all attitude, Ford employees carefully studied cars by other manufacturers and examined their best features. For example, Ford noted the accuracy of the Toyota fuel gauge and the good tire storage of the BMW. Ford also tested various seats on male and female drivers of all ages. Through extensive market studies, Ford learned about other customer preferences.
>
> The chairman, Donald Petersen, credits Ford's turnaround to his team. But he is the one who took the biggest risk in developing the new line of cars. He delegated authority down the organizational hierarchy to the ranks of the workers. Petersen practiced "management by wandering around." In other words, he visited and listened to the workers. This style of management put Ford back in the running. [Adapted from Harold Koontz and Heinz Weihrich, *Essentials of Management*]

ACTIVITY

14.15 **Using Tense and Voice**

In each blank in the following passage about Native American music, fill in the correct form of the verb in parentheses.

The Native American population, which _____ had declined _____ (decline) to half a million or less by the end of the nineteenth century, _begon_ (begin) again to grow at a rapid rate and now numbers well over a million. Automobiles, radio, and television _ended_ (end) the isolation of reservation life, and a large-scale movement of Indian people toward urban centers since the end of World War II _intensified_ (intensify) cultural contact not only between Indians and whites but also between Indian peoples of different tribal nations. It is important to recognize, then, that the indigenous and inherited culture of over one million Native Americans _isn't been_ (be, negative) dead. It is true that there _was_ (be) an irreversible loss of much of the older music. And the exploitation of Indian music—at fairs, rodeos, and other tourist attractions and for Hollywood films—_gave_ (give) currency to a certain standardized and stereotyped product. But music _has been_ (be) part of a strong general movement of cultural revival since the 1950s. The pan-tribal *pow-wows* _held_ (hold) annually on the large Plains reservations are primarily great social events today, but they also _include_ (include) the performance of songs and dances that maintain distinct tribal identity and characteristics.

The movement of Native Americans off the reservations and into the cities _given_ (give) extra impetus in the 1950s by a Bureau of Indian Affairs program aimed at terminating the special status of the Indians and the reservations themselves. This program has since been abandoned, but not all the Indians who _have been relocated_ (relocate) returned to the reservations, and there _ex?_ (exist) sizable communities of Native Americans in virtually every small city in the West and in and around large urban areas. These urban Indian communities also regularly _enjoyed_ (enjoy) large social gatherings, at which Indian songs and dances _had been performed_ (perform). Thus there _has been_ (be) a preservation of the music that comes from the tribes of yesterday. [Adapted from Daniel Kingman, *American Music*]

14g VERB TENSE AND VOICE: COMPREHENSIVE CHECK

ACTIVITY
14.16 Diagnostic Retest

Complete Activity 14.1 again. If you still miss or have difficulty with any items, review the relevant sections of the workbook.

FINDING AND REVISING ERRORS WITH CONDITIONALS, HYPOTHETICALS, AND THE SUBJUNCTIVE

Conditional and **hypothetical** sentences are similar in that they are introduced by an *if* clause. Each of the following sentences represents a relationship between two ideas. Each asserts that if one thing happens, another will also.

> If a tree is cut down, carbon dioxide is released.

This statement is *conditional;* if the first thing happens, the second thing is *certain* to happen. Conditional statements reflect possible situations and are sometimes referred to as *real conditionals.*

> If people had lots of money, they would never work.

This *hypothetical* statement is often called an *unreal conditional* because the situation is very unlikely or impossible.

The **subjunctive** is one of the three moods in English (the others are the *indicative* and the *imperative*). Subjunctive forms express nonfacts—actions or states that cannot or may not occur or exist. The subjunctive also appears in clauses following statements of command and request:

> My friend acts as if he were a millionaire.

> I insist that Tom wipe the counters.

15a DIAGNOSTIC ACTIVITY: CONDITIONALS, HYPOTHETICALS, AND THE SUBJUNCTIVE

ACTIVITY

15.1 **How Much Do You Know?**

Read each sentence to determine if there is an error in conditional, hypothetical, or subjunctive form. If there is such an error, correct it. Not all sentences contain errors.

> *Example:* I recommend that Lawrence calls the loan officer at the bank.

1. If it was raining, I wouldn't have been able to walk to school today.

2. Jim wishes that he has a bigger apartment.

3. Whenever I ride in an airplane, I will get an earache.

4. If participation had been greater this year, money might be raised for a new stadium.

5. It is vital that students be informed of the new registration process.

189

6. If he had been there earlier, the director would have saw him.

7. Unless I finish my research paper by Tuesday, I will be able to go to the concert.

8. If the police officer had asked me, I would have told her my speedometer wasn't working.

9. If I were you, I would call the telephone company and ask for a refund.

10. More people would have come to the party if the invitations were sent out earlier.

11. If you had lost your credit card, what would you do?

12. Bob acts as if he was the director of the center.

13. If I hadn't dropped off that package by ten o'clock today, it won't have arrived until Wednesday.

14. The law requires that students be in school a certain number of hours each day.

15. Provided that all children are immunized, the virus spreads.

Determine which items you missed in this Diagnostic Activity. If you missed or had trouble with any of the items, please go to the appropriate section in *The HarperCollins Concise Handbook for Writers* and this workbook for further practice and study.

It is important to know which items cause you difficulty. When revising your writing, you might want to go through your paper one time checking only for use of the conditional, hypothetical, and subjunctive forms. Concentrate on items that you had difficulty with in this activity.

15b CONDITIONALS

Conditional sentences are formed by combining a conditional clause with a main independent clause (the result clause). The verb form in each of these clauses will change, depending on the meaning of the sentence.

VERB FORMS WITH CONDITIONAL STATEMENTS			
Meaning	Verb Form in *if* Clause	Verb Form in Result Clause	Example
General truth (present time frame)	Simple present	Simple future	If you heat water to 212 degrees Fahrenheit, it will boil.
Habit (present or past time frame)	Simple present or past	Simple present or past	If I eat dinner early, I sleep well. If we came to class late, we needed a note from our parents.
Prediction (future time frame)	Simple present	*will, be going to, should, may, might, can, ought to* + base form of verb	If the population increases, there might not be enough food to feed everyone.

The following examples illustrate conditional sentences with subordinators other than *if*. The subordinator is italicized.

When you heat water to 212 degrees Fahrenheit, it will boil.

Whenever I eat dinner early, I sleep better.

Statements about general truths or habits can be introduced by *when* or *whenever*. The grammar of the sentence remains the same, and these words simply replace the word *if*.

Unless water is heated to 212 degrees Fahrenheit, it will not boil.

Unless I pass the test, I will have to take the course again.

The subordinator *unless* means "if not" and can be used with general truth, habit, or prediction statements.

There might not be enough food to feed the people *in the event that* the population increases.

The subordinator *in the event that* is in a category with *in case, given that, on condition (that), provided (that)*, and *supposing (that)*. These subordinators can be used with general truth, habit, or prediction statements. Usually, the result clause precedes the conditional clause.

ACTIVITY
15.2 **Using Conditionals**

In the following sentences, make the conditional forms suggested using the verb in parentheses.

1. *Prediction:* Unless it _____ (rain) this week, the corn crop _____ (be) good this year.

2. *Habit, present time:* Whenever Jonas _____ (see) Ginger, his face _____ (turn) bright red.

3. *General truth, present time:* If a policeman _____ (catch) you driving too fast, he _____ (give) you a speeding ticket.

4. *Prediction:* We _____ (hire) five new English teachers this year, provided that we _____ (receive) the funding.

5. *Habit, past time:* If I _____ (arrive) late for that job, the boss _____ (become) a monster.

ACTIVITY
15.3 **Editing Sentences for Correct Usage of Conditionals**

Correct the verbs in the following sentences so that they make sense in the context. Not all sentences contain errors.

1. When Nathan quits the soccer team, Woody takes his place.

2. Unless I write to my mother very often, she is very happy.

3. On the condition that Danny will promise not to have an accident, Shirley lets him borrow her van.

4. When something goes wrong at the office, nobody blames the boss.

5. If cars are going to be parked in the wrong places, they will most likely be given tickets by the university police.

15c HYPOTHETICALS

VERB FORMS WITH HYPOTHETICALS

Meaning	Verb Form in *if* Clause	Verb Form in Result Clause	Example
Speculation (what might be in the present or future)	Past tense; *were (to); should*	*would, should, might, ought to could* + simple form	If more people voted, election results would change. Were more people to vote, election results would change. Should more people vote, election results would change.
Hindsight (what might have been in the past and would have affected the present)	*had* + participle	*would, could, might, should, ought to* + simple form of verb	If I had not stayed out late last night, I would not be tired now. Had I not stayed out late last night, I would not be tired now.
(what might have been in the past and would have affected the past)	*had* + participle	*would have, could have, might have, should have, ought to have*	If Sabine had found a horse, she could have entered the competition. Had the president run a stronger campaign, he might have been reelected.

The following sentences illustrate a type of hypothetical statement using the word *wish*.

Speculation: I *wish* I knew more about computers so that I could get a job. (present or future time)

Hindsight: I *wish* I had known more about computers, so that I could have gotten the job I applied for last week. (past time influencing the past)

Hindsight: I *wish* I had learned more about computers in college so that I could find a job. (past time influencing the present)

Wish statements (*wish* + noun clause) are used when the speaker wants reality to be different or exactly the opposite of what it is. The verb forms in *wish* statements are similar to those in hypothetical statements. One difference is that only the modals *could* and *would* can follow wish statements.

COULD: I *wish* I could fly.

      Could gives the meaning of hypothetical ability or possibility.

WOULD: I *wish* my boyfriend would buy me some jewelry.

      Would implies hypothetical promises or certainties.

ACTIVITY 15.4   **Writing Hypothetical Statements**

Complete the following statements.

> *Example:* If he had won the election, *I would have given up my position as chairperson.*

1. If people didn't learn foreign languages, _____

2. If all the males in the world suddenly became females, _____

3. If I find strange hair in my cafeteria food, _____

4. If my best friend were fifty pounds overweight, _____

5. If the sun rose in the west tomorrow morning, _____

6. I could have slept until eleven o'clock this morning if _____

7. If Gandhi had not been born, _____

8. We would all be rich if _____

9. I wish traveling were cheaper _____

10. I wish I had studied harder for the exam last week _____

ACTIVITY 15.5   **Writing Conditional and Hypothetical Statements**

Write two sentences using the information given, the first version in conditional future time and the second in hypothetical past time. An example is provided.

> *Example:* If she (come) to the office, I (give) her the package.
> *Conditional future time:* If she comes to the office, I will give her the package.
> *Hypothetical past time:* If she had come to the office, I would have given her the package.

1. If Greg and Peter (play) football in the house, someone (get hurt).

   _____

   _____

2. Amy (buy) a new truck if she (have) enough money at the end of the month.

   _____

   _____

3. John (go) to Michigan State University if he (finish) the statistics course at the community college.

_____

_____

4. If Deana (see) her cousin this weekend, she (ask) him for his new phone number.

_____

_____

5. If I (find) your watch, I (bring) it to work with me on Monday.

_____

_____

ACTIVITY

15.6 **Hypotheticals with Inverted Word Order**

Change each sentence to one in which *if* is not used, and write this sentence below the original.

> *Examples:* If you have any questions, ask your doctor.
> *Should you have any questions, ask your doctor.*
>
> If I were able to help him, I would.
> *Were I able to help him, I would.*
>
> If he had the time, he would build a new deck.
> *Had he the time, he would build a new deck.*

1. If Harry had enough money, he would buy a car.

2. If you want to borrow money, see the loan officer.

3. If I were a millionaire, I would travel more.

4. If I had studied harder, I would have passed the exam.

5. If it were winter, I would go skiing.

6. If the people arrive late, cancel their reservations.

7. If you had told me earlier, I could have helped you.

8. If the present arrives early, hide it in the closet.

9. If my dog were human, she would talk to me.

10. If I had a new computer, I could work faster.

15d SUBJUNCTIVE MOOD

The English language has three moods for verbs: indicative, imperative, and subjunctive. The indicative mood is used to state facts or opinions and to ask questions:

I generally wait thirty minutes after eating before I swim.

The imperative mood is used for commands and requests:

Close the door and turn out the lights when you leave.

Use of the Subjunctive

The subjunctive mood is used in two situations:

1. In clauses introduced by *as though* or *as if*
2. After verbs, nouns, or adjectives of command and request

Clauses with *as though* or *as if*

Michael acts **as though** he were unaware that any struggle is going on.

He acts as **if he** were oblivious to the problem.

Use the subjunctive verb *were* rather than the indicative *was* in any clause beginning with *as though* and *as if*.

After Verbs, Nouns, or Adjectives of Command and Request

Common decency **requires** that Michael not challenge the instructor's authority.

The **suggestion** that he take a calmer approach is a good one.

It was **mandatory** that he cooperate with the instructor.

Use the subjunctive mood in *that* clauses following verbs, nouns, or adjectives that express a demand, a request, a requirement, or a suggestion. The subjunctive verb in the complement is the base form of the verb. Note in the first example to use *not* before the verb in the subjunctive clause to make the sentence negative.

VERBS THAT REQUIRE SUBJUNCTIVE COMPLEMENTS

advise	insist	prefer	require
beg	move	propose	stipulate
command	order	recommend	suggest
demand	pledge	request	urge
determine	pray		

NOUNS THAT REQUIRE SUBJUNCTIVE COMPLEMENTS

advice	necessity	recommendation
command	suggestion	request
desire	order	requirement
importance	preference	
insistence	proposal	

ADJECTIVES THAT REQUIRE SUBJUNCTIVE COMPLEMENTS

advisable	important	recommended
better	mandatory	requested
desirable	necessary	suggested
essential	obligatory	urgent
imperative	preferable	vital

There are two grammatical differences between the indicative and subjunctive moods:

1. In the present tense subjunctive mood, verbs do *not* add an -*s* ending when the subject is singular:

   Each morning the instructor requests that Michael stops leaving class early.

2. In the present tense subjunctive mood, the verb *be* always takes the form *be* rather than *am, is,* or *are:*

   It is important that Michael ~~is~~ *be* on time for the next few weeks.

15.7 Using the Subjunctive

Decide whether the verbs in the following sentences should be in the subjunctive or the indicative; then write in the proper form of each verb.

1. It is mandatory that Rachel _____ (be) at work at eight o'clock.

2. If she isn't, the supervisor demands that she _____ (fill) out a form giving the reason that she _____ (be) late.

3. What's more, he asks that she _____ (do) twice as much work as the rest of us, as though she _____ (be) superhuman!

4. But Rachel never complains that her job _____ (be) too difficult.

5. She never says that she wishes Mr. Tapie _____ (be) more reasonable.

6. She just keeps on going, acting as if it _____ (be) completely normal that she continue working through her lunch hour.

7. What is even more amazing is that she _____ (claim) to like this job more than her last one.

8. I really can't believe that her old job _____ (be) harder!

9. Whatever the case, if I _____ (be) in her position, I would ask Mr. Tapie, nicely, to be a little less severe.

10. I would also kindly request that he _____ (find) someone else to pick on once in a while!

15.8 The Subjunctive

A. Put a C in the blank if the sentence is correct, or an X if there is an error in the verb that occurs in the noun clause after the subjunctive. Then write the corrected sentence below the original.

_____ 1. My professor insisted that we arrive on time for class.

_____ 2. The manager recommended that all employees took a seminar in accounting.

_____ 3. It is important that the taxi is on time.

_____ 4. It was essential that the train left punctually.

_____ 5. They request that you be dressed appropriately.

B. Complete the following sentences using the subjunctive.

6. A suggestion was made that _____

7. My mother asked that _____

8. The football players demanded that _____

9. It is essential that _____

10. I would prefer that _____

15e CONDITIONALS, HYPOTHETICALS, AND THE SUBJUNCTIVE: COMPREHENSIVE CHECK

ACTIVITY 15.9   Diagnostic Retest

Complete Activity 15.1 again. If you still miss or have difficulty with any items, review the relevant sections of the workbook.

ACTIVITY 15.10   Putting It All Together

Correct all the errors in conditional, hypothetical, and subjunctive forms in the following passage. Rewrite the passage, incorporating your corrections.

Many armchair historians are prone to speculation. They like to ask questions like "If Abraham Lincoln wasn't assassinated, what had happened after the Civil War?" or "If Kennedy isn't born, how is our world today?" At times, I wish I was more knowledgeable in the study of history, but I still find it amusing to hear people carry on about such questions as if there was some great conclusion to be reached. If one was to continue speculating on the results of a certain person or event having never existed, one will eventually come to the same conclusion that I reached.

We must not question history. We all wish that we can relive the countless possibilities of our past, but we cannot. Unless we accept the reality of our own personal and collective past, we will be able to concentrate on what is really important: our personal and collective future.

16 FINDING AND REVISING ERRORS WITH VERBALS

In English, it is possible to use verbs as nouns or adjectives in sentences by changing their form slightly. When verbs are used this way, they are no longer verbs; they are **verbals.** There are three types of verbals in English: infinitives, gerunds, and participles.

16a DIAGNOSTIC ACTIVITY: VERBALS

ACTIVITY
16.1 How Much Do You Know?

Identify the verbals (gerunds, infinitives, and participles) in the following passage by underlining them. Determine which are used incorrectly (not all of them are). Rewrite the corrected version of the paragraph.

> To find work in another country is never easy. Understanding what you are expected doing in a strange new workplace is even more difficult. This is precisely what Larry was made to discover after to arrive as a university instructor in Paris. One thing he liked, having a close relationship with his supervisors, was nearly nonexistent. He was surprising when they even let him see them. Of course, the positive side to this was that he was nearly always able doing what he wanted doing in the classroom without much interference. He appeared to enjoy this at first. He found his teaching excited. But after a few months, it did become difficult to continue without any guidance. He was never sure what teaching. In the end, by asking many questions, he was able taking control of the situation. By the time he was about to leave, he finally wanted staying!

Determine which items you missed in this Diagnostic Activity. If you missed or had trouble with any of the items, please go to the appropriate section in *The Harper-Collins Concise Handbook for Writers* and this workbook for further practice or study.

It is important to know which items cause you difficulty. When revising your writing, you might want to go through your paper one time checking only for the use of gerunds, infinitives, and participles. Concentrate on items that you had difficulty with in this activity.

16b IDENTIFYING INFINITIVES, GERUNDS, AND PARTICIPLES

The **infinitive** is the base form of the verb, preceded by *to*. Infinitives can be used as nouns (as they are in the following sentences) or, occasionally, as adjectives or adverbs, but never as verbs.

199

The point of the game is *to collect* as much money as possible.

To lose my gloves was irritating.

Verbs with *-ing* endings are either **gerunds** or **participles,** depending on their use in the sentence. If they are used as nouns, as in the first example below, they are gerunds. If they are used as adjectives, as in the second example, they are participles.

Odysseus warned his men against *opening* the bag of winds.

A *moving* target is difficult to hit.

16c FUNCTION OF INFINITIVES AND GERUNDS

Both infinitives and gerunds can be used as nouns in sentences. Deciding whether to use an infinitive or a gerund is sometimes difficult. It may help to think first about the function of these verbals, as outlined in the accompanying chart.

FUNCTIONS OF INFINITIVES AND GERUNDS

Function	Example
Infinitives	
Subject	*To study* for a test is important for a good grade.
Subject complement*	He seems *to like* going to the movies.
Object of a verb	Students don't like *to study.*
Appositive	His reason, *to earn* a better salary, was convincing.
Adjective modifier	I was happy *to lend* her a hand.
Object of the preposition *about*	I was about *to leave* when the phone rang.
Noun modifier	Her decision *to go* to the bank was a good one.
Verb phrase modifier	I quit smoking (in order) *to save* my health.
Special uses of the infinitive	
With *what, who, whom, where,* or *when* in a noun clause as object	She wasn't sure what *to take* to the party.
With *too* and *enough*	He is rich enough *to afford* a new car.
With *make, let,* or *have* (omit *to*)	It is too cold *to go* outside.
	She made me *go* to bed.
	They let us *watch* television.
	They had me *grade* the papers after school.
With *force, allow,* or *got*	She forced me *to go* to bed.
	They allowed us *to watch* television.
	They got me *to grade* the papers at school.
With *help* (*to* is optional)	They helped him *(to) work* in the yard.
With verbs of command or request	The teacher told the class *to sit down.*
	She asked the man *to give* her money.
With modals (omit *to*)	I must *study* English every day.
Gerunds	
Subject	*Working* in a bank is not very exciting.
Subject complement	She doesn't like *working* in a bank.
Object of a verb	She loved *singing* in a choir.
Appositive	The next step, *writing* the conclusion, is easy.
Object of a preposition†	I'm not used to *eating* so late.

*The infinitive is often used with the verbs *be, seem,* and *appear.*
†When *to* is a preposition rather than part of an infinitive, the *-ing* form of the verb must follow it. Some typical expressions in which *to* is a preposition are *adapt to, adjust to, admit to, agree to, be accustomed to, be used to, change to, get accustomed to, get used to, limit to, look forward to, put a stop to,* and *submit to.*

Identifying the Function of Verbals

Underline the infinitives or gerunds in the following sentences, and write in the blank the type of verbal and the function it serves.

> *Example:* Looking at the sun is bad for your eyes. *gerund, subject* _____

1. Nobody ever said it would be easy to be a big rock star. _____

2. My duty, naming the finalists, comes near the end of the contest. _____

3. Malachi told me that he could deliver the copies by morning. _____

4. Everyone was amazed to find the office so neat and orderly. _____

5. Sophie passed the course by studying with her roommates. _____

6. Minhua's greatest aspiration, to be a policeman, was finally realized. _____

7. The director of the program, Mr. Pham, is someone who likes being challenged. _____

8. Mr. Peters made our study group hand in ten copies of each research paper. _____

9. To join the armed forces was never one of my greatest ambitions. _____

10. Francine raised money to help pay for the new day-care center. _____

16d CHOOSING BETWEEN INFINITIVES AND GERUNDS

Infinitives and gerunds can both function as subjects, subject complements, appositives, objects of prepositions, and objects of verbs. Six rules govern the use of these verbals.

1. Gerunds and infinitives can both function as subjects of a sentence. The meanings of these examples are the same, and they are both grammatically correct. However, it is more common to use gerunds as subjects:

   Eating spaghetti is fun.

   To eat spaghetti is fun.

2. Gerunds and infinitives can also both function as appositives. Again, the meaning is the same, and both sentences are grammatically correct. However, it is more common to use gerunds as appositives.

   The next step, *writing* the conclusion, is easy.

   The next step, *to write* the conclusion, is easy.

ne object of a preposition, the gerund is required. The infinitive can follow only the prepo-
.ion *about*.

You can seal an envelope by *licking* the back.

I was about *to leave* when the phone rang.

4. Gerunds and infinitives can both function as objects of verbs. Some verbs can be followed
    only by a gerund, as in the first example; some verbs can be followed only by an infinitive, as
    in the second. These verbs can be found in the accompanying chart.

    They enjoy *going* to the movies.

    She wants *to eat* ice cream.

5. The verbs *forget, quit, remember,* and *stop* can take either a gerund or an infinitive, but the
    meaning differs. For example, in the first sentence, the man no longer buys a newspaper; in
    the second, the man stopped and bought a newspaper. (See chart.)

    He stopped *buying* a newspaper.

    He stopped *to buy* a newspaper.

6. Some verbs can be followed by gerunds or infinitives with no effect on the meaning. For ex-
    ample, both of the following sentences tell us that the person enjoys visiting Paris. The chart
    lists verbs of this type.

    I like *going* to Paris.

    I like *to go* to Paris.

VERBS THAT TAKE VERBAL OBJECTS

Verbs that take only infinitives as objects
The infinitive follows these verbs directly:

agree	decide	offer	refuse	swear
appear	hope	pretend	seem	wish

The infinitive either follows these verbs directly or follows a noun or pronoun:

- With the same meaning: *promise*

  He promised to go. (He gave his word he would go.)
  He promised me to go. (He gave me his word he would go.)

- With different meanings: *ask, expect, get, need, want*

  He asked to go. (He requested permission to leave.)
  He asked me to go. (He wants me to go with him or in his place.)

After these verbs, the infinitive must follow a noun or pronoun:

command	force	order	remind	tell
compel	instruct	persuade	require	warn
encourage	invite			

(continued)

VERBS THAT TAKE VERBAL OBJECTS *(continued)*

Verbs that take only gerunds as objects

admit	deny	enjoy	imagine	postpone
appreciate	discuss	escape	keep	put off
avoid	endure	finish	mind	risk
delay				

Verbs that can take either gerunds or infinitives as objects

- With the same meaning: *begin, continue, hate, like, prefer, stand, start, try*

  I hate playing the piano. (I dislike this activity.)

  I hate to play the piano. (I dislike this activity.)

- With different meanings: *forget, quit, remember, stop*

  I remember winding my grandfather's watch every night. (I recall performing this action regularly in the past.)

  I remember to wind my grandfather's watch every night. (I perform this action regularly in the present.)

ACTIVITY 16.3

Editing Sentences for Infinitives and Gerunds

The following sentences contain errors in infinitives and gerunds. Correct them, indicating in the blank the number of the rule in section 16d that you used to make your decision. An example is provided.

> *Example:* ~~To know~~ *Knowing* the rules of football makes watching the game more exciting. *Rule 1*

1. I can't imagine to move as often as Joy does. _____

2. I forgot buying milk at the store. _____

3. Her favorite hobby, eating, was not good for her health. _____

4. I was about going to the store when my aunt called. _____

5. I prefer exercising in the morning. _____

6. I expect winning the lottery. _____

7. Kwon offered helping with the dishes. _____

8. After to consider the proposal, I accepted it. _____

9. She encouraged me to write as often as I could. _____

10. To have a good friend is an important part of life. _____

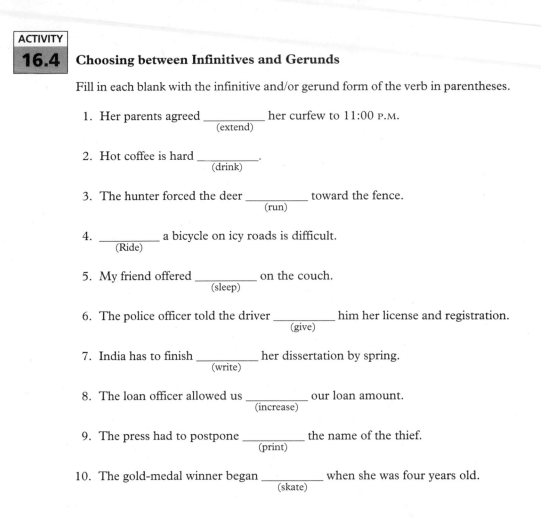

ACTIVITY

16.4   **Choosing between Infinitives and Gerunds**

Fill in each blank with the infinitive and/or gerund form of the verb in parentheses.

1. Her parents agreed _____ her curfew to 11:00 P.M.
   (extend)

2. Hot coffee is hard _____.
   (drink)

3. The hunter forced the deer _____ toward the fence.
   (run)

4. _____ a bicycle on icy roads is difficult.
   (Ride)

5. My friend offered _____ on the couch.
   (sleep)

6. The police officer told the driver _____ him her license and registration.
   (give)

7. India has to finish _____ her dissertation by spring.
   (write)

8. The loan officer allowed us _____ our loan amount.
   (increase)

9. The press had to postpone _____ the name of the thief.
   (print)

10. The gold-medal winner began _____ when she was four years old.
    (skate)

16e PARTICIPLES

Participles are used in verb phrases to form tenses or they can serve as adjectives or adverbs. Present participles are formed by adding *-ing* to the base form of the regular verb. The past participle form of the verb ends in *-ed, -en,* or *-t.* For a discussion of participles used to form tenses, see Chapters 13 and 14.

Differentiating between Participles Used as Verb Forms and Adjectives

Students sometimes confuse participles used with the progressive and passive verb forms and participles used as adjectives. One way to differentiate these uses is to add an intensifier such as *very* before the *-ing* or *-ed/en/t* word in the sentence. The sentence will only be correct when the participle is functioning as an adjective:

CORRECT: The sound is very annoying (*-ing* adjective).

INCORRECT: The sound is very annoying me (progressive verb).

Participles Used as Adjectives with Emotive Verbs

One common mistake when participles are used as adjectives is the following:

INCORRECT: I am *amazing* at the price.

INCORRECT: The price is *amazed* to me.

Deciding which participle to use is difficult when the verbs show mental states or opinions (see the chart). If the adjective applies to the person or animal that experienced the mental state or opinion, as in the first example, use the past participle. If the adjective applies to the cause of the mental state or opinion, use the *-ing* form.

CORRECT: I am *amazed* at the price.

CORRECT: The price is *amazing* to me.

FORMS OF VERBS SHOWING MENTAL STATES OR OPINIONS	
amazing/amazed	frightening/frightened
amusing/amused	irritating/irritated
annoying/annoyed	interesting/interested
confusing/confused	satisfying/satisfied
depressing/depressed	surprising/surprised
disappointing/disappointed	worrying/worried
embarrassing/embarrassed	

ACTIVITY 16.5   **Using the Right Participle**

Fill in the blanks in the following sentences with the correct participle form of the verb in parentheses.

1. Uwe was _____ (startle) by the presence of Alan when he entered the room.

2. The instructions on the label were very _____ (confuse).

3. Yuko has a _____ (surprise) capacity for learning languages. Even she is a little _____ (amaze).

4. Tatsuo is _____ (do) his homework. He'll go out when it's _____ (finish).

5. Florence is _____ (annoy) by her math class because she finds it a little _____ (bore).

6. Nick jumped, _____ (frighten) by the lightening.

7. _____ (Irritate) that bears had invaded the camp, the family left.

8. The school director was _____ (impress) by the students' progress.

Participles Functioning as Reduced Adjective and Adverb Clauses

Present and past participles can be used to introduce reduced **adjective** clauses:

> ADJECTIVE CLAUSE: People *who live* in cities have more cultural opportunities.

> REDUCED ADJECTIVE CLAUSE: People *living* in cities have more cultural opportunities.

Present participles can be used in **adverb** clauses when both sentences have the same subject and same verb forms:

> ADVERB CLAUSE: After we had finished dinner, we took a walk.

> REDUCED ADVERB CLAUSE: (After) having finished dinner, we took a walk.

Adverb clauses showing *cause* can be reduced to *-ing* phrases or *-ed* phrases as long as the subjects are the same.

> ADVERB CLAUSE: *Because John was tired* from playing soccer all afternoon, he went to bed.

> REDUCED ADVERB CLAUSE: *Tired* from playing soccer all afternoon, John went to bed.

> ADVERB CLAUSE: *Since they wanted* to travel, they bought a new car.

> REDUCED ADVERB CLAUSE: *Wanting* to travel, they bought a new car.

See 11d for a discussion of dangling modifiers, a common error that occurs when using adverb modifiers at the beginning of a sentence.

ACTIVITY

16.6   **Reduced Adjective and Adverb Clauses**

Reduce the adjective and adverb clauses in the following sentences.

> *Example:* Because the dogs were barking in the yard, they annoyed the neighbors.
>
> *Barking in the yard, the dogs annoyed the neighbors.*

1. Since Corey was excited about her new car, she drove it everywhere.

2. When the boy jumped off the building, he landed on the trampoline below.

3. As Larry was running toward the train, he slipped on a banana peel.

4. The water that surrounds the island is crystal blue.

5. The books that are on the table need to be moved.

16f VERBALS: COMPREHENSIVE CHECK

16.7 Diagnostic Retest

Complete Activity 16.1 again. If you still miss or have difficulty with any items, review the relevant sections of the workbook.

16.8 Putting It All Together

Read the following passage, underlining gerunds, infinitives, present participles, and past participles. Change all misused verbals or participles to the correct form.

I arrived in Perth with five dollars and a determination getting a job in the mines. I was too late. Every company, it seemed, had just recruited a small army of miners; the quotas were full. To face the urgent necessity of to find work that day, I went to the employment office and invented some agricultural experience. I wanted being somewhere isolated, without the need or opportunity spending my earnings. A farmer arrived and agreed collecting me when his wife had finished her shopping.

At seven-thirty the next morning, I was driving a tractor for the first time in my life, being taught plowing a straight furrow. These fields were huge—over a thousand acres apiece—and I felt, at first, overwhelming by the desolate vastness of the place. We were miles from the nearest house, and every tree was a landmark, to stretch almost featureless to a far horizon. It was poor soil, virtually sand, exhausting by the monoculture of wheat, fertilizing by tons of superphosphate. In parts it was even poisoning by salinity.

Gradually, however, I began relishing the space, the scale, the shadow of the clouds passing across the enormous landscape. Alone on my tractor, I plowed around and around in ever-diminishing rings. I became proud of my expertise. I came knowing where I might find an iguana, lurking like a miniature dragon in the shade of a rock, and I became accustomed to the harsh cawing of the flocks of red and gray birds. [Adapted from Simon Loftus, *A Pike in the Basement*]

17 FINDING AND REVISING SUBJECT-VERB AGREEMENT ERRORS

Subject-verb agreement requires using the form of the verb that agrees with the subject in a sentence. Some writers have trouble with the basic concept; others have trouble with just one or two special cases. Activity 17.1 will help you determine some of the areas where you may have trouble.

17a DIAGNOSTIC ACTIVITY: SUBJECT-VERB AGREEMENT

ACTIVITY
17.1   **How Much Do You Know?**

Read each sentence. If it contains an error in subject-verb agreement, correct the error. An example is provided.

> *Example:*   That student speak͜three languages: English, Japanese, and Spanish.

1. Our neighbor enjoys gardening in the springtime.

2. That silk shirt look great with my skirt.

3. The children asks to watch cartoons every morning.

4. I enjoy reading the newspaper with my breakfast.

5. You never call me anymore.

6. I is happy to be studying in this country.

7. Cathy is sick with a stomachache today.

8. My classmates is surprised at their test scores.

9. My brother has played football for the Chicago Bears.

10. The students are being tested in Room C210.

11. Sue might goes to New Mexico over the semester break.

12. Joey's younger brother can eats so much.

13. My roommate will have three exams next Tuesday.

14. Zeynep and I walked five miles yesterday.

15. The attention of young boys often wander during long speeches.

16. Fishing, as well as camping, are my favorite things to do in the summer.

17. Joon and Carlos always studies together in the library.

18. Hot tea with lemon make me feel better.

19. Macaroni and cheese is my daughter's favorite meal.

20. Each teacher and student want a copy of the new schedule.

21. Every man, woman, and child in the United States learns the Pledge of Allegiance.

22. Kris or Paul have lost the telephone message.

23. The nurses or the doctor answers the patient's questions.

24. My staff are willing to work overtime.

25. Every night, the audience shout and beg the musician to continue.

26. A number of my classmates are advancing to the next language level.

27. There is a huge bug in my bathtub!

28. There is many ways to get to my house from Washington Street.

29. In the newspaper yesterday were two excellent articles on health and fitness.

30. Tom's biggest complaints about the movie was the price and a weak ending.

31. This restaurant's most famous dish are spaghetti and meatballs.

32. Linguistics is the study of language.

33. The *New York Times* is a reputable newspaper.

34. One hundred miles were the distance to the campground.

35. Each of the letters was typed beautifully.

36. Anything my sister does is okay with my mother.

37. Most of the graduation cakes are gone.

38. Some of the money have been spent on groceries.

39. The quiet woman who is in your writing class called yesterday.

40. People who live in glass houses shouldn't throw stones.

Determine which items you missed in this Diagnostic Activity. If you missed or had trouble with any of the items, please review the appropriate section of *The HarperCollins Concise Handbook for Writers* and this workbook for further practice and study.

It is important to know which items cause you difficulty. When revising your writing, you might want to devote one complete revision to checking each sentence for subject-verb agreement, concentrating on items that you had difficulty with in this activity.

Let us begin with the basic principles of subject-verb agreement and then discuss a series of special situations. Note that in the examples in this chapter, subjects are underlined once and verbs twice to help you see how subject-verb agreement works.

17b BASIC SUBJECT-VERB AGREEMENT

Examine these sentences:

> One <u>dog</u> <u>barks</u> every morning.
>
> Two <u>dogs</u> <u>bark</u> every morning.

ACTIVITY

17.2 Basic Rule

A. Based on your observations of the sentences in 17b, complete the basic rule for subject-verb agreement in English.

1. If the subject is singular, the verb must end in _____

2. If the subject is plural, the verb _____

B. Apply the basic rule by filling in each blank with the appropriate *present-tense* form of the verb provided.

> *Example:* Each summer, my girlfriend ___*buys*___ (buy) a new swimsuit.

1. My older sister _____ (write) me every week.

2. Those boys _____ (make) a lot of noise!

3. Your cat _____ (like) to have plenty of attention.

4. The monkeys _____ (swing) on the rope all day long.

5. My father _____ (help) my mother with the cooking every weekend.

6. That woman _____ (teach) at the Language Institute.

7. My husband _____ (work) for IBM Corporation.

8. Mountain bikes _____ (cost) hundreds of dollars.

9. This semester, my teachers _____ (assign) homework every night.

10. His brother _____ (exercise) at 5:30 every morning!

In addition to knowing the basic principle of subject-verb agreement, it is important to know some special cases.

17c SUBJECT-VERB AGREEMENT WITH *I* AND *YOU* AS THE SUBJECT

Examine these sentences:

> One <u>student</u> <u>leaves</u> early every Friday.
>
> Two <u>students</u> <u>leave</u> early every Friday.
>
> <u>I</u> <u>leave</u> early every Friday.
>
> <u>You</u> <u>leave</u> early every Friday.

The first two sentences follow the basic rule for subject-verb agreement, but the last two sentences illustrate an exception. Even though the subjects *I* and *you* are singular, the verbs used with them do not have -*s* endings.

ACTIVITY

17.3   **Subject-Verb Agreement with *I* and *You***

Complete each sentence by using the correct form of each listed verb. Use each verb only once. Pay special attention to subject-verb agreement. An example is provided.

live	eat	swim	speak	work
visit	study	fly	love	look

Example: My little sister ____*talks*____ on the phone every single night!

1. I _____ in Akers Hall on campus.

2. My father _____ for General Motors.

3. Your roommate _____ in the library every day.

4. You _____ English very well.

5. Those students _____ lunch together every day.

6. You _____ very beautiful today!

7. I _____ to watch mystery movies late at night.

8. Our kids _____ their grandparents on Thanksgiving.

9. You _____ to Korea twice a year, don't you?

10. I _____ in the outdoor pool three times a week.

17d SUBJECT-VERB AGREEMENT WITH THE VERB *BE*

The most common verb in the English language is also the most irregular: the verb *be*. The various forms of the verb *be* do not always follow the standard rules.

The following sentences illustrate how subject-verb agreement works for the various forms of the verb *be* in the present tense:

He <u>is</u> tired of feeling helpless.   We <u>are</u> tired of feeling helpless.
Max <u>is</u> tired of feeling helpless.   I <u>am</u> tired of feeling helpless.
They <u>are</u> tired of feeling helpless.   You <u>are</u> tired of feeling helpless.
My <u>parents</u> <u>are</u> tired of feeling helpless.

ACTIVITY

17.4   **Writing Sentences with the Verb *be***

A.   Based on your observations of the sentences in 17d, complete the rules for subject-verb agreement with the verb *be* in the *present tense*.

1. If the subject is the pronoun *I*, the correct form of the verb *be* is _____

2. If the subject is singular and not *I* or *you*, the correct form of the verb *be* is _____

3. If the subject is plural or the pronoun *you*, the correct form of the verb *be* is _____

B.   Using the rules in part A, write sentences with the following subjects and the verb *be*. Use the present tense.

     Example: You *are a considerate friend.* _____

1. He _____

2. Your girlfriend _____

3. My cat _____

4. They _____

5. Those books _____

6. We _____

7. I _____

8. You _____

ACTIVITY

17.5   **Editing for Subject-Verb Agreement with the Verb *be***

A.   The following passage contains ten errors in subject-verb agreement. Read the passage, and identify and correct these errors.

     Let me tell you a little about my family. I comes from a family of seven; I have three sisters and one brother. My father is a businessman. He own a little jewelry store where he sells and repairs beautiful gold and silver pieces. My mother is a homemaker, but she often help my father at the store on the weekends. My oldest sister, Cathy, are a nurse at the local hospital. I admires Cathy; she works full-time and also care for her husband and two children. My sister Judy is an artist. Her specialty are watercolors, but she is also good with pen and ink. My brother, Paul, is an architect. Paul also have artistic talent, and he designs eye-catching buildings. Currently, his newest design is being considered by the city. And finally, my youngest sister, Sharla, is a high school science teacher. She love her work and plan to teach for many years to come.

B.   Now write a paragraph about your family in the present tense like the one in part A. When you have finished, edit your paragraph for subject-verb agreement errors.

17e SUBJECT-VERB AGREEMENT WITH HELPING VERBS

The following sentences illustrate how subject-verb agreement works when you use a form of the verb *be* as a helping verb in front of a main verb:

One of my neighbors is helping my mother.

Two of my neighbors are helping my mother.

One bird is driving me crazy every morning at six.

Several birds are driving me crazy every morning at six.

In the first sentence, the main verb is *help; is* is the helping verb. When you use a form of the verb *be* as a helping verb in front of a main verb, the helping verb agrees with the subject, and the main verb takes the ending *-ing.*

Notice that *only the helping verb* agrees with the subject. The main verb remains the same. Two other common helping verbs, *do* and *have,* work much the same way:

Does Suzanne live in the city?

Do Suzanne and Stephen live in the city?

Paula Skolnik has played extremely well this year.

Paula Skolnik and Yuri Sher have played extremely well this year.

These sentences show that you must use *does* and *has* as the helping verb with singular subjects and *do* and *have* as the helping verb with plural subjects. Whenever there is a helping verb, the main verb remains unchanged.

The following sentences show how to handle subject-verb agreement when more than one of these helping verbs is used with a main verb:

The airplane has been searched, and no bomb was found.

The airplanes have been searched, and no bombs were found.

My Macintosh is being repaired, so I cannot let you use it.

My Macintosh and my IBM are being repaired, so I cannot let you use them.

Note that when more than one helping verb is used, *only the first helping verb* changes to reflect subject-verb agreement.

In the English language, there are nine other helping verbs—*can, could, may, might, must, shall, should, will,* and *would*—known as **modals,** that work somewhat differently from *be, do,* and *have:*

That nurse can take blood without the patient even feeling the needle.

Many nurses can take blood without the patient even feeling the needle.

Mrs. Nakamura might buy my car this weekend.

Mr. and Mrs. Nakamura might buy my car this weekend.

From these examples, you can see that this group of helping verbs does not add *-s* when the subject is singular; they are an exception to the basic rule for subject-verb agreement.

ACTIVITY

17.6 Editing for Subject-Verb Agreement with Helping Verbs

The following passage about outdoor clothing contains seven errors in subject-verb agreement, primarily errors involving helping verbs. Read the passage, and identify and correct these errors. The first error has been corrected for you.

The outerwear system you need depend on the weather conditions you anticipate. Experience has shown that design of the outerwear is very important in making your backpacking trip successful. Design includes everything from the fit to the hood closure to the number of pockets. Key considerations are as follows:

Outerwear should never fits tightly. You needs room to wear a bulky sweater and pants underneath. Shell jackets intended for winter should accommodate a down sweater, too. Look twice before buying a jacket that doesn't includes an attached hood. If you tend to overheat, your outerwear should ventilate easily. So-called "breathable" gear won't keeps you cool when lumbering uphill with a heavy pack. We assume you'll be wearing a pack, so don't choose a short-waisted jacket that will crumples up under your waistbelt. [Mark Jenkins and Steve Gorman, "Creating the Perfect Clothing System"]

17f SUBJECT-VERB AGREEMENT WITH PAST AND FUTURE TENSES

The following sentences show how subject-verb agreement works with tenses other than the present:

One dog barked last week.

Two dogs barked last week.

One dog will bark tomorrow morning.

Two dogs will bark tomorrow morning.

Verbs do *not* change form to agree with their subjects in the past or the future tense. The one exception to this generalization is revealed by the following:

One dog was barking last week.

Two dogs were barking last week.

The only verb that changes its form to indicate a subject-verb agreement in the past tense is the verb *be*, which takes the form *was* for singular subjects and *were* for plural subjects.

ACTIVITY

17.7 **Using Past and Future Tenses with Correct Agreement**

Read the following paragraphs written in the present tense. Rewrite each as indicated, making sure that the subjects and verbs agree.

1. Change this paragraph to the past tense.

   It is a beautiful day! The sun is shining, and the birds are singing. On cool spring days, I wake up at sunrise and walk my dog, Fido. Fido likes to sniff the wet ground. He also enjoys watching the birds in the trees. Sometimes Fido sees a small rabbit in the bushes. He chases the frightened animal, but he is only playing. He never harms the animals we encounter on our early morning walks.

2. Change this paragraph to the future tense.

   My roommate and I ride our bicycles each morning before our classes. We see the countryside at its most peaceful moments. The roads are free of traffic; the air is clean. Then we eat a healthy breakfast at the small diner on the corner of Main and Berkeley streets. Our day begins in a wonderful way!

17g SUBJECT-VERB AGREEMENT WITH INTERVENING PHRASES AND COMPOUND SUBJECTS

The cause of these incidents has not been discovered.

A series of misunderstandings is likely to occur if we don't communicate often.

The losses by my mother's company are not as large as expected.

What makes these sentences difficult is the presence of a second noun between the subject and the verb. This second noun can be mistaken for the subject if you are not careful. It may be helpful to remember that the subject can never be in a prepositional phrase.

The nurse, as well as the patients, was confused by the sounding of the alarm.

My father, together with his dog, is a real sight to see.

Again, the presence of a second noun between the subject and the verb makes these sentences a little tricky. Phrases introduced by *as well as, together with, along with, in addition to, including,* and *not to mention* are not considered part of the subject.

Cardinals and kingfishers are my favorite birds.

Alice and Nancy never speak to each other.

Oil, vinegar, and basil are essential ingredients in my salad dressing.

When subjects are composed of two or more words joined by the conjunction *and,* they are said to be *compound.* Compound subjects joined by *and* are always plural. The only exceptions involve subjects that *look* compound but in fact are not. For example, the terms joined by *and* may form a single idea:

The winner and new champion of the world is Bouncing Bill Bennett.

Ham and cheese is the only sandwich she will eat.

In the first sentence, the subject is *winner and champion.* These terms refer to a single person, and so *winner and champion* is treated like a singular subject and takes a singular verb. In the second sentence, *ham and cheese* refers to a single item, a sandwich, and so it too is treated as a singular subject even though it is composed of two nouns joined by *and.*

The terms *each* and *every* can cause confusion:

Each man and woman receives a sterling silver lapel button as a remembrance of this night.

Every dog, cat, and parakeet in this neighborhood needs to be tested for rabies.

When a compound subject joined by *and* is preceded by *each* or *every,* the subject is treated as singular.

Sam and Carrie each ride with a neighbor to work every morning.

My mother and father each live in a condominium.

When a compound subject is *followed* by *each,* however, it is treated as plural.

Now see what happens when a compound subject is formed with *or:*

Butter or sour cream on a potato is too fattening for me, so I use a little nonfat yogurt.

Raisins or bananas are good in cream of wheat.

If two *singular* subjects are joined by *or,* the subject is singular; if two *plural* subjects are joined by *or,* the subject is plural. But what happens when singular and plural subjects are mixed?

Raisins or brown sugar is good on cream of wheat.

Brown sugar or raisins are good on cream of wheat.

The <u>teacher</u> or the <u>students</u> <u><u>have</u></u> to apologize.

The <u>students</u> or the <u>teacher</u> <u><u>has</u></u> to apologize.

The rule is that the verb agrees with the subject nearest to it, the one that *follows* the word *or*.

ACTIVITY

17.8   Identifying and Editing Sentences for Subject-Verb Agreement

Read the following sentences, underlining each subject once and each verb twice. Then determine whether the subjects and verbs agree in the sentences. If there is an error in agreement, correct the sentence.

> *Example:*   Each <u>undergraduate student</u> and <u>graduate student</u> <u><u>receive</u></u> a school ID card $\overset{s}{\wedge}$ in the mail.

1. The newsletter, as well as the booklet, has to be published this week.

2. My coworkers or Mr. Wald have the original file.

3. Chinese, Mexican, and Italian are my favorite ethnic foods.

4. The report by the committee and its board members have been reviewed and revised.

5. Robert, along with Susan and Anne, attend weekly discussion meetings.

6. A review of the tax proposals were conducted last week.

7. My mother or my father gives me $20 each week.

8. Confusion about subject-verb agreement and pronoun agreement causes many problems.

9. After each of the placement exams are corrected, the students receive their scores.

10. My wife and my mother each are excellent cooks!

ACTIVITY

17.9   Editing for Subject-Verb Agreement

The following passages contain six errors each in subject-verb agreement. Read each passage, and identify and correct the errors. One error has been corrected for you.

1.   Warm drinks like thick, sweet Turkish coffee *is* served in demitasse cups to whet $\overset{are}{}$ the appetite. *Chay* (tea) has a special place in every Turk's heart. Small glasses of the carefully brewed beverage is sipped throughout the day. The tea leaves, ~~grown~~ on the Aegean or Black Sea coasts, is steeped in a small teapot perched atop a larger steaming kettle for fifteen minutes. The strong brew that results are tempered with hot water to the personal taste of the drinker. A teaspoon of sugar or a squeeze of lemon add the final touch to the smoothest glass of *chay* in the world.

     Before breakfast, it is common to take a brisk walk to the neighborhood baker to buy a fragrant, just-baked loaf of bread. For the morning meal, generous slices are topped with chunks of feta cheese, black olives, and juicy tomatoes. Homemade jams, boiled down from seasonal fruit combined with sugar, is served with butter churned from fresh milk. [Adapted from Judy Erkanat, "Turkish Delight"]

2. Meet one of the world's largest land mammals, the common hippopotamus. Hippos spends most of their lives in the water, napping and relaxing. During dry seasons, they cool off in wallows, or mud holes. Then a coating of mud and dirt protect the animals' skin from the sun. Although the Greek word *hippopotamus* means "river horse," the hippo most resemble its cousin the pig.

   The hippo may look awkward, but the river giant swims and dives with grace and ease. Underwater, the hippo's eyes narrow to slits and its ears flatten to form a seal. Pores in the hippo's skin produces a pink, sticky fluid that waterproofs the animal. Even the toes on its feet, which aids in paddling, are designed for its watery environment.

   A calf, or young hippo, are born—you guessed it!—underwater. Right away it can push off the bottom and rise to the surface to breathe. When in water it often rides on its mother's back. There it can breathe easy, safe from crocodiles. [Adapted from Ann L. Di Fiore, "Hip, Hip, Hippo!"]

17h SUBJECT-VERB AGREEMENT WITH COLLECTIVE NOUNS

The jury is waiting for the lawyers' closing arguments.

The class wants to take the final exam on Friday.

A group of bicyclists rides past my house each Saturday morning.

In each of these subjects, *jury, class,* and *group,* the people are being considered *as a unit.* They are not acting as individuals but rather as one group. Therefore, each of these collective nouns is singular.

Occasionally, a collective noun is used in such a way that the members of the group are being considered as individuals. In these unusual instances, it is correct to consider the collective noun plural:

The committee are not able to agree on a meeting time.

My family seem to be unable to communicate with each other.

Even in these cases, it seems awkward to most writers to use these nouns as plurals. A less awkward solution is to add words to make the subjects more clearly plural:

The committee members are not able to agree on a meeting time.

My parents and my sisters seem to be unable to communicate with each other.

The word *number* is an unusual collective noun:

The number of students who drop out of school is too large.

A number of students are planning to quit school this spring.

The phrase *the number* is always singular; the phrase *a number* is always plural.

ACTIVITY

17.10 **Using the Correct Verb with Collective Nouns**

In the following sentences, underline each subject. Then, using the rules of subject-verb agreement with collective nouns, circle the appropriate form of the verb.

Example: The student <u>committee</u> ((is)/are) unhappy with the university's decision to cancel Homecoming festivities.

1. <u>Management</u> ((disagrees)/disagree) with our proposal for a four-day workweek.

2. The <u>number</u> of international students attending American universities ((has)/have) increased greatly in the past five years.

3. The newly married <u>couple</u> ((is)/are) going to the Bahamas for a honeymoon.

4. A <u>number</u> of similarities ((appears)/appear) in two of my students' research papers.

5. The <u>members</u> of the jury (debates/(debate)) the man's innocence or guilt.

6. The <u>people</u> on my soccer team (is/(are)) extremely competitive.

7. A <u>number</u> of my friends ((lives)/live) off campus.

8. A baseball <u>team</u> ((needs)/need) at least nine players.

9. My family <u>members</u> (loves/(love)) good food, music, and celebrations!

10. At our school, the <u>number</u> of female engineering students ((has)/have) doubled since last year.

17i   SUBJECT-VERB AGREEMENT WHEN THE SUBJECT FOLLOWS THE VERB

Sentences with *there*

Ordinarily in English sentences, the subject comes first and the verb comes later. However, exceptions to this normal word order do occur:

There <u>are</u> three <u>cups</u> of coffee left.

There <u>is</u> a <u>reason</u> for his sudden absence.

There <u>are</u> two <u>reasons</u> why I cannot go to the meeting on Monday.

In these sentences, notice that the subject follows the verb. Notice also that all of these sentences start with the word *there*. When sentences start with *there,* the subject almost always follows the verb. In these cases, subject-verb agreement works exactly as it does in any other sentence, but the subject is a little harder to find. To gain practice in identifying the subject in sentences that begin with *there,* complete Activity 17.11.

ACTIVITY
17.11   Subject-Verb Agreement in Sentences Beginning with *there*

Each of the following sentences illustrates an exception to the normal subject-verb word order. Underline the subject in each sentence; then supply the correct form of the verb *be.*

Example: There ____*is*____ a huge bug in my bathtub!

1. Unfortunately, there _____ many unhappy people in this world.

2. There _____ no one at the early-bird movie yesterday!

3. There _____ an excellent book on sale at Wheeler's Bookstore.

4. There _____ not enough equipment to play volleyball.

5. There _____ several interesting courses in the schedule book last semester.

Sentences Beginning with Prepositional Phrases

Here is a second type of sentence in which the subject follows the verb:

In the closet on the left are my best suits.

Under that bed live four of the cutest kittens in the Western Hemisphere.

In the basement is a complete set of carpenter's tools.

In addition, notice that each of these sentences starts with a prepositional phrase. Finally, notice that subject-verb agreement works the same way it has in earlier examples, once the subject has been identified.

Now look at the following sentences, which also begin with prepositional phrases:

In the closet, Greg found several new suits.

Under that bed, four of the cutest kittens in the Western Hemisphere were born.

In the basement, Marcy hid a complete set of carpenter's tools.

These sentences begin with prepositional phrases, but the subject does not follow the verb; it comes in its normal position. To make sure the verb agrees with the subject in sentences that begin with prepositional phrases, you must be careful to find the actual subject of the sentence—it can come either *before* or *after* the verb. To gain practice in identifying the subject in sentences like these, complete Activity 17.12.

ACTIVITY

17.12 Subject-Verb Agreement in Sentences Beginning with a Prepositional Phrase

In each of the following sentences, underline the subject once and the verb twice. An example is provided.

> *Example:* In the metal file cabinet is my birth certificate.

1. At the corner of Sunset and Mission is a wonderful new coffee shop.

2. In the top left drawer are love letters from India's boyfriend.

3. On the table in the dining room is the vase for the roses.

4. Under the kitchen sink are my cleaning supplies.

5. In the garage is your birthday present: a red BMW.

17j SUBJECT-VERB AGREEMENT WITH LINKING VERBS

Subject-verb agreement can be a little complicated when the verb is a linking verb. As you recall, a linking verb connects the subject of the sentence with something that comes after the verb. Linking verbs include *be* and sensory verbs such as *appears, feels, looks, seems, smells, sounds,* and *tastes*.

My favorite dessert is strawberries and cream.

A major social problem in America is the many people who are homeless.

Gloria's dogs smell terrible when they are wet.

In the first sentence, even though *strawberries and cream* is plural, the subject, *dessert,* is singular, so the verb is the singular *is*. In the second sentence, even though *people* is plural, the subject, *problem,* is singular, so the verb is the singular *is*. In the third sentence, the subject is *dogs,* which is plural, so the verb is the plural *smell*.

To gain practice in identifying the subject in sentences like these, complete Activity 17.13.

ACTIVITY

17.13 **Identifying Subjects and Verbs in Sentences with Linking Verbs**

In each of the following sentences, underline the subject once and the verb twice. An example is provided.

> *Example:* Emre's <u>friends</u> <u>are</u> a bad influence on him.

1. My biggest worry after graduation is the many student loans I have.

2. My children's favorite game is cards.

3. Grades are a major concern for Hoon.

4. The cheapest item on the menu is the peanut butter and jelly sandwich.

5. Romeo's greatest interest is women.

6. Mr. Hong's wife seems lonely living here.

17k SUBJECT-VERB AGREEMENT WHEN THE SUBJECT IS PLURAL IN FORM BUT SINGULAR IN MEANING

Some nouns that end in -*s* are not plural:

<u>Mathematics</u> <u>is</u> an easy subject for me.

The <u>news</u> <u>was</u> very bad when I called the doctor.

Both of these subjects end in -*s* but are nevertheless singular and take singular verbs. Names and titles are singular:

<u>General Motors</u> <u>is</u> located in Detroit, Michigan.

<u>Hard Times</u> <u>is</u> a novel about working conditions in Victorian England.

Quantities are also considered singular:

<u>Two miles</u> <u>is</u> the distance from my house to my work.

<u>Twenty dollars</u> <u>is</u> a good price for that sweater.

<u>Five hours</u> <u>is</u> a long time to talk on the telephone.

ACTIVITY

17.14 **Recognizing Singular Subjects in Plural Form**

In each of the following sentences, underline the *complete* subject once and the verb twice. Then indicate the rule that explains the subject-verb agreement, as follows:

     a. Noun ending in -*s* in subject is singular, so verb is singular.
     b. Name or title is considered singular, so verb is singular.
     c. Quantities are considered singular, so verb is singular.

     Example: _____*a*_____ Economics <u>is</u> one of my most difficult classes this semester.

_____ 1. Two and one-half hours is long for a multiple-choice exam.

_____ 2. *American Challenges* is a book about business and government in the 1990s.

_____ 3. Years ago, ten dollars was a lot of money.

_____ 4. The workshop series on environmental issues was very interesting.

_____ 5. Eighty miles isn't too far to commute by train.

17l SUBJECT-VERB AGREEMENT WITH INDEFINITE PRONOUNS

The chart groups the most common indefinite pronouns according to whether they are singular, plural, or variable, depending on the context.

NUMBER WITH INDEFINITE PRONOUNS			
Always Singular		**Always Plural**	**Singular or Plural**
another	everything	both	all
anybody	neither	few	any
anyone	nobody	many	half
anything	no one	several	more
each	nothing	two (*any number greater than one*)	most
either	one		much
every	somebody		none
everybody	someone		some
everyone	something		

     The following sentences illustrate how subject-verb agreement works with most indefinite pronouns.

<u>Each</u> of these plants <u>requires</u> watering twice a week.

<u>Everyone</u> <u>likes</u> to receive flowers.

<u>Someone</u> in the next booth <u>is</u> listening to us.

<u>Everything</u> <u>points</u> to a recession within the next year.

As you can see, most indefinite pronouns are singular and require the singular form of the verb. Be especially careful with the pronouns *each* and *everyone*, which can seem plural in meaning but are grammatically singular.

     A much smaller group of indefinite pronouns are always plural:

<u>Many</u> <u>are</u> called, but <u>few</u> are chosen.

<u>Two</u> of my brothers <u>play</u> professional baseball.

A third group of indefinite pronouns are singular or plural depending on the noun in the prepositional phrase that follows the pronoun:

Some of the wine is cabernet sauvignon.

Some of the cookies are chocolate chip.

All of Melia's personality does not come from her father.

All of Melia's sweaters do not fit in the closet.

In these sentences, the prepositional phrase following the indefinite pronoun determines whether the subject is plural or singular. If the noun in the prepositional phrase is singular, the indefinite pronoun preceding the phrase is singular. Likewise, if the noun in the prepositional phrase is plural, the indefinite pronoun preceding the phrase is plural.

ACTIVITY

17.15 **Subject-Verb Agreement with Indefinite Pronouns**

Study the indefinite pronouns in the chart on the previous page. Then circle the appropriate verb form in each of the following sentences.

1. None of the one-bedroom apartments (is/are) available this month.

2. Whenever one of my favorite songs (is/are) played on the radio, I increase the volume.

3. Most of my fellow classmates (has/have) returned to their native countries.

4. Neither my aunt nor my grandmother (is/are) coming to my graduation party.

5. Either the Eastland Mall or the West Towne Plaza (is/are) having a clearance sale.

6. None of those textbooks (is/are) in stock at the bookstore.

7. Neither of you (appreciates/appreciate) the things your parents do for you.

8. Everything you ordered from the menu (was/were) delicious.

9. Either my little brother or the post office (has/have) lost my important letter.

10. One of those women (becomes/become) president of the company next month.

11. Some of my biology textbook (is/are) interesting.

12. All of my friends this semester (is/are) dedicated, intelligent students.

17m SUBJECT-VERB AGREEMENT IN CLAUSES BEGINNING WITH *WHO, WHICH,* OR *THAT*

Difficulty with subject-verb agreement may arise in clauses in which the subjects are *who, which,* or *that.*

A student who is late for class should enter the room quietly.

Students who are late for class should enter the room quietly.

A bird that migrates across the Gulf of Mexico is exhausted when it reaches the coast.

Birds that migrate across the Gulf of Mexico are exhausted when they reach the coast.

When the relative pronouns who, which, and that are subjects, it is impossible to tell whether they are singular or plural because they use the same form for both singular and plural. The only way to know is to determine what their antecedent is and whether it is singular or plural.

In the examples, the arrows make this process clear. In the first sentence, the antecedent of *who* is *student*. *Student* is singular, which means that *who* is singular and requires the singular verb *is*. In the second sentence, the antecedent of *who* is *students*. *Students* is plural, so *who* is plural, requiring the plural verb *are*. In the third sentence, the antecedent of *that* is the singular *bird*, so *that* is singular, and the verb that agrees is *migrates*. In the last sentence, the antecedent of *that* is the plural *birds*, so *that* is plural, and the verb that agrees is *migrate*.

At this time, it might also be helpful to separate each of the above sentences into its two original sentences. This way, it is easy to see whether the pronoun is singular or plural:

A student who is late for class should enter the room quietly.=

A student is late for class. A student should enter the room quietly.

It is now clear that *who* refers to the singular *student* and hence should take a singular verb.

ACTIVITY

17.16 **Subject-Verb Agreement with Relative Pronouns**

Break each of the remaining examples of sentences with relative clauses into two separate sentences.

1. Students who are late for class should enter the room quietly.

2. A bird that migrates across the Gulf of Mexico is exhausted when it reaches the coast.

3. Birds that migrate across the Gulf of Mexico are exhausted when they reach the coast.

The following sentences illustrate a situation in which subject-verb agreement with *who, which,* and *that* is particularly complicated:

Ronnie is one of those people who are always punctual.

This is one of those problems that are easy once you know the answer.

Ronnie is the only one of those people who is always punctual.

This is the only one of those problems that is easy once you know the answer.

The first sentence is saying that many people are always punctual and Ronnie is one of them, so the antecedent for *who* is *people,* not *one.* Therefore, *who* is plural and takes the plural verb *are.* In the second sentence, *that* similarly refers to *problems,* not *one.* Therefore, *that* is plural and takes the plural verb *are.* By contrast, the third sentence does not say that *many people* are punctual; it says that *only one* person is punctual. Therefore, the antecedent for *who* is the singular *one,* so it takes the singular verb *is.* In the fourth sentence, *that* likewise refers to *one,* not *problems,* and is therefore singular and takes the singular verb *is.* (In fact, you may have noticed by now that if the phrase *the only one* appears, the referent is always singular.)

As before, to see whether the pronoun is singular or plural, it may be helpful to separate the complex sentence into two separate sentences:

> Ronnie is one of those people who are always punctual. =
>
> Ronnie is one of those people. Those people are always punctual.

It is now clear to see that *who* refers to the plural *people* and hence should take a plural verb. If the phrase **the only one** is in the sentence, the referent is always singular.

ACTIVITY 17.17   Subject-Verb Agreement with Relative Pronouns

Break each of the following sentences with relative clauses into two separate sentences.

1. This is one of those problems that are easy once you know the answer.

2. She is the only one of those women who is always punctual.

3. This is the only one of those problems that is easy once you know the answer.

ACTIVITY 17.18   Using the Correct Form of the Verb with Relative Pronouns

Each of the following sentences contains the relative pronoun *which, who,* or *that.* Circle the appropriate form of the verb. An example is provided.

> *Example:* This is one of those days that (seems/ seem) to last forever.

1. Yesterday, we saw the man who (was/were) in our class last semester.

2. That was one of those movies that (makes/make) people feel happy about life.

3. Students who (studies/study) English in England often speak differently from students who (studies/study) English in America.

4. She was looking at the flowers, which (is/are) absolutely gorgeous.

5. He is the only one of my friends who (calls/call) me each year on my birthday.

6. The essay that (wins/win) the competition must be creative and interesting.

7. This was one of those easy-to-make pie crusts that (takes/take) only thirty minutes to bake.

8. Ms. Swenson is the only one of my teachers who (gives/give) us a quiz every week.

17n　SUBJECT-VERB AGREEMENT: COMPREHENSIVE CHECK

ACTIVITY
17.19　**Diagnostic Retest**

Complete Activity 17.1 again. If you still miss or have difficulty with any items, review the relevant sections of the workbook.

ACTIVITY
17.20　**Putting it All Together**

The following passage contains errors in subject-verb agreement. Read the passage, and identify and correct these errors.

In 1985, my friend and I was sent to Madagascar to look for an almost extinct form of lemur, called the aye-aye. Only a few of these animals is known to exist on a tiny island off the northeastern coast of Madagascar. This nocturnal animal, like everything else that live on the island, do not exists anywhere else on earth. It look a little like a large cat with a bat's ears, a beaver's teeth, a tail like a large ostrich feather, a middle finger like a long dead twig, and enormous eyes that seems to peer past you into a totally different world that exist just over your left shoulder.

When Madagascar broke off Africa and drifted into the Indian Ocean, it became isolated from all evolutionary changes that took place in the rest of the world. The major change that passed this island by were the arrival of the monkeys. They descended from the same ancestors as the lemurs, but they had bigger brains and was aggressive competitors for the same habitat. The monkeys were ambitious and interested in all sorts of things, especially twigs, with which they found they could do all kinds of things that they couldn't do by themselves—dig, probe, hit. The monkeys took over the world, and the lemur branch of the primate family died out everywhere—except on Madagascar. There was no monkeys for millions of years.

Then, fifteen hundred years ago, the monkeys finally arrived, or at least the monkeys' descendants—us. Thanks to astounding advances in twig technology, we arrived in canoes, then boats, and finally airplanes and started to competes for the same habitat. Today, the lemurs once again is fighting for survival. [Adapted from Douglas Adams and Mark Cawardine, *Last Chance to See*]

18 FINDING AND REVISING PRONOUN AGREEMENT AND REFERENCE ERRORS

A **pronoun** is a word that stands for or takes the place of a noun and its modifiers. The noun or pronoun that a pronoun refers to is called its **antecedent.** Problems involving pronouns and their antecedents are known as **pronoun agreement** problems. If the relationship between a pronoun and its antecedent is not clear, the sentence has a problem with **pronoun reference**.

Before we begin, let's determine how much you already know about pronoun agreement and reference.

18a DIAGNOSTIC ACTIVITY: PRONOUN AGREEMENT AND REFERENCE

ACTIVITY
18.1 **How Much Do You Know?**

Read each sentence. If it contains an error in pronoun agreement or reference, correct the error. Not all sentences contain errors. An example is provided.

they
Example: Some of the apples are rotten; ~~it~~ will have to be thrown away.

1. My teacher, Mrs. Collins, asked Ali to pass out the papers for them.

2. I believe that the two Japanese men in our English class improved because they participated in class activities.

3. My roommate goes to the library every night because you must complete a research paper.

4. Two friends will transfer to Georgia State University because they prefer the warmer climate.

5. My sister didn't come home for the holidays because he had research to do.

6. A conscientious student must submit his papers on time.

7. I hope all parents will attend the spring recital with their children.

8. Each employee should submit their health insurance questionnaire by Wednesday.

9. Every person who sees the movie will think about their relationship with their own father.

10. A cat or a dog is allowed in the apartment only if they are quiet and clean.

226

11. Neither Tom nor Mohammed attended his class this morning.

12. The reason my parents and brother called was that he wanted to wish me a happy birthday.

13. Anyone who has a question about their paper should see me after class.

14. A few of my friends have questions on their papers.

15. Some of the instructors have office hours posted on his or her door.

16. One of the instructors offers coffee to her students who visit during office hours.

17. Some of the fruit is expensive because it is out of season.

18. My committee decided to revise the bylaws, but it took us about a month.

      Determine which items you missed in this Diagnostic Activity. If you missed or had trouble with any of the items, please go to the appropriate section in *The HarperCollins Concise Handbook for Writers* and this workbook for further practice and study.

      It is important to know which pronoun agreement principles cause you difficulty. When revising your writing, you might want to go through your paper one time checking only for pronoun agreement or reference. Concentrate on items that you had difficulty with in this activity.

Let us review the basic principles of pronoun agreement and then discuss other special situations.

18b BASIC PRONOUN AGREEMENT

A pronoun must agree with its antecedent in number, in person, and in gender. In the following sentences, the editing shows changes necessary to make sure that the pronouns agree with their antecedents in all three ways. The antecedent in each sentence is underlined once, and the pronoun is underlined twice.

Number

Pronouns must agree with their antecedents in number: if the antecedent is singular, the pronoun must be singular; if the antecedent is plural, the pronoun must be plural.

                                         he
Julio worked until ten every night at a record store, but ~~they~~ still came to class every morning at eight.

                                         her
Ms. Gardner, his boss, asked him to manage the store for ~~them~~.

Person

Pronouns must agree with their antecedents in person (first person, second person, or third person).

                                     he or she
Ms. Gardner preferred a strong manager because ~~you~~ often had to close the store alone late at night.

Employees never like to be promoted because of some kind of favoritism or bias on the part of
their
~~your~~ boss.

Gender

Pronouns must agree with their antecedents in gender.

Julio talked to ~~her~~ ^{his} mother about the possible promotion.

His mother pointed out that the manager's <u>position</u> would involve many additional hours of work and that ~~she~~ ^{it} did not include a raise in pay.

ACTIVITY 18.2   Editing for Number, Person, and Gender

The following letter contains six errors in basic pronoun agreement. Find and correct these errors.

Dear Acme Company Customer Service Representative:

Recently, I purchased one of your company's products, the Handy Dandy Kitchen Tool. The Acme Company advertised that a person doesn't need to spend their precious evenings cooking. Acme guaranteed that this product would save valuable time in the kitchen.

I am a working mother who wants to spend his free time relaxing with his children. When I bought your product, my husband laughed at me. She said that the product was a waste of money. I want to inform you that my husband was wrong! I use the Handy Dandy Kitchen Tool every day and have more time to spend with your children.

People should try your product. I think he will be pleasantly surprised!

Thanks, Acme Company!

Sincerely,

A Happy Customer

18c AVOIDING SEXISM WITH PRONOUNS

Sexism in the use of pronouns can be eliminated in three ways.

He or She

A writer should think for a while before ~~he~~ *he or she* starts to write.

Thoughtful writers no longer use *he* to refer to an antecedent that may in fact be male or female. Instead, they refer to both sexes, using *he or she*. However, the phrase *he or she* can be awkward, especially when used repeatedly in a short piece of prose.

Plural

Sometimes, however, the best way for a writer*s* to think is to start writing and see what ideas come to ~~him~~ *them*.

Here the sexism in the original sentence has been eliminated by changing the singular *writer* to the plural and using the plural pronoun *them*, which does not indicate any gender.

No Pronouns

A writer should use the technique that makes it possible ~~for him~~ to come up with good ideas.

In this example, the words *for him* were deleted, making the sentence more concise and eliminating the need to use any pronoun at all.

ACTIVITY

18.3 Three Methods of Avoiding Sexism with Pronouns

The use of pronouns in the following sentences is sexist. Rewrite each sentence in three ways, using each of the methods described in 18c to eliminate sexism.

1. I believe that each citizen should volunteer to help clean up his neighborhood.

   a. _____

   b. _____

   c. _____

2. A teacher must have her credentials to teach in the public school system.

   a. _____

   b. _____

   c. _____

ACTIVITY

18.4   Eliminating Sexism in Writing

Here is a business memorandum. Revise the memo, eliminating sexism where necessary by using the three methods mentioned in 18c.

To: All employees

From: Frank Richardson, Manager of Human Resources, Peachtree Corporation

Re: Promotion procedure

Date: May 20, 1995

Recently, many questions have been asked regarding promotion possibilities at Peachtree Corporation. The following is the promotion procedure used at Peachtree:

1. All positions are posted on the Human Resources Bulletin Board.
2. If an employee is interested in a position, he must complete an application form.
3. When applying for a position, each employee should bring his employment identification card.
4. An employee will be required to interview for the desired position, and his department manager will notify him of the outcome.

Where possible, Peachtree Corporation has always tried to promote from within the company. We encourage professional advancement for all employees. If you have any additional questions, please contact me at extension 9801.

18d PRONOUN AGREEMENT WITH COMPOUND ANTECEDENTS

The following sentences have been edited to reflect the basic rules for pronoun agreement with compound antecedents. Antecedents are underlined once, and pronouns are underlined twice.

Compound Antecedents Joined with *And*

Compound antecedents joined with *and* are plural if they refer to more than one person or thing:

W. E. B. Du Bois and Booker T. Washington wrote books in which ~~he~~ *they* described the African-American experience in the early years of the twentieth century.

They are singular if both nouns apply to a single person or item:

The author and educator spoke frequently to audiences in the North and the South, but ~~their~~ *his* book *Up from Slavery* was what really made ~~them~~ *him* famous.

Compound Antecedents Joined with *or* or *nor*

Singular antecedents joined with *or* or *nor* require singular pronouns appropriate to all persons or items mentioned:

Du Bois agreed that a man or a woman could be free only if ~~they~~ *he or she* were educated.

his
Neither Du Bois nor Washington believed that ~~their~~ people were being educated satisfactorily.

Plural antecedents require plural pronouns:

they
Washington argued that men or women should be educated so that ~~he or she~~ could perform useful work.

If both singular and plural words are joined by *or* or *nor,* the pronoun refers to the one that is closest to the pronoun:

Du Bois argued that neither the teacher nor the students should be satisfied if the final goal of
their
~~his or her~~ work was simply a job and the income that it would provide.

Du Bois argued that neither the students nor the teacher should be satisfied if the final goal of
his or her
~~their~~ work was simply a job and the income that it would provide.

ACTIVITY

18.5 | **Editing for Pronoun Agreement with Compound Antecedents**

Read the following sentences, underlining each complete antecedent once and each pronoun twice. Correct any errors in pronoun agreement. Not all sentences contain errors. An example is provided.

their
Example: Either Peter or his parents will loan you ~~his~~ car for the weekend.

1. My grandfather and grandmother were taught the meaning of hard work and honesty when he was young.

2. Aunt Helen and Uncle Gene sold the house in which he lived for over twenty years.

3. Neither dogs nor cats enjoy baths, even if they like water.

4. My mentor and friend is a hardworking person who enjoys their career immensely.

5. Roses or tulips are wonderful anniversary gifts because they are beautiful.

6. Employees and spouses will receive his or her invitation in the mail.

7. Waffles or an omelet is part of a good breakfast because they contain carbohydrates.

8. It is important that students receive an education so that he or she can be productive members of society.

9. Either my parents or my older sister will drive me to the airport when they return from work.

10. My husband and son couldn't attend the party because they went to a baseball game.

18e PRONOUN AGREEMENT WITH INDEFINITE PRONOUN ANTECEDENTS

There are three ways to correct an error involving pronoun agreement with indefinite pronouns, as illustrated by the revisions of the following sentence:

INCORRECT: Everyone should bring their disks to class this week.

You can change the pronoun to a singular form:

CORRECT: Everyone should bring his or her disks to class this week.

You can change the antecedent to a plural form:

CORRECT: All students should bring their disks to class this week.

Or you can recast the sentence so that no pronoun is needed:

CORRECT: Everyone should bring some disks to class this week.

Some indefinite pronouns are always singular. The most common indefinite pronouns are listed in the chart in 17l.

ACTIVITY

18.6 Revising Sentences for Pronoun Agreement with Singular Indefinite Pronoun Antecedents

The following sentences contain indefinite pronouns that are always singular. Pronoun agreement in these sentences is incorrect. Rewrite each sentence using the three methods suggested in 18e.

1. Anybody who knows how to cook should volunteer their time to the food drive.

    a. _____

    b. _____

    c. _____

2. Each of the students in this class will write their next paper using a computer.

    a. _____

    b. _____

    c. _____

3. Anybody who has questions about the computer will have a chance to ask those questions as they work on their papers.

    a. _____

    b. _____

    c. _____

A few indefinite pronouns are always plural (see the chart in 17l). These pronouns are not difficult to recognize because their plural sense is quite obvious.

A few of the students in this class have used computers in ~~his or her~~ *their* writing before.

Several of these students have volunteered to share ~~his or her~~ *their* expertise with anyone who is having trouble.

Another group of indefinite pronouns can be either singular or plural (see the chart in 17l). Study the following sentences, and see if you can determine when the indefinite pronouns are singular and when they are plural. Antecedents are underlined once, pronouns twice.

Singular: Some of the writing is quite good, but it is not very effective because of the frequent grammar errors.

Plural: Some of the students will write their papers on IBM computers.

Singular: All of the paper is already gone, and it was very expensive.

Plural: All of the Macintoshes have hard disks built into them.

Singular: Most of my day was spent dealing with customer complaints; it was very long!

Plural: Most of the IBMs have a hard drive, and they have black-and-white monitors.

If you concluded that the indefinite pronoun is singular or plural depending on the noun in the following prepositional phrase, you were correct! Go back to the sentences, putting parentheses around the prepositional phrases. This will make it easier to see whether the indefinite pronoun is singular or plural.

The chart in 17l lists all the indefinite pronouns and specifies whether they are always singular, always plural, or variable, depending on the context.

ACTIVITY

18.7 **Revising Sentences for Pronoun Agreement with Indefinite Pronoun Antecedents**

Read each sentence, underlining the indefinite pronoun twice, the antecedent once, and the pronoun three times. Check to see if the antecedent agrees with the indefinite pronoun. If it does not, revise the sentence so that it does agree. An example is provided. If you change the pronoun, you may also need to change the verb.

> *Example:* Some of the computers are Macintoshes, but ~~it is~~ *they are* kept in another computer room.

1. All of my sisters are coming home for the holidays; she will be traveling great distances.

2. Most of the books in the library are out of date; they do not provide the information needed to complete my research.

3. Much of my second language, Spanish, was taught by my mother; it was her native language.

4. None of the local television stations have female broadcasters; I wonder if it is violating the equal employment opportunity regulations.

5. Half of my breakfast remained on my plate; they were not very good!

6. Several journalists used their recorders during the press conference.

18f PRONOUN REFERENCE

Make sure that a pronoun has one clear antecedent:

INCORRECT: My brother gave Mr. Williams a package before *he* left.

It is not clear whether *he* refers to *brother* or *Mr. Williams*.

CORRECT: Before my brother left, he gave Mr. Williams a package.

Look at another example.

INCORRECT: My committee decided to revise the bylaws, but *it* took us about a month.

Does *it* refer to deciding on the revision or actually doing it?

CORRECT: My committee decided to revise the bylaws, but the revision took us about a month.

Avoid using pronouns with an implied antecedent:

INCORRECT: After we camped in Baxter State Park this weekend, I knew *it* was something I would like to do more often.

It seems to refer to *camping*, but *camping* isn't mentioned in the sentence; it is merely implied.

CORRECT: After we camped in Baxter State Park this weekend, I knew *camping* was something I would like to do more often.

Avoid placing pronouns far from their antecedents:

INCORRECT: Richard Wright wrote a powerful autobiographical novel called *Black Boy*, *who* was a leading figure in the Harlem Renaissance.

The pronoun *who* is so far from its antecedent that it is difficult for the reader to figure out what the antecedent is.

CORRECT: Richard Wright, *who* was a leading figure in the Harlem Renaissance, wrote a powerful autobiographical novel called *Black Boy*.

ACTIVITY

18.8 Identifying Pronoun Referents

Read the following passage. For each double-underlined pronoun, draw an arrow to the noun or noun phrase it refers to, and underline that antecedent. The first item has been done for you as an example.

Monterey is a city with a long and brilliant literary tradition. It remembers with pleasure and some glory that Robert Louis Stevenson lived there. More recently in Carmel there have been a great number of literary men about, but there is not the old flavor, the old dignity of the true belles-lettres.

Where the new post office is, there used to be a deep gulch with water flowing in it and a little foot bridge over it. On one side of the gulch was a fine old adobe and on the other the house of a doctor who handled all the sickness, birth, and death in the town. He worked with animals too and, having studied in France, he even dabbled in the new practice of embalming bodies before they were buried. Some of the old-timers considered this sentimental and some thought it wasteful and to some it was sacrilegious since there was no provision for it in any sacred volume. But the better and richer families were coming around to the idea and it looked to become a fad. [John Steinbeck, *Cannery Row*]

ACTIVITY 18.9   Editing for Pronoun Reference Errors

Edit the following sentences for pronoun reference errors. Indicate in the blank the type of pronoun problem involved, using the following key:

     a. lack of a single clear antecedent
     b. lack of an explicit antecedent
     c. placement too far from the antecedent

_____ 1. The car sped and turned from the dangerous oncoming vehicle, but it managed to pull away.

_____ 2. Dina and Bill decided to move back to Minneapolis, but it took them almost three months.

_____ 3. When André took his nephews to the Vail ski area, he knew it was something they would like to do again.

_____ 4. When Abdul went to Erfan's house for dinner, he told him that he wasn't hungry.

_____ 5. Francisco thought about staying at his job in Seville or moving to Chicago, but he decided against it.

18g   PRONOUN AGREEMENT AND REFERENCE: COMPREHENSIVE CHECK

ACTIVITY 18.10   Diagnostic Retest

Complete Activity 18.1 again. If you still miss or have difficulty with any items, review the relevant sections of the workbook.

ACTIVITY 18.11   Putting It All Together

Read the following passage about careers in robotics, and find the errors in pronoun agreement and reference. Rewrite the passage, incorporating your corrections.

       Veteran robot expert Roy Morley, a senior development engineer in Peoria, Illinois, has been interested in it since he was a robot in her fifth-grade Halloween parade. A certified robotic engineer, Morley has been with his company for twenty-seven years.

His first full-time assignment was to locate the best place for the company to install its first robot. At that time, the robot was required to work with a heat treatment furnace—it got as high as 1,500 degrees Fahrenheit.

Getting the robot operational wasn't easy. Morley recalls having to rearrange the plant area to make room for him and planning his functions carefully. Intensive job analysis was another of their responsibilities. He not only wrote the programs for the robot but also trained the operators.

More than twenty years after the first installation, Morley is still enthusiastic about robots. Now that he's helping her daughter choose a college and a career, Morley suggests strongly that everyone who is considering working with robotics tour industrial plants, research labs, and manufacturing environments as much as possible while they are still in high school. He especially recommends summer career institutes in engineering like those offered by the Bradley Institute, which give young people a chance to take field trips and meet industry leaders.

He points out that new engineering graduates are rotated through company assignments for one to two years, and they take on a variety of company projects so that company managers can evaluate how well they do on the jobs. "Every man and woman is rated on their initiative, desire, quality, and quantity of work," he says. "It's better to have as broad an engineering background as possible, rather than just a specialty in robotics." [Adapted from Jan Bone, *Opportunities in Robotics Careers.*]

FINDING AND REVISING PRONOUN CASE ERRORS

Changing the form of a pronoun to indicate how it is functioning in a sentence is what we mean by pronoun **case.** In English, there are only three cases:

Subjective: *I* am going to the movies.

Objective: Hand that stapler to *me.*

Possessive: That is *my* stapler.

In English, only the pronouns *I, we, he, she, they,* and *who* have different forms of all three cases. Other pronouns and all nouns have only subjective and possessive forms.

19a DIAGNOSTIC ACTIVITY: PRONOUN CASE

ACTIVITY
19.1 **How Much Do You Know?**

Read each sentence to determine if it sounds awkward or is ungrammatical. If so, correct it. Not all sentences require revision. An example is provided.

> *Example:* Warren knows how to fix the car, but he won't tell ~~I~~ *me*.

1. Boyd asked her to give he a break.

2. Even though operas are long, they are very beautiful.

3. The person who will be president is her.

4. It was I who broke the window.

5. Sam was convinced that both he and them had played terribly in the baseball game.

6. Just between you and me, Sandra took the teacher's pen.

7. The greatest fishermen, Rodney and me, caught more than twenty bass yesterday.

8. Save some food for your best friend, I.

9. We women have to work harder than ever these days.

10. It is clear that us liberals are a minority.

11. Mohammad can run faster than me.

12. Bernard can't write as well as I.

13. Violet liked the man whom was wearing the red hat.

14. My aunt Marilyn, who is a feminist, is very involved.

15. Who did you write to?

      Determine which items you missed in this Diagnostic Activity. If you missed or had trouble with any of the items, please go to the appropriate section in *The HarperCollins Concise Handbook for Writers* and this workbook for further practice and study.

      It is important to know which items cause you difficulty. When revising your writing, you might want to go through your paper one time checking only for pronoun case errors. Concentrate on items that you have difficulty with in this activity.

19b SUBJECTS VERSUS OBJECTS

The chart shows the subjective, objective, and possessive case forms for pronouns that have both subjective and objective forms.

FORMS FOR PRONOUN CASE

Subjective	Objective	Possessive
I	me	my, mine
he	him	his
she	her	her, hers
we	us	our, ours
they	them	their, theirs
who	whom	whose
whoever	whomever	

      The basic principle for choosing between subjective and objective cases is relatively clear-cut.

Subjective Case

A pronoun used as the subject must be in the subjective case.

SUBJECTIVE: *She* is not sure what kind of job *she* wants.

She is the subject of each verb with which the pronoun is used; hence it is in the subjective case.

SUBJECTIVE: *She* wanted to be an architect when *she* was younger.

She is also the subject of the dependent clause, so the pronoun is in the subjective case.

Objective Case

A pronoun used as a direct object, an indirect object, or the object of a preposition must be in the objective case.

OBJECTIVE: I urged *her* to think it over carefully.

Because *her* is the direct object in the sentence, the pronoun is in the objective case.

OBJECTIVE: I also asked my mother to talk to *her*.

Since *her* is the object of the preposition *to*, the pronoun is in the objective case.

ACTIVITY

19.2   Using Pronouns in the Subjective and Objective Cases

Choose the correct case for the pronoun in each of the following sentences.

> *Example:*   Ellie asked Carol if (she, her) would go to the store.

1. John is the secretary in our office, and only (he, him) is allowed to answer the phone.

2. Kyra and Whiskey were playing, but Kyra wanted to get the ball back from (he, him).

3. It is impossible for (they, them) to attend the party.

4. Although it is dreary, (she, her) decided to go for a walk anyway.

5. Randy wanted to go camping, but (he, him) got sick.

19c   SUBJECTIVE CASE AFTER LINKING VERBS

Use the objective case after action verbs, the subjective case after linking verbs.

LINKING VERB: Even though Elsie didn't think she sang very well, it was <u>she</u> who won the talent contest.

She is a subject complement, not an object, so it is in the subjective case. Subject complements always follow a linking verb.

ACTION VERB: The judges called <u>her</u> to the stage for the award.

Called is an action verb, so *her* is a direct object and is therefore in the objective case.

ACTIVITY

19.3   Using the Subjective Case after Linking Verbs

Read the following sentences. If a linking verb precedes or follows the pronoun, write "L" in the blank; if an action verb, write "A" in the blank. Then circle the correct pronoun and underline the verb.

> *Example:*   Even though the scores on Mrs. Johnson's test were low, (she, her) <u>was</u> proud. __*L*__

1. It was (he, him) who broke the window with the baseball. _____

2. The person who is going to win will be (I, me). _____

3. The music compelled (her, she) to sing along. _____

4. Rudolph admitted that the robber was (he, him). _____

5. We were surprised to learn that the guilty person was (she, her). _____

6. The teacher asked (we, us) to stand up. _____

19d CASE IN COMPOUND STRUCTURES

Even though the same principles that you learned in 19b and 19c apply, some writers have difficulty with sentences like the following:

> *I*
> Franklin and ~~me~~ are going to talk to the dean.

Because the subject is compound, some writers make the error of using *me* instead of *I*. However, since *Franklin and I* is the subject, the subjective case must be used for the pronoun.

A good way to figure out the correct case in sentences with compound constructions is to split the sentence mentally into two sentences without compound structures:

> *Franklin* is going to talk to the dean.
> *I* am going to talk to the dean.

Clearly, it would be incorrect to say, "Me is going to talk to the dean."

Mistakes are even more common with compound constructions involving prepositional phrases, particularly when those phrases come at the beginning of the sentence:

> *her*
> According to Walter and ~~she~~, Julie's house is not for sale.

Because *her* is the object of a preposition, it must be in the objective case. If this sentence is separated to eliminate the compound construction, it becomes clear that the pronoun must be *her*:

> According to Walter, Julie's house is not for sale.
> *her*
> According to ~~she~~, Julie's house is not for sale.

The most frequent error with pronoun case involves the phrase "between you and me":

> *me*
> Just between you and ~~I~~, this restaurant's prices are very reasonable.

Because *me* is the object of the preposition *between*, the pronoun must be in the objective case.

ACTIVITY

19.4 Choosing Correct Pronoun Case in Compound Structures

Edit the following sentences for correct pronoun usage. Some of the sentences are correct. If the sentence is incorrect, supply the correct pronoun.

1. Reynaldo and me are going to the movies tonight.

2. Just between you and I, the food tastes terrible.

3. After class, my friends and me went for a bite to eat.

4. Come with Julie and me to see Paul McCartney in concert.

5. My mother asked my sister and I to help her.

19e CASE IN APPOSITIVES

You will recall that an appositive is a noun that, together with its modifiers, follows another noun and stands for the same person or thing as the first noun.

The case of a pronoun used as an appositive is the same as the noun or pronoun it is in apposition to:

me
Professor Starr gave the book to the only person in the room, ~~I~~.

Me is in apposition to the noun *person*, which is the object of a preposition, so *me* must be in the objective case.

Sometimes compound constructions are used as appositives:

I
The winners, *Janice and ~~me~~,* are going to compete in the national tournament next month.

Because *Janice and I* is in apposition to the subject, *winners,* the pronoun must be in the subjective case.

me
Trophies were presented to the winners, Janice and ~~I~~.

Because *Janice and me* is in apposition to *winners,* the object of the preposition *to,* the pronoun must be in the objective case.

ACTIVITY

19.5 **Using Correct Pronoun Case with Appositives**

Edit the following sentences to ensure that the correct pronoun is used in the appositive. Some of the sentences do not contain errors.

1. The project scientists, Dr. Watson and I, concluded the test results last Friday.

2. The university supplied us, Dr. Watson and me, with a beautiful laboratory.

3. The coaches, Gloria and me, decided to replace the pitcher.

4. My father gave flowers to his favorite daughter, me.

5. The director asked us, Carol and I, to lead the seminar.

19f *WE* AND *US* BEFORE A NOUN

Occasionally in English, the pronouns *we* and *us* are used before a noun for emphasis:

We
~~Us~~ students must insist that the requirements not be changed.

Because *we* is used before the subject *students,* it must be in the subjective case.

                                                                        us
The administration should consider how the new requirements will affect ~~we~~ students.

Here *us* is used before *students,* which is the direct object, so the objective form *us* is correct.

When *we* or *us* is used before a noun, its form must correspond to the case of that noun.

ACTIVITY

19.6 **Using Pronoun Case Correctly in Sentences with *we* and *us* before a Noun**

Fill in the blanks with either *we* or *us,* as appropriate.

1. Because our health insurance was canceled, _____ workers must strike.

2. The union will decide the best plan to help _____ workers.

3. Employment issues have come a long way for _____ minorities, but we must continue to fight.

4. _____ minorities demand equal pay.

5. _____ teachers work hard with little pay.

19g CASE IN SENTENCES WITH *THAN* AND *AS*

                                                    I
Wilson can swim better than ~~me~~.

Notice that this sentence really means the following:

Wilson can swim better than I (can swim).

The phrase *can swim* is not actually written following the final pronoun, but it is understood to be there. Once you add this phrase, it is clear that the pronoun should be *I.*

In sentences that make a comparison using *than* or *as,* the phrase that would be repeated is often omitted, but it is understood to be there. To figure out whether to use the subjective or objective form of the pronoun, mentally fill in the understood phrase; that will usually make the correct form clear:

                                                    I
Wilson is not as good a student as ~~me~~.

When the understood word *am* is supplied, it becomes clear that the pronoun should be the subjective *I.*

In sentences with *as* and *than,* the choice of a pronoun can greatly affect meaning. Notice the difference in the meaning of these sentences:

Wilson likes Vivian better than *I.*
Wilson likes Vivian better than *me.*

This is what these sentences actually mean:

Wilson likes Vivian better than I (like Vivian).
Wilson likes Vivian better than (he likes) me.

Mentally filling in the understood phrase in a comparison lets you select the correct form of the pronoun.

ACTIVITY

19.7 Using the Correct Form of the Pronoun in Sentences with *Than* and *As*

To decide if the correct form of the pronoun is used, fill in the phrase that is not actually written but understood to be there. Then correct the pronoun if necessary.

Example: I can't believe my little brother is stronger than ~~me~~ (_____am_____). *I*

1. Although he is fine, Tom can't cook as well as me (_____).

2. Chen-ling is smarter than me (_____).

3. My sister envies my brother more than (_____) me.
   My sister envies my brother more than I (_____).

4. Wally and Sandy are best friends, but she is stronger than he (_____).

5. Rover's whining annoys him more than I (_____).
   Rover's whining annoys him more than (_____) me.

19h *WHO* AND *WHOM, WHOEVER* AND *WHOMEVER*

The distinction between *who* and *whom* and between *whoever* and *whomever* has become less important, especially in spoken language. Still, in certain formal speaking and writing situations, it is necessary to choose the correct form. This choice occurs primarily in subordinate clauses and in questions.

To decide which form to use, follow these principles:

1. Use *who* or *whoever* in the subjective case, *whom* or *whomever* in the objective case.
2. Determine how the pronoun is being used *in its clause.*

Activity 19.8 will help you learn to use these pronouns correctly.

ACTIVITY

19.8 Determining When to Use *who* and *whom*

Study the following sentences. Then answer the questions after each.

1. Donald Johanson, *who/whom* is a paleontologist, discovered Lucy, the world's most famous fossil.

   a. What is the subordinate clause in this sentence? _____

   b. Insert a personal pronoun *(he, she, him, her)* in place of *who/whom:* _____

    c. Does this personal pronoun act as a subject or an object?_____

    d. So which is the correct pronoun, *who* or *whom?*_____

2. Johanson showed the fossil to Richard Leakey, *who/whom* he admired.

    a. What is the subordinate clause in this sentence? _____

    b. Insert a personal pronoun *(he, she, him, her)* in place of *who/whom:* _____

    c. Does this personal pronoun act as a subject or an object?_____

    d. So which is the correct pronoun, *who* or *whom?*_____

3. Leakey, *who/whom* people often showed fossils to, was not impressed.

    a. What is the subordinate clause in this sentence? _____

    b. Insert a personal pronoun *(he, she, him, her)* in place of *who/whom:* _____

    c. Does this personal pronoun act as a subject or an object?_____

    d. So which is the correct pronoun, *who* or *whom?*_____

ACTIVITY

19.9   **Choosing between *who and whom, whoever* and *whomever***

Using the method you learned in Activity 19.8, fill in *who, whom, whoever, or whomever* in the blank.

1. Quinton was nice to the man _____ walked into his office.

2. Are those the people _____ you asked for directions?

3. He acted like a man _____ was crazy.

4. She was the person to _____ I was speaking.

5. _____ is interested in receiving a brochure should contact the agency.

19i CASE BEFORE A GERUND

You will recall that a gerund is a form of the verb ending in *-ing* that is used as a noun.

        his
We didn't even hear ~~him~~ whistling until he stopped.

In this sentence, *whistling* is a gerund. When pronouns modify gerunds, the possessive case is used. In this sentence, the possessive form *his* is correct.

           's
We didn't even hear Gerald/whistling until he stopped.

Notice that we also use the possessive case for nouns that are modifying gerunds. In this case, the noun *Gerald's* is modifying *whistling,* so it is in the possessive case.

The objective case may on occasion be used before a gerund if the meaning requires it. Consider the difference in meaning between the next two sentences:

The teacher didn't notice *him* sleeping in the back of the room.

The teacher didn't notice *his* sleeping in the back of the room.

In the first sentence, the teacher didn't notice *him*. In the second sentence, what the teacher didn't notice was the fact that he was sleeping. When the emphasis is on the person rather than the action, it is correct to use the objective rather than the possessive case. Be aware, however, that such instances are extremely rare.

ACTIVITY

19.10 **Using Pronoun Case Correctly with Gerunds**

Circle the appropriate pronoun depending on whether the sentence is focused on the person or on the action.

> *Example:* My boyfriend likes my dog, but he is annoyed with ((his), him) barking. (action)

1. The editor thought that (him, his) writing was good. (action)

2. The woman found (us, our) laughing too loud. (action)

3. The priest was upset about (them, their) lying. (person)

4. The spectators said that (his, him) diving was elegant. (action)

5. The doctor didn't like (them, their) running. (person)

19j PRONOUN CASE: COMPREHENSIVE CHECK

ACTIVITY

19.11 **Diagnostic Retest**

Complete Activity 19.1 again. If you still miss or have difficulty with any items, review the relevant sections of the workbook.

ACTIVITY

19.12 **Putting It All Together**

Read the following passage, correcting all errors involving pronoun case.

> The eldest daughter, Rose, is a big husky girl of twenty-one, the "big sister" of the family, the mother's constant companion and helper, a robust creature full of hilarity and vigor and warmth. Her possesses a large and generous nature. She

walks around the kitchen with the heavy steps of a pachyderm that make the dishes in the pantry rattle and jingle, and she hauls in the wash in huge baskets from the yard. When her favorite brother, whom is Joe, comes home from him constant wanderings, she yells and chases he around the house. Joe is faster than her.

The few boyfriends who she goes out with are all big husky creatures like she whom work on farms or drive trucks or handle the heavy work in factories. When one of them cuts his finger or burns his hand, she and him sit down and she administers the necessary aid and scolds he furiously. She is the first member of the family to get up in the morning, and the last in bed. As far back as her can remember, she has been a "big sister." At dusk, we, my other sister and me, can see her standing in the yard taking down her wash, packing it in baskets, and starting back to the porch. [Adapted from Jack Kerouac, *The Town and the City*]

 # FINDING AND REVISING ADJECTIVE AND ADVERB ERRORS

Because adjectives and adverbs perform similar functions in sentences, some writers have difficulty with them. Both adjectives and adverbs modify other words or groups of words. The term *modify* covers a number of similar functions: to describe (a *yellow* dress; walking *slowly*), to identify (the *first* customer), to quantify (*three* mistakes), to intensify (a *very* large spider), to limit (*slightly* damaged), or to place in time (arrived *early*). In this chapter you will learn to distinguish between adjectives and adverbs and to use them correctly in various situations. You will also learn about several special problems with adjectives and adverbs.

The first chart summarizes the forms of regular and irregular adjectives and adverbs.

FORMS OF ADJECTIVES AND ADVERBS			
Regular		**Irregular**	
Adjective Form	**Adverb Form**	**Adjective Form**	**Adverb Form**
angry	angrily	good	well
beautiful	beautifully	fast	fast
perfect	perfectly	hard	hard
quick	quickly	late	late
rapid	rapidly	lovely	—
		—	here
		—	very
		—	often

20a DIAGNOSTIC ACTIVITY: ADJECTIVES AND ADVERBS

ACTIVITY

20.1 **How Much Do You Know?**

Read the sentences carefully to see if there is an adjective or adverb error. If so, correct it.

bad
Example: Naomi was ~~badly~~ in class today.

1. Annette does her work very good.

2. Since his accident, Darnell thinks different about his life.

3. The dog went in the water, and now she smells badly!

4. Mrs. Applebee was curious about her new neighbors.

5. Larry is more bigger than Jeff.

6. Stephanie was more pregnant than Allison.

7. Thad always arrived to class earliest.

8. I know I won't be dissatisfied with the meal.

9. I don't understand nothing about nuclear energy.

10. Kaye tells always the truth.

Determine which items you missed in this Diagnostic Activity. If you missed or had difficulty with any of the items, please go to the appropriate section in *The HarperCollins Concise Handbook for Writers* and this workbook for further practice and study.

It is important to know which adjective and adverb errors cause you difficulty. When revising your writing, you might want to go through your paper one time checking only for adjective and adverb errors. Concentrate on items that you had difficulty with in this activity.

20b DISTINGUISHING BETWEEN ADJECTIVES AND ADVERBS

Although both adjectives and adverbs serve as modifiers in sentences, the parts of speech they can modify are completely distinct: adjectives modify only nouns or pronouns, and adverbs modify only verbs, adjectives, or other adverbs. It is also possible to distinguish between adjectives and adverbs by the questions they answer. The accompanying chart summarizes these differences.

ADJECTIVES AND ADVERBS

Words Modified	Example	Questions Answered
Adjectives		
Nouns	*contemporary* novelist	What kind?
Nouns	*first* novel	Which?
Nouns	*one* novel	How many?
Pronouns	it was very *interesting*	What kind?
Nouns	the hero, completely *alone*	What kind?
Nouns	made the *young* man *tense*	What kind?
Adverbs		
Verbs	*nervously* gives a speech	How? In what manner?
Adjectives	*exceedingly* cruel	To what degree?
Other adverbs	*very* innocently	To what degree?
Verbs	arrives *there*	Where?
Verbs	*then* he moves	When?
Verbs	he *frequently* thought	How often?
Clauses	*Unfortunately*, he was unable . . .	How? In what manner?

ACTIVITY 20.2 **Identifying and Using the Correct Form of Adjectives and Adverbs**

A.   In the following paragraph, underline each adjective and adverb. Write "Adj." above the word if it is an adjective and "Adv." above the word if it is an adverb.

> The sun has just gone down. I am sitting alone on a smooth log that is slightly moist from the previous rainstorm. I sit quietly, taking in the sights around me. It is a place I often come to at this time of the day. In front of me is a lake that is still, except for the few ripples where fish are eagerly eating their dinner. Suddenly, a bird calls out above me. It is the cry of a lonely raven, perhaps looking for its mate. The sky is still light, and the clouds are moving swiftly. There is a warm glow that only this time of day can provide. It is intensely beautiful, and I am peaceful.

B.   Read the following paragraph, circling the correct choice of adjective or adverb.

> When Berlin was carved up in 1945, the old city center, with its bombed-out churches, palaces, and museums, fell into the eastern section. Most of the buildings in West Berlin were less than a century old. After the split, the two Berlins went their own ways, a course made (striking/strikingly) permanent in 1961 by the building of the Berlin Wall. It gave visitors a (special/specially) chance to compare the workings of capitalism and socialism side by side. Access was (surprising/surprisingly) easy. Tourists (constant/constantly) bouncing back and forth from the west to the east were left with conflicting impressions. Today, tourists are given an even more (unique/uniquely) opportunity to see the (considerable/considerably) changes in the (new/newly) unified Germany. Because these changes are happening so (quick/quickly), tourists are sure to get a (different/differently) but very (interesting/interestingly) view of life in Berlin. [Adapted from David Stanley, *Eastern Europe on a Shoestring*]

20c USING ADJECTIVES AFTER LINKING VERBS

Linking verbs (forms of the verb **be** and sensory verbs) link the subject of the sentence with something that comes after the verb. Look at the following sentences, all of which contain adverbs:

CORRECT: Naomi behaved *badly* in class today.

INCORRECT: Naomi was *badly* in class today.

CORRECT: Phillip acted *seriously* in the situation.

INCORRECT: Phillip was *seriously* in the situation.

Can you see the difference between the correct and incorrect sentences? The incorrect sentences use a linking verb; the correct sentences use an action verb. Adverbs are used to modify action verbs, whereas adjectives are needed with linking verbs.

Based on this rule, is the following sentence correct or incorrect?

Naomi feels badly about the way she had behaved.

It is incorrect because *feel* is a linking verb, which requires an adjective, not an adverb.

Writers can become confused sometimes because sensory linking verbs can also be used as action verbs.

Because it was dark, we didn't really *look* well for the hubcap last night.

Here *look* is an action verb; it is describing something we did—using our eyes to examine the ground for a hubcap.

We *look* good in our tuxedos.

Here the same verb, *look*, is being used as a linking verb. Notice that we are not talking about our using our eyes to search for something; in fact, *we* are not "doing" anything. Instead, a statement is being made about our appearance—the way we look or appear to others.

To help you tell the difference, remember that when *look* is used as an action verb, it is always followed by the word *for* or *at*. When *look* is a linking verb, it is not accompanied by *for* or *at*.

ACTIVITY
20.3   **Recognizing Linking and Action Verbs with Adjectives and Adverbs**

Decide if the following sensory verbs are operating as linking verbs or as action verbs. Underline the sensory verb, and write "L" in the blank if it is a linking verb or "A" if it is an action verb. Adjectives and adverbs in the sentences will give you clues.

1. Mother smelled the milk to see if it was sour. _____

2. The dinner smelled wonderful. _____

3. Cassandra touched the soft, luxurious carpet. _____

4. Raoul was touched deeply by the opera. _____

5. He carefully tasted the hot soup. _____

6. The soup tastes wonderful. _____

ACTIVITY
20.4   **Common Mistakes with Adjectives and Adverbs Used with Linking and Action Verbs**

Circle the appropriate word of each pair in the following sentences.

1. Mary sang the song so (sad/sadly).

2. Ionia felt (bad/badly) about spilling coffee on my dress.

3. My sister looked especially (bad/badly) after the accident.

4. The food tastes (real/really) (good/well) at my favorite restaurant.

5. Getting a good night's sleep is important to doing (good/well) on exams.

20d USING COMPARATIVE AND SUPERLATIVE FORMS

Most adjectives and adverbs have alternative forms that are used for making comparisons.

Julio is *tall*.

Here we use the regular form of the adjective *tall* because no comparison is being made.

Of the two men in my chemistry class, Julio is the *taller*.

Here we are using a form known as the **comparative** because we are comparing *two* items: the two men in the chemistry class.

Of the six men in my chemistry class, Julio is the *tallest*.

This time we have used a form called the **superlative** because we are comparing more than two items—in this case, six.

COMPARATIVE AND SUPERLATIVE FORMS OF ADJECTIVES AND ADVERBS

Regular	Comparative	Superlative
Short adjectives		
big	bigger	biggest
smart	smarter	smartest
early	earlier	earliest
Long adjectives		
beautiful	more beautiful	most beautiful
terrible	more terrible	most terrible
Adverbs		
carefully	more carefully	most carefully
sadly	more sadly	most sadly
soon	sooner	soonest

Regular adjectives and adverbs form the comparative and the superlative in fairly predictable ways. Comparatives of adjectives are formed by adding an *-er* ending to the regular form; superlatives are formed by adding an *-est* ending. Note, however, that this applies only to adjectives and adverbs that are one syllable long and to two-syllable adjectives ending in *-y*. For longer adjectives and adverbs (and all adverbs ending in *-ly*), form the comparative by placing the word *more* before the adjective or adverb. Form the superlative by using the word *most*.

The principle that short adjectives and adverbs add *-er* and *-est* is generally true, but there are many exceptions. In addition, many two-syllable adverbs take *more* or *most* rather than the *-er* and *-est* endings. If you are in doubt, consult a dictionary. If the word takes the *-er* and *-est* endings, these forms will appear in the definition; otherwise, use the words *more* and *most*.

It is also possible to compare things downward, as the accompanying chart shows. And as the chart after that demonstrates, a small group of fairly common adjectives and adverbs form their comparatives and superlatives in irregular ways.

DOWNWARD COMPARISON OF ADJECTIVES AND ADVERBS

Regular	Comparative	Superlative
Adjectives		
expensive	less expensive	least expensive
impressive	less impressive	least impressive
Adverbs		
hurriedly	less hurriedly	least hurriedly
angrily	less angrily	least angrily

FORMS OF IRREGULAR ADJECTIVES AND ADVERBS

Regular	Comparative	Superlative
Adjectives		
good	better	best
bad	worse	worst
many	more	most
much	more	most
some	more	most
little	less, littler	least, littlest
Adverbs		
well	better	best
badly	worse	worst
little	less	least

Although there are two different ways to form comparatives and superlatives and there are even some words like *steady* that can be formed either way *(steady, steadier, steadiest or steady, more steady, most steady)*, it is never correct to combine both forms for the same word, as you can see from the following sentence.

She was a ~~more~~ steadier player than he was.

The following pairs illustrate another possible problem with adjectives.

dead	*but not*	more dead
infinite	*but not*	more infinite

You probably find that the comparative forms in the right-hand column sound odd. That's because it is just not logical to say that someone is *more dead. Dead* is an absolute concept—either you are dead or you aren't. The same is true of *infinite*—it means "unlimited" or "without bound." If something is *unlimited,* it has *no* limits, so it would be impossible for something else to be *more limitless.* Other absolute adjectives include *blind, empty, fatal, impossible, perfect, pregnant, unique, and wrong.* In speech and casual writing, some writers persist in comparing these terms (often for dramatic or comic effect), even though to do so defies logic. To be formally correct, however, you should avoid using the comparative or superlative of absolute adjectives.

ACTIVITY

20.5 Choosing the Correct Form of Comparatives and Superlatives

Read the following paragraph about demographic trends in the world. Decide if a comparative or a superlative is needed in each blank. If so, write the correct term in the blank. All comparisons are upward *(more)* rather than downward *(less)*.

Demographic trends are fairly predictable and provide a good basis for the analysis of structural change and the associated economic and social policy issues of the next decade. Against a background of generally _____ (slow) population growth resulting in a world population of 6 billion just before the turn of the century, there will be considerable regional diversity. The _____ (fast) growth (an annual rate of 3 percent) will occur in Africa, where the task of economic recovery and restoration of self-sustained growth will be particularly difficult. There will be, however, less diversity in labor force growth rates in the developing world, averaging 2.5 to 3 percent. In contrast, labor force growth rates in developed countries will be less than 1 percent. Employment is _____ (likely) to grow _____ (slow) than the labor force in most countries, and unemployment will be a concern for all groups of countries. Urban population in the developing countries will continue to grow even _____ (fast) than total population, as large numbers of people leave rural areas to seek jobs and education. [United Nations, *Global Outlook 2000*]

ACTIVITY

20.6 Using Comparatives and Superlatives

A. Write sentences using the form identified.

Example: tall building (superlative)

The tallest building in the United States is the Sears Tower.

1. good food (superlative)

_____

2. early event (comparative)

_____

3. busy agenda (comparative)

_____

4. much luck (superlative)

_____

5. leaking slowly (comparative)

_____

B. Read the following information about three provinces in Canada. Write a comparative summary of the information.

	QUEBEC	BRITISH COLUMBIA	MANITOBA
Total area	1,648,000 km^2	947,800 km^2	650,000 km^2
Population	6,438,403	2,883,367	1,026,241
Year of admission	1774	1871	1870
Range of elevation	sea level to 4,663 m	sea level to 1,268 m	sea level to 832 m
Highest point	Mount Fairweather	Mount Jacques Cartier	Baldy Mountain
Largest city	Montreal (pop. 1,214,352)	Vancouver (pop. 1,268,183)	Winnipeg (pop. 594,551)
Primary economic activity	Manufacturing	Logging	Manufacturing

ACTIVITY

20.7   Editing for Correct Usage of Comparatives and Superlatives

Edit the following sentences so that the comparatives and superlatives are used correctly.

1. The backhand in tennis is the most impossible swing.

2. _Dracula_ is the most scariest movie ever made.

3. Konishki is the fatter of all the sumo wrestlers.

4. My puppy was the baddest of all the dogs in the park.

5. Peter was the happiest of the two brothers.

20e   AVOIDING DOUBLE NEGATIVES

The following sentences illustrate another problem some writers have with adjectives and adverbs.

                               anything
I don't understand ~~nothing~~ about nuclear energy.

This sentence contains a **double negative.** The *not* contracted in *don't* conveys a negative meaning, and so does the *no* in *nothing.* These two negatives cancel each other out, conveying the unintended meaning that I do know something.

It does not make ~~no~~ *any* sense to me to produce poisonous materials that we don't know how to dispose of.

Again, the writer intends to say that it doesn't make sense, but the two negatives (*not* and *no*) cancel each other out, conveying the opposite meaning.

There are ten negatives in English: *neither, never, no, nobody, none, no one, nor, not, nothing,* and *nowhere.* In addition, five **frequency adverbs**—*barely, hardly, rarely, scarcely,* and *seldom*—are considered negative and create double negatives when used with each other or with any of the ten negatives:

We can't hardly keep the environment safe as it is, without creating tons of highly toxic materials in nuclear power plants.

Here the *not* in the contraction *can't* cancels out the negative meaning of *hardly,* so that the sentence means that we *can* keep the environment clean, the opposite of the writer's intention.

When an adjective is made negative by a prefix, a double negative is acceptable in English:

I would not be unhappy to learn that all nuclear power plants were being closed down.

Here the two negatives cancel each other out to convey the meaning that I would be happy, which is exactly what the writer intends, so the double negatives are correct.

Thus you may use double negatives when the positive meaning created by the two negatives canceling each other out is what you intend. However, it is more direct and hence usually more effective to use a positive expression rather than two negatives:

I would be very pleased to learn that all nuclear power plants were being closed down.

ACTIVITY

20.8 **Avoiding Double Negatives**

Write the exact meaning of the original sentence. Then revise the sentence to eliminate the double negative and convey the intended meaning.

Example: I couldn't barely get out of bed this morning.

Meaning: *I could get out of bed this morning.*

Revision: *I could barely get out of bed this morning.*

1. Erfan isn't disinterested in history; he prefers geography.

Meaning: _____

Revision: _____

2. The weather doesn't rarely get above 30°C in London.

   Meaning: _____

   Revision: _____

3. Nobody isn't going to the arts and crafts show.

   Meaning: _____

   Revision: _____

4. Kristin's son doesn't never clean his room.

   Meaning: _____

   Revision: _____

20f DETERMINING THE ORDER OF ADVERBS AND ADJECTIVES

Adverbs

The position of adverbs is quite flexible in English:

CORRECT: *Anxiously,* he opened the envelope containing the last letter from Dr. Bledsoe.

CORRECT: He *anxiously* opened the envelope containing the last letter from Dr. Bledsoe.

CORRECT: He opened the envelope containing the last letter from Dr. Bledsoe *anxiously.*

But notice that not *all* positions are acceptable for adverbs:

INCORRECT: He opened *anxiously* the envelope containing the last letter from Dr. Bledsoe.

In general, avoid placing the adverb between the main verb and the direct object.
When a form of *be* is the only verb in the clause, the adverb follows it:

CORRECT: My ankle is *continually* bothering me.

Frequency adverbs are most often placed between the subject and any main verb other than *be*. Note that frequency adverbs *cannot* come between the main verb and the direct object:

CORRECT: The door *always* swings open when it's windy.

INCORRECT: The door swings *always* open when it's windy.

Adjectives

When a series of modifiers comes before a noun, the modifiers should be sequenced according to the accompanying chart. The order is somewhat more flexible than the chart indicates; however, the order shown will generally be correct. For example, you might say *the first expensive wide green felt hat,* but you could not say *the felt green wide expensive first hat.* You might talk about *a simple green picture frame,* but you could never say *a picture simple green frame.*

ORDER OF ADJECTIVES

Determiner	Number	Quality or Characteristic	Size or Shape	age	Color	Other Noun	Main Noun
the	one	expensive	large		green	bamboo	chair
these	six	impressive	small		red	picture	frames
this	first	Swedish	round			dining room	table
a	third		wide		black	automobile	tire
her		simple				felt	hat
Joe's		new				fountain	pen
some		noisy			brown		chickens
many		smart				high school	students

ACTIVITY 20.9   Putting Adjectives and Adverbs in Order

Rewrite the following sentences, putting the adjectives and adverbs in the right order.

1. The queen is wearing a satin, impressive mauve evening gown to the ceremony.

   _____

2. The agent opened carefully the suspicious package.

   _____

3. My mother's scissors seldom are where she expects them.

   _____

4. The movie had a green slimy grotesque small alien in the beginning.

   _____

5. The wicker, small, uncomfortable chair is in the corner.

   _____

20g ADJECTIVES AND ADVERBS: COMPREHENSIVE CHECK

ACTIVITY 20.10   Diagnostic Retest

Complete Activity 20.1 again. If you still miss or have difficulty with any items, review the relevant sections of the workbook.

ACTIVITY
20.11 Putting It All Together

Read the following passage, looking for errors in adverb and adjective form or placement. Rewrite the paragraph, making any necessary revisions.

Most technological gizmos seem extraordinarily for a time, then either go away because nobody doesn't need them (electric knives) or blend into the world of things we take for granted (remote-control television). No one isn't amazed or troubled anymore (as people once were) by the implications of a horseless carriage, a transistor radio, or a personal computer. But isn't it strangely how these plastic, small, impressive answering machines, which are over a quarter-century old, still make a lot of people act so funny?

Some callers are rendered speechless. For many, refusing to leave a message on the tape is a gesture of principle: they consider answering machines a symbol of the fact that the world is becoming less personally. These people believe that personal attention is more dead. Then, too, there are people who experience stage fright when talking to an answering machine. Few other occasions in life call on you to sum up your thoughts and express them clear and concise and have them neatly saved on a recording device.

If talking to a machine makes some callers seem rudely or foolishly, programming the machine has quick transformed normally reserved people into entertainers. For the time it takes to deliver their message, they have something that is rarely even for professional actors: a captively audience, which sits waiting patient and polite for a beep. And while it waits, this audience has the privilege of listening to whatever humorous routine the machine owner has programmed. Has any other technologically invention made us act so different? [Adapted from Jane Stern and Michael Stern, *Encyclopedia of Culture*]

21 FINDING AND REVISING ERRORS WITH ARTICLES

Three determiners—*a, an,* and *the*—are known as **articles.** The articles *a* and *an* are called **indefinite articles;** *the* is known as the **definite article.**

21a DIAGNOSTIC ACTIVITY: ARTICLES

ACTIVITY
21.1 **How Much Do You Know?**

Read the sentences to determine if there are any errors in article usage. Correct any errors you find. Not all sentences require revision.

> *Example:* We took many interesting pictures at ‸Louvre.
> *the*

1. The Illinois Wesleyan University has an average enrollment of 1,700 students.

2. My mother prefers a̶ umbrella rather than a raincoat.

3. When Gary swims for a couple of hours, he usually gets a̶ earache.

4. Most people agree that touring Europe on̶ train is better than flying.
   taking a

5. Kristie goes to the̶ church on Sunday morning and Wednesday night.

6. The staff at the East Lansing Public Library is helpful.

7. My professor suggested that I add a̶n̶ appendices to my research paper.

8. My sister will wear the wedding dress that my mother wore twenty-five years ago.

9. ‸Credit card is not necessary for a university student.

10. A bridal shop is located on the̶ Michigan Avenue in Chicago.

11. A̶ apple is a refreshing snack on a hot day.

12. Many elementary school students carry the̶ lunch boxes to school every day.

13. Did you turn in a homework that Professor Bach assigned for today? *(the)*

14. Prague is one of most beautiful cities in Europe. *(the)*

15. The AIDS is becoming one of the most common killer diseases.

16. I prefer Pepsi to Coca-Cola.

17. Telephone was invented by Alexander Graham Bell. *(A)*

18. In general, the cats are much smarter than the dogs.

19. I love to take walks on the beach when moon is full. *(the)*

20. Would you go to the store and buy a rice?

Determine which items you missed in this Diagnostic Activity. If you missed or had trouble with any items, please go to the appropriate section in *The Harper-Collins Concise Handbook for Writers* and this workbook for further practice or study.

It is important to know which items cause you difficulty. When revising your writing, you might want to go through your paper one time checking only for the use of articles. Concentrate on items that you had difficulty with in this activity.

21b DETERMINERS

Determiners are words that precede nouns, gerunds, and sometimes pronouns and modify their meaning. The characteristics of the modified word—countable or noncountable noun, singular or plural, even pronunciation in some cases—tells which determiner is possible.

Articles are determiners; so are a number of other words, as shown in the chart.

DETERMINERS IN ENGLISH

Articles	Other Determiners				
a, an the	any each every many much some	this that these those	my his her its your our their	possessive nouns	first second third the last one two three

Whereas most native speakers of English have little trouble with articles, writers for whom English is a second language often find articles one of the most difficult aspects of English to master. The rules for determining when not to use an article, when to use *the*, and when to use *a* or *an* are complex and subtle. Many languages, such as Chinese, Japanese, Korean, most Slavic languages, and most African languages, do not use articles at all. And those that do, such as French, Spanish, Persian, and most Semitic languages, use the articles in ways that are different from the way English uses them.

21c CHOOSING BETWEEN *A* AND *AN*

We use *a* before a word starting with a consonant *sound* and *an* before a word starting with a vowel sound. The choice of *a* or *an* depends on the word that immediately follows the article, not necessarily the noun it modifies.

ACTIVITY
21.2 **Choosing between *a* and *an***

Read the paragraph below, filling in the blanks with *a* or *an,* as appropriate.

Ecology is defined as the study of how all living things interact with one another and their nonliving environment. The study of ecology is concerned with five levels: organisms, populations, communities, ecosystems, and the biosphere. __The__ organism is __a__ unit, or __an__ individual living thing that belongs to the same species, such as __the__ squirrel. Organisms of the same species that live in the same geographic area are called populations. __The__ habitat is the place where __the__ organism lives. The habitat for __the__ squirrel is __the__ oak tree. __a__ community includes all the populations of organisms that live and interact with one another in __a__ given area at __a__ given time. The community where __the__ squirrel lives might include birds, cats, insects, and other animals. __An__ ecosystem consists of interactions between the community and the physical environment. In other words, the ecosystem that __a__ squirrel lives in could be __an__ urban ecosystem or __a__ forest. Finally, the biosphere is the thin layer of air, water, and soil and rock that surrounds the earth.

21d ARTICLE USAGE WITH PROPER NOUNS

To select the correct article (or the option of using no article), you must first decide if the noun is a common noun or a proper noun.

A **proper noun** is the name of a particular person, place, or thing. There are three basic rules for using articles with proper nouns, but there are many exceptions (see the accompanying chart). You might find it useful to keep a list of the proper nouns you encounter and the article that is used before them.

Rules for Articles with Proper Nouns

1. Singular proper nouns do not take the indefinite articles *a* or *an.*
2. *In general,* singular proper nouns do *not* take the definite article, *the.*
3. *In general,* plural proper nouns *do* take the definite article, *the.*

EXCEPTIONS TO THE RULES FOR ARTICLES WITH PROPER NOUNS

Names of nations	*Geographic areas*	*Colleges and universities*
the Ivory Coast, the Sudan (*countries named for regions*)* the Republic of China (*republics*)	the American South (*regions*) the Mojave (*deserts*) the Iberian Peninsula the Pacific Ocean the Sargasso Sea the Gulf of Mexico the Yellow River the Panama Canal the North Channel (*but* Cape Cod, Point Barrow, Biscayne Bay)	the University of Hawaii, the University of Colorado (*but* Hawaii State University, Colorado State University)
Empires and dynasties the Roman Empire the Ching Dynasty	*Museums and libraries* the Louvre the Library of Congress	
Organizations the Red Cross the American Association for Retired People the National Honor Society	*Languages* the English language (*but not* the English)	*Historical periods and events* the Great Depression the Holocaust the Mesozoic Era

*Country names that are grammatically plural (*the United States, the Netherlands, the Philippines*) follow rule 3 for plural proper nouns, even though they are construed as singular: *The Netherlands* lies *entirely below sea level.*

ACTIVITY

21.3 **Using Articles with Proper Nouns**

Fill in the blank with the correct article. Write a short dash if no article is needed.

> *Example:* ___The___ University of California is located in ___-___ Los Angeles.

1. ___—___ Charles Darwin proposed his theory of speciation by observing ___the___ Galápagos Islands.

2. ___The___ Minneapolis Institute of Art recently acquired a famous Monet painting.

3. The end of communism in ___the___ Czech Republic and ___—___ Slovakia is referred to as ___the___ Velvet Revolution.

4. ___—___ Mount McKinley, part of ___the___ Alaska Range, is the tallest mountain in ___—___ North America.

5. Notre-Dame is a good example of Gothic architecture in ___the___ Middle Ages.

6. One of the largest deserts in the world is ___the___ Sahara.

7. _The_ Mississippi River flooded in the summer of 1993.

8. _____ John Steinbeck wrote his famous novel *Cannery Row* while living on _the_ Monterey Peninsula.

9. The climate of the world was changed when _the_ Mount Pinatubo erupted in _the_ Philippines in 1992.

10. Volunteers dress like _____ Santa Claus and ring bells every _____ Christmas for _the_ Salvation Army.

21e ARTICLE USAGE WITH COUNTABLE AND NONCOUNTABLE SINGULAR AND PLURAL COMMON NOUNS

If a noun is not proper, it is common. A **common noun** is a word that represents a person, place, or thing but is not its name. The rules governing article use with common nouns depend on three distinctions:

1. Is the noun countable or noncountable?
2. Is the noun singular or plural?
3. Is the noun definite, generic, or indefinite?

Once you understand the difference between each of these distinctions, then you can apply the rules of article usage. The next section will review these distinctions; however, you might want to review the rules for using articles with common nouns on page 269 as you read through the next few pages.

Countable versus Noncountable

One concept essential to understanding the use of articles with common nouns is the distinction between countable nouns and noncountable nouns. As the name implies, you can count or quantify countable nouns but not noncountable nouns. Also, countable nouns have separate singular and plural forms, whereas noncountable nouns do not.

The distinction between countable and noncountable nouns is difficult for some students because nouns that refer to the same type of item may be countable in one language but not in another. *Furniture,* for example, is noncountable in English but countable in Spanish. *Chalk* is a noncountable noun in English but is countable in Japanese. Because of the complexity of this distinction, it would be a good idea to keep a list of noncountable nouns as you discover them. It is easier to list the noncountable nouns because there are fewer of them; most nouns in English are countable.

ACTIVITY

21.4 Identifying Noncountable Nouns

A. The chart lists noncountable nouns in categories. Look at the nouns given in the left-hand column, and try to name the category they belong to. Some have already been done for you.

Noncountable Nouns	Category
biology, chemistry, economics	
politics, pollution, violence	*general topics*
air, oxygen, carbon dioxide	
rain, gravity, sunshine	*natural phenomena*
rice, sand, sugar	
milk, water, coffee	
basketball, soccer, table tennis	
chicken pox, flu, measles	
fruit, furniture, jewelry	*groups of items*
Arabic, Japanese, Russian	
parking, smoking, studying	
sadness, happiness, anger	
intelligence, courage, honesty, luck	*qualities*

B.   Match the following noncountable nouns to their correct category and write them in the chart.

equipment	music	education
chess	luggage	learning
patience	money	darkness
garbage	flour	lightness
oatmeal	blood	smoke
gravel	dancing	weather

It is also possible for a noun to be both countable and noncountable, with little change in meaning:

Countable: I see two *beauties* over there.

Noncountable: The *beauty* of the mountains in Alaska is incredible.

Nouns such as these mean "an instance of" the noncountable commodity when they are made countable. Other nouns in this category include *truth, crime, law,* and *education.*

Another category of noncountable nouns that can be countable includes certain nouns that represent "a type of," as in the following sentences:

Countable: The waiter can recommend a *wine* for your dinner.

Noncountable: I had some excellent *wine* for dinner.

Other nouns that fall into this category are *cheese* and *tea.*

Finally, the third type of noncountable nouns that can be made countable are those that represent a "unit or serving of," as in the following sentences:

Countable: I had a delicious *coffee* at Espresso Royale this morning.

Noncountable: I usually drink *coffee* in the morning.

Other nouns in this category are *aspirin, pastry,* and *chocolate.*

Singular versus Plural

This distinction applies only to countable nouns. The plural form of regular nouns is formed by adding *-s* to the singular form. However, many nouns in English are *irregular* and form their plurals in unpredictable ways. Be careful to recognize these irregular spellings so that you will use the appropriate article.

The accompanying chart presents the rules for spelling irregular plural nouns.

PLURALS OF IRREGULAR NOUNS*

	Examples		
Noun Ending	**Singular**	**Plural**	**Rule**
consonant + *y*	baby community	babies communities	Change *y* to *i* and add *-es.*
f or *fe*	shelf wife hoof *belief* *chief*	shelves wives hooves *beliefs* *chiefs*	Change *f* or *fe* to *ves.*
ch, sh, ss, x, z	church dish mass box waltz	churches dishes masses boxes waltzes	Add *-es.*

*Exceptions are printed in italics.

(continued)

PLURALS OF IRREGULAR NOUNS* (continued)

Noun Ending	Singular	Plural	Rule
o	potato tomato *piano* *zoo*	potatoes tomatoes *pianos* *zoos*	Add -*es*.
is	analysis crisis	analyses crises	Change *is* to *es*.
um	bacterium medium	bacteria media	Change *um* to *a*.
on	phenomenon criterion	phenomena criteria	Change *on* to *a*.
us	stimulus nucleus	stimuli nuclei	Change *us* to *i*.
a	vertebra formula	vertebrae formulae†	Add -*e*.
ex	index	indices	Change *ex* to *ices*.

*Exceptions are printed in italics.
†Often spelled as *formulas* rather than *formulae*.

The following irregular nouns form their plurals in unusual ways. You will simply have to memorize them:

child	children	woman	women	tooth	teeth
man	men	deer	deer	fish	fish
mouse	mice	species	species	series	series
sheep	sheep	ox	oxen		
foot	feet	goose	geese		

ACTIVITY

21.5 **Using Irregular Plural Nouns**

In the following dialogue, change all the singular countable nouns to plural nouns. Also correct the grammar as a result of the change if needed.

TAKESHI: Professor Bird, can you tell me the criterion for completing my thesis?

DR. BIRD: All you need to do is finish your research. How is it going?

TAKESHI: Well, I still don't understand the formula that measures the radius of the nucleus of an atom.

DR. BIRD: Did you read my article on the analysis of that formula in the *Chemical Journal?* You can find it in the index.

TAKESHI: No, I didn't know about it.

DR. BIRD: It's on the shelf over there.

TAKESHI: Thank you so much, Professor Bird.

DR. BIRD: You're welcome. Good luck, Takeshi!

21f ARTICLE USAGE WITH DEFINITE, GENERIC, AND INDEFINITE COMMON NOUNS

A third distinction important to the use of articles is whether a noun is definite, generic, or indefinite. The following sentences represent these three types of common nouns:

The Japanese student who is in Susanna's class is smart.

Japanese students are generally good at math.

A Japanese student left her wallet in the classroom.

In the first example, the noun phrase, *Japanese student,* is definite because the phrase *who is in Susanna's class,* which follows the noun, specifies exactly which Japanese student. The noun phrase in the second example is generic because it refers to all members of a group in general. In the third example, the noun phrase is indefinite because the Japanese student is not clearly identified.

Definite Common Nouns

A definite noun requires the definite article, *the.* A noun is considered definite if it meets any one of the following six criteria.

1. If it has been mentioned in a previous sentence or earlier in the same sentence:

   Last week Mr. Tranh looked at *a car* that was advertised in the newspaper. *The car* was a 1989 Pontiac.

2. If it is identified by a phrase or clause that follows it:

   The car that he is driving now is ten years old.

3. If it is modified by a comparative or superlative adjective:

   The most expensive *car* that he looked at this weekend was a Buick Riviera convertible.

4. If it stands for a unique and therefore specific person or thing:

   The convertible would be great when *the sun* was shining.

5. If it stands for parts of a whole that are being discussed:

   As he looked at the Buick, Mr. Tranh noticed that *the windows* were power operated.

6. If the context or situation makes the specific identity of the noun clear:

   Mr. Tranh is now looking at cars at Russell Ford. I hope *the salesperson* realizes that he cannot spend more than $10,000 for a car.

ACTIVITY 21.6 Identifying the Criteria for Using the Definite Article

Decide which of the six criteria in 21f applies to the use of the definite article in each of the following sentences. Write the number of that criterion in the blank following the sentence.

1. *The classroom* where I study English is terrible. _____

   The chairs are uncomfortable. _____

The chalkboard is so scratched, I can't read it, and *the floor* is terribly dirty.

_____ _____

2. *The house* where Ramon lives has *the* most beautiful *view* of Mount Buffalo.

_____ _____

3. This morning when I woke up, there was a bird outside my window. When I let

my dogs out, *the bird* flew away. _____

Generic Common Nouns

There are three ways to express generic meaning:

The automobile is a part of many households in America.

Automobiles are a part of many households in America.

An automobile is a part of many households in America.

Using the definite article, *the,* is the most formal way to indicate generic meaning. This format is usually used in technical or informative writing about animals, plants, musical instruments, or complex inventions or devices. However, it cannot be used with simple inanimate objects, such as a book:

INCORRECT: *The book* is a wonderful escape on a rainy day.

CORRECT: *Books* are a wonderful escape on a rainy day.

Indefinite Common Nouns

The indefinite article *a* or *an* is used with singular countable nouns, and the word *some* or no article is used with plural countable and noncountable indefinite nouns:

I need to get *a* faster computer.

I went to see *some* computers at the store.

I'd like some *sugar* for my coffee.

ACTIVITY

21.7   **Differentiating among Generic, Definite, and Indefinite Usage of Articles**

Examine the following sentences, and write "G" if the italicized noun is generic, "D" if it is definite in meaning, or "I" if it is indefinite.

1. *Teachers* are underpaid and overworked. _____

2. A *dog* is a friendly animal. _____

3. The *car* Cheryl drives is old and rusty. _____

4. A *desk* in the classroom is broken. _____

5. *Pigs* are very intelligent animals. _____

6. There were some beautiful antique *lamps* at the show. _____

7. The largest *city* in Austria is Vienna. _____

21g RULES FOR USE OF ARTICLES WITH COMMON NOUNS

In the preceding section, you learned three distinctions for common nouns:

1. Countable versus noncountable.
2. Singular versus plural.
3. Definite, generic, or indefinite.

Now that you understand these distinctions, look at the rules for usage of articles with common nouns.

RULES FOR THE USE OF ARTICLES WITH COMMON NOUNS

Rule	Example
Always use an article with singular countable nouns.	Tomorrow he is going to look at *a used car*.
Use the article *a* or *an* with singular countable nouns that are indefinite.	Tranh has to buy *a car* to drive to work on Monday.
Use the article *the* with singular countable nouns that are definite.	*The* **building** where he works is not located near a bus line.
Use the article *the* with definite plural nouns.	He looked at *the* **cars** that Jan had recommended.
Use the determiner *some* or no article at all with indefinite plural nouns.	There must be *some* **cars** for sale under $6,000.
Do not use an article with generic plural nouns.	**Car dealers** expect **customers** to bargain with them.
Use the article *the* with definite noncountable nouns.	Tranh was aware of *the reputation* of car dealers for driving hard bargains.
Use the determiner *some* or no article at all with indefinite noncountable nouns.	Tranh experienced *some nervousness* when the dealer started pressuring him to sign a contract.
Use no article with generic noncountable nouns.	The dealer assured Tranh that *nervousness* was a normal reaction.

21h EXCEPTIONS TO THE RULES FOR THE USE OF ARTICLES WITH COMMON NOUNS

The box presents rules for article use with common nouns, but there are many exceptions, especially in the following areas.

Diseases

Diseases use articles in unpredictable ways. Those with formal names *(pneumonia, AIDS, influenza)* are frequently referred to by the singular noun and no article. Those with more informal names sometimes take *the (the flu, the plague)* and sometimes take *a* or *an (a cold, an earache).* Those with informal names and plural forms can often be used with no article *(measles* or *the measles; chicken pox* or *the chicken pox).* Note also that names of diseases are not capitalized.

Body Parts

Remember that generic common nouns normally take one of two forms. If they are countable, like *marbles* or *lions*, the generic form is the plural with no article. If they are noncountable, like *wine* or *pollution*, the generic form is the singular with no article. However, the parts of the body are an exception to these rules:

The heart is the most common organ to malfunction.

The eyes of a child are not fully developed at birth.

For generic use, body parts use *the* + noun. The noun is singular or plural depending on whether the human body has one or more than one of the part.

Radios and Telephones

It is common for English speakers to use the definite article, *the*, instead of *a* or *an* when referring to radios and telephones.

CORRECT BUT RARE:	I listened to the baseball game on *a radio*.
	I talked with my father on *a telephone*.
CORRECT AND MORE COMMON:	I listened to the baseball game on *the radio*.
	I talked with my father on *the telephone*.

Trains and Buses

Train and *bus* can take the definite article, *the*, even when a specific train or bus is not known to the reader and writer.

CORRECT BUT RARE:	Mr. Rodriguez came to town on *a train*.
	Ms. Rodriguez rides *a bus* every day to work.
CORRECT AND MORE COMMON:	Mr. Rodriguez came to town on *the train*.
	Ms. Rodriguez rides *the bus* every day to work.

Destinations

For destinations, the *preferred* form is with the definite article, *the*, even if the reader is unfamiliar with the particular place involved:

Maria is going to *the store*.
Maria is going to *the beach*.
Maria is going to *the library*.

School and *church* are exceptions, perhaps because we think of them primarily as activities rather than buildings:

Maria is going to *school*.
Maria is going to *church*.

Notice what happens when we think of *school* and *church* as buildings:

Maria took a picture of *the school.* (specific school in mind)

Maria took a picture of *a school.* (no specific school in mind)

Maria took a picture of *the church.* (specific church in mind)

Maria took a picture of *a church.* (no specific church in mind)

When *school* and *church* are used to denote buildings rather than the activity that takes place in them, they follow the regular rules for articles with common countable nouns.

Items in a Series

When a series of items is joined by *and* or *or* and the same article is needed for each of them, it can be placed in front of the first item and omitted from the others.

I looked for my dog in *the* kitchen, basement, and backyard.

At the hardware store, she purchased *a* hammer, saw, and screwdriver.

21i ARTICLES: COMPREHENSIVE CHECK

ACTIVITY

21.8   **Diagnostic Retest**

Complete Activity 21.1 again. If you still miss or have difficulty with any items, review the relevant sections of the workbook.

ACTIVITY

21.9   **Putting It All Together**

A.   Fill in the blanks in the following passage with *a, an,* or *the.* If no article is required, write a short dash.

_____*The*_____ bubonic plague, or "Black Death," killed one-fourth of Europe in three long years (1347–1350). ___*The*___ disease spread quickly, killing horribly, and then moved on, leaving whole cities devastated in its wake. ___*The*___ economic, physical, and emotional shock is unsurpassed in European history. Most saw ___*the*___ plague as not just ___*a*___ disease but ___*a*___ heavenly curse "sent down upon ___—___ mankind for our correction by ___*the*___ just wrath of God." Whatever ___*the*___ cause, it killed with such power and swiftness that "___*the*___ living could scarcely bury ___*the*___ dead."

 ___*The*___ plague came out of ___—___ Central Asia, passing to

_____ Marseilles on ___*the*___ infested Genovese ship. ___*The*___ disease is caused by ___*a*___ bacterium carried by fleas (which travel on _____ rats). Humans get it when bitten by ___*the*___ fleas and then spread it by coughing. ___*The*___ unsanitary conditions in medieval Europe allowed ___*the*___ disease to move rapidly northward. In _____ Florence alone, 100,000 people died within _____ four months. In some cities, 90 percent of ___*the*___ population was wiped out.

___*The*___ symptoms were quick and harsh. ___*The*___ first sign was sneezing, followed by ___*the*___ appearance of lumps, or "buboes," in ___*the*___ groin or armpits. This was followed by _____ diarrhea, _____ pneumonia, and almost inevitably, _____ death within three days. [Rick Steves and Gene Openshaw, *Europe 101*]

B. Correct the following sentences for article usage by adding articles where they are needed and omitting them where they are not needed.

1. An excellent dry cleaner is on ~~the~~ Pennsylvania Avenue.

_____

2. Each greenhouse gas has *an* influence on *the* greenhouse effect.

_____

3. Jose went to ~~an~~ *the* hospital in Tucson.

_____

4. Many students ride ~~the~~ bicycles in a university town.

_____

5. Fahad saw ~~a~~ *an* eagle on our field trip.

_____

6. Recently, market share of Coca-Cola has declined.

_____

7. Alex tried *the* clams that Brian had recommended.

---

8. My roommate goes to ~~the~~ church every Sunday morning.

---

9. Writing a research paper is *a* criterion for completing this course.

---

10. Mrs. Robbins had ~~a~~ patience and she was very honest.

The accompanying charts provide a visual summary of the conventions for using articles with nouns in English.

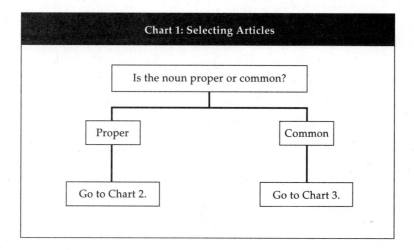

Chart 1: Selecting Articles

Is the noun proper or common?

Proper

Common

Go to Chart 2.

Go to Chart 3.

diary —
diarrhea —

Chart 2: Selecting Articles with Proper Nouns

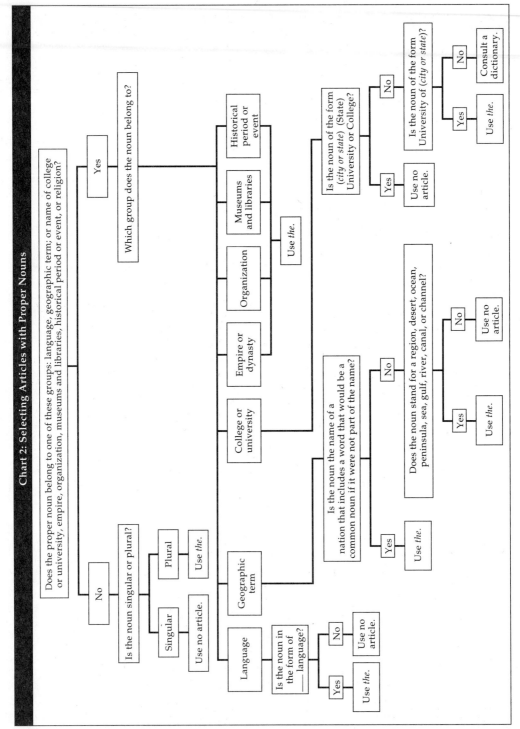

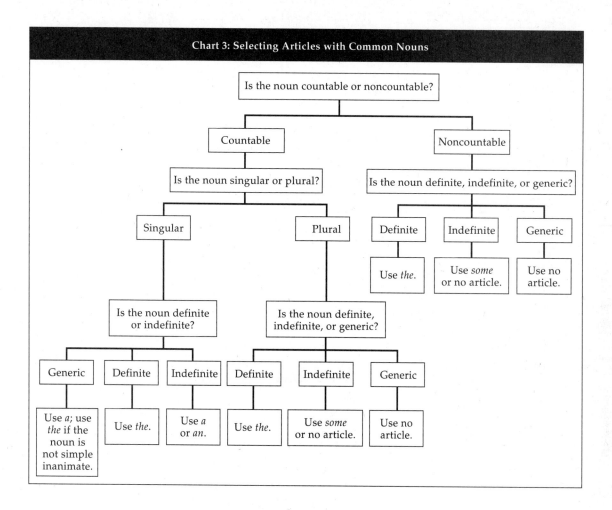

Chart 3: Selecting Articles with Common Nouns

FINDING AND REVISING ERRORS WITH PREPOSITIONS

Prepositions are words that indicate a connection between the noun at the end of the phrase and another word in the sentence. They often define direction, location, or time. Prepositions are particularly troublesome for many ESL students, especially since each preposition may have several meanings. A dictionary will list these various meanings; however, we suggest keeping a journal of sentences you come across with prepositions so that you can remember their meanings within context.

22a DIAGNOSTIC ACTIVITY: PREPOSITIONS

ACTIVITY 22.1 **How Much Do You Know?**

Read each sentence to see if it sounds awkward or is ungrammatical. If so, correct it. Not all sentences require revision. An example is provided.

Example: Max was getting bored ~~of~~ *with* the discussion, so he suggested that we leave.

1. Maria has been studying in Budapest since early July.
2. My boss needs the reports by lunchtime.
3. Albert arrived at this country three days ago.
4. Traveling in the desert can be very dangerous.
5. That behavior isn't consistent to our friendship.
6. My mind was churning out ideas on the opportunities before us.
7. My mother made a cake to me.
8. The table is made out of walnut and oak.
9. The concert was canceled because of they were sick.
10. It is difficult to provide families in Romania because of the low wages.
11. Please explain me what you mean.
12. My boss is difficult to talk to.
13. With whom are you going to the movie?
14. The chair's leg is unstable.
15. Kirby Puckett's swing is one of the most powerful in baseball.

276

Determine which items you missed in this Diagnostic Activity. If you missed or had trouble with any of the items, please go to the appropriate section in *The HarperCollins Concise Handbook for Writers* and this workbook for further practice and study.

It is important to know which items cause you difficulty. When revising your writing, you might want to go through your paper one time checking only for the use of prepositions. Concentrate on items that you had difficulty with in this activity.

22b THE NINE MOST COMMON PREPOSITIONS

The nine prepositions used most commonly in English are explained in the accompanying chart.

NINE COMMON PREPOSITIONS

Preposition	Meaning	Examples
in, on, at	Time	The earthquake occurred *in* the evening. The earthquake occurred *on* October 17. The earthquake occurred *at* 5:04 P.M.
	Place	I was living *in* Monterey, California. I lived *on* Eighteenth Street. I lived *at* 216 Eighteenth Street.
from	Source or origin	I got the book *from* my friend. I was tired *from* working out.
to	Direction toward place	We drove *to* Grand Rapids.
	Direction toward person	Laura gave some chocolate eggs *to* Kathy.
by	Agent	*Silent Spring* was written *by* Rachel Carson. We went to the baseball game *by* bus.
	Deadline	I have to complete Chapter 12 *by* next week.
	Location	The chair is *by* the table.
for	Purpose	Joe had to study *for* his chemistry final.
	Length of time	I was traveling in Asia *for* six months.
	In favor of	The Republican candidate is *for* lowering taxes.
	To be given to someone	Carlos baked a cake *for* Lucy.
	Cost	Susan bought new shoes *for* seventy dollars.
of	Relationship between part and whole	Many *of* the people in Somalia were starving.
	Reference	She is afraid *of* heights.
with	Association	Annette has long conversations *with* her mother. Donald often eats dinner *with* me.
	Implement	The Japanese usually eat *with* chopsticks.
	Description	Catherine's dress was purple *with* small blue flowers.
	Manner	She spoke *with* grace and poise.

22c PREPOSITIONS OF TIME AND SPACE

The accompanying charts list prepositions of time and prepositions of space.

PREPOSITIONS OF TIME

after	before	in	till
as late as	by	on	to
as soon as	during	prior to	until
at	for	since	up to

PREPOSITIONS OF SPACE

above	before	far (away) from	next to	round
across	behind	from	off	through
against	below	in	on	throughout
along	beneath	in back of	onto	to
among	beside	in front of	opposite	toward
around	between	inside (of)	out (of)	under
as far as	beyond	in the middle of	outside (of)	underneath
at	by	into	over	up
away from	down	near	past	

ACTIVITY 22.2   **Using the Appropriate Preposition of Time**

Read the following letter, filling in each blank with the appropriate preposition of time from the chart.

Dear Amanda:

I had the most wonderful trip to Europe! I left Atlanta ____on____ May 22

___in____ the evening and arrived in Amsterdam ___till.___ sunrise the

next morning. I stayed there ___until___ May 25 and saw such wonderful

sights as the Anne Frank Huis and the Rijksmuseum. _____ Friday,

I traveled to Paris for the first time _____ I lived there _____

1989. It was wonderful to be back. _____ my stay there, I saw many

old friends and visited the typical tourist spots again—Notre-Dame, the

Louvre, and Versailles. _____ five days, I left Paris and flew to

Barcelona. What a wonderful city! _____ I left the United States, my

mother had told me about the wonderful architecture in the city by a man

named Gaudi. I had no idea how incredible his works really were

_____ I saw them. Unfortunately, I stayed in Barcelona _____

only three days as I had to be back in Amsterdam _____ the end of May. I can't wait to go back next summer and see more. Write soon and tell me how your life is!

Love,

Bernadette

ACTIVITY
22.3 **Using the Appropriate Preposition of Space**

Study the following picture. Then fill in each blank in the paragraph that follows it with the appropriate preposition of space from the chart.

   Michigan's first state park is located _____on_____ an island. The adventure begins when you step _____onto_____ the ferry that brings you _____from_____ Saint Ignace _____to_____ Mackinac Island. Throughout the year, this island, located _____in_____ the Straits of Mackinac, attracts thousands of tourists. Some of them even come ___from___ _____ Europe or Asia to enjoy the various historic sites _____at_____ this state park. The picture shows Huron Street, the main shopping area _____ the island. Here visitors can rent bikes or horses to tour _____ the island. Since no cars are allowed _____on_____ the island, many visitors walk _____down_____ the streets and take the opportunity to stop _____at_____ one of the little stores. If you look _____toward_____ the picture carefully, you can see a group of tourists leaning _____ a store window to get a closer look _____ a product that Mackinac is famous for—fudge. A couple is walking hand in hand _____ the street, and a young gentleman is walking with a puppy _____ him. Behind these buildings is Fort Mackinac, perched _____ a promontory looking _____ the harbor. As you walk _____ the fort, you will see the visitors' center, where you will find the information you need for a great day on the island.

ACTIVITY 22.4

Writing Directions Using Prepositions of Space

Look at the map of Omonia Square in Athens. Locate the X, which means "You are here." From this point, write directions to the five locations listed. An example is provided.

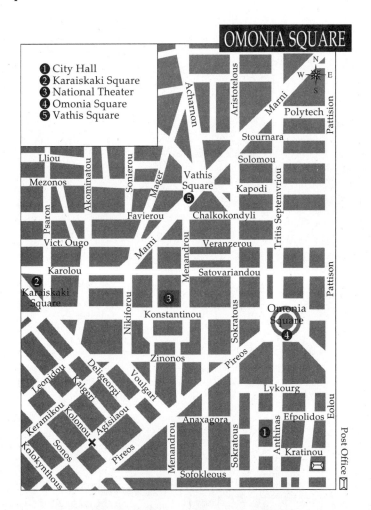

OMONIA SQUARE

❶ City Hall
❷ Karaiskaki Square
❸ National Theater
❹ Omonia Square
❺ Vathis Square

Example: To get to City Hall, go north up Agisilaou until you come to Deligeorgi. Turn right. Go one block until you hit Pireos and turn left. Walk until you come to Anaxagora. Turn right here. Walk for two blocks until you come to Sokratous and turn right. At the first street you come to, make a left. City Hall will be in front of you.

22d PREPOSITIONS SHOWING LOGICAL RELATIONSHIPS

The accompanying chart lists common prepositions that show logical relationships.

PREPOSITIONS OF LOGICAL RELATIONSHIP				
about	by	from	of	to
as	despite	in spite of	on	with
but	except for	like	out of	

ACTIVITY
22.5 Identifying the Meaning of Prepositions Showing Logical Relationships

Examine the following sentences. Indicate the meaning conveyed by each italicized preposition by writing the corresponding letter in the blank. Use each definition only once.

a. association
b. instrument/tool
c. purpose
d. subject
e. concession
f. description
g. origin or source
h. origin or source
i. in favor of

j. part of a whole
k. means or method
l. similarity
m. favor
n. receiver
o. omission
p. in the role of
q. agent

Example: __q__ A peace plan was proposed *by* the secretary of state.

_____ 1. Pablo goes to work *by* subway.

_____ 2. The rugs in Anwar's living room come *from* Turkey.

_____ 3. Pesto is made *from/of/out of* olive oil, basil, and nuts.

_____ 4. The rest *of* the team was too tired to go out for pizza.

_____ 5. Red wine goes well *with* pasta.

_____ 6. I always underline my textbooks *with* a highlighter.

_____ 7. The new wallpaper for the nursery has white puppies *with* red collars.

_____ 8. Andrea is going *for* an interview tomorrow.

_____ 9. Elka often teaches my class *for* me.

_____ 10. My friend prays *for* world peace every day.

_____ 11. We decided to go to Saugatuck Beach *despite* the bad weather.

_____ 12. We are learning *about* the Russian Revolution in my history class.

_____ 13. India gave the journal guidelines *to* Cheryl yesterday.

_____ 14. The escalators in the Prague subway are just *like* the escalators in the Budapest subway.

_____ 15. Everyone *but* Wayne saw the raccoon in the tree.

_____ 16. I asked for money from Anne *as* a landlord and not *as* a friend.

ACTIVITY
22.6

Using Prepositions That Show Logical Relationships

Insert the correct preposition showing logical relationships in the following sentences.

1. Salt consists _____ sodium and chlorine.

2. Yasuo sent a letter _____ Joy.

3. Shane wants to learn more _____ the company where he hopes to work.

4. Lottie's wedding cake was decorated _____ roses and carnations.

5. Everyone was able to go to the soccer game _____ Carlos, who was sick.

6. People who belong to the Libertarian party are _____ less government involvement.

7. Her mother insisted that Amelia go _____ a haircut.

8. Australians insist that the best beer comes _____ their country.

9. The countries finally signed a peace treaty _____ their differing opinions.

10. The team captain insisted that the new rule be approved _____ everyone.

22e THREE COMMON ERRORS WITH PREPOSITIONS

When using prepositions, writers commonly make three kinds of errors: omitting a preposition, adding a preposition where one is not needed, and using the wrong preposition.

                                                                        of
Omitted preposition: Marius didn't pay his bill in time on account ˄ several kinds of difficulties.

Unnecessary preposition: Global warming does not influence ~~on~~ manufacturers since their buildings have air conditioning.

Wrong preposition: The Third World countries are highly dependent ~~in~~ *on* cheap energy sources.

ACTIVITY

22.7 Identifying Errors with Prepositions

Each of the following sentences contains one of the three common errors in using prepositions. First, find the error in the sentence and decide what kind of error it is. In the blank, write "O" for an omitted preposition, "U" for an unnecessary preposition, or "W" for a wrong preposition. Then revise the sentence so that it is correct.

1. You could ride a bike, but a motorcycle will get you in there faster. _____

_____

2. Sometimes you are stuck on traffic for half an hour without moving. _____

_____

3. Parents who punish their children by hitting them and not listening them are often despised. _____

_____

4. PepsiCo is moving aggressively into foreign markets, pushing harder to sell into its soda brands such as Mountain Dew and Slice. _____

_____

5. Ben did not come to class because of he was sick. _____

_____

6. Police are very strict to the speed limit. _____

_____

7. Shelly believed and donated to the ASPCA. _____

_____

22f ENDING SENTENCES WITH PREPOSITIONS

Several grammatical problems are common with prepositions. One of these is demonstrated by the following sentences:

INFORMAL: The boss is difficult to talk *to*.

BETTER: It is difficult to talk *to* the boss.

The first sentence ends with the preposition *to*. Many writers feel that sentences should not end with prepositions, so this is a construction you should avoid except perhaps in your most informal writing. The problem has been corrected in the second sentence, a perfectly natural sentence that avoids the problem of ending with a preposition.

Sometimes, however, a sentence sounds awkward when the preposition is placed anywhere but at the end. Consider the following sentences:

INFORMAL: Physics was the topic I was thinking *about*.

FORMAL: The topic *about* which I was thinking was physics.

BEST: I was thinking *about* physics.

The first example ends with a preposition and so is appropriate only in informal writing. The formal sentence corrects the problem, but it sounds stuffy. It would be acceptable in very formal writing such as a research paper. The third sentence both corrects the problem and avoids sounding too formal.

In academic writing, it is usually best to avoid using prepositions at the ends of sentences without, however, creating an overly formal style.

ACTIVITY

22.8 **Revising Sentences That End with Prepositions**

Revise each of the following sentences to remove the preposition from the end. Try to do this without creating a sentence that is overly formal.

1. My mother is difficult to get along with.

   _____

2. George doesn't understand what the book is about.

   _____

3. My friend recommended that I go to Hudson's to try a dress on.

   _____

4. Marilee's boyfriend came to her house to pick the car up.

   _____

5. Rhonda really needed someone to talk to.

   _____

22g CHOOSING BETWEEN *OF* AND *'S* FOR POSSESSIVES

Another problem with prepositions occurs when a writer has to choose between using a prepositional phrase beginning with *of* or using the possessive form *'s:*

Judy's car
~~The car of Judy~~ was damaged in the accident.

The original version of this sentence is stilted and awkward. It is preferable in English to form the possessive of nouns referring to humans with *'s*.

Possession in English is used to indicate a much broader range of relationships than just literal ownership, as the chart illustrates.

USES OF POSSESSIVES WITH NOUNS REFERRING TO HUMANS	
Thing Possessed	**Examples**
Belongings	Judy's car, Judy's coat, Judy's wallet
Parts of the body	Judy's hair, Judy's ears, Judy's voice
Qualities	Judy's style, Judy's reputation, Judy's ambition
Products	Judy's essay, Judy's painting, Judy's dance
Relatives	Judy's mother, Judy's husband, Judy's uncle
Associates	Judy's friend, Judy's neighbor, Judy's teacher

The rules for forming possessives with nouns referring to inanimate objects are a little different.

The *pencil's tip* is not very sharp.

The *tip of the pencil* is not very sharp.

Both sentences are correct. In the past, however, many grammarians preferred the form used in the second sentence. More recently, many writers have abandoned this preference. If you are writing for a traditional audience, you should probably avoid using *'s* to form a possessive with inanimate nouns.

Practices for forming possessives with animals, which are not human but also not inanimate, are a compromise. The closer the animal is to human, the more likely writers are to use *'s* to form the possessive:

Rover's bowl has been a feature of our kitchen for more than ten years.

The *antlers of the deer* were enormous.

The writer of the first sentence used *'s* to form the possessive because the dog Rover has been a member of the family so long that he is thought of as almost human. The writer of the second sentence, by contrast, was discussing an animal that was considered much less human.

ACTIVITY

22.9 **Choosing between *of* and *'s* for Possessives**

Write a possessive phrase with the words provided using either the preposition *of* or *'s,* as appropriate.

Example: flower, stem   *the stem of the flower* _____

1. brother, arm _____

2. car, door _____

3. Whiskers, toy _____

4. eagle, claws _____

5. Alex, stereo _____

22h VERB + PREPOSITION COMBINATIONS

Certain prepositions can be used only with certain verbs, adjectives, or nouns. The accompanying charts contain verb + preposition combinations and *be* + adjective or noun + preposition combinations. Do not memorize this list. Instead, keep a list in your journal of sentences you hear that contain these phrases, and try to remember each phrase in context.

VERB + PREPOSITION COMBINATIONS

account for	disapprove of	pay for
accuse (someone) of	dream about/of	plan on
adapt to	excuse (someone)	prefer to
add to	for (something)	prepare for
agree on (something)	explain (something) to (someone)	prevent from
agree to (something)	forgive (someone)	protect from
agree with (someone)	for (something)	provide for
apologize for (something)	get along with	provide (someone) with
apologize to (someone)	get back from	recover from
apply for	get rid of	refer to
approve of	get through with	relate to
argue about (something)	get used to	rely on
argue with (someone)	graduate from	remind (someone) of
arrive at	happen to	search for
ask for	have an opportunity for	see about
become of	have a reason for	send for
believe in	have a talent for	separate from
belong to	have confidence in	show up at
blame (someone) for	have influence over	spend (money) on
blame (something)	have patience with	stare at
on (someone)	hear about/of	stop from
borrow from	hear from	substitute for
care about	help (someone) with (something)	subtract from
catch up with	hope for	succeed in
come from	insist on	take advantage of
comment on	introduce to	talk about
communicate with	invite (someone) to	talk over
compare with	keep for	talk to
complain about/ of	keep from	thank (someone)
compliment (someone)	know about/of	for (something)
on (something)	laugh about	think about
concentrate on	laugh at	think of
congratulate (someone)	learn about/of	throw away
on (something)	listen for	travel to
consent to	listen to	vote for
consist of	look at	wait for
convince (someone)	look for	wait on
of (something)	look forward to	waste (money) on
decide between	matter to	wish for
decide on	object to	worry about
depend on	participate in	

BE + ADJECTIVE OR NOUN + PREPOSITION COMBINATIONS

be absent from	be envious of	be jealous of
be accustomed to	be equal to	be known for
be acquainted with	be essential to	be lazy about
be afraid of	be excited about	be made from/of
be angry at/with	be exhausted by/from	be married by (someone)
be appropriate for	be faithful to	to (someone)
be ashamed of	be familiar with	be opposed to
be aware of	be famous for	be out of
be bad for	be fed up with	be patient with
be bored by/with	be finished with	be polite to
be capable of	be fond of	be prevented from
be certain of	be friendly to/with	be proud of
be clear to	be frightened by/of	be relevant to
be committed to	be generous about	be responsible for (something)
be composed of	be glad about	to (someone)
be concerned about/by	be good at	be satisfied with
be content with	be good for	be scared by/of
be dedicated to	be grateful to (someone)	be sensitive to
be delighted at/with	for (something)	be sorry about/for
be devoted to	be guilty of	be suitable for
be different from	be happy about/for/with	be sure about/of
be disappointed by/in/with	be incapable of	be surprised at/by
be divorced from	be in charge of	be terrified of
be done with	be in danger of	be thankful for
be dressed in	be in favor of	be tired from/of
be engaged in	be innocent of	be used to
be engaged to	be interested in	be worried about
be enthusiastic about	be in touch with	

PREPOSITIONS: COMPREHENSIVE CHECK

ACTIVITY

22.10 Diagnostic Retest

Complete Activity 22.1 again. If you still miss or have difficulty with any items, review the relevant sections of the workbook.

ACTIVITY

22.11 Putting It All Together

Read the following passage about Leeds Castle in England, putting the correct preposition in each blank. (More than one preposition may be appropriate.)

Leeds Castle, the oldest and most romantic _____ England's "stately homes," was first built _____ stone _____ a Norman baron _____ the reign _____ William the Conqueror's son, Henry I, almost nine hundred years ago. A century and a half later, _____ the accession of

Edward I, the castle came _____ the possession _____ the Crown. _____ the next three centuries, it was a royal palace and the "lady's castle" _____ six _____ England's medieval queens. One _____ the most famous owners _____ Leeds Castle was Henry VIII, who liked it very much. He went there _____ time _____ time and expended large sums to enlarge and beautify the property. _____ the same time, he was careful to retain all the defenses _____ the castle, for he often had cause to fear a French invasion. Later it passed _____ the hands _____ three famous English families—the St. Legers, the Culpepers, and the Fairfaxes—_____ it was bought _____ Lady Baillie _____ the twentieth century. It was Olive Baillie's lifelong love _____ and devoted restoration _____ this ancient and beautiful castle that brought about its rededication _____ the service _____ the nation. [Adapted from Sir Arthur Bryant, *Leeds Castle*]

PART V

PUNCTUATION, MECHANICS, AND SPELLING

23 Editing for Commas, Semicolons, Apostrophes, and Quotation Marks

24 Editing for Other Punctuation

25 Mechanics

26 Spelling

23 EDITING FOR COMMAS, SEMICOLONS, APOSTROPHES, AND QUOTATION MARKS

23a DIAGNOSTIC ACTIVITY: COMMAS, SEMICOLONS, APOSTROPHES, AND QUOTATION MARKS

ACTIVITY
23.1 How Much Do You Know?

Read each sentence to determine if it contains an error in punctuation. If so, correct the error. Not all sentences contain errors.

Example: Running for the bus, Zelda tripped and fell.
⌃

1. I don't have a computer, but I want to buy one soon.

2. Most junior colleges do not have student housing however they do refer students to apartments.

3. I graduated from high school on 25 May 1978.

4. Allison explained, "At the end of the movie, the butler said, 'I didn't do it.' "

5. My teacher told us that it is common to confuse the words accept and except.

6. When the semester was finally over, we all relaxed and went to the beach.

7. Mom always told us "not to play ball in the house."

8. Most American students in my opinion are more serious than foreigners think.

9. The student, who usually comes to class late, is named Simon.

10. My mother's-in-law birthday is the same day as mine.

11. We told Michelle that she should'nt worry about her upcoming exam.

12. Because Margie didn't finish writing her research paper, she wasn't able to go skiing with us.

13. You didn't think you could leave without saying good-bye did you?

14. The private detective searched each lawyers files for evidence.

15. Whenever a dog thinks its time to go for a walk, it usually barks.

16. Did Michael actually say, "I need to know how much money you make?"

17. "Registration will begin tomorrow morning at nine," said the program director.

18. John Grisham's first novel was *A Time to Kill.*

19. In several professors opinions, the university needs better-qualified graduate students.

20. Art King who ran for city council last August is a good friend of mine.

Determine which items you missed in this Diagnostic Activity. If you missed or had trouble with any of the items, please go to the appropriate section in *The HarperCollins Concise Handbook for Writers* and this workbook for further practice and study.

It is important to know which items cause you difficulty. When revising your writing, you might want to go through your paper one time checking only for punctuation. Concentrate on items that you had difficulty with in this activity.

23b COMMAS AND SEMICOLONS

Commas with Introductory Elements

An introductory element is ordinarily set off with a comma:

Dependent clause: Because it was raining **,** Angel did not go to the soccer game.

Relative clause: When I saw my professor **,** she was having a cup of coffee.

Participial phrase: Glancing at her watch **,** Juanita realized she was late for class.

Prepositional phrase: In the booth next to us **,** two young men were having a loud argument.

Single word: Yes **,** you may ride home with us this afternoon.

Two special situations with introductory elements warrant attention:

Two elements: If you work hard and if you have some luck **,** you could win a part in this play.

If there are two introductory elements, a comma follows only the second.

Short element: In December we had eight inches of snow.

The comma may be omitted after a short introductory element, but it would not be wrong to leave it in, either.

Commas and Semicolons with Items in a Series

A comma is required after each item in a series:

Strawberries **,** blueberries **,** and plums are in season right now.

You can buy them from the supermarket **,** from a roadside stand **,** or from a health food store.

I eat blueberries for breakfast **,** I eat strawberries for dessert **,** and I eat plums for a snack.

If the items in a series are long or contain commas of their own, use semicolons to separate them:

Recently, some unusual fruits have come on the market, including kiwi fruit, which originated in New Zealand **;** papayas, which are grown in Hawaii **;** and mangoes, which come from Mexico.

ACTIVITY
23.2 Using Commas with Introductory Elements and Commas and Semicolons with Items in a Series

Read the following text about meditation. First, underline the introductory elements. Then insert commas and semicolons wherever they are needed.

> Gandhi kept a day of silence once a week. No matter what happened or who came to visit he would spend that day quietly. Most of us are unable to maintain an entire day of silence. However we can establish regular periods of meditation.
>
> There are as many forms of meditation as there are temperaments. Some of these forms of meditation are elaborate some are simple and some are unstructured. In alphagenetics people select a number and count slowly biofeedback monitors body processes with machines transcendental meditation focuses on a personal mantra and psychosynthesis uses visual images and guided daydreams.
>
> Slow conscious breathing focuses our energy. When the mind slows down it channels deep beneath the noise and surface clutter. After meditation we emerge renewed refreshed and peaceful. [Diane Dreher, *The Tao of Inner Peace*]

Commas and Semicolons in Sentences with Two Independent Clauses

Two independent clauses may be joined in three ways:

1. With a coordinating conjunction:

   Lin is moving into the city to be nearer the university **,** *and* she is looking for a housemate.

2. With a semicolon:

   Michelangelo painted a series of frescoes on the ceiling of the Sistine Chapel in Rome **;** a fresco is a painting made on a plaster surface while the plaster is still wet.

   A semicolon signals that the next independent clause will be closely related to the previous one. Sometimes the second clause explains the first one; sometimes it gives an example to support it.

3. With a conjunctive adverb or a transitional expression:

   Bird watching is not an expensive hobby **;** *however* **,** you do need to invest in a pair of binoculars.

   Bird watching is not an expensive hobby **.** *However* **,** you do need to invest in a pair of binoculars.

   Bird watching is not an expensive hobby **;** you do **,** *however* **,** need to invest in a pair of binoculars.

   Bird watching is not an expensive hobby **;** you do need to invest **,** *however* **,** in a pair of binoculars.

   Bird watching is not an expensive hobby **;** you do need to invest in a pair of binoculars **,** *however.*

ACTIVITY
23.3 Forming Sentences with Two Independent Clauses

Combine each pair of independent clauses into one sentence using the coordinating conjunction or conjunctive adverb provided.

Example: The truck is not running well.
I am going to take it back to the dealer. (so)

The truck is not running well, so I am going to take it back to the dealer.

1. Glenora was very excited about her high school reunion.
   She couldn't go. (but)

2. Nuclear power is beneficial because it doesn't contribute to the greenhouse effect.
   Nuclear power has many problems with safety and disposal issues. (on the other hand)

3. The newly established baseball team has a winning record.
   The fans are going to the game in droves. (and)

4. The water was found to be heavily contaminated in Cooperstown.
   The townspeople have to buy bottled water. (as a result)

5. The Johnsons could leave their puppy with us.
   They could pay to leave it in the kennel. (or)

Commas with Restrictive and Nonrestrictive Clauses

The following sentences are both correct, but they describe different circumstances:

Restrictive: Americans who live in Alaska tend to be interested in nature.

Nonrestrictive: Americans **,** who have one of the highest standards of living in the world **,** do not eat the healthiest diet.

Restrictive clauses restrict the nouns they modify to a particular one. They contain information essential to understanding who or what the noun stands for. Nonrestrictive clauses, by contrast, simply provide extra information.

Commas with Restrictive and Nonrestrictive Phrases

Prepositional Phrases

Restrictive: Spring weather in upstate New York can be unpredictable.

Nonrestrictive: San Francisco **,** in the middle of an earthquake zone **,** is the home of the San Francisco Giants.

Participial Phrases

Restrictive: Women running for political office are often asked about their husbands.

Nonrestrictive: My mother **,** driving home from work **,** did not notice the protest.

Commas with Restrictive and Nonrestrictive Appositives

Restrictive: The movie *Dr. Strangelove* was popular during the 1960s.

Nonrestrictive: John Barth's first novel **,** *The Floating Opera* **,** is set in Maryland.

ACTIVITY
23.4   ## Using Commas with Restrictive and Nonrestrictive Elements

Examine each pair of sentences. Decide which sentence has a nonrestrictive element, and insert the commas where necessary.

> *Example:*   The boy who is eating is my brother.
> My brother, who is always eating, is younger than I.

1. Dogs that are more than twenty inches long are not allowed in the apartment complex.
   Emily's dog who always barks at strangers is a golden retriever.

2. My friend who lives in Japan is coming to visit.
   My friend Naomi who lives in Japan is coming to visit.

3. Sheila running to catch the train did not see the small rock.
   People driving to work in rush hour traffic are often under stress.

4. The light at dusk my favorite time of day is perfect for taking moody pictures.
   The light from my bedroom lamp is blue.

5. My professor Dr. Moriarity is famous for his research on pesticides.
   The song *Yesterday* is still one of the most popular Beatles tunes.

Commas to Set off Parenthetical Expressions

This camera **,** in my opinion **,** is overpriced.

Cora Lee can come to the party **,** I suppose.

Commas with Nouns of Direct Address

Jose **,** do you wish you were back in California?

With a little luck **,** Monica **,** you will be in England in June.

The time has come **,** fellow bird lovers **,** to demand restrictions on the cats of America.

Commas with *yes* and *no*

Yes **,** I have gotten better at using commas since I read this book.

No **,** I cannot go to the movies tonight.

Commas with Interjections

Well **,** I suppose I should stay home and study this weekend.

Oh **,** I spent about eighty dollars on the party.

Commas with Tag Questions

You were born in Hawaii **,** weren't you?

Tony is good at headstands **,** isn't he?

You didn't hurt yourself **,** did you?

Commas with Coordinate and Cumulative Adjectives

Coordinate adjective: Anneke was carrying a wet **,** muddy kitten into the kitchen.

Cumulative adjective: The gray electric blanket was folded up at the end of the bed.

When two or more adjectives precede a noun, they can be categorized as either **coordinate adjectives** or **cumulative adjectives.** The distinction is subtle; two tests, however, help distinguish them. First, if the word *and* can be inserted between the adjectives, they are coordinate. Second, if their order can be reversed without the sentence sounding odd, they are coordinate.

The rules for punctuating two or more adjectives before a noun are as follows: Use a comma *between* (but not before or after) coordinate adjectives. Do *not* use a comma between cumulative adjectives.

Commas with Absolute Phrases

An **absolute phrase** consists of a noun and the *-ed* or *-ing* form of a verb (past or present participle) used to modify the whole sentence rather than any specific word in it:

Her homework finished **,** Samona went for a bicycle ride.

Samona drove off to Gunpowder State Park **,** her bicycle firmly mounted on the back of her car.

Her bicycle **,** its tires pumped up **,** was ready for an all-day ride.

Commas with Contrasted Elements

Paula is the one who is pregnant **,** not her sister.

Stan is teaching level three **,** not level two **,** on Saturday mornings.

Commas with Quotations

"Get out of here before I throw you out **,** " said Arnie Becker.

She replied **,** "You've known about this deadline since September."

The rule "Do unto others as you would have them do unto you" exists in many cultures.

"My mother **,** " said Francine **,** "does not sound like she is from the South."

Commas with Dates, Places, Numbers, and Titles

Dates

May 15 **,** 1993 **,** was a day I will always remember.

My mother was born on April 30 **,** 1922.

The warranty on my car expired on Monday **,** March 29.

I was discharged from the army on 30 November 1988.

My loan will be paid off in December 1998.

Places

Kansas City **,** Missouri **,** was the first stop on our trip.

My aunt lives in Birmingham **,** Alabama.

Ms. Jennifer Johnson **,** 11308 South Shore Road **,** Stockton **,** CA 95202 **,** was the address on the envelope.

Numbers

64 **,** 000   10 **,** 000 **,** 000   398 **,** 754 **,** 230 **,** 819

For numbers of more than four digits, use commas to separate the digits into groups of three, starting from the right. (In four-digit numbers used alone, the comma is optional.)

Never use commas in telephone numbers, street numbers, zip codes, social security numbers, or years more recent than 10,000 B.C.

Titles

Dr. Martin Luther King **,** Jr. **,** was buried in Atlanta.

Donald L. Slowinski **,** Ph.D. **,** has been selected as the next president of the college.

Commas to Prevent Misreading

In my class, students who are able to **,** write their papers on computers.

The day before **,** the professor had assigned a ten-page paper.

My uncle stormed in **,** in a seersucker jacket and plaid pants.

ACTIVITY
23.5 **Editing for Comma Usage**

Read the sentences to determine if commas are used in them correctly. Mark unnecessary commas for deletion, and add commas where they are needed. Not all sentences contain errors.

Example: The black**,** leather briefcase belongs to Dr. Thompson.

1. Anne likes to talk a lot, doesn't she?

2. Boulder Colorado is where Heather lives not Denver.

3. "Your deadline" said my boss "is August 28."

4. Their car all packed, the Wilsons left, for a wonderful vacation.

5. "Yes I will do my homework I promise" the little boy told his mother earnestly.

6. The sea was very stormy and it was difficult to navigate.

7. François likes many kinds of cheese, including Gouda, Jarlsberg, and Swiss.

8. "I will hold your daughter" snarled the kidnapper, "until, you bring me $325000 in cash."

9. Sam caught a slimy wet salamander and put it in his mother's closet.

10. Bungee jumping, in my opinion, is extremely dangerous.

ACTIVITY
23.6   Using Commas and Semicolons

Read the following passage, inserting commas and semicolons wherever they are necessary.

> On a wintry day in November 1823 a tall beefy wanderer with a bland open face like a rising sun stood with his scrawny wife pudgy eleven-year-old son and three hunting dogs in the western reaches of the new state of Louisiana. A straggler from Tennessee who had fled to avoid bankruptcy and jail he was not pleased with what faced him.
>
> "Don't mind the water we can wade through it. Done so many times on our exploration but I do worry about this next stretch between here and Texas."
>
> "We'll get through" his red-headed wife mumbled. Reaching for her rather unpleasant son she warned "You're to stay close Yancey. Help us load the guns if they attack."
>
> The three were dressed in buckskin garments laboriously cut and sewn by the mother who appeared to be responsible for all vital decisions on the other hand her husband thrashed about deciding issues which never seemed to matter. Each member of the family carried guns an axe pots extra articles of clothing and bundles of food. Useful items protruded from every angle of their body so that they looked like three porcupines waddling through the woods. [James A. Michener, *Texas*]

23c   APOSTROPHES

Forming Possessives of Nouns

All these sentences illustrate situations that are grammatically possessive in English:

I found *Carmella's* umbrella in the back seat of my car.

Jeff's back has not bothered him for the past six months.

Corretta's grandmother is coming to visit.

Al's sense of humor makes the office a pleasant place to work.

Alyce's essay was the best in the class.

This *school's* policy on plagiarism is printed in the catalog.

Today's students are likely to hold jobs and may also be parents.

One *hour's* delay will not wreck our plans.

PROCEDURE FOR FORMING POSSESSIVES WITH NOUNS

1. Ask yourself whether the word in question is possessing anything. Is it in a possessive situation? If not, do not make it possessive.
2. Ask yourself whether the word in question is a noun or indefinite pronoun. If not, do not use 's to make it possessive. Pronouns other than indefinite pronouns never form their possessives with an apostrophe.
3. Ask yourself if the word is singular or plural. Write the word on scrap paper or in your head in its singular or plural form as appropriate. At this point you are merely determining number; do *not* make the word possessive until step 4.
4. Form the possessive as follows:

   - If the word is singular, add an apostrophe and an *s*: 's.
   - If the word is plural and ends in *s*, add an apostrophe only: '.
   - If the word is plural and ends in anything other than *s*, add an apostrophe and an *s*: 's.

The procedure outlined in the box and the accompanying flowchart are two different ways of representing the same process. Use whichever is more helpful to you.

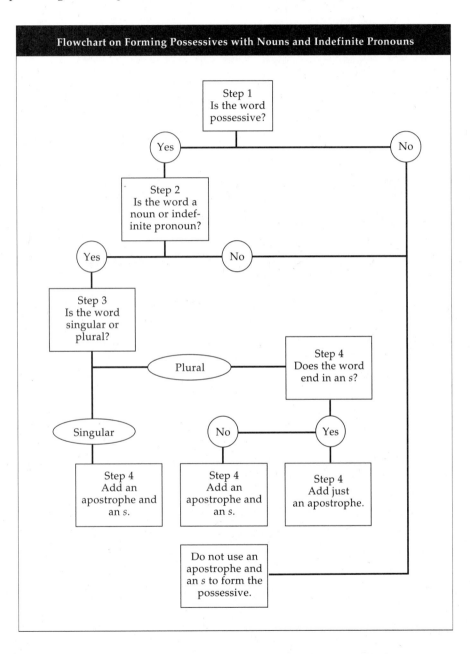

Flowchart on Forming Possessives with Nouns and Indefinite Pronouns

Step 1
Is the word possessive?

Yes   No

Step 2
Is the word a noun or indefinite pronoun?

Yes   No

Step 3
Is the word singular or plural?

Plural

Step 4
Does the word end in an *s*?

Singular   No   Yes

Step 4
Add an apostrophe and an *s*.

Step 4
Add an apostrophe and an *s*.

Step 4
Add just an apostrophe.

Do not use an apostrophe and an *s* to form the possessive.

In general, when the noun that is possessing something is a human being or an animal, it is preferable to use 's to show possession. When the noun that is possessing something is inanimate, it is preferable to use the preposition *of* to show possession. (See 22g.)

Lon's haircut made him look different.

My *dog's bowl* has his name on it.

The *tip of the pencil* is very sharp.

Forming Possessives with Hyphenated, Group, and Compound Nouns

Hyphenated: Her sister-in-law **'s** house is on the same block as mine.

Group: The dean of faculty **'s** policy is quite clear.

Joint compound: Polly Walker and John Schumaker **'s** business has really taken off.

Polly and John own the business together, so the apostrophe goes on the final noun only.

Separate compound: Polly Walker **'s** and John Schumaker **'s** businesses have really taken off.

Polly and John each own a separate business, both of which have taken off.

Forming Possessives with Pronouns

As the chart shows, personal pronouns do not use apostrophes to form possessives.

POSSESSIVE FORMS OF PERSONAL PRONOUNS			
Singular		**Plural**	
Pronoun	**Possessive**	**Pronoun**	**Possessive**
I	my, mine	we	our, ours
you	your, yours		
he	his	they	their, theirs
she	her, hers		
it	its	who	whose

Pronouns that have two forms for the possessive use them as indicated in the following sentences:

Min has lost *her* notebook.

That notebook is *hers*.

I have finished *my* essay.

The essay that won the prize was not *mine*.

All other pronouns form the possessive with *'s*, just like nouns:

I found *someone's* wallet behind the bookcase.

ACTIVITY 23.7   **Forming Possessives**

Form a new sentence with the material in parentheses, using either of the methods you learned for forming possessives.

Example: The collar (belonging to Whiskey) got caught on a tree.

Whiskey's collar got caught on a tree.

1. I must prepare for the visit (of my mother-in-law).

_____

2. The delay (of two weeks) will cost the company thousands of dollars.

_____

3. The legs (belonging to the table) are not very sturdy.

_____

4. The dresses (belonging to the bridesmaids) are peach.

_____

5. The decisions (made by the committee) made the workers angry.

_____

6. The book on the table is (belonging to me).

_____

7. The time the play begins is a guess (belonging to anyone).

_____

8. The policy on abortion (belonging to the president of the United States) is controversial.

_____

9. The computer (belonging to him) is a Macintosh.

_____

10. The back (belonging to the room) is for standing only.

_____

Apostrophes with Contractions

Aki _can't_ come to the meeting because he is working on a research paper.

_We'll_ join you for coffee.

Nicole _shouldn't_ wear such expensive clothes to work.

Apostrophes with Plurals of Letters, Numbers, Signs, Abbreviations, and Words Used as Words

Use _'s_ to form the plural of lower-case letters:

Ned dotted his _i_ **'S** with little circles.

Add just -*s* to form the plural of capital letters:

Angela had received A **S** on all the quizzes.

Add just -*s* to form the plural of numbers and years:

Gertrude made her 7 **S** with little crossbars.

I hope the economy improves before the end of the 1990s.

Use just -*s* to form the plural of symbols such as & and $:

She always used & **S** instead of writing out the word *and*.

Use '*s* to form the plural of abbreviations ending with a period:

Very few R.N. **'S** work on the night shift at this hospital.

Use just -*s* to form the plural of abbreviations that do not end with a period:

Two BMW **S** were parked in front of Nancy Hume's house.

Because a simple -*s* added after an abbreviation spelled with lower-case letters might be misread, use '*s* to form the plural of such abbreviations:

Professor Schwartz's collection of lp **'S** was destroyed in the fire.

Use '*s* to form the plural of words used to represent themselves.

The opening paragraph of Donna's essay contained five *consequently* **'S**.

Confusion of Contractions and Possessives

Examine these sentences:

My dog was chasing *its* tail.

My dog thinks *it's* time for dinner.

In the first sentence, *its* expresses a possessive situation—the tail belongs to the dog—and no apostrophes are used to show possession with personal pronouns. In the second sentence, *it's* has nothing to do with a possessive situation—the time does *not* belong to the dog. *It's* is the contraction formed from *it is*.

ACTIVITY

23.8   **Editing for Apostrophe Usage**

The following letter includes many errors involving apostrophes. Correct these errors.

Dear Huong,

How are you? Things are okay here, but Im a little upset about the writing class Im taking. The teachers grades are incredible. I received Cs on my first two compositions. I couldnt believe it. When I went to talk to her about it, she told me my writing was good, but I had to learn the proper format for papers in an American university. Also, she said I had to learn how to use the spelling checker on the computer as all of my *separates* and *accepts* were spelled wrong. Whats really frustrating is that I could barely read her comments because of her writing. Her *as* look more like *os*, and the handwriting is terrible. Shes nice, though, and was helpful when I went to see her about my paper.

Now Im working on a research paper about life in America in the 1960s. Its really interesting! Mostly Im focusing on the big events that reflect the cultural attitudes of that time, like President Kennedys assassination. Im working hard to understand the style of writing research papers here. I didnt know there were so many rules, and its so different from the way we write. Oh, well, I guess Im learning!

Hope everythings well with you. Cant wait to see you in December. Write soon.

Love,

Hajin

23d QUOTATION MARKS

Quoting Other People's Words

The following examples illustrate the difference between direct and indirect quotation and paraphrasing.

Direct Quotation **Direct quotation** repeats a person's exact words, enclosed in quotation marks:

In *No Easy Walk to Freedom,* Nelson Mandela wrote, "I have fought against White domination, and I have fought against Black domination" (189).

When using direct quotation, be sure that the words of the original are reproduced exactly, including spelling, capitalization, and interior punctuation.

Indirect Quotation Reporting what someone else has written by changing the tense and person to fit into your context is known as **indirect quotation:**

In *No Easy Walk to Freedom,* Nelson Mandela wrote that he had fought against white domination, and he had fought against black domination (189).

Note that indirect quotation does not use quotation marks but does require a citation to credit the source.

Paraphrase Paraphrasing is expressing a person's meaning in different words:

In *No Easy Walk to Freedom,* Nelson Mandela wrote that he had opposed both white and black domination (189).

As with indirect quotation, paraphrased passages are not placed in quotation marks, but they do require a citation to credit the source.

Using Quotation Marks with Dialogue

The following conversation between Sid and Sam shows how dialogue—the representation of conversation between two or more people—should be handled:

> "I told you I don't have any advice." He poured coffee for both of them. "Do me a favor, Sam. Whatever happens between your Mom and me, or between you Mom and Dad, stick with me. Will you? Like a brother—I haven't got a brother."
>
> "Sure. But that's a funny idea."
>
> They looked into each other's eyes, maybe for the first time. The intimacy was a shock and a joy.
>
> Sid told him, "Your Mom's coming back." [John Jacob Clayton, *What Are Friends For?*]

In dialogue, place the words of each speaker in quotation marks and start a new paragraph each time the speaker changes. This makes it unnecessary to use a phrase like "he said" each time the speaker changes. Place text that is not spoken in the paragraphs along with the spoken text, but use no quotation marks with it.

Using a Quotation within a Quotation

In his book *Working,* Studs Terkel describes Dolores Dante, a waitress whose "pride in her skills helps her make it through the night: 'When I put the plate down, you don't hear a sound'" (xv).

When a quotation occurs within a quotation (in this case, the words of Dolores Dante within the words of Studs Terkel), the inner quotation is set off with single quotation marks rather than double ones. At the end of the quotation shown here, the writer has used both a single and a double quotation mark. The single quotation mark signals the end of the quotation from Dante; the double marks signal the end of the quotation from Terkel.

Using Quotation Marks with Titles of Short Works

I've just finished reading "O Yes" by Tillie Olsen.

Short works are pieces that are included within complete books, journals, or newspapers, or are of such length that they could be included in a book. Examples of short works include short stories, most poems, one-act plays, chapters, articles, essays, songs, and episodes of radio or television programs.

Larzer Ziff's article "The Ethical Dimensions of 'The Custom House'" argues that Hawthorne was dissatisfied with his novel *The Scarlet Letter.*

The writer has placed the title of Ziff's article in quotation marks and the title of the Hawthorne short story, "The Custom House," which is part of the larger title, in single quotation marks.

Using Quotation Marks with Words Used as Words

Professor Chavez used *hegemony* fourteen times in her speech yesterday.

Professor Chavez used "hegemony" fourteen times in her speech yesterday.

Using Quotation Marks with Words Used Ironically

Alvin's "limousine" was actually a Volkswagen Rabbit.

Using Quotation Marks with Definitions

Ms. Lewis is using *affect* to mean "a feeling or emotion."

Punctuation with Quotation Marks

Periods

My aunt said, "I believe that Malcolm X was a great leader."

Periods go *inside* quotation marks in American English. In other parts of the world, the convention may be different.

It is clear, as Michael Millgate points out, that "the doom of the Compson family seems about to be finally accomplished" (107).

Periods do not go inside the quotation marks when a citation immediately follows the sentence.

Agnew's "effete corps of impudent snobs" ultimately had the last laugh.

Periods do not go inside the quotation mark if nonquoted material completes the sentence in which the quoted material appears. In such cases, the period goes at the end of the sentence.

Commas

"I would like a cup of coffee," shouted Mr. Chang.

Place commas inside quotation marks.

Colons and Semicolons

The letter from the Department of Motor Vehicles said, "You owe a total of $129 for overdue fines"; I've never gotten a ticket in my life, so I know there is some mistake.

Place colons and semicolons *outside* quotation marks.

Question Marks, Exclamation Points, and Dashes

Nan asked, "What did you get on the test?"
Did Joan say, "I don't care about grades"?

Place question marks inside the quotation marks only when the quoted words form a question; place them outside the quotation marks when the whole sentence is a question but the quote itself is not.

When the couch fell on her foot, Corretta shouted one word: "Damn!"
I will never use the words "I give up"!

Place exclamation points inside quotation marks when they apply to the quoted material and outside if they apply to the whole sentence.

"I will not open my—" began Mitchell, until Carlo's look silenced him.

Place dashes inside the quotation marks if they clearly belong to the quoted material; otherwise, place them outside.

Using Quotation Marks with Direct Quotations

Add quotation marks wherever they are needed in the following sentences.

1. In President Kennedy's inaugural address, he stated, Ask not what your country can do for you; ask what you can do for your country.

2. Marius used the transitional expression however more than twenty times in his research paper!

3. Greg stared at Penelope, who looked away. That's a lot of money to spend on a trip, Greg said.

4. When will you be home? asked Mrs. Cleaver. Before supper, said Beaver. I promise.

5. In his book *Dictators*, Jules Archer cites Karl Marx and Friedrich Engels: Let the ruling class tremble at a Communist revolution. The proletarians have nothing to lose but their chains. They have a world to win. Working men of all countries, unite! (17).

6. Paula stated defiantly, I ate the turkey, mashed potatoes, and stuffing! No wonder nothing remained for the other guests.

7. The *Wall Street Journal* article Flooded by Refugees, Western Europe Slams Doors on Foreigners was fascinating.

8. Texans, replied Jake, are a tough breed.

9. The actor was upset about the writer using skinny rather than slender to describe him.

10. Did the policeman say Please sign the warrant?

Distinguishing between Direct and Indirect Quotations

Decide if the following sentences are direct or indirect quotations. If they are indirect, place a check next to the sentence; if they are direct, add quotation marks, punctuation, and capital letters where necessary.

> *Example:* Jason said he would not be able to join us for the trip to Reading. __✓__

1. My father said that I could drive his BMW to Colorado. _____

2. Cheryl blurted out when my laundry is done, I'm out of here. _____

3. The United Nations Population Fund states that population growth will be the greatest in Africa in the 1990s. _____

4. The chairperson asked the stockholders if they wanted to sell some shares. _____

5. The little boy screamed to his mother Mindy did it! _____

Using Quotation Marks with Dialogue

Add quotation marks to the following dialogue wherever they are necessary.

> When we have France, said Casson, there will be no shortage—
> Cash, said the Englishman. Half in advance and half on completion.
> How much? asked Rodin.
> Half a million.
> Rodin glanced at Montclair, who grimaced. That's a lot of money, half a million new francs—
> Dollars, said the Englishman.
> Half a million dollars? shouted Montclair, rising from his seat. You are crazy!
>
> No, said the Englishman calmly, but I am the best, and therefore the most expensive. [Frederick Forsythe, *The Day of the Jackal*]

23e COMMAS, SEMICOLONS, APOSTROPHES, AND QUOTATION MARKS: COMPREHENSIVE CHECK

Diagnostic Retest

Complete Activity 23.1 again. If you still miss or have difficulty with any items, review the relevant sections of the workbook.

Putting It All Together

All of the commas, semicolons, apostrophes, and quotation marks have been omitted from the following passage. Add these marks wherever they are needed.

> It was two oclock in the morning when Pilar waked him. As her hand touched him he thought it was Maria and he rolled toward her and said Rabbit. Then the womans big hand shook his shoulder and he was suddenly completely and absolutely awake. His hand was around the butt of the pistol that lay alongside of his right bare leg he was as cocked as the pistol with its safety catch slipped off.
>
> In the dark he saw it was Pilar and he looked at the dial of his wristwatch with the two hands shining in the short angle close to the top. Seeing it was only two he said What passes with thee woman?

Pablo is gone the big woman said to him.

Robert Jordan put on his trousers and shoes. Maria had not waked.

When? he asked.

It must be an hour.

And?

He has taken something of mine the woman said miserably.

So. What?

I dont know she told him. Come and see.

In the dark they walked over to the entrance of the cave ducked under the blanket and went in. Robert Jordan followed her in the dead-ashes bad-air and sleeping-men smell of the cave. He shined his electric torch so that he would not step on any of those who were sleeping on the floor. [Ernest Hemingway, *For Whom the Bell Tolls*]

EDITING FOR OTHER PUNCTUATION

DIAGNOSTIC ACTIVITY: OTHER PUNCTUATION MARKS

ACTIVITY
24.1 **How Much Do You Know?**

Read each sentence to determine if it contains an error in punctuation concerning periods, question marks, exclamation points, colons, ellipses, parentheses, dashes, brackets, or slashes. If so, correct the error. Not all sentences contain errors.

> *Example:* The exam sections are as follows: grammar, vocabulary, and dictation.

1. Pam had two goals for the summer: moving to Chicago and finding a job.

2. Boris ate thirty-five hamburgers at lunch.

3. I still remember the old Irish priest's words, "Let the sun shine warmly on your face."

4. Wayne had to contact the director (a woman who was also the chairperson of the Modern Language Association MLA and whom he had already met at the previous convention).

5. Anita's plane was scheduled to arrive at O'Hare International Airport at 3;00 A.M.

6. U.S. educators are concerned with the low scores on the Scholastic Achievement Test SAT.

7. I tried to get French Open tickets for: the men's quarterfinals and the women's finals.

8. You should contact your state senator and-or state assembly representative.

9. "Don't you think you should buy a foreign car instead"? my uncle asked me.

10. Since his arrival in Chicago, Terry has had several jobs: restaurant manager, cook, and baker.

11. Her purpose—to win the race was second only to the money.

12. The proportion of students to teachers is 15–1.

13. The interest on her student loan amounted to five hundred and fifty dollars ($550).

14. The bill that I had neglected to pay was dated 11/2/92.

15. The ingredients for guacamole are as follows—avocados, tomatoes, garlic, and hot peppers.

Determine which items you missed in this Diagnostic Activity. If you missed or had difficulty answering any of the items, please go to the appropriate section in *The HarperCollins Concise Handbook for Writers* and this workbook for further practice and study.

It is important to know which items cause you difficulty. When revising your writing, you might want to go through your paper one time checking only for punctuation. Concentrate on items that you had difficulty with in this activity.

24b USING PERIODS, EXCLAMATION POINTS, AND QUESTION MARKS TO END SENTENCES

Periods

A snake entered the garden .

At that moment, I noticed that it was 3:00 P . M .

When a sentence ends with an abbreviation, the period also serves as the end punctuation for the sentence; never use two periods in succession.

Question Marks

Could this be the same snake that tempted Eve ?

Should I say yes ? Say no ? Run away ?

I finally responded, "Are you talking to me ? "

Hadn't I read a sign that said, "Don't eat the fruit of the tree in the middle of the garden" ?

In the third sentence, the quoted material is a question, so the question mark goes inside the quotation marks. In the fourth, the complete sentence is a question, but the quoted portion is not, so the question mark goes outside the quotation marks.

Exclamation Points

The snake asked me my name !

ACTIVITY

24.2 Using End Punctuation

Read the following advertisement, from which all of the end punctuation (periods, question marks, and exclamation points) has been omitted. Determine where the sentences end, and add the appropriate punctuation marks.

Are you happy with your life Have you been feeling worthless lately How would you like to turn your life around We have the answer

JOIN
the School of Snappy Comebacks

Millions of people have turned their lives into successful, profitable, and happy ones The School of Snappy Comebacks teaches you how to take charge of your life No longer will you find bullies kicking sand in your face at the beach or your boss humiliating you in front of your clients You will be well prepared with all kinds of interesting, humorous, and forceful comebacks to any situation

Read the following quote from one of our clients:

"When I first arrived at the School of Snappy Comebacks, I had never been so low in my life I was at the end of my rope In just six short weeks, I was a new person I got a new job and was recently promoted to vice-president of the company It's unbelievable I never could have done it without the help of your school"

If you call today, you will receive the first week's tuition absolutely free Classes are offered in the A.M. and P.M. Don't hesitate to call Isn't it time to turn your life around

555-3333

24c COLONS

When to Use a Colon

A colon can be used only after an independent clause. It indicates a break between two grammatical elements greater than that marked by a semicolon but less than that indicated by a period:

Two issues are at the center of her campaign : employment and health care.

One use for a colon is to introduce specific instances or examples of general ideas mentioned in the independent clause preceding the colon. Often the number of examples is specified in the independent clause preceding the colon.

I could never live in a big city, for two reasons : I grew up on a farm, and I love the wide-open spaces.

The material following the colon explains or justifies the fact stated in the first independent clause.

What Can Follow a Colon

Appositives:	The museum will be exhibiting one of the twentieth century's most famous paintings : van Gogh's *Starry Night*.
Quotation:	At times like these, we should remember the words of Franklin Delano Roosevelt : "We have nothing to fear but fear itself."
Word:	There was one explanation for her success : luck.
Phrase:	Max was hiding in the one place we never thought to look : under his bed.
List:	My collection features three kinds of recipes : salads, appetizers, and desserts.
Independent clause:	The teacher did the only thing he could under the circumstances : he dismissed the class.

Capitalization with Colons

In general, a complete sentence or series of sentences that follows a colon begins with a capital letter. There is one exception, however:

Jake did the one thing he could do : he ran out of the room.

Jake did the one thing he could do : He ran out of the room.

If only one sentence follows the colon, it may be capitalized or lower-cased. Either approach is correct, but be consistent throughout a given piece of writing.

President Kennedy's words echoed in my ears : "Ask not what your country can do for you; ask what you can do for your country."

It puzzled us : Who put them up to it?

If the complete sentence after a colon is a quotation or a question, it must begin with a capital letter.

Bruce acted erratically after the accident : He jumped out of his car. He started shouting at passing cars. Then he lay down on the shoulder of the road and went to sleep.

When a colon introduces material that consists of more than one sentence, each sentence must begin with a capital letter, including the one following the colon.

Colons with *the following* and *as follows*

A colon is required after *the following* and *as follows* when they introduce a list:

You should bring the following : a pen, a pad, and a dictionary.

The ingredients are as follows : corn, flour, salt, and milk.

Other Uses of the Colon

TIME: The train arrived at 6 **:** 38 P.M.

SUBTITLES: The text for my psychology course is *Understanding Human Behavior* **:** *An Intro-duction to Behavioral Psychology.*

RATIOS: The ratio of water to salt is 10 **:** 1 in this solution.

CHAPTER/VERSE: We preferred the version of creation in Genesis 1 **:** 27 to that in Genesis 2 **:** 22.

Note that the current trend is to use a period rather than a colon to separate chapter and verse.

A colon is also used after the salutation of a business letter:

Dear Mr. Vasquez **:**

ACTIVITY
24.3   **Editing for Use of Colons**

Check the following sentences for the use of colons. Some sentences have unnec-essary colons, some are missing colons, and some are correct. Rewrite the incor-rect sentences.

> *Example:*   My father was: tired, angry, and flabbergasted over my brother's accident.
>
> *My father was tired, angry, and flabbergasted over my brother's accident.*

1. The committee decided on two important recommendations, to raise taxes and to limit spending.

   _____

2. Nan's ring had three kinds of stones: rubies, emeralds, and diamonds.

   _____

3. Don is currently reading *Peer Editing. What Do Students Really Think?*

   _____

4. I'll never forget my grandmother's words. "An apple a day keeps the doctor away."

   _____

5. Sue's son suffered a terrible injury: when he was out late at night, a piece of glass from a bottle flew into his eye.

   _____

ACTIVITY
24.4   Writing Sentences Using Colons

Use the following prompts to create your own sentences using colons.

> *Example:*   Ingredients for an omelette—eggs, milk, cheese, salt, pepper
>
> *The ingredients for an omelette are as follows: eggs, milk, cheese, salt, and pepper.*

1. The time is thirty-five minutes after six o'clock.

   _____

2. A saying your mother often used

   _____

3. The title and subtitle of a book

   _____

4. An explanation for the hot weather

   _____

5. A salad recipe

   _____

24d ELLIPSES

An **ellipsis** (plural, *ellipses*) is a series of three dots separated by spaces used to indicate that material has been left out. To type an ellipsis, you first press the space bar, then type a period, hit the space bar again, type another period, hit the space bar once more, type a third period, and hit the space bar one last time.

Ellipses to Show Omissions in Quotations

A quote from Annie Dillard's *Pilgrim at Tinker Creek* will illustrate how ellipses are used to show that part of a direct quotation has been omitted. The original passage appeared as follows:

> When I was six or seven years old, growing up in Pittsburgh, I used to take a precious penny of my own and hide it for someone else to find. It was a curious compulsion; sadly, I've never been seized by it since. For some reason I always "hid" the penny along the same stretch of sidewalk up the street. I would cradle it at the roots of a sycamore, say, or in a hole left by a chipped-off piece of sidewalk. Then I would take a piece of chalk and, starting at either end of the block, draw huge arrows leading up to the penny from both directions. After I learned to write I labeled the arrows: SURPRISE AHEAD or MONEY THIS WAY. I was greatly excited, during all this arrow-drawing, at the thought of the first lucky passer-by who would receive in this way, regardless of merit, a free gift from the universe. But I never lurked about. I would go straight home and not give the matter another thought until, some months later, I would be gripped again by the impulse to hide another penny.

Now observe how ellipses are used to mark omissions:

Annie Dillard tells about hiding a penny in the sidewalk near her home in Pittsburgh. "Then I would take a piece of chalk and . . . draw huge arrows leading up to the penny from both directions."

The writer has omitted the words *starting at either end of the block* and has indicated this omission with an ellipsis. (Note that punctuation no longer necessary to the new context has been omitted also.)

After hiding her penny, Dillard reports that she never waited to see who would find it but rather "would go straight home and not give the matter another thought. . . . "

Here the writer has quoted a part of a sentence, omitting both the beginning and the end. Note that an ellipsis is *not* used to indicate omitted material at the beginning of a quotation. Note also that the omission at the end coincides with the end of the writer's sentence; the ellipsis therefore follows the sentence period.

Annie Dillard tells a story about a curious activity she engaged in when she was a child. "When I was six or seven years old, growing up in Pittsburgh, I used to take a precious penny of my own and hide it for someone else to find. . . . For some reason I always 'hid' the penny along the same stretch of sidewalk up the street."

In this quotation, a period and an ellipsis are used because a complete sentence precedes the omission.

INCORRECT: "I would go straight home and . . . would be gripped again by the impulse to hide another penny."

This sentence is not a legitimate use of ellipsis because even though it reproduces the original words accurately and indicates where words have been omitted, it distorts the meaning of the original passage. In this case, the quoted passage implies that Annie would go home and immediately be gripped by the desire to hide another penny; in fact, the original passage indicated that some months would pass before she would again feel such a compulsion. Distorting the original author's meaning through the use of ellipses is unethical.

Omissions of Lines of Poetry

In quoted poetry of more than three lines, a full line of spaced periods is used to indicate the omission of one or more lines of the original poem:

> Let me not to the marriage of true minds
> Admit impediment. Love is not love
> Which alters when it alteration finds
> Or bends with the remover to remove
> . . . .
> Love alters not with his brief hours and weeks,
> But bears it out even to the edge of doom.
>   If this be error, and upon me proved,
>   I never writ, not no man ever loved.
>
> —William Shakespeare, Sonnet 116

Ellipses to Indicate Interrupted Speech

An ellipsis may be used to indicate hesitation or an interruption in the words of a speaker or writer or to suggest speech or writing left unfinished:

I wonder what would happen if . . .

The ellipsis indicates that the speaker's voice trails off without finishing the sentence.

ACTIVITY
24.5 **Using Ellipses**

This activity is based on the following passage about Mustafa Kemal Atatürk, dictator of Turkey from 1919 to 1938. The sentences have been numbered for easy reference. First read the passage; then follow the instructions. An example is provided.

(1) He was a great man and he was a terrible man. (2) He freed Turkey from European colonialism—and burned alive tens of thousands of Greek civilians in Smyrna, pitching their charred bodies into the harbor. (3) He brought Turkey out of the Middle Ages into the twentieth century—and lived a personal life of barbaric depravity. (4) He preached democracy for Turkey—and ruled as an absolute dictator, torturing and hanging his opponents.

(5) Born in the Turkish quarter of Salonika, Greece, in 1881, he had only a first name, Mustafa, as was the custom of the old Ottoman Turks. (6) He won a second name, Kemal ("Perfection"), from his teachers, who were impressed with his brilliance as a student. (7) His third name, Atatürk ("Father of Turks"), he awarded to himself as dictator. [Jules Archer, *Dictators*]

Example: Begin with this sentence: *The Turkish dictator had many names.* Quote sentence 5, omitting the place of birth and the comment on Turkish custom.

The Turkish dictator had many names. "Born . . . in 1881, he had only a first name, Mustafa. . . ."

1. Begin with this sentence: *Mustafa Kemal Atatürk, Turkey's dictator, was both a great man and a terrible man.* Quote sentence 2, omitting the final phrase, "pitching their charred bodies into the harbor."

2. Using the same beginning, quote sentence 3, omitting the prepositional phrase "into the twentieth century."

3. Using the same beginning, quote sentences 2 and 4, omitting sentence 3 completely.

24e **PARENTHESES**

Parentheses, always in pairs, are used for a variety of purposes:

1. To set off information that is supplementary to the main idea of the sentence:

   Mayor Schmidt (now in his third term) announced a twenty percent budget cut.

My mother never learned to drive an automobile. (She grew up in rural China.) She did, however, get her pilot's license in 1972.

When a complete sentence is used parenthetically, as in the second example, the sentence begins with a capital letter and ends with appropriate end punctuation. Do not place a complete sentence parenthetically inside another sentence.

2. To introduce an acronym:

The Modern Language Association (MLA) publishes a guide to research and documentation.

An acronym is an abbreviation written in capital letters without periods. If you are going to use an acronym throughout a piece of writing, introduce the reader to it by first using the spelled-out name, followed by the acronym in parentheses. Thereafter, you can use the acronym alone.

3. To restate sums of money:

The interest on this debt amounts to six thousand four hundred dollars ($6,400) per year.

In some business writing, it is common to spell out amounts of money and then to indicate the same amount parenthetically in numbers.

4. To enclose numerations:

The causes of the accident were (1) excessive speed, (2) faulty brakes, and (3) foggy conditions.

When presenting a numbered or lettered list within a sentence, it is conventional to place the numbers or letters in parentheses.

5. To set off citations:

Wagenknecht observes that Hawthorne was "a solitary, introspective man" (5) .

Use parentheses to enclose citations indicating the sources of quotations and paraphrases in your writing. (Parenthetical documentation is discussed in Chapter 27 of this workbook.)

24f DASHES

A dash—more precisely, an **em dash** (because it is the width of the letter *m*) is not the same as a hyphen. It is longer than a hyphen. On a typewriter, use two hyphens to represent a dash; in most word processing programs, there is a key combination that will produce a true dash. Do not put spaces at either end of a dash.

Use dashes to set off parenthetical information that you want to emphasize:

The president—with only three weeks remaining in his term—should not appoint a new chief of staff.

Supplemental material, asides, and minor digressions can be set off by commas, parentheses, or dashes. Dashes give the material the most emphasis, indicating that it is important. Commas give less emphasis, and parentheses give even less, indicating that the material can be ignored if the reader is in a hurry.

24g BRACKETS

Brackets, always in pairs, are used to set off inserted material:

John Dean reports that "within a month of coming to the White House, [he] had crossed an ethical line."

Use brackets to show where the writer has inserted material or made minor changes in the wording of direct quotations. In the original text quoted here, John Dean wrote, "I had crossed an ethical line." The writer using this quotation placed *he* in brackets to indicate that the word has been changed from the original *I*. Many writers prefer to avoid such changes.

I had to meet with a representative of the neighborhood organization (a man who was rumored to work for the Central Intelligence Agency [CIA] and whom I had avoided for years).

Normally, the acronym *CIA* would be placed in parentheses; here, however, it is placed in brackets because it appears within a larger element already in parentheses.

24h SLASHES

The slash—also called the *virgule* or the *solidus*—is useful in the following circumstances in English:

1. To form fractions:

   An error of 1 / 32 inch can make the tool inoperable.

2. To express dates:

   The memo was dated 3 / 12 / 93.

   Use this format only in informal communications.

3. To indicate that either of two words is or may be appropriate:

   Your mother and / or your father may also attend the banquet.

   A student should always make sure he / she understands an assignment before beginning to work on it.

   To avoid sexism, the third-person pronoun is sometimes written *he / she* (or *s / he*), indicating that it is referring to either a man or a woman. Opinion is divided over this usage. Many readers find it clumsy or distracting. We recommend that you either write *he or she* or revise the sentence to permit the use of a plural pronoun.

4. To mark line breaks in song lyrics and poetry:

   Emily Dickinson's self-effacing style can be seen in her lines, "I'm nobody. Who are you? / Are you nobody too?"

   The slash is used to separate lines of lyrics or poetry when they are run into the text instead of set off from it. This is the only situation in which you leave a space before and after the slash.

ACTIVITY

24.6   Using Parentheses, Dashes, Brackets, and Slashes

Read the following passage, inserting parentheses, dashes, brackets, and slashes wherever they are needed. Not all of these punctuation marks are necessary in this passage.

The British anthropologist Sir Edward Burnett Tylor introduced the term *culture* as scientists use it today. In his book *Primitive Culture* 1871, Tylor defined culture as "that complex whole which includes knowledge, belief, art, morals, law, custom, and any other capabilities and or habits acquired by man as a member of society." Tylor's definition includes three of the most important characteristics of culture: 1 Culture is acquired by people a process called *enculturation*. 2 A person acquires culture as a member of society. Social life would be impossible without understandings and practices shared by all people. 3 Culture is a complex whole. Its units are called *cultural traits*. They may include a customary place for the dead, a device such as a plow, or a gesture such as a handshake.

Culture must be in two places at once. First, it must be in the environment, where it appears as *artifacts* things made by human beings or as *behavior*. Some of the culture in this environment such as a gesture or the telling of a story is short-lived. But other culture such as a stone ax or a written story lasts for a very long time. Second, culture must be in some person's mind as a set of ideas for understanding and evaluating artifacts and behavior. An artifact that nobody understands is incomplete culture.

Development of a culture can bring change. For example, a society may switch from food gathering to farming as a result of population growth and the disappearance of game. A still larger population, in turn, brings even greater specialization and division of labor. The United Nations Population Fund UNPF is now studying the effects of these changes in Third World countries. Whenever environmental changes or other pressures make new ways of doing things desirable, a culture changes. [Paul Bohannan]

24i ■ OTHER PUNCTUATION: COMPREHENSIVE CHECK

24.7 Diagnostic Retest

Complete Activity 24.1 again. If you still miss or have difficulty with any items, review the relevant sections of the workbook.

24.8 Putting It All Together

Read the following passage about Taoism and how it can be applied to the story of *Winnie the Pooh*. Then answer the questions that follow the passage.

The essence of the principle of the Uncarved Block is that things in their original simplicity contain their own natural power; this power is easily spoiled and lost when that simplicity is changed. For the written character *P'u*, the typical Chinese dictionary will give a definition of "natural, simple, plain, honest." *P'u* is composed of two separate characters combined: the first, the "radical" or root-meaning one, is that for tree or wood; the second, the "phonetic" or sound-given one, is the character for dense growth or thicket. So from "tree in a thicket" or "wood not cut" comes the meaning of "things in their natural state"—what is generally represented in English versions of Taoist writing as the "uncarved block."

The basic Taoist principle applies not only to *things* in their natural beauty and function but to people as well. Or bears. Which brings us to Pooh, the very epitome of the Uncarved Block. As an illustration of the principle, he may appear a bit *too* simple at times:

"I *think* it's more to the right," said Piglet nervously. "What do *you* think, Pooh?"

Pooh looked at his two paws. He knew that one of them was right, and he knew that when you had decided which one of them was right, then the other one was left, but he never could remember how to begin.

"Well," he said slowly—

But no matter how he may seem to others, especially those fooled by appearances, Pooh, the Uncarved Block, is able to accomplish what he does because he *is* simple-minded. [Benjamin Hoff, *The Tao of Pooh*]

A.   Write down all the words, phrases, or sentences in the passage that are examples of each of the following items. Certain words, phrases, or sentences may be used in more than one instance. The number in parentheses indicates how many examples there are of that item.

1. Commas with introductory elements (6)

2. Commas with items in a series (1)

3. Semicolon with items in a series containing commas (1)

4. Commas in sentences with two independent clauses (1)

5. Semicolon in two closely related independent clauses (1)

6. Commas with a nonrestrictive appositive (3)

7. Commas with a noun of direct address (1)

8. Commas with an interjection (1)

9. Commas to set off parenthetical information (1)

10. Commas with quotation marks (2)

11. Apostrophe in a contraction (1)

12. Quotation marks used around a direct quotation (3)

13. Quotation marks around definitions (7)

B. Now answer the following questions.

1. There are two colons in the passage. Based on what you know about what can follow a colon, what does each colon in this example introduce?

2. The first dash in this passage is used for the function you learned about in 24f. What function is this?

3. The second dash serves a different function. What do you think this function is?

 **MECHANICS**

25a DIAGNOSTIC ACTIVITY: MECHANICS

25.1 How Much Do You Know?

Read each sentence to determine if it contains an error in mechanics. If so, correct the error. Not all sentences contain errors.

Example: The chicago tribune and the chicago sun-times are rival newspapers.

1. Meade high school will be hosting the track invitational this Saturday.

2. "When you arrive at the airport," my sister said, "Give me a call."

3. 25,000 people marched in the parade last week.

4. Kathy's grand-parents came to the United States from England.

5. Dallas was a popular television drama.

6. I explained to the secretary that I had an appointment with my prof.

7. I can't decide whether to take art history 101 or film aesthetics 110 this semester.

8. Boat rides on the Mississippi river are more popular than ever.

9. There were 115 presenters at the conference.

10. The legal drinking age in most states is twenty one.

11. Have you ever read a shakespearean poem?

12. "The Purloined Letter" is one of my favorite Edgar Allan Poe short stories.

13. The governor asked senator Bower to speak at the meeting.

14. The failed coup d'état jeopardized the lives of many people.

15. My neighbor is so good-natured; she quickly forgave me for breaking her window.

16. When told that the peasants had no bread, Marie-Antoinette retorted: "let them eat cake!"

Determine which items you missed on this Diagnostic Activity. If you missed or had trouble with any of the items, please go to the appropriate section in *The HarperCollins Concise Handbook for Writers* and this workbook for further practice and study.

It is important to know which items cause you difficulty. When revising your writing, you might want to go through your paper one time checking only for mechanical items. Concentrate on items that you had difficulty with in this activity.

25b CAPITALIZATION

Prose and Poetry

Capitalize the first word in every sentence:

This coffee is great.

Capitalize each line of a poem (unless the poet prefers otherwise):

To fling my arms wide
In the face of the sun,
Dance! Whirl! Whirl!
Till the quick day is done.
Rest at pale evening . . .
A tall, slim tree . . .
Night coming tenderly
    Black like me.
—Langston Hughes, "Dream Variations"

Some contemporary poets do not capitalize the first word in every line of their poetry. When quoting poetry, reproduce the poet's capitalization exactly.

Text after a Colon

A single independent clause (or complete sentence) that follows a colon may be capitalized or lower-cased:

My mother is a determined woman: she went back to college at the age of forty-five.

My mother is a determined woman: She went back to college at the age of forty-five.

Whichever style you choose, be consistent throughout a given piece of writing.

If the complete sentence after a colon is a quotation, a question, or the first in a series of sentences, it must be capitalized:

Early in "Civil Disobedience," Thoreau makes a paradoxical observation: "That government is best which governs not at all."

The question was on everyone's mind: Who shot J.R.?

My boss treats me well: He listens to my suggestions. He gives me credit when I do well. Most important, he explains what I've done wrong when I make a mistake.

Proper Nouns versus Common Nouns

An important use of capitalization involves proper nouns. The following lists indicate the basic difference between proper and common nouns.

PROPER NOUN	COMMON NOUN
Doctor Williams	my doctor
Arkansas	the state
the Pacific Ocean	the ocean
Mathematics 101	a math course
Rover	my collie
Uncle Jake	her uncle

As you can see, you should capitalize **proper nouns,** nouns that are the **names** of specific persons, places, or things.

The chart gives general guidelines for capitalizing proper and common nouns. Be aware, however, that different publications and professions may take a different approach to capitalization.

CAPITALIZING NOUNS

Category	Proper Noun	Common Noun
Names	Julie Moriarty Tracey Robertson Professor Scheper Colonel Adams Dean Snope	my neighbor a freshman the professor a colonel the dean
Groups	African American Republicans Chicano Hispanic Muslim Libertarians	
Place names	Indian Ocean Delaware River the South	the ocean the river walking south
Organizations	the Boy Scouts New York Court of Appeals Miami Dade Community College Groveton High School	my club traffic court the college my high school
Historical periods	the Great Depression the Vietnam War the Age of Enlightenment	the next depression the war the eighteenth century
Time	Wednesday March	winter the third month
Religious terms	God Allah Buddha the Koran	a Greek god the painting of a goddess a prophet a hymnal
Scientific terms	*Homo sapiens* *Quercus palustris* *E. coli*	man oak tree bacteria
Heavenly bodies	Mars the Milky Way Crab Nebula	planet galaxy star

(continued)

CAPITALIZING NOUNS (continued)

Category	Proper Noun	Common Noun
Chemical elements	—	uranium sulfuric acid
Diseases	Hodgkin's disease	cancer pneumonia
Laws	Boyle's law	the second law of thermodynamics
Trademarks	Kleenex Coca-Cola Advil Xerox	tissues soda, pop, soft drink aspirin photocopier
School courses	Sociology 101 Early Childhood Psychology	sociology psychology

Proper Adjectives

Adjectives that are derived from proper nouns should ordinarily be capitalized:

French	Shakespearean
Roman	Christian

I and *O*

Capitalize the pronoun *I* and the interjection *O:*

When I heard the phone ring, I answered it.

I replied, "I will do whatever you wish, O mighty one."

Quotations

Within a sentence, only a quotation that is a complete sentence and is presented as such should be capitalized:

My father asked us not to "besmirch the family's name."

Besmirch the family's name is not a sentence by itself, so the first letter is not capitalized.

My father said, "Be home by midnight," as we walked out the door.

Be home by midnight is a sentence by itself, so it is capitalized.

"When you get home," my father said, "don't wake me up."

The second part of the quotation is not capitalized because it is not a sentence by itself; it is the continuation of the sentence begun in the first part of the quotation.

Titles

Titles of books, poems, paintings, plays, musical compositions, movies, radio and television programs, and periodicals are capitalized as in the following:

The Floating Opera

Paradigms Lost: Images of Man in the Mirror of Science

Sundiata: An Epic of Old Mali

Capitalize the first word, last word, and all other important words in titles. Articles, prepositions, co-ordinating conjunctions, and *to* in infinitives are not capitalized, regardless of their length, unless they are the first or last word of the title or subtitle. Pronouns and verbs are always capitalized, regardless of their length.

Questions in a Series

The convention for capitalizing a series of questions that are not complete sentences varies:

What will the government tax next? Our children? Our underwear? Our garbage?

What will the government tax next? our children? our underwear? our garbage?

Use either style, but be consistent throughout a single piece of writing.

ACTIVITY
25.2 **Editing Sentences for Capitalization**

Edit the following sentences for capitalization. Then state the principle that applies.

Example: The M̶aple tree in my back yard has beautiful fall colors.
(m above the crossed-out M)

Don't capitalize common nouns.

1. The results of the exam were incredible: Not one person passed!

2. My Doctor, who is Hispanic, comes from Guadalajara.

3. My favorite novel is *Travels With my Aunt.*

4. Based on my visit to Europe last summer, I find the french more interesting than the germans.

5. She summed it up succinctly: "the place is a dump!"

ACTIVITY
25.3 **Writing Sentences with Capitalized Words**

Write sentences using the prompts given.

Example: Use a proper noun for an organization and a common noun for a location.

Midland High is on the southeast corner of the street.

1. Write a sentence containing a full-sentence quotation.

_____

2. Write a sentence with a colon followed by an independent clause.

_____

3. Write a sentence containing a trademark and a common noun.

_____

4. Write a sentence about two of the classes you are taking and your professors.

_____

5. Write a sentence with a title in it.

_____

ACTIVITY
25.4 | **Using Capitals**

No capital letters have been used in the following passage about unusual dreams. Insert them where they are needed.

a popular dreamer was professor john chapman from swaffam, england. he had three dreams that told him to journey to london and meet on london bridge a man who would make him rich. he obeyed and met a man who asked, "what are you doing on this bridge?" he answered, "a dream has sent me here." the man remarked that a recent dream had instructed him to journey to swaffam and dig up a jar of gold coins that rested under the only tree of john chapman. chapman kept quiet, went home, and became a rich man.

sir e. w. budge had a triple dream on the night before his fateful examination in ancient oriental languages 101, between midnight and 2 A.M., showing him just what the test would be. he got up and studied the obscure material from 2 A.M. until it was time for the examination. his dream had been accurate in every detail, and he won the fellowship that made possible his career as keeper of egyptian antiquities at the british museum.

abraham lincoln was oppressed for two weeks by a dream that foretold his assassination. when lincoln next looked into his bible, he turned by chance to jacob's dream and then discovered how much emphasis the entire bible puts on dreams and visions. He remarked that in his day, dreams were regarded as very foolish, but if we believe the bible, we must accept the fact that in the old days, god used dreams. lincoln shared that observation shortly before he died, hoping that his dream would not come true. [Adapted from Kathryn Lindskoog, *The Gift of Dreams*]

25c ABBREVIATIONS AND ACRONYMS

Personal Titles

Abbreviate titles only when used with names. Use only one title at a time.

Ms. Hillary Rodham Clinton   Dr. Marie Williams

Mr. Jacob Miller	Mr. Castleton
George Scheper, Ph.D.	Nancy Hume, M.A.
Ursula Gudrun, D.D.S.	Martin Villanueva, M.S.W.
Henry Wadsworth, Jr.	Kent G. Stockdale III
Prof. Ralph Stephens	Professor Stephens
Sen. Barbara Boxer	Senator Boxer
Col. L. Dow Adams	Colonel Adams

Abbreviations with Numbers

Periods have traditionally been used with many abbreviations but not with others. In recent years, the trend has been toward using fewer periods with abbreviations, a trend we encourage. Nevertheless, for writers who prefer a more conventional approach, the examples here show periods where they have been traditionally required. The trend toward omitting periods is especially strong in technical writing.

10:30 P.M. *or* 10:30 p.m.	Typesetters normally use small caps—letters the size of lower-case letters but in the form of capital letters. If your typewriter or computer doesn't permit small caps, use lower case for A.M. or P.M.
400 B.C. *or* 400 B.C.	Again, use small caps, if you can; if not, use *full capitals.*
A.D. 1492 *or* A.D. 1492	B.C. follows the date; A.D. precedes it. B.C. is the abbreviation for *before Christ* and indicates the number of years before the birth of Christ that an event occurred. A.D. stands for *anno Domini,* Latin for "in the year of the Lord." It is used to indicate dates of events after the birth of Christ.
400 B.C.E. *or* 400 B.C.E.	B.C.E. stands for "before the Common Era" and is the equivalent of B.C. It is used to avoid the Christian connotation of B.C.
1492 C.E. *or* 1492 C.E.	C.E. stands for "Common Era" and is the equivalent of A.D. It is used to avoid the Christian connotation of A.D. Note that C.E. follows the date rather than precedes it, as A.D. does.
No. 10 or no. 10	The abbreviation for *number* may be either capitalized or lower-cased. Just be consistent throughout a piece of writing.
$19.95	Use a dollar sign with numbers and a decimal point to indicate dollar and cent amounts. Never use a dollar sign and a cent sign (¢) with the same numbers.
32°F 0°C 273 K	A small superscript circle stands for the word *degrees.* The capital *F* indicates that the temperature is being measured on the Fahrenheit scale; the capital *C,* that the Celsius (centigrade) scale is being used; the capital *K,* that the Kelvin scale is being used. Note that no degree mark is used with temperatures expressed in Kelvin.

Avoid the errors illustrated by the following sentences:

INCORRECT: I will meet you in the P.M.

The abbreviations A.M. and P.M. should be used only with times expressed in numbers and should not substitute for the word *morning* or *afternoon* in other contexts.

INCORRECT: I found a $ bill in my pocket.

Use a dollar sign only with a number amount, not to indicate the word *dollar* or *dollars* by itself.

INCORRECT: We have ordered a no. of spare parts for the computer.

Use the abbreviation for *number* only in conjunction with a number, not to represent the word *number* by itself.

Organizations, Companies, and Government Agencies

CIA	Central Intelligence Agency
NAACP	National Association for the Advancement of Colored People
IBM	International Business Machines
NOW	National Organization for Women
CBS	Columbia Broadcasting System
GM	General Motors

Such abbreviations are acceptable in most writing; today they are almost always written without periods. Be careful, however, not to use an abbreviation with which your reader may be unfamiliar, unless you introduce it first as in the following sentence:

> We sent a grant proposal to the National Endowment for the Humanities (NEH), and we expect to be funded. The NEH is giving priority to proposals related to cultural diversity this year.

Use abbreviations such as *Inc., Co., Corp.,* or the ampersand (&) only if they appear in the official name of the company or organization.

Abbreviations of Latin Terms

In general, avoid Latin terms and the abbreviations for them in your writing. They are intended primarily for use in documenting sources.

cf.	compare *(confer)*
e.g.	for example *(exempli gratia)*
et al.	and others *(et alii)*
i.e.	that is *(id est)*
loc. cit.	in the place cited *(loco citato)*
N.B.	note well *(nota bene)*
op. cit.	in the work cited *(opere citato)*
q.v.	which see *(quod vide)*

In written text, use the English translation in place of the Latin term:

for example

This college has many support services for students: e.g., counseling, job placement, tutoring, and assessment.

Periods with Abbreviations

The use of periods with abbreviations varies, although the trend is strongly away from the use of periods with most abbreviations. If there is a principle behind current use, it is illustrated by the following:

ABBREVIATIONS	ACRONYMS AND INITIAL ABBREVIATIONS
St.	CARE
Blvd.	UNICEF
Nov.	IRS

In general, true **abbreviations**—words shortened by the omission of letters—are often followed by a period. An **acronym,** which consists of the first letter of a series of words used as a shortened version and pronounced as though it were a word (CARE, UNICEF, MIRV), is generally used without periods. **Initial abbreviations,** which are made up of the first letter of a series of words and are pronounced by saying each letter (IRS, IBM, AFL-CIO), are also commonly written without periods.

When periods are used with abbreviations (as in A.M., U.S.A., or B.C.), do not leave a space between the period and the next letter. For initials in a personal name (G. K. Chesterton), however, *do* leave a space between the period and the next letter.

ACTIVITY

25.5 **Using Abbreviations and Acronyms**

Write a sentence using abbreviations for each of the following items.

> *Example:* A senator who promotes a certain organization
>
> *Sen. Pat Wilson is a supporter of NOW.*

1. A professor and a dentist meeting at a company at a certain time

2. A definition introduced by the Latin abbreviation for *that is*

3. The address of a social worker who charges a certain amount per hour for her counseling

4. The title of a person who works for a government agency

25d ITALICS

Italic print is generally used to indicate that certain words are being emphasized. Most type-writers and many computers are not capable of producing italics, and you should never attempt italics if you are handwriting your paper. If you are not able to produce italics, underline the words that you intend to italicize. Underlining has exactly the same meaning as italicizing text.

Titles of Works

Use italic type or underlining to indicate the titles of longer works and works in the visual arts. The following examples should help clarify this principle:

WORKS THAT SHOULD BE ITALICIZED OR UNDERLINED

Books:	*A Brief History of Time*	A Brief History of Time
Plays	*King Lear*	King Lear
Long musical works:	Haydn's *Creation*	Haydn's Creation
Long poems:	*The Waste Land*	The Waste Land
Visual art:	Matisse's *Pink Nude*	Matisse's Pink Nude
Magazines:	the *Atlantic Monthly*	the Atlantic Monthly
Newspapers:	the *St. Louis Post-Dispatch*	the St. Louis Post-Dispatch

Television programs:	*60 Minutes*	60 Minutes
Films:	*Rebel without a Cause*	Rebel without a Cause
Journals:	*Modern Fiction Studies*	Modern Fiction Studies

Legal documents, religious books such as the Bible or the Koran, and parts of these works are not italicized, underlined, or placed in quotation marks:

| the Declaration of Independence | the Bible | the Talmud |
| the Constitution | the Book of Tao | Exodus |

Note that for titles of newspapers, magazines, and journals, an initial *the* is not italicized or underlined even when it is part of a title:

the *Baltimore Sun*   the *New Yorker*   the *American History Review*

In citations of such works, the initial *the* is usually omitted.

Names of Spacecraft, Ships, Airplanes, and Trains

The official names of spacecraft, ships, airplanes, and trains are italicized or underlined:

| *Apollo IX* | Apollo IX | the *Titanic* | the Titanic |
| the *Orient Express* | the Orient Express | *Air Force One* | Air Force One |

Italicize or underline only the *names* of specific spacecraft, ships, airplanes, and trains. Do *not* italicize or underline types of models of such vehicles:

space shuttle   Boeing 747   aircraft carrier

Words Used as Words, Letters Used as Letters, Numbers Used as Numbers

Use italics or underlining to indicate a word, letter, or number used not with its normal meaning but rather as the word, letter, or number itself. For example, look at the following sentences:

My boss uses advice whenever it is given.

My boss uses *advice* the way other people use *command*.

In the first sentence, *advice* has its usual meaning, but in the second, it is the word *advice* itself that is intended; hence it is italicized in the second sentence.

Words from Other Languages

When used in English sentences, foreign words are italicized or underlined.

Adios was all he said as he drove away.

She ended up taking a position as a *bonne à tout faire*.

However, words or phrases from foreign languages that are commonly used by English speakers are not italicized or underlined. If you are in doubt, consult a dictionary, where foreign words that should be italicized or underlined are identified by a symbol, italicized, or marked with their language of origin.

Emphasis

Italics may be used to indicate stress or emphasis on a word or phrase, but do not overuse italics for this purpose. When italics are used too often, they quickly lose their force and become just a distraction.

Notice how the meaning in the following sentences changes as the emphasis changes:

I can't believe *you* did that.

I can't believe you *did* that.

I can't believe you did *that.*

ACTIVITY 25.6 **Using Italics**

Underline all the words in the following sentences that need to be italicized.

1. The Washington Post carried a piece on the recent discovery of remains from the Titanic.

2. The Catcher in the Rye tells the story of Holden Caulfield.

3. La Señorita has the best margaritas and burritos; however, the churritos are terrible.

4. Not only did Bob Rullo put the goldfish in his mouth, but he actually swallowed it!

5. I saw John Grisham talk about his book The Firm on the Today show.

25e HYPHENS

A hyphen and a dash are not the same thing; a hyphen is about half the length of a dash. The hyphen is usually available on the top row of a keyboard on the right—often just to the right of the zero key.

End-of-Line Word Division

Late in the afternoon on Friday, August 21, Lynn checked into the Refuge Motor Inn on Chinco ▬ teague Island. She wasn't sure how long she was going to stay.

Most computers have a feature called wrap-around that fits words between the margins in such a way that hyphenation becomes unnecessary. However, if you are handwriting a paper or using a typewriter, remember to observe the following conventions:

- Divide words only between syllables. If you have any doubt about where the syllables divide, consult a dictionary.
- Never divide one-syllable words.
- When you divide a word, never leave a single letter at the end of one line or fewer than three letters at the beginning of the next line.
- When dividing a word that is already hyphenated, always divide it at the hyphen.

Compound Words

Compound words take three different forms: two words, hyphenated words, and run-together words. Use the correct form as it appears in your most reliable dictionary.

Here are some examples of the three types of compound words.

Two Words	Hyphenated	Run-Together
nurse practitioner	blue-collar	blueberry
cross section	cross-reference	crosswalk

Two Words	Hyphenated	Run-Together
high school	water-repellent	waterproof
parking meter	city-state	textbook
floppy disk	go-between	extraterrestrial
guinea pig	self-government	notebook
attorney general		

Compound Modifiers

When two or more words modify a noun *as a unit,* they should be hyphenated:

a well-known actor   a late-starting movie
an English-speaking tour guide   a blood-curdling scream

When such terms come after the noun, they are hyphenated unless one of them is an adverb:

The scream was blood-curdling.   That actor is not wellknown.

Adverbs ending in *-ly* are never hyphenated and words in comparative or superlative forms are never hyphenated:

a carefully ironed shirt   a thoroughly disgusting film
the most expensive ring   a less provocative position

Fractions and Numbers

Use a hyphen for two-word numbers between *twenty-one* and *ninety-nine:*

thirty-six   five hundred

When writing out fractions in words, use a hyphen between the numerator and the denominator.

one-half   one-fourth

You should not, however, use a hyphen between the numerator and denominator if either of them already contains hyphens:

three thirty-seconds   sixty-four hundredths

Prefixes and Suffixes

Use a hyphen with the prefixes *self-, all-, ex-* (when it means "former"), and *quasi-* and with the suffix *-elect:*

self-confident   self-employed   all-inclusive
ex-wife   quasi-official   president-elect

Hyphenate prefixes when either the base word or the prefix begins with a capital letter:

A-frame   non-African   un-American

Sometimes a hyphen is used to clarify meaning or facilitate reading:

re-creation   recreation
anti-intellectual   bell-like

Re-creation means "creating again"; *recreation* is what we do on weekends. Misreading can also occur when a prefix or suffix results in the repetition of a vowel or a triple consonant.

Suspended Hyphens

When two or more prefixes are used to modify the same word, each prefix retains its hyphen even though the base word appears only once.

full- and part-time employees   English- or Chinese-speaking students

ACTIVITY
25.7 **Using Hyphens to Divide Words at the End of a Line**

Decide if the words at the end of the line have been divided appropriately. If they haven't, rewrite the word, using a hyphen to show where it should be divided. If the division is already correct, write "OK" in the blank.

> *Example:* When my mother returned from Ecuador, she brought me a fragi-le vase. *fra-gile*

1. Racial tensions on campus have recently been ignited, leading to serious head-aches for administrators. _____

2. To make a perfect Waldorf salad, mix raisins, grapes, walnuts, and peel-ed apples with yogurt. _____

3. The southwestern United States, especially Arizona, is home to ma-ny Native Americans. _____

4. When the detective questioned him, the criminal said he acted a-lone. _____

5. The Peace Corps was established to assist developing countries, primarily with agr-icultural activities. _____

6. During the presidential election between Bush and Clinton, the vote of the blue-collar workers was very important. _____

7. In the movie *Dances with Wolves*, the Indians, who relied on the buffalo for their livelihood, were portrayed as slightly barbaric when they mas-sacred the buffaloes. _____

ACTIVITY
25.8 **Using Hyphens**

In the following passage, decide if the underlined words should be hyphenated, written as two words, or run together. Write the correct version above each term. If already correct, write a check mark.

A Whimsical Look at Hats

Clothes make the man. The truth in this truism can be found starting at the top with our hats. We use hats to define ourselves, make fashion statements, and once in a while for a real purpose.

Hats give us added stature. The best example of this is a Texan's <u>ten gallon</u> hat, a <u>cow boy</u> hat that could also be used to carry water to the horses. Sometimes hats define physical stature. One foot ball player's helmet has been widely reported as size fourteen and seven eighths—the largest in the NFL.

A hat can help us create vivid descriptions, as rock star Prince did with his top forty hit, "Rasp berry Beret." Radio news announcers frequently mention the blue helmets of the United Nations peacekeeping forces.

Often hats serve to identify a person's perceived role in society.

An honorably battered fly fishing hat is a requirement for any self respecting fisher man, with a few spare hooks in the band. This is a hat that serves some purpose, but for real utility, we turn to the helmet of bicycle racing's Greg Lemond. Finding himself in second place on the last day of the Tour de France, Lemond wore an aero dynamic helmet, while his opponent wore none. The difference in wind drag enabled Lemond to win the last leg by more than the sixteen and three-tenths seconds needed to capture first place over all.

Next week, we'll take a look at neck ties.

25f NUMBERS

In writing with many numbers, such as scientific, technical, or business writing, use words for the numbers *one* to *nine;* use numerals for the numbers 10 and higher:

> We had nine respondents to our survey.

> We sent out 25 questionnaires.

In writing with few numbers, use words for all numbers that can be expressed in one or two words; use numerals for all others:

> A total of ninety-nine respondents answered the question in the affirmative.

> A total of 104 respondents answered the question in the negative.

Do not begin a sentence with a numeral. Either write the number out in words, or recast the sentence so that the number comes later.

> **INCORRECT:**   126 people applied for the job.

> **CORRECT:**   There were 126 applicants for the job.

If you write out lengthy numbers, use *and* only between a whole number and a fraction; do not use *and* between the hundreds and the tens:

> One hundred twenty-six people applied for the job.

> The stock fell to eleven and three-eighths.

Be sure to hyphenate the numbers from *twenty-one* to *ninety-nine.*

Numbers greater than *one million* may be expressed as follows:

> four million   4.5 million   780 billion

When expressing time of day, use numerals when you use A.M. or P.M.; use words when you use *o'clock:*

> 9:00 P.M.   nine o'clock

When two numbers occur next to each other, express one of them in words and the other in numerals:

> We saw 8 two-masted sailboats.

Even in a text that otherwise uses words for most numbers, numerals are used in many situations:

Dates:	May 8, 1956	A.D. 1056	1697
Divisions of books, plays, or poems:	Chapter 4	pages 33–41	Act 3
Decimals:	3.1416	0.55	0.0001
Money:	$4.50	$1.2 million	$1,187.25

In writing with few numbers, write out amounts of money that can be expressed in one or two words: *ten dollars, one thousand dollars, fifty cents.*

Mixed Numbers: $8\frac{1}{2}$ $32\frac{3}{4}$ 99 98/100

Fractions that can be written in one or two words should be written out: *one-half, three-fourths.*

Addresses:	11308 South Road, #12J
Scores and statistics:	the odds were 3:1
	the Rangers won 6–2
	the ratio of wounded to killed was 5 to 1

25.9 Using Numbers

Read the following passage about the population of England in comparison with the number of English speakers from the years 1500–1900. Assume that this passage comes from a text with few numbers, and edit the passage so that all the numbers are written correctly.

By the end of the 11th century, shortly after the Norman Conquest, the total population of England seems to have been about 1.5 million. In the year 1500, there were about five million speakers of English, as against ten million speakers of German, 12 million of French, eight and a half million of Spanish, and 9 $\frac{1}{2}$ million of Italian. By 1700, the population of England stood at less than six million, but there were about 8 million speakers of English. By the year 1790, when the first American census was taken, some four million persons were counted, 90 percent of whom were of British stock. By 1900, the English population stood at thirty-two and a half million. 123 million people spoke English, outstripping German with 80, Russian with eighty five, French with 52, Spanish with 58 million, and Italian with fifty-four. [Adapted from Mario Pei, *The Story of the English Language*]

25g MECHANICS: COMPREHENSIVE CHECK

25.10 Diagnostic Retest

Complete Activity 25.1 again. If you still miss or have difficulty with any items, review the relevant sections of the workbook.

ACTIVITY 25.11 **Putting It All Together**

Read the following news release, correcting all mechanics errors.

This article was first printed in the Sunday Times on may 4 1974.

in Septem., 1971, author George Feifer lent an impatient friend an advance copy of his novel, *The Girl from Petrovka* he'd been reluctant, for it was a unique copy, bearing marks of intensive work. major errors in the american proofs of the same book persuaded his new york editor to publish an americanized version of the english edition—which itself had been specially anglicized, since he was an American. his red marks, 4 or 5 to a page, indicated necessary changes (e.g., *labour* to *labor* and *theatre* to *theater*). these marks gave the copy almost as much sentimental as practical value for him.

within a week, his friend had lost it from his car in Bayswater. frantic searches and proffered rewards failed. it was an oddly painful experience that seemed to jinx the book.

26 months later, in Novem., 1973, feifer traveled to vienna to write an article about the novel's filming and quickly fell submerged in the haunted lives of the persons on whom the characters are based. anthony hopkins, a well known actor who plays one of the strongest characters, told feifer of a puzzling incident the previous summer.

having signed to do the part, hopkins went to Central London to buy a copy of the book. returning home after a fruitless trip, he noticed an abandoned book on a bench in the leicester square subway station. turning it over, he read the title: The Girl From Petrovka. he was still confounded by the red marks scattered on most pages. "Might that copy," hopkins asked feifer, "Have some personal meaning for you?"

One wonders how many journeys the book had made, in the nearly 2 years since it had been stolen, before it chanced to be abandoned in leicester square for the movie character, anthony hopkins. [Adapted from Alan Vaughn, *Incredible Coincidence*]

 **SPELLING**

DIAGNOSTIC ACTIVITY: SPELLING

ACTIVITY
26.1 **How Much Do You Know?**

Read the following passage, noting all nineteen spelling errors. Write the correct spelling in the margin.

Today, enviromental problems, such as overpopulation, global warming, and acid rain, are important issues worldwide. Overpopulation is a problem primarily in the developing countrys, where people lack akcess to education and medical facilities or where religious beleifs may prevent the use of birth control. Cultural traditions also may encourage large families as a source of labour. Some goverments have established laws that families may not excede more than one child.

When population grows beyond a sustainible point, there are bound to be disasterous consequenses. More people means that more resources must be developped and ultimately used. Since the Industrial Revolution and the subsequent rise in population, problems from the burning of coal, oil, and gas have occured. One affect has been an increase in the temprature of the earth. This increase could result in the melting of the polar ice cap, which would raise the sea level, and a change in whether patterns that could shift agricultural production. Another problem, acid rain, results from the burning of coal, which increases the acidity of precipitation. This acidity can have negative health consequences for humans and also damages aquatic ecosystems.

Can the earth adjust to these incredable changes? What's more important, will people be able to adapt their behaviour to lesson the impact on the earth? Regretably, we do not have any choice.

PRONUNCIATION AND SPELLING

Read the following poem. Underline all the words that you are not sure how to pronounce.

Of *tough* and *bough* and *cough* and *dough,*
Others may stumble, but you, oh, no!
Of *hiccough, thorough, although,* and *through,*
Well done! And now you wish, perhaps,
To learn of less familiar traps?

Beware of *heard,* a dreadful word
That looks like *beard* and sounds like *bird.*

And *dead;* it's said like *bed,* not *bead;*
For goodness sake, don't call it *deed.*
Watch out for *meat* and *great* and *threat*
(They rhyme with *suite* and *straight* and *debt*).
A *moth* is not a *moth* in *mother,*
Nor is *both* in *bother* or *broth* in *brother.*

And *here* is not a match for *there,*
Nor *dear* and *fear* for *wear* and *pear.*
And then there's *dose* and *rose* and *lose.*
Just look them up, and *goose* and *choose*
And *cork* and *work* and *card* and *ward*
And *front* and *font* and *thwart* and *cart*—
Come, come, I've hardly made a start!

A dreadful language, why, man alive,
I'd learned to talk it when I was five,
And yet to write it, despite my tryin',
I hadn't learned it at fifty-nine!

The poem gives the impression that pronunciation in English has nothing to do with spelling. However, that is not entirely true. Research in linguistics has shown that the English language is approximately 85 percent phonetic, and many spelling patterns are predictable. Therefore, it is important to be aware of pronunciation to assist you with your spelling.

Look back at the words you underlined in the poem. If you are unsure of how to pronounce a word, what can you do to learn? Think of at least three things and write them here:

1. _____

2. _____

3. _____

Just as there are words in English that are spelled the same but pronounced differently, there are words in English that are pronounced differently from the way they are spelled. This difference in spelling can result from a variety of things. First, consonants can have both a hard sound and a soft sound, and they can also be pronounced differently in conjunction with another consonant.

The following words show the different pronunciation for the consonant *c:*

ice   cookie   church

Second, certain words in English contain letters that were once pronounced but now stand for no sound at all:

debt   dumb   ghost   knife   receipt

Third, words can be misspelled because of their pronunciation in informal speech or in nonstandard dialects. The following words are especially troublesome in this respect:

accidentally	handkerchief	prejudice
business	history	probably
definitely	incidentally	sophomore
environment	mischievous	temperature
government	muscle	

One way to help spell these words is to practice pronouncing them exactly as they are written. For example, most people would omit the *d* sound when saying the word *handkerchief*. However, if you intentionally repeat the word to yourself several times with the *d* included, you may recall the "funny" pronunciation the next time you need to write the word. The charts in section 26c contain many more examples of these types of words.

Finally, pronunciation may lead to misspelling when the past-tense ending *-ed* is not pronounced. Be careful when you write any of these that you do not leave off the *-ed* ending.

asked	fixed	pronounced
basked	frightened	risked
concerned	improved	supposed to
developed	prejudiced	used to

26c WORDS COMMONLY MISSPELLED OR CONFUSED

The first chart lists words whose spelling gives many people trouble. The second lists **homonyms,** words that are frequently confused because they have the same sound but different spellings and meanings.

COMMONLY MISSPELLED WORDS

absence	believe	dessert	fulfill
accidentally	benefited	develop	genius
accommodate	bureaucracy	development	government
actually	business	dilemma	grammar
adequately	calendar	dining room	guarantee
adolescence	category	disappoint	guidance
amateur	changeable	disastrous	happened
among	cigarette	discussion	height
analyze	coming	disease	heroes
annually	committee	eighth	hoping
answer	completely	eligible	humorous
apologize	condemn	embarrass	illogical
applying	conscience	environment	immediately
appreciate	conscientious	exaggerate	independence
appropriate	controlled	excitable	inoculate
argument	convenience	exercise	intelligent
assassination	courtesy	familiar	interest
athlete	criticize	fascinate	interruption
attendance	cruel	favorite	jewelry
available	deceive	February	judgment
beautiful	definite	finally	knowledge
becoming	dependent	financially	laboratory
beginning	desert	foreign	leisure
behavior	desperate	forty	length

(continued)

COMMONLY MISSPELLED WORDS *(continued)*

library	possess	roommate	together
license	preferred	sandwich	tragedy
losing	prejudice	schedule	transferred
luxury	privilege	seize	truly
lying	probably	separate	twelfth
marriage	proceed	similar	unnecessary
mathematics	professor	sincerely	until
medicine	psychology	skiing	usually
necessary	pursue	sophomore	vacuum
nickel	quarrel	speech	valuable
niece	receipt	studying	villain
ninety	receive	succeed	visibility
nuclear	recommend	sufficient	vitamin
nuisance	recommendation	surprise	weather
omission	religion	swimming	Wednesday
oppressed	religious	technique	writing
parallel	repetition	temperature	written
paralyze	rhythm	thoroughly	
personnel	ridicule	though	
persuade	ridiculous	thought	

HOMONYMS AND NEAR HOMONYMS

Words	Definitions
accept	to receive
except	excluding
advice	suggestions about a course of action (noun)
advise	to give advice (verb)
affect	to influence (verb); *in psychology,* feeling or emotion (noun)
effect	result of something (noun); *rarely,* to bring about a change (verb)
aisle	walkway between seats
isle	island
allusion	indirect reference
illusion	false idea
all ready	completely prepared
already	by now
altar	platform for religious ceremony (noun)
alter	to change (verb)
all together	all in one place or at one time
altogether	completely
all ways	every way
always	forever
ascent	climb
assent	agreement
bare	nude, naked (adjective)
bear	to carry (verb); an animal (noun)

(continued)

HOMONYMS AND NEAR HOMONYMS *(continued)*

Words	Definitions
board	slab of wood
bored	uninterested
brake	device for stopping a vehicle
break	to damage, to fracture
buy	to purchase
by	near, next to, through the agency of
capital	city where government is located
capitol	building where government meets
choose	to make a choice (present tense)
chose	made a choice (past tense)
cite	to quote, to make reference to (verb)
sight	view, something to be seen (noun)
site	location (noun)
clothes	garments
cloths	pieces of fabric
coarse	rough
course	path, college subject
complement	something that completes
compliment	praise or flattery
conscience	moral sense
conscious	awake, alert
council	governing body
counsel	advice
dairy	place with cows
diary	personal journal
decent	following accepted behavior
descent	downward movement
dissent	disagreement
desert	dry, barren area (noun); to abandon (verb)
dessert	sweet food at the end of a meal (noun)
device	tool, implement
devise	to invent, to construct
die	to cease living (verb); one of a pair of dice (noun)
dye	to alter the color (verb); substance used to alter color (noun)
discreet	modest, not showy
discrete	separate, individual
dominant	controlling (adjective)
dominate	to control (verb)
elicit	to ask for, to draw out
illicit	illegal
eminent	prominent
immanent	inherent
imminent	about to happen
envelop	to surround
envelope	sheath for a letter
fair	light in color; just (adjective); festival (noun)
fare	cost of transportation; food (noun)

(continued)

HOMONYMS AND NEAR HOMONYMS *(continued)*

Words	Definitions
forth *fourth*	forward in position number four
hear *here*	to use one's ears in this place
heard *herd*	used one's ears group of animals
hole *whole*	opening, gap complete, entire
its *it's*	belonging to it it is
know *no*	to be mentally aware of opposite of *yes*
later *latter*	subsequent in time second of two things
lead *led*	to guide (verb); a heavy metal (noun) past tense of *lead* (verb)
lessen *lesson*	to make less (verb) something learned (noun)
lightening *lightning*	making lighter electrical discharge in the sky
loose *lose*	not tight to misplace
may be *maybe*	might be perhaps
meat *meet*	food from an animal to encounter
miner *minor*	person who works in a mine person who is underage
moral *morale*	having to do with right and wrong (adjective); lesson from a fable or story (noun) attitude, spirit (noun)
of *off*	belonging to opposite of *on*
hour *our*	sixty minutes belonging to us
pair *pare* *pear*	two of a kind to slice a fruit
passed *past*	past tense of *pass* previous, earlier
patience *patients*	calm endurance people in a hospital
peace *piece*	opposite of *war* part of a whole
personal *personnel*	intimate employees

(continued)

HOMONYMS AND NEAR HOMONYMS *(continued)*

Words	Definitions
plain	simple, not fancy (adjective); flat land (noun)
plane	to shave wood (verb); airplane (noun)
precede	to come before
proceed	to continue, to move forward
presence	attendance
presents	gifts
principal	foremost, main (adjective); school administrator (noun)
principle	basic truth (noun)
quiet	calm, silent (adjective)
quite	very (adverb)
quit	to give up; to resign (verb)
rain	precipitation (noun)
reign	to rule (verb); rule (noun)
rein	strap used to guide a horse (noun)
right	correct; opposite of *left* (adjective)
rite	ritual (noun)
write	to put words on paper (verb)
road	path (noun)
rode	past tense of *ride* (verb)
scene	place of action; section of a play (noun)
seen	past tense of *saw* (verb)
stationary	standing still
stationery	writing paper
straight	not bent
strait	waterway between two landmasses
taught	past tense of *teach*
taut	tight, rigid
than	compared to
then	at that time
their	belonging to them
there	in that place
they're	they are
thorough	exhaustive, methodical (adjective)
threw	past tense of *throw* (verb)
through	finished (adjective); passing into and out of (preposition)
to	toward; in the direction of; particle in infinitives
too	also; excessively
two	one more than one
track	course, path
tract	pamphlet; system of organs
waist	area above the hips (noun)
waste	to use excessively and carelessly (verb); material to be thrown away (noun)
waive	to forgo, to give up (verb)
wave	to move to and fro (verb); water breaking on shore (noun)
weak	not strong
week	seven days

(continued)

HOMONYMS AND NEAR HOMONYMS *(continued)*	
Words	**Definitions**
weather	atmospheric conditions
whether	if
wear	to have on one's body, as clothes
where	in which place
which	what; that
witch	sorcerer
who's	who is
whose	belonging to whom
yore	long ago
your	belonging to you
you're	you are

ACTIVITY 26.2   Editing for Commonly Misspelled Words

Read the following letter of complaint, and find all the spelling errors. Write the correct spelling above each misspelled word.

May 24, 1995

Mrs. Polly Polton, Manager
Gray's Department Store
Baltimore, MD 21212

Dear Mrs. Polton:

I am writing to complain about the interaction I had with a member of you're personel, André, last Saturday afternoon, May 20.

I was in a dilemna about a gift to buy for my neice. I was intrested in buying her a piece of jewlery, but I was financially a little bit strapped at the time. I explained my situation to André and told him that I prefered to stay within a certain price range. Well, he must not have been paying attention because he proceded to bring out increasingly expensive items. I was embarassed to keep telling him that I couldn't afford the items, and the situation became more and more uncomfterable. I could tell he was losing his pacience. I repeated that I was looking for something a little less elegant, and he began to get angry. Then another customer interruptted us, and André completly ignored me and began to help the new customer.

I found André's behavoir inappropriate and unnecesary. I would apreciate it if you would remind him that although some people may not have a lot of money, they still deserve to be treated as valuabale customers. I would also like him to apologize for his rudeness. Thank you very much for your attention to this matter.

Sincerly,

Gladys Kravitz

ACTIVITY
26.3   **Using Homonyms and Near Homonyms Correctly**

Circle the correct word in the parentheses.

1. My sister decided to (altar, alter) her wedding plans at the last minute.

2. Her parents have always been (fair, fare) in their discipline.

3. The shortstop (through, threw) the ball over the pitcher's head.

4. Agnes finally decided to (except, accept) her boyfriend's proposal of marriage.

5. The letters are (all ready, already) to be mailed.

6. The bus driver tried to (break, brake) for the squirrel crossing the road, but it was too late.

7. The (advice, advise) given by Professor Gass was to turn the paper in on time.

8. When you don't have a hammer available, a handy (devise, device) to use is a heavy shoe.

9. When Juan spit his gum at Eloise, he was sent to the (principle, principal).

10. Light travels faster (than, then) sound.

26.4 Writing Sentences with Homonyms and Near Homonyms

Write a sentence for each of the words listed below. Be careful to use the correct spelling in the proper context.

1. capitol _____

2. capital _____

3. precede _____

4. proceed _____

5. your _____

6. you're _____

7. altogether _____

8. all together _____

26d SPELLING RULES

Several rules are of some help in spelling. Because English spelling is so irregular, however, there are a number of exceptions to each rule. Nevertheless, here you will learn the most useful spelling rules and the most common exceptions to each one.

RULE 1: Use *i* before *e* except after *c* or when sounded like *ay* as in *neighbor or weigh*.

believe   The *i* comes before the *e*.
receive   The *e* comes before the *i* because they follow *c*.
eight   The *e* comes before the *i* because they sound like *ay*.

EXCEPTIONS

either	leisure	seize
foreign	neither	their
height	protein	weird

RULE 2: Adding suffixes to words ending with consonants. When a suffix that begins with a vowel (such as *-er, -est, -ed,* or *-ing*) is added to a word, the consonant is doubled if all of the following are true: (1) the word ends in a single consonant; (2) the final consonant before the suffix is preceded by a single vowel; and (3) the accent (stress) is on the last syllable or the word has only one syllable.

Let's take a look at how this rule applies to some specific cases.

occur   This word ends in a single consonant, *r.* This consonant is preceded by a single vowel, *u.* The accent is on the final syllable (oc-CUR). Since all the conditions under rule 2 are met, the final consonant must be doubled when a suffix beginning with a vowel is added: *occurred.*

listen This word ends in a single consonant, *n*, preceded by a single vowel, *e*. However, the accent is not on the final syllable (the word is pronounced LIS-en). Since one of the three conditions of rule 2 is not met, the final consonant before ending is not doubled: *listening*.

meet This word ends in a single consonant, *t*, that is not preceded by a single vowel (it is preceded by two vowels, *ee*.), so the final consonant is not doubled: *meeting*.

RULE 3: Adding suffixes to words ending in silent *e*. When a word ends in a silent *e*, the *e* is dropped before adding a suffix that begins with a vowel. The *e* is retained before a suffix that begins with a consonant.

SUFFIXES BEGINNING   **SUFFIXES BEGINNING**
WITH VOWELS   **WITH CONSONANTS**

move + *-ing* = *moving*   *move* + *-ment* = *movement*
love + *-ing* = *loving*   *love* + *-less* = *loveless*

EXCEPTIONS

argument	changeable	judgment	mileage	truly
canoeing	courageous	manageable	noticeable	

RULE 4: Changing the final *y* to *i*. When adding a suffix to a word ending in *y*, change the *y* to *i* if both of the following conditions are met: (1) the letter preceding the *y* is a consonant, and (2) the suffix is not *-ing*.

happier *Happy* ends in *y*, and the preceding letter, *p*, is a consonant. The suffix *-er* begins with a vowel and is not *-ing*, so the *y* is changed to *i*.

happiness *Happy* ends in *y*; the preceding letter, *p*, is a consonant; and the suffix is not *-ing*; hence *y* is changed to *i*.

delayed *Delay* ends in *y*, but the preceding letter, *a*, is a vowel, so the *y* is retained.

worrying *Worry* ends in *y*, and the preceding letter, *r*, is a consonant. However, the suffix is *-ing*, so the *y* is retained.

EXCEPTIONS

said   paid   laid   daily

RULE 5: Deciding between *-cede*, *-sede*, and *-ceed*. Of these three endings, *-cede* is the most common. Only one word ends with *-sede: supersede*; only three words end with *-ceed: proceed, succeed*, and *exceed*. All other rhyming words end with *-cede*.

concede   precede   secede   intercede

RULE 6: Deciding between *-able* and *-ible*. Words that end in *-able* can usually stand alone; words that end in *-ible* cannot.

comfortable   laughable   advisable

These words can "stand alone" without the suffix *-able:* comfort, laugh, advise. The following words, however, cannot stand alone.

horrible   terrible   incredible

RULE 7: Prefixes do not change the spelling of the base word.

prehistoric   unnecessary   rearrange

RULE 8: Irregular spelling of plural nouns. See 21e for a discussion about an activity on spelling irregular plural nouns.

ACTIVITY 26.5   Using Spelling Rules

Edit the following passage for spelling errors. Then decide which rule applies to the misspelling.

On Waverly Street, everybody knew everybody else. It was only one short block, after all—a narrow strip of patched and reppatched pavment, bracketted between a high stone cemetery wall at one end and commercial clutter at the other.

Each house had its own particular role to play. Number Nine, for instance, was foreign, with an assortment of Middle Eastern graduate students attending classes at Johns Hopkins. Number Six was refered to as the newlyweds', although the Crains had been marryed two years now and were begining to look a bit worn around the edges. And Number Eight was the Bedloe family. They were never just the Bedloes but the Bedloe family, Waverly Street's version of the ideal apple-pie household.

Ian was seventeen and, like the rest of his family, large-boned and handsome and likable. He had the noticeible Bedloe golden-brown hair and golden skin, although his mouth was his mother's pale biege mouth quirking upward at the corners. He liked to wear ragged jeans and unbuttonned plaid shirts. His teachers were forever sending him home to put on something more presentible. Also, there were complaints about the quality of Ian's schoolwork. It was the spring of his junior year, and if he didn't soon mend his ways, he would not succede in finding a self-respecting college.

Ian listened to all this with a tolerant, bemused expression. Things would turn out fine, he felt. Crowds of loyal friends had surroundded him since kindergarten. His sweetheart, Cicely Brown, was the prettyest girl in the junior class. His father was the baseball coach and claimed that Ian had talent. In fact, sometimes Ian daydreamed about pitching for the Orioles, but he knew he didn't have that much talent. He was a medium kind of guy, all in all. Even so, there were moments when he beleived someday, somehow, he was going to end up famous. [Adapted from Anne Tyler, *Saint Maybe*]

26e STRATEGIES FOR IMPROVING SPELLING

The first step to improve your spelling is to keep a list of the words you misspell. Every time you have to look a word up to see how it is spelled, add it to your collection.

After your collection grows to fifty words or so, you are ready to spend some time analyzing it.

1. Write the words on cards, arrange the cards in alphabetical order, and identify the words you misspelled more than once.
2. Look at each word, and write on the card a brief description of the error.
3. Group similar patterns together.

To help you understand how to analyze your spelling list, let's take a look at a typical list of spelling problems.

Misspelling	Correct Spelling
begining	beginning
relavence	relevance
ammendment	amendment

MISSPELLING	CORRECT SPELLING
ommission	omission
personel	personnel
enterred	entered
seperate	separate
existance	existence
occuring	occurring
refered	referred
innaccurate	inaccurate
equivilant	equivalent

If you followed the three recommended steps, you would end up with the following groupings according to the types of errors:

MISSPELLING	CORRECT SPELLING	TYPE OF ERROR
ammendment	amendment	*mm/m*
ommission	omission	*mm/m*
innaccurate	inaccurate	*nn/n*
personel	personnel	*nn/n*
equivilant	equivalent	*i/a, a/e*
existance	existence	*a/e*
relavence	relevance	*a/e, e/a*
seperate	separate	*e/a*
begining	beginning	Final consonant before ending
enterred	entered	Final consonant before ending
occuring	occurring	Final consonant before ending
refered	referred	Final consonant before ending

Once you have analyzed your list of spelling errors, what next? How do you actually learn to spell these words? There are three basic strategies. Each strategy works with different spelling problems.

1. If some of the mistakes are covered by one of the rules in 26d, you can learn that rule and thereby learn to spell those words. (On our sample list, the words with errors involving the final consonant before an ending are in this category.)
2. Other groups of words don't follow a rule but involve a similar problem. These will just require memorizing the groups. (On our list, the words with errors involving the doubling of the letters *m* and *n* are in this group.)
3. Finally, the mistakes in some words will have little to do with mistakes in any other words. These you will just have to memorize the spelling, one word at a time.

The goal for memorizing the spelling of certain words is to retain that word in your long-term memory, where you can recall it days, weeks, months, or even years later. Two approaches can help you memorize the spelling of words: rote learning and mnemonic devices.

Rote learning involves writing the word down over and over, or if you have a patient friend, you can ask your friend to read your words aloud while you write them down. You can also read the words on your list into a tape recorder and replay them several times.

A mnemonic device is a gimmick that helps you remember something. For example, I used to have trouble remembering whether the correct spelling is *restaurant* or *restaraunt*. One evening, I lost my temper and ranted to the waiter in a restaurant. I made a fool of myself, but from that night on, I knew how to spell *restaurant* because I remembered that *restaurant* has a *rant* in it. A friend of mine always remembers the two *a*'s in *separate* because they are *separated* by an *r*.

Finally, it is important to proofread your papers carefully. One technique that helps is to read your paper backward. This will force you to read one word at a time, which may help you see your spelling errors more readily.

Begin your spelling list by writing the words you have spelled incorrectly in this chapter's activities.

26f   AMERICAN VERSUS BRITISH SPELLING

The spelling of some words in British English differs from that in American English. This can be particularly confusing for students who have previously studied British English. The most common of these words are listed here.

AMERICAN	BRITISH
acknowledgment	acknowledgement
anemia	anaemia
anesthetic	anaesthetic
apologize	apologise
behavior	behaviour
canceled	cancelled
center	centre
check	cheque
civilization	civilisation
color	colour
connection	connexion
criticize	criticise
defense	defence
dreamed	dreamt
endeavor	endeavour
fetus	foetus
harbor	harbour
honor	honour
humor	humour
inflection	inflexion
judgment	judgement
labor	labour
licorice	liquorice
mold	mould
neighbor	neighbour
realize	realise
smolder	smoulder
theater	theatre
traveled	travelled
vigor	vigour

26g   HOW TO FIND WORDS IN A DICTIONARY WHEN YOU DON'T KNOW HOW TO SPELL THEM

Certain strategies will allow you to find a word in a dictionary even if you don't know how to spell it. The most straightforward strategy is merely to write down two or more ways in which you think the word might be spelled and then look up each possibility. Chances are, one of them will be correct.

More difficult words—ones you have no idea how to spell—require a more complicated strategy: Focus on the first three to five letters of the word. Figure out as many options for spelling those sounds as you can think of. Then look up each option to see if there is a word beginning with that set of letters. If there is, check its definition to see if it means the same thing as the word you want. Continue until you have found the word you are seeking.

As you sound out the word, trying to think of possible ways it could be spelled, pay particular attention to the vowel sounds—that is where there are usually the most possible variations. Also watch for the following alternative consonant sounds:

1. The letters *c* and *sc*, as well as *s*, can represent the *ss* sound (for example, *bicycle* and *science*).
2. The letters *ch* and *ss*, as well as *sh*, can represent the *sh* sound (for example, *chauffeur* and *tissue*).
3. The letters *k, ck, qu*, and *ch*, as well as *c*, can represent the *k* sound (for example, *kill, lick, liquor*, and *school*).
4. The letters *s* and *ss*, as well as *z*, can represent the *zz* sound (for example, *his* and *scissors*).
5. The letters *ph* and *gh*, as well as *f*, can represent the *ff* sound (for example, *phone* and *rough*).
6. Watch for double letters that sound like one (as in *alloy, giddy*, or *inning*).

26h USING COMPUTER SPELLING CHECKERS

Most word processing programs feature a "spelling checker." After you have finished a draft of a paper or other writing on a word processor, you can just run it through the spelling checker. This program highlights each word that might be misspelled and gives you a chance to change it. You decide whether or not it is spelled the way you want it to be. The screen lists suspect words and may suggest alternative choices. These programs can be a real blessing for people who are weak spellers. If your office or school has computers, ask about spelling checkers.

Unfortunately, the computer cannot tell when a misspelled word actually forms a correctly spelled word. For example, if you mistakenly write *effect* when the word you mean is *affect,* the computer cannot detect the error. Similarly, if you type in *king* when you mean *kind,* the computer will not recognize the error. You will have to catch such errors when you proofread your writing.

ACTIVITY

26.6 Checking Up on the Spelling Checker

The following passage has been edited by a spelling checker. Find the errors that still have to be corrected.

I clearly remember when its all begun. Just before he retired, a journalist fiend of mine returned from the Austria-Hungary border in mid-September 1989, crying with excitement. "East German are crossing the border bye the thousand. I didn't think I would every live to see this." Neither did I. That is show you are trained in this part off the world, note to believe that change is possible. You a retrained to fear change, so that when change eventually begins to take place, you are suspicious, afraid, because every change you ever experiences was always for the worst. Much as I desired the collapse of the mold system, the ground was shaking beneath my fee. The world I had thought of as permanent, stable, and secure was suddenly falling apart wall around me. It was not a peasant experience. [Adapted from Slavenka Drakulic, *How We Survived Communism and Even Laughed*]

26i SPELLING: COMPREHENSIVE CHECK

ACTIVITY 26.7 Diagnostic Retest

Complete Activity 26.1 again. If you still miss or have difficulty with any items, review the relevant sections of the workbook.

PART VI

WRITING A RESEARCH PAPER

27 Using and Documenting Material for a Research Paper

27 USING AND DOCUMENTING MATERIAL FOR A RESEARCH PAPER

27a REVIEW: WRITING A RESEARCH PAPER

ACTIVITY 27.1 **What Is a Research Paper?**

A. For each statement, write "T" if the statement is true and "F" if it is false.

1. A research paper is the summary of an article or a book. _____

2. A research paper synthesizes your discoveries about a topic. _____

3. A research paper is based on personal opinion. _____

4. A research paper is a collection of summaries of articles on a single topic. _____

5. In a research paper, you may choose to take a stand on an issue or to remain neutral. _____

B. When writing a research paper, the first step is to decide on a topic. Identify at least three important aspects to think about when choosing a topic.

C. Once you have decided on a tentative topic, you need to begin collecting information. Identify at least six sources of information for your research paper.

A research paper is your own original work that answers some question you are interested in. Perhaps you are a student majoring in child development and you want to compare the raising of children in the United States and in your own country. You might go to the library and find an excellent article that describes this topic. You would not be writing a research paper if you summarized this article. Of course, you may take information from the article, but your job as a researcher is to check a variety of sources to decide how you want to present the topic and what you want to say about it. In this way, the research paper becomes your own paper, even though much of the information in it comes from outside sources.

Once you have decided on a topic, collected the information, and started to write a first draft, you will need to learn how to use the information properly in your research paper.

27b USING INFORMATION FROM OTHER SOURCES IN YOUR PAPER

Whenever you use information from another source in your paper, you must tell your readers where the information came from. This is called *documenting* or *citing sources*. Before learning how to go about documenting sources, you must first decide how to incorporate information into your paper and then decide what does and doesn't need to be documented.

There are two primary methods for incorporating material into your paper: direct quotation and paraphrasing. The citations are shown in these examples; you will learn what they mean later in the chapter. For now, work on learning how to use the tools of direct quotation and paraphrasing.

Direct Quotation

In *No Easy Walk to Freedom*, Nelson Mandela wrote, "I have fought against White domination, and I have fought against Black domination" (189).

Quotation marks indicate where the exact words of the person being quoted begin and end. When using quotation marks, be sure that the words of the original are reproduced exactly, including spelling, capitalization, and interior punctuation.

Paraphrase

In *No Easy Walk to Freedom*, Nelson Mandela wrote that he had opposed both black and white domination (189).

Paraphrasing is expressing a person's meaning in different words. Paraphrased passages are not placed in quotation marks, but they do require a citation to credit the source.

Deciding whether to paraphrase or use direct quotations is sometimes difficult. The accompanying guidelines should help you.

WHEN TO QUOTE THE ORIGINAL SOURCE

- When the language is so eloquent that it shouldn't be changed
- When you cannot find an effective way to paraphrase
- When the original is a famous saying, such as "To be or not to be—that is the question" (*Hamlet* 3.1.56)
- If there is a danger that a paraphrase will change the original meaning
- When you present an expert's testimony to support your opinions, especially when the person is highly regarded in that particular area

---

ACTIVITY

27.2 Distinguishing between Direct Quotations and Paraphrases

In each blank, write "DQ" if the sentence is a direct quotation or "P" if it is a paraphrase. (Quotation marks and citations have been removed.)

1. Mary Cassatt's paintings were greatly influenced by Manet. _____

2. The basic principle is the higher the clouds, the finer the weather. _____

3. Dr. Vernon Suomi claims that a really accurate three-day forecast will result in a savings of $86 million a year just for growers of wheat in the state of Wisconsin. _____

4. The *Journal of Medical Technology* uses the example of the oximeter, which measures the amount of oxygen in the brain, to dramatize recent advances in laser technology. _____

5. In their book *Against the Grain,* Tony Jackson and Deborah Eade of Oxfam detail the many ways in which disaster relief aid often goes wrong. _____

27c DECIDING WHAT NEEDS TO BE DOCUMENTED IN YOUR PAPER

Plagiarism—neglecting to acknowledge your debt to others for ideas incorporated into your paper—is irresponsible and dishonest. Each school or department has its own policies regarding plagiarism, usually ranging from simple grade reduction to expulsion. Most instances of plagiarism are not intentional, but ignorance of the rules is no excuse.

Many cultures do not have strict rules regarding documentation. In fact, in a number of countries, it is perfectly acceptable to copy words from others without citing the source. In addition, many ESL students mistakenly think that if they paraphrase a passage, source credit is not necessary. Plagiarism can also occur when students are pressured by time constraints or worried about using language they are not comfortable with. Remember that using other people's words or ideas without documenting them is intentional plagiarism and is treated as a serious offense at American colleges and universities.

Often it is difficult to decide what needs to be documented and what doesn't. Information that is common knowledge to almost every well-informed person does not have to be documented. For example, you would not need to document the statement that Bill Clinton was elected president of the United States in 1992.

There are three types of information for which you *must* document your sources:

- Opinions, judgments, theories, and personal explanations by other individuals
- Assertions of fact that are open to dispute and virtually all statistics regarding human behavior
- Factual information gathered by a small number of observers

ACTIVITY 27.3   **Deciding What Information Needs to Be Documented**

Read the passages. Decide if the information in the sentences that follow each needs to be documented, and explain why or why not.

A.   Fire—chemistry at its most basic. Substances made of carbon and hydrogen react with oxygen and release energy. The by-products: water and carbon dioxide. That equation propelled the Industrial Revolution. Today the world's factories, cars, and power plants burn enough gas, coal, and oil to spew more than 5.5 billion tons of carbon into the earth's atmosphere yearly. [Adapted from Emily T. Smith, "The Global Greenhouse Finally Has Leaders Sweating"]

1. Every year more than 5.5 billion tons of carbon is released into the atmosphere.

    a. Document? _____
    b. Explain:

2. When carbon and hydrogen react with oxygen, energy is released.

    a. Document? _____
    b. Explain:

B. Getting rid of garbage is a problem, in some places a serious one. Mainly it involves handling trash at an acceptable cost. But this crisis doesn't threaten the earth's future, and even if it did, disposable diapers wouldn't matter too much: the 15.8 billion used annually constitute less than 2 percent of all garbage. [Adapted from Robert J. Samuelson, "The Way We Diaper"]

1. Every year, 15.8 billion disposable diapers are thrown away, accounting for 2 percent of all garbage.

    a. Document? _____
    b. Explain:

2. Garbage disposal is becoming a sometimes serious problem.

    a. Document? _____
    b. Explain:

3. Despite its small contribution to the total percentage of garbage, I feel disposable diapers are still potentially a problem.

    a. Document? _____
    b. Explain:

27d PARAPHRASING

Paraphrasing other people's words and ideas is one of the most difficult skills in writing. You must not only understand the meaning but also rewrite the language without distorting its original meaning. Paraphrasing requires a great deal of practice and skill.

ACTIVITY 27.4 Recognizing Techniques for Paraphrasing

Read the following original passage and a paraphrase of it. Then answer the questions.

ORIGINAL

In today's world, despite the fact that 730 million people in thirty-seven developing countries (excluding China) do not get enough calories to support an active working life, food is much more abundant than cash. This fact is at the heart of most food aid issues. Nations with food surpluses tend to be much more interested in getting rid of that food in ways that benefit the producing countries rather than the recipient countries. This is little understood by northern taxpayers, who assume that the term "food aid" means "food transfers that help the hungry." It all too often means "food transfers that help the rich." [Lloyd Timberlake, "The Politics of Food Aid"]

PARAPHRASE

In the thirty-seven developing countries (except China), 730 million people do not get enough nutrition to be active. Food is plentiful, but money isn't. Developed countries that have a surplus of food are more interested in getting rid of the excess food, which helps them, rather than helping the people that are hungry. Many people whose taxes contribute to food aid programs do not realize this fact.

1. What techniques has this writer used to paraphrase?

2. Is the meaning the same as that of the original? _____

Paraphrases that parallel the original too closely are the most common form of plagiarism. It is imperative that you restate the meaning of the original in *your own* words. Not only is this intellectually honest, but it also makes sense stylistically. When you restate the original in your own words, the style of the material you are incorporating into your research paper will match your written style.

The following example shows one way that a paraphrase has become plagiarism. The italicized words in the faulty paraphrase are also found in the original.

ORIGINAL

Americans produce 160 million tons of solid waste every year—more than three pounds per person each day—which is the highest per capita rate among industrialized nations. Along with the natural increase in population and the resulting increase in the volume of waste materials, the cost of traditional landfill disposal in some locations has skyrocketed, doubling and even tripling in recent years. These cost increases reflect the growing awareness that landfill sites around the country have already closed or will close soon.

FAULTY PARAPHRASE

Americans create *160 million tons of* garbage *every year*—greater *than three pounds per person* per day—which is the most per person of any developed country. In addition to the rise in population and the *increase* in garbage, the expense of *landfill disposal* has *skyrocketed* by two or three times. This expense shows that people know that landfill areas have *closed or will close* shortly.

This is plagiarism in two senses: first, the writer does not credit the author as the original source of the information, and second, the phrasing is too similar to the original. The sentence structure is almost identical, and words and phrases from the original are presented without quotation marks. This paraphrase would not be acceptable, even if it were correctly cited, because it is too similar to the original.

ACCEPTABLE PARAPHRASE

Rising population has led to the highest rate of solid waste disposal in the United States. In fact, each American produces 160 million tons of solid waste annually, which is an average of more than three pounds per person each day. As a result, the expense of disposing of solid waste in landfills has "skyrocketed," causing some landfill areas to close or face the possibility of closing in the near future (Council on Solid Waste, 5).

Here the writer has put the source's information *completely* into his or her own words. The writer has put the word *skyrocketed* in quotations because it is not a typical adjective and is clearly taken from the article. The writer has also added a citation.

To avoid plagiarism when paraphrasing, follow the suggestions in the box.

WRITING EFFECTIVE PARAPHRASES AND AVOIDING PLAGIARISM

- Read the passage very carefully to make sure you understand the meaning.
- Put the material aside, and then write in your own words what you remember. Use different vocabulary when possible, but retain technical terms, proper names, and numbers and statistics.
- Check your writing against the original by rereading the passage to make sure that you have conveyed the same meaning. Your paraphrase must have the same meaning as the source and reflect the same relationship between the main ideas and the supporting details.
- The length of the paraphrase should be approximately the same as the original passage.
- The style of the paraphrase should sound like your own style of writing.
- Cite the source.

ACTIVITY

27.5 **Recognizing Acceptable and Unacceptable Paraphrases**

Read the following original passage; then decide if the paraphrases that follow are acceptable.

The Old Jewish Cemetery in Prague is one of the most important features of the old Jews' Town and, as some would have it, one of the ten most interesting sights in the world. It was established in the first half of the fifteenth century and remained in use until 1787. Under its elder trees are no fewer than twenty thousand gravestones. The restricted area of the cemetery was inadequate for the large number of burials, and additional earth had to be brought in to accommodate more graves. The result is that in places there are anything up to nine superimposed layers of burials. Hence the extraordinary accumulation of gravestones, huddled together in picturesque confusion. [*Baedeker's Prague*]

1. The Old Jewish Cemetery in Prague is a very impressive part of the old Jews' Town in Prague. Since the first half of the fifteenth century until 1787, more than twenty thousand people have been buried there. The area was restricted, so they brought in more dirt to have more graves. In some places, there are more than nine layers of people buried on top of each other. It is quite a sight!

   a. Is this paraphrase acceptable or unacceptable? _____
   b. Why?

2. From the mid-1400s to 1787, the Old Jewish Cemetery in the Jewish quarter of Prague was used to bury more than twenty thousand people. Because the area is small, they had to add more earth on top of the existing graves in order to accommodate all the people. In some areas of the cemetery, there are as many as nine layers of burials. The incredible collection of gravestones packed together makes this monument a very interesting and important sight.

   a. Is this paraphrase acceptable or unacceptable? _____
   b. Why?

3. One very interesting and important sight in Prague is the Old Jewish Cemetery. It is one of the biggest cemeteries, with over twenty thousand graves. It was used from the beginning of the fifteenth century until 1787. Some people say it is one of the ten most interesting sights in the world.

   a. Is this paraphrase acceptable or unacceptable? _____
   b. Why?

ACTIVITY 27.6   Writing Paraphrases

Paraphrase the following passages.

1. Desertification, the spread of deserts in Africa, Asia, Australia, and the Americas, is a result of overgrazing, overcropping, and denudation by firewood gatherers.

2. Most persons use their hands when speaking to punctuate the flow of conversation, to refer to objects or persons, to mimic or illustrate words or ideas. Often, gestures are used in place of words. Generally, Japanese speakers use fewer words and fewer gestures than American speakers; French use more of both, and Italians much more. [Philip T. Harris and Robert T. Moran, *Managing Cultural Differences*]

3. When buying auto or homeowner's insurance, shop around for the best price, and self-insure by taking as much of the risk yourself as you can comfortably afford. You do this by choosing the highest possible deductible category. In the case of auto collision insurance, this usually means paying the first $250 or $500 of damage yourself. Unless you are a dreadfully unskilled or unlucky motorist, your savings in premiums will more than cover the extra money you might have to pay out in accidents. Allstate not long ago was charging an adult driver in Columbus, Ohio, $208 for collision and comprehensive coverage on an '81 Chevy Citation with $100 deductible. The same driver who chose a $500 deductible exposed himself to—at most—$400 more risk per accident but cut his annual premium by $94. [Adapted from Andrew Tobias, *The Only Investment Guide You'll Ever Need*]

27e DOCUMENTING SOURCES IN A TEXT

To ensure uniformity and to simplify the researcher's task, each academic discipline has its own strict rules for documentation. These rules dictate the ways in which borrowed and quoted material is acknowledged and presented in notes and in bibliographies. In the humanities (literature, language studies, and foreign languages), the style guide of the Modern Language

Association (MLA) is used most often. However, you should always consult with your instructor before choosing a style guide.

To acknowledge your debt to other authors, you must attribute material to sources and incorporate those references into your writing. The usual method for doing this is called **parenthetical** or **in-text citation.** Your aim is to give the reader enough information in the text to refer to the Works Cited list at the end of your paper and to determine the exact page in the source on which the original material, be it a quotation, a summary, or a paraphrase, appears.

Some style guides require that the information about sources be placed at the end of the paper (as **endnotes**) or at the bottom of the page (as **footnotes**). A small number in the text alerts the reader to the citation.

Acknowledging Direct Quotations in MLA Style

If possible, introduce quoted material by acknowledging the author or both the author and source. This makes referencing easier and adds authority to your own work.

Short Quotations

```
    According to Martin Pawley, in his landmark book, Building for Tomorrow:

Putting Garbage to Work, recycling's "chief drawback is that the energy that

went into giving the bottle its distinctive shape or the can its remarkable

dimensional shape is lost" (109).
```

Because you have mentioned the author's name, you need only write the page number in parentheses after the quote. Notice that the sentence period *follows* the closing parenthesis.

If your paper cites more than one work from the same author, you'll have to give an abbreviated form of the title along with the page number:

```
    According to Pawley, "No mention is made of the plastic recovery process

known as 'reintegration' before 1990" (Remanufacturing 343).
```

In-text acknowledgments can be introduced by many expressions, including these:

according to X	X concludes by saying that
X states that	X points out that
in the words of X	X says that
X remarks that	X claims that

Longer Passages
Quotation marks are used for passages that are relatively short—ones that can be written in four lines or less. Longer passages should be set off, as follows:

```
    Sylvia Plath opens her novel, The Bell Jar, with her narrator's thoughts

about the execution of the Rosenbergs:

        It was a queer, sultry summer, the summer they electrocuted the

        Rosenbergs, and I didn't know what I was doing in New York. I'm

        stupid about executions. The idea of being electrocuted makes me

        sick, and that's all there was to read about in the papers--goggle-

        eyed headlines staring up at me on every street corner and at the

        fusty, peanut-smelling mouth of every subway. It had nothing to do

        with me, but I couldn't help wondering what it would be like, being

        burned alive along your nerves. (1)
```

Because the quoted material is more than four lines long, it is not put in quotation marks; instead, it is set off by double spacing and indenting the left margin ten spaces if you are following MLA style. If you want to bring special emphasis to a passage of fewer than four lines, you may set it off in this same manner.

If the quoted material is more than one paragraph, indent the first line of each paragraph an additional three spaces. If the material is more than one paragraph but the first section is not a complete paragraph, indent the first line of the first paragraph ten spaces; indent the first line of succeeding paragraphs an additional three spaces.

Acknowledging Paraphrases

Paraphrases need not contain an in-text acknowledgment, but if they do not, the author's name and the page number follow the paraphrase in parentheses:

```
Some countries, including China and the Republic of

South Africa, have tried to reduce the movement of people from

rural to urban areas by putting restrictions on migration

(Miller 284).
```

ACTIVITY

27.7 **Using In-Text Citations**

Edit the following excerpt from a paper on drunk driving. Check the author's use of in-text citations in MLA style. Mark any places where you think citations are missing and should be added.

Drinking is a pervasive and deep-rooted feature of American life. In a survey of U.S. drinking behavior, a Gallup poll found that the proportion of adults 21 or older who drank at least occasionally rose from 65% of men and 40% of women before World War II to nearly 80% of men and 60% of women by the end of the 1960s (Calahan, 1988, 64). According to Olson, in his report on alcohol usage, the per capita consumption of pure alcohol in the United States is about 2 3/4 gallons per year, which corresponds to approximately two drinks a day. (Olson, 32).

Today the most severe problem caused by alcohol is traffic accidents. According to the National Highway Traffic Safety Administration (NHTSA), alcohol-related crashes are the leading cause of death for young Americans between 16 and 24 years of age (1). On the average, more than three Americans are killed and eighty are injured by drunk drivers every hour of the day. (Starr, 34)

The effort of one grassroots organization, Mothers Against Drunk Driving (MADD), has had a tremendous impact on educating the public about this problem. Specifically, more police resources, such as roadblocks, have been directed against drunk drivers, penalties have been increased, and plea-bargaining has been cut in drunk driving cases.

A MADD publication distributed worldwide describes the tragic story of how the organization began. "A Los Angeles mother named Cindy Lightner had the misfortune of losing her lovely 13-year-old daughter Cari in an accident. By chance, Cari was walking to school in a bicycle lane when she collided with a hit-and-run drunk driver who had been arrested a few days before for a Driving Under the Influence (DUI) charge. Her death sparked the nationwide movement of MADD, which demands reform of the drunk-driving problem which Cindy Lightner has had to endure." (2) [Ronnie J. C. Hsu, Taiwan]

SAMPLE CITATIONS IN THE MLA SYSTEM OF DOCUMENTATION

Books

Single author:	Piccione, Anthony. Seeing It Was So. Brockport, NY: BOA Editions, 1986.
Other works by the same author:	Everwine, Peter. Collecting the Animals. New York: Atheneum 1976. ---Keeping the Night. New York: Atheneum, 1977.
Two or three authors or editors:	Knoblauch, C. H., and Lil Brannon. Rhetorical Traditions and the Teaching of Writing. Upper Montclair, NJ: Boynton/Cook, 1984.
More than three authors or editors:	Belanoff, Pat, et al. The Right Handbook. Upper Montclair, NJ: Boynton/Cook, 1986.
Single editor:	Franzosa, Bob, ed. Grateful Dead Folktales. Orono, ME: Zosafarm Publ., 1989.
Corporate or group author:	Environmental Defense Fund. Secondary Containment: A Second Line of Defense. New York: Environmental Defense Fund, 1985.
Translation:	Botwinik, Berl. Lead Pencil: Stories and Sketches by Berl Botwinik. Trans. Philip J. Klukoff. Detroit: Wayne State UP, 1984.
Republished book:	Polyani, Michael. Personal Knowledge: Towards a Post-Critical Philosophy. 1958. Chicago: U of Chicago P, 1962.
Edition other than the first:	Ruggiero, Vincent Ryan. The Art of Thinking: A Guide to Critical and Creative Thought. 3rd ed. New York: Harper, 1991.
Work in two or more volumes:	Bonfantamantin, Reginald. The Jewish Mystique. 3 vols. New York: Achshav, 1977.
Work in an anthology:	Bettelheim, Bruno. "The Informed Heart." Out of the Whirlwind: A Reader of Holocaust Literature. Ed. Albert Friedlander. New York: Schocken, 1976. 48-63.
Unpublished dissertation:	Wilensky, Harold L. "The Staff 'Expert': A Study of the Intelligence Functions in American Trade Unions." Diss. U of Chicago, 1953.

Periodicals

Article in a weekly or twice-monthly magazine:	Corliss, Richard. "Do Stars Deliver?" Time 26 Aug. 1991: 38-40.
Article in a monthly or bimonthly magazine:	Murphy, Bob. "Modern Neo-Pagans." Utne Reader Nov.-Dec. 1991: 22-26.
Article in a journal paginated continuously by volume:	Coles, Robert. "Public Evil and Private Problems: Segregation and Psychiatry." Yale Review 54 (1965): 513-31.
Article in a journal paginated separately by issue:	Revell, Donald. "Abesces': The Oz and Sheol of James Tate." Willow Springs 25.2 (1990): 63-89.

(continued)

SAMPLE CITATIONS IN THE MLA SYSTEM OF DOCUMENTATION (continued)

Unsigned article in a periodical:	"Dough Conditioners: Pizzeria Question Mark." Pizza World Jan. 1990: 23-24.
Book review in a periodical:	Smith, Raymond J. "Some Poetic Self-Revelations." Rev. of American Poets in 1976, ed. William Heyen. Ontario Review 5 (1976-77): 102-04.
Signed article in a newspaper:	Sullivan, Barbara. "Burning Ambition." Chicago Tribune 21 May 1992, late ed., sec. 7: 11.
Letter to an editor:	Lovis, Adrian C. Letter. AWP Chronicle 24.1 (1991): 17-18.
Other sources	
Lecture:	Anderson, Mary Victoria. Class lecture, English 095. Loyola U of Chicago. 21 Oct. 1993.
Interview:	Avrahami, Nir, and Ilene Greenberg. Personal interview. 6 July 1994.
Dictionary entry:	"Experimental Design." Modern Dictionary of Sociology. Ed. George A. Theodorson and Achilles G. Theodorson. New York: Crowell, 1969.
Encyclopedia entry:	Fussell, Paul. "Meter." Encyclopedia of Poetry and Poetics. Ed. Alex Preminger. Princeton, NJ: Princeton UP, 1965.
Audio recording:	Garcia, Jerry. Jerry Garcia Band. With John Kahn, Melvin Seals, David Kemper, Jackie La Branch, and Gloria James. Arista, 07822-18690-2, 1991.
Computer software:	Sweitzer, Keith. Backup Master: High Performance Hard Disk Backup Utility. Computer software. Intersecting Concepts, 1986. IBM, 160kb, 5.25" disk.
Videotape or film:	Teenage Mutant Ninja Turtles: The Shredder Is Splintered. Based on characters and comic books created by Kevin Eastman and Peter Laird. Mirage Studios, 1988.
Television or radio program:	"Youth." Writ. Roseanne Arnold. Roseanne. Prod. Marcey Carsey and Tom Warner. With John Goodman. WABC, New York. 29 Oct. 1991.
Government publication:	United States. Environmental Protection Agency. Chemicals in Your Community: A Guide to the Emergency Planning and Community Right-to-Know Act. Washington, DC: GPO, 1988.

27f THE LIST OF WORKS CITED

Researchers following the guidelines of the MLA system of documentation call the list of sources for a paper *Works Cited*. (You may have heard this section referred to as the "references" or the "bibliography.") The Works Cited list is a record of all the sources you have used in writing your paper. Each entry contains information regarding authorship; title of text, article, or other work; place and date of publication; and related details.

The chart on pages 367 and 368 contains sample citations for various types of sources (books, periodicals, and others). If you cannot find the style for a source you are using in your paper, consult the MLA handbook, or ask your instructor to help you.

ACTIVITY

27.8 **Writing References for the Works Cited List**

Use the information provided to write a reference for the Works Cited list in a paper.

1. The book *Alaska,* written by James A. Michener in 1988 and published by Random House, Inc., in New York.

2. An article by Robert B. Cox called "City under Grass" in the bimonthly magazine *Sierra.* This article appeared in the September-October 1993 issue on pages 28, 29, and 30.

3. The second edition of a textbook called *Guiding Children's Social Development* by Marjorie Kostelnik, Laura C. Stein, Alice Phipps Whiren, and Anne K. Soderman, published in 1993 by DelMar Publishers, Inc., in New York.

4. A personal interview with Paul McCartney and Ringo Starr on February 7, 1993.

5. An article by Shirley Brice-Heath called "Inner City Life through Drama: Imagining the Language Classroom," on pages 173 to 193 of the journal *TESOL* (which is paginated by volume), volume 27, number 2 for Summer 1993.

6. An article in a newspaper, the *Lansing State Journal,* on page 11A of the September 19, 1993, edition, with no author given. The article is headlined "Many Britons Dream about Queen Elizabeth."

27g MANUSCRIPT PREPARATION

When following the MLA style of manuscript preparation and documentation, here are some basic considerations to keep in mind:

- Type or print clearly on white paper. Check with your instructor before submitting a paper printed with a dot-matrix printer.
- For your protection, always keep a copy of the original.
- As a rule, double-space your text (including the Works Cited list and any notes). Indent five space to indicate the beginning of a paragraph. Indent ten spaces from the left margin to show a set-off quotation.
- Allow for one-inch margins at the top and bottom and on both sides of your paper (page numbers may be placed closer to the top).
- Title page and report cover are optional. You may include all relevant information on the first page.
- Indicate your last name and page number on *all* pages beginning with the first (including notes, Works Cited, and appendixes).

Always check with your instructors regarding their preferences for manuscript formatting and presentation.

ANSWER KEY

Chapter 1

ACTIVITY 1.1

Answers will vary. Possible answers:

Writing a letter
Taking a phone message
Writing a paper for a class
Taking notes during a lecture
Writing in a journal or diary
Creatively writing for one's own pleasure

ACTIVITY 1.2

1. W 2. B 3. W 4. S 5. B 6. W 7. S

Chapter 2

ACTIVITY 2.3

1. a 2. d 3. f 4. e 5. c 6. b

ACTIVITY 2.4

A. MEMO 1: TO: Mr. Rodini
              SUBJECT: Plans for Mr. Hannuschke's visit
        MEMO 2: TO: Krystyna Rumisek/Donald Busman
              SUBJECT: Plans for Mr. Hannuschke's visit

Possible answers:

The first memo uses complete sentences, more formal vocabulary, a request for permission, and full names. The second memo uses incomplete sentences, less formal vocabulary, and no full names.

B. Possible answers:

Differences in Writing	Essay	Letter
Content		specific details (drama club, washing clothes, etc.)
Organization	formal introduction, conclusion topic sentences, paragraphs	no paragraphs
Sentence structure	embedded sentences use of passive	simple sentences (subject-verb-object)

(continued)

Differences in Writing	Essay	Letter
Word choice	"increase your language ability" "opportunities to speak/interact"	"get so much better at speaking English" "hang around with Americans"
Use of pronouns	it, one	I, you

ACTIVITY 2.5

B. 1. organization, parents **2.** to convince

ACTIVITY 2.6

A. 1. S **2.** P **3.** S **4.** P **5.** P **6.** S

Chapter 3

ACTIVITY 3.1

1. Definition of drafting
2. Keeping the plan in mind
3. Postponing editing
4. Drafting on the computer

ACTIVITY 3.2

1. F 2. T 3. F 4. F

ACTIVITY 3.3

Answers may vary.

A. 1. The purpose of this paper is difficult to determine. Perhaps it could be to explain the effects of earthquakes, to explore the writer's feelings about earthquakes, or to persuade readers to think about where they should live as a result of earthquakes.
   2. He should add the purpose of his paper at the beginning. He could discuss earthquakes in general and then talk about the San Francisco earthquake and his experience. He needs more details on his personal experience.
   3. The audience needs more details about the San Francisco earthquake. Some of the language is a bit technical ("transform fault zones," "shallow-focus earthquakes," "deep-sea trenches").
B. 1. Nothing.
   2. Purpose of the paper in the first paragraph, topic sentence in the second paragraph, definitions of *mid-ocean ridges* and *transform fault zones*, much more details of his personal experience.
   3. The paragraph describing the effects of earthquakes was split.
C. 1. Yes, but he might use actual geographic names to describe where earthquakes occur.
   2. Yes.

ACTIVITY 3.4

Answers may vary.

A. 1. The second worksheet is much more specific with concrete suggestions for the writer. The peer editor also tells the writer where exactly in the paper the changes could be made. The second worksheet uses suggestive language and also makes positive statements about the paper. The first worksheet tells the writer something is "stupid," which is not appropriate or helpful.

B. 1. Racism is the cause of high black mortality.
  2. General readers.
  3. Answers will vary but you might suggest looking for more concrete examples of racism and giving more supporting details.
  4. Answers will vary. Some of the writer's arguments are a little weak.

Chapter 4

ACTIVITY 4.1

A. 1. The three types of sushi
  2. Cannot tell
  3. Cannot tell

B. Topic sentence 2 is too specific; there is nothing left to say. Topic sentence 3 is too general; the reader has no idea what will follow.

ACTIVITY 4.2

1. During the winter, some mammals become dormant; that is, they *hibernate*.
2. Temperature can act as a limiting factor.
3. Animals that maintain themselves at their optimum temperature are warm-blooded, or *homeothermal,* animals.
4. Temperature may have a significant effect on the appearance of organisms.

ACTIVITY 4.3

1. The beautiful beach and the scenic lighthouse have made Holland a very, very popular park.
2. Another important piece of the communication picture is nonverbal communication.
3. And until recently, the choices open to elderly Japanese were dismal.

ACTIVITY 4.4

Answers will vary. Possible answers:

1. Presidential debates are useful to help voters decide on their candidates.
2. The homicide rate for black males is higher than for white males.
3. Developing countries with lower income groups have lower literacy rates.

ACTIVITY 4.5

Format 2 is more appropriate.

ACTIVITY 4.6

Omit these sentences:

1. Reward the dog with treats for positive behavior.
2. Choosing these musical pieces can be fun for the trained volunteers who work with the mentally retarded.
3. This land has rolling hills and pleasant landscapes, making Turkey a beautiful place to visit.

ACTIVITY 4.7

Possible answers:

1. near; As a result
2. Hence
3. For example; In contrast
4. For instance; In addition
5. for example; As a result; However; For instance; In addition; Thus; also

ACTIVITY 4.8

Possible answers:

1. there; the restaurant; Hong Sing's
2. them; they; them; Bats; They; these animals

ACTIVITY 4.9

Possible answers: these ribs; these bones; this injury; This accumulation

ACTIVITY 4.10

Possible revision:

In Thailand, the biggest holiday is Songkran, or the Thai New Year. This holiday is a water-throwing festival and is held on April 13, during the hottest month of the year.

Usually, early in the morning of April 13, we go to the temple to put food in the bowls of Buddhist priests. Then we go to visit our close relatives and pour a special kind of water with rose and jasmine in their hands. After we pour it, they give us good words and money.

Teenagers throw water at each other with bowls, and some children play with water guns; however, the children don't get angry if they get wet. Some people use powder mixes with water, and they wipe this mixture on other people's faces. The people look so funny because the powder makes their faces white.

In the evening, we have a beauty contest in the national park. The one who wins is called "Miss Songkran." She wears a real Thai costume and walks on the stage showing it to the people. Then they have fireworks. Most of the people celebrate this holiday until the next day.

ACTIVITY 4.11

TOOL	EXAMPLE
Opening sentences with introductory phrases	To his horror, the man watched . . . Hating coyotes anyway, he decided . . .
Inverted word order	At the edge of the clearing where he was camped . . .
Compound sentences	So he tied a stick of dynamite . . . . . . and ran over behind some trees to watch . . . . . . and drag himself over to the camper. . . . and blew himself and much of the camper to bits.
Complex sentences	There was nothing he could do as the coyote pulled . . .

ACTIVITY 4.12

Possible revision:

> People complain about how dark it is in the morning, but this is often the best time of the day, when the dawn peers gray and silent into my pale windows. My bright little table lamp becomes a blazing spotlight, flooding over the big black shadow of my desk. Last week it really felt marvelous. I sat engrossed in *The Idiot,* translated a few lines, wrote them down in an exercise book, made notes, and suddenly it was 10 o'clock. Then I felt: yes, that's how you should always work, so deeply immersed that you forget time. This morning I am wonderfully peaceful.

ACTIVITY 4.13

Each of the following sentences should begin a new paragraph:

Coca-Cola is one of the most famous beverages in the world.

The popularity of Coca-Cola abroad started in 1907 when the company set up shop in Hawaii.

This popularity has certainly led to financial reward for the company.

Coca-Cola has been in competition with other brands, both in and out of the United States.

The Coca-Cola Company is involved in activities other than the production of the beverage.

In the beginning, Coca-Cola was sold as a medicine for headaches.

ACTIVITY 4.14

Possible revision:

> Death is a normal thing for every living creature. Man is not immortal. In order to live long everybody need some facilities such as healthcare, nutrition, hospital service. Though the United States has all the facilities still black mortality rate is higher than any other developed nation. It has been found that mortality rate among blacks is twice that of whites.
>
> Racism is a totally biological concept that promotes the ordering of human variations. Humans are classified on genetically determined anatomical and chemical features. The modern fallacy that races differ genetically from the other is not justified scientifically. God has created us in different ways. All of

us have different looks. But beneath our skin all of us are same. To be racist is harmful to society.

Infant mortality in the United States during 1989 was the lowest it has ever been, but it is still higher than in other developed countries. In 1989, the infant mortality rate for blacks was twice that of whites, and infant deaths among blacks have decreased at a much slower rate than among whites. Black infants have over twice the risk of dying in their first year of life compared to white infants.

Between 1988 and 1989, the main causes of infant death were premature birth and low birth weight, respiratory distress syndrome, and complications associated with pregnancy. Prematurity is the primary cause of newborn deaths and illness, and poverty and unplanned pregnancies are important causes of preterm births. Teenagers, unmarried black women, and women receiving Medicaid are at greatest risk for both poverty and unplanned pregnancy.

It seems that racism is a contributing factor to the high infant mortality rate. Poor black women who have no education and cannot get the same health care as whites are giving birth to these premature babies. Black women are often the victims of a national policy that prevents them from receiving information about family planning, including ready availability of contraceptives. Poverty, illiteracy, and unplanned pregnancy are responsible for premature births.

The United States has the best health care system in the world technologically but is lacking in measurements of good health care service. Services are not easily available, nor are health care resources used efficiently. The United States spends 40 percent more than Canada for health care and much more than England, though England's level of health care is equivalent to that of the United States. There is not distributional equity. A specific level of health care is not available to all citizens.

The differences in the quality of health care among people in the United States are persistent and often substantial, with considerable disparity between white and black people. Differences also exist in need for and access to health care. It appears that even when blacks are treated, they are less likely to receive certain kinds of treatment. Treatment of some conditions, such as pneumonia, was found to be more aggressive for white people. Differences in the rates of cesarean sections were noted, with more being performed for white women. Here racial prejudice is probably the factor.

In addition, blacks living in urban areas of the United States are generally more disadvantaged in economic, social, and health care areas than whites. Blacks are more likely to be sick and disabled and to have lower incomes and education levels.

The leading cause of death among young black males is homicide and "legal intervention"—in other words, being shot by police officers. These two causes accounted for 98.9 per 100,000 deaths of black males aged 24 to 34 in 1987. For white males of the same age, the rate was 13.2 per 100,000. The probability of a black male being killed is 500 percent greater than it is for his white counterpart.

In this case, racism is also a factor. In most of the cases, the blacks are being shot without any reason. Sometimes the police officers killed black people only under suspicion. As the blacks have no power or very little power against the whites, the police officers are killing these people without any hesitations. Because they know that they are not going to be charged.

High mortality rates for a nation is always bad. The white people are using their power over the black people. As a result, the black people are being deprived from their rights. It is always wise to find out the key reason of any problem. Because it helps a person to solve the problem in a meaningful way.

Chapter 5

ACTIVITY 5.1

Possible answers:

TYPE OF SUPPORT	EXAMPLE
Facts or statistics	opened in 1970, shortly before 8583 fish turned belly up . . . In October 1970, two workers were contaminated . . . Twenty-two more workers were exposed . . .
Examples	In October 1970, two workers were contaminated . . . Twenty-two more workers were exposed . . . The protective "glove boxes" . . . Sometimes the drums . . . One day a worker bent down . . .
Personal experiences	"When I got down there," . . .
Expert testimony	According to . . . Wes McGovern . . .
Descriptive details	it exploded, ripping through his hand and tearing off the top of his face.

ACTIVITY 5.3

Possible answers:

1. It has increased the speed of carrying out simple tasks.
2. Mass transportation can help reduce pollution in large cities.
3. The advantages include more cultural activities and good restaurants.

ACTIVITY 5.4

behind; above; below; over it; under his elbows; Below; that rose from; across; at each end

ACTIVITY 5.6

Correct order: 5, 2, 4, 1, 6, 3

ACTIVITY 5.8

1. *General idea:* The past four decades have not been kind to poor old Mount Everest.
   Specific details: (all remaining sentences)
2. *General idea:* This war was thus considered the first modern war.
   Specific details: (all remaining sentences)

ACTIVITY 5.9

A. 1. e   **2.** f   **3.** a   **4.** b   **5.** d   **6.** h   **7.** c   **8.** g
B. 1. f   **2.** h   **3.** e   **4.** g   **5.** b
C. Possible answers:

PATTERN OF DEVELOPMENT	LANGUAGE	TOPIC
Description	feels, tastes, smells, sounds like, looks like	a favorite person
Comparison and contrast	like, similar, as with, but in the same way, although, compared with, however, in contrast, as opposed to	cultures
Division and analysis	There are several aspects/types/features/characteristics/parts/properties X can be broken down into . . .	the engine of a car
Definition	X is defined as/means/is/refers to	a scientific term
Narration	(depends on the story)	a frightening experience
Process	first, then, finally, next, eventually, following this, before, after	training dogs; recipe
Cause and effect	because, reasons, effects, results, due to, therefore, thus, then, as a result of	environmental problems
Classification	divided into, types of	diets

Chapter 6

ACTIVITY 6.1

A. 1. Iraq's invasion of Kuwait on 2 August 1990 plunged the world . . . Cold War.
   2. However, beyond the conventional . . . in shaping American foreign policy.
   3. In the past, . . . and the desire to shape a new world order.
B. 1. On February 14, 1989, . . . and the Holy Koran.
   2. The motive . . . not religiously motivated.
   3. The social, political, and economic . . . the basic necessities of life for its people.

ACTIVITY 6.2

A. 1. How culture differs in Korea and the United States
   2. Educational differences, food differences, social customs
   3. Yes. The reader knows what the essay will be about; the thesis is not too broad or too narrow.

B. 1. Not sure
   2. No
   3. It is too narrow; there is nothing left to say.
C. 1. Not sure
   2. No
   3. It is too broad for an essay.

ACTIVITY 6.3

Possible answers:

1. The process of recycling depends on the materials being recycled.
2. Retirement homes offer an incredible service to the elderly.
3. Compact cars offer more advantages than other automobiles on the market.
4. There are advantages and disadvantages to living on or off campus.
5. Socialized medicine is one solution to the current health care crisis.

ACTIVITY 6.4

A. Opening with a striking image or description
B. Opening with a startling fact.

ACTIVITY 6.5

A. 1. Emphasizing the action you want the reader to take
   2. A job application
B. 1. Referring to an image or event from the opening
   2. Traffic in Washington and Maryland—possibly in comparison with Los Angeles
C. 1. Using a question
   2. What jazz is

ACTIVITY 6.6

Correct order:

Gauguin and van Gogh: 3, 2, 5, 4, 1
Aunt Arie: 3, 1, 4, 5, 2

ACTIVITY 6.7

Possible answers:

Introduction: Mortality rates for black people in the United States are twice that of whites, higher than in any other developed nation. Yet the United States has the best health care system in the world technologically. It appears that racism—hatred or prejudice against another group—is a contributing factor.

Conclusion: Poverty, lack of education, and inequity in hospital services are some of the racial prejudices contributing to the high black mortality rate. The modern fallacy that races differ genetically from each other is not justified scientifically. God has created us in different ways. All of us have different looks. But beneath our skin, all of us are the same.

Chapter 7

ACTIVITY 7.1

1. Luke and Murphey already know how the four of them will pair up if such a final ever takes place.
2. The scene shifts to the future; *cue:* "if such a final ever takes place."
3. On the way to the hospital to see their newborn sisters twenty years ago, the brothers picked their doubles partner.
4. The scene shifts to the past; *cue:* "twenty years ago."

ACTIVITY 7.2

1. When I entered the classroom, I noticed immediately that something was wrong. One student *was* standing in the front of the room looking very disturbed, and everyone else *was* crowded against the back wall. Several chairs *were* turned over, and no one *was* saying anything. Then I *noticed* that the student in the front of the room *was* pointing a large, shiny pistol at everyone else. As I *walked* in, he *ran* past me, out of the room, and down the hall. Everyone breathed deeply and started talking at once. I finally figured out that the student with the gun had robbed everyone else and then fled.
2. Anyone familiar with a large opera house would testify that it is an extraordinary labyrinth of people and passageways, but the Paris Opera House of the last quarter of the nineteenth century *is* remarkable by any standards. This opera house, which was the inspiration for the book *The Phantom of the Opera,* was built between 1861 and 1875. At the time in which the novel *is/was* set, the Opera House *boasted* over fifteen hundred employees and *had* its own stables. Even today it employs over a thousand people and contains two permanent ballet schools within the building.
3. The Park Service, established by Congress in 1916, *was* directed not only to administer the parks but also to "provide for the enjoyment of same in such a manner and by such means as will leave them unimpaired for the enjoyment of future generations." This appropriately ambiguous language, employed long before the onslaught of the automobile, has been understood in various and often opposing ways ever since. The Park Service, like any other big organization, *includes* factions and factions. The Developers, the dominant faction, *place* their emphasis on the words "provide for the enjoyment." The Preservers, a minority but also strong, *emphasize* the words "leave them unimpaired." It is apparent, then, that we cannot decide the question of development versus preservation by a simple referral to holy writ or an attempt to guess the intention of the founding fathers; we must make up our own minds and decide for ourselves what the national parks should be and what purpose they should serve.

ACTIVITY 7.3

1. If you take yoga classes, you do not have to do any meditation. You can just do the various positions, which are good for your posture and for reducing tension. If you practice the various positions about three times a week, you will experience considerable progress within six months. You will get out of yoga as much as you put in.

2. If people take yoga classes, they do not have to do any meditation. They can just do the various positions, which are good for their posture and for reducing tension. If they practice the various positions about three times a week, they will experience considerable progress within six months. They will get out of yoga as much as they put in.

ACTIVITY 7.4

1. People should eat right and exercise if they want to live a long life.
2. A dog is a very loyal pet, and it loves to play.
3. You must sign in when entering the pool area, or else you can't swim.
4. I went to see my teacher about my grades, but she wouldn't talk to me.
5. Last week we went to the ballpark. When we entered the stadium, we could hear the roar of the crowd.

ACTIVITY 7.5

Possible answers:

1. Doctors advise against playing in the woods during tick season. They also advise that you check your pets carefully.
2. If Ross Perot were elected, I would leave the country.
3. Don't walk on campus late at night, and carry mace with you at all times.
4. The principal asks that students come to class on time and that they sit in their seats during class.
5. If you want to learn how to sail, read the book *All about Sailing* and then take lessons.

ACTIVITY 7.6

Possible answers:

1. The students went to the library and checked out books.
2. Jack washed and cut the vegetables and prepared the salad.
3. The attorney elicited the information from the witness and documented the details.
4. The scientist identified the insect and concurred that it had hurt many people.
5. Many trees were blown down by the tornado, and several houses were destroyed.

ACTIVITY 7.7

Possible answers:

1. I wonder if the defense secretary knew of the attack and if he authorized it.
2. My doctor said that eating garlic will lower cholesterol and that the garlic should be eaten fresh.
3. The newscaster reported that the queen of Thailand looked lovely as she approached the limousine.
4. My veterinarian said that my puppy is healthy but that I should give him more exercise.
5. The dean recommended that each department trim its budget and that he expected to receive a statement by the end of the month.

Chapter 8

ACTIVITY 8.1

Relevant section of chapter is indicated in parentheses. Answers may vary.

1. The train is convenient; in addition, it is cheaper. (8c)
2. (Correct as written; 8c)
3. (The ideas are not coordinated; 8d)
4. Seth didn't like to go camping; nonetheless, he went with his family over the holiday. (8d)
5. The swimming pool is located behind Building A; it is open from 9 to 5. (8e)
6. (Correct as written; 8e)
7. Betty's aunt, who runs a catering business, will cook lunch for us. (8g)
8. (Correct as written; 8g)
9. Since the game was on at seven o'clock, we decided to eat early. (8h)
10. (Correct as written; 8h)
11. Mary wondered whether the windows were shut. (8i)
12. Helena decided that Pan will begin preschool this year. (8i)
13. The river is so wide because of the tremendous amount of rain in the last few days. (8j)
14. The periods Picasso went through were diverse. For example, he had a blue period, pink period, and Cubist period. (8j)

ACTIVITY 8.2

CATEGORY	COORDINATING CONJUNCTIONS	CONJUNCTIVE ADVERBS
Additive	and, or, nor	accordingly, also, besides, certainly, for example, for instance, further, furthermore, in addition, incidentally, in fact, indeed, in other words, likewise, moreover, similarly
Adversative	but, yet	after all, also, anyway, even so, however, instead, nevertheless, nonetheless, of course, on the other hand, otherwise, still
Causal	so, for	as a result, consequently, hence, subsequently, then, therefore, thus
Sequential	(none)	finally, meanwhile, next, thereafter

ACTIVITY 8.3

A. Possible answers:
1. I've been a flight instructor for ten years, so I know that students tend to make easy things hard.
2. There are many different options to think about when buying a computer; for instance, you must choose the size of the hard drive, the type of monitor, and the amount of memory.
3. Garbage is a big problem in the United States; every American produces 3.5 pounds of garbage a day.

4. André complained that he was very hungry. In fact, he said he was so hungry he could eat a horse.

5. Ramon has never visited Alcatraz, and he doesn't ever want to.

B. Possible revision:

A Garden of Eden

Old legends say that all Indian people lived as one in a big village. The Great Spirit fulfilled all their needs. In the middle of the village grew a huge tree. It bore all sorts of fruits and vegetables; for example, it had apples, pears, peaches, potatoes, beans, and carrots. The people depended on the tree for their food.

Soon the people began to argue and grow angry with one another. One day the Great Spirit told them to change their ways and get along; however, they didn't listen, so the Great Spirit sent a violent storm. The storm blew the tree over.

The people looked at the tree, lying on the ground. Their existence depended on the tree, but now it was gone. They tried to exist on the fish and animals, but they went hungry, and many of them grew sick and weak.

They held a council. Many things were discussed, yet it all came back to the big tree. They knew they must try to appease the Great Spirit. Perhaps they should talk to Penaywog (Many Partridge), for he was an old man who knew everything.

They went to Penaywog and told him of their plight. Penaywog knew that the Great Spirit had destroyed the tree because they had careless ways of living. He told them that this was their punishment. As a result, they must now raise their own food. "How do we do that?" they asked. Penaywog said, "Go to the tree, pick up the leaves and branches, dig up the ground, and put them in. You will have to tend these plants forever."

They went back to the village, took the leaves from the trees, and planted them. They worked in the hot sun and pulled weeds and hoed. Then, fruits and vegetables began to appear, and they harvested the crops. They remembered that they should get along with one another and live in balance with the Earth Mother.

ACTIVITY 8.4

Possible answers:

1. Chincoteague Island is my idea of a perfect place for a vacation, for it has something for everyone.
2. Chincoteague Island is my idea of a perfect place for a vacation; it has something for everyone.
3. Chincoteague Island is my idea of a perfect place for a vacation; moreover, it has something for everyone.
4. Chincoteague Island is my idea of a perfect place for a vacation. It has something for everyone.

ACTIVITY 8.5

Possible answers:

1. Diving in the Cayman Islands is spectacular, because the fish are brig
2. (Correct as written)

3. Music can be used to stimulate and help in a variety of situations; there are two different kinds.
4. (Correct as written)
5. Shanghai is one of the most crowded cities in the world. Its population density is five times that of Paris.

ACTIVITY 8.6

Possible answers:

1. Mr. Jensen, whose car is a Mercedes-Benz, works for a computer company.
2. There is a great restaurant on Grant Street that serves *tapas*.
3. The best time [at which] you can see an eclipse is in winter.
4. The woman who cuts my hair is from Argentina.
5. Garlic, [which is] a great flavor enhancer, can lower your cholesterol.
6. The house [that is] on the corner is for sale.
7. The committee of which Geraldo is a member will not meet on Saturday.

ACTIVITY 8.7

A deletion has been made wherever [ ] appears.

When Erfan first came to the United States, he stayed with a family that lived on a lake. The Ripples had three children. Mike, [ ] the oldest, was interested in water-skiing and playing the guitar. The sister [ ] Erfan liked best was the second oldest. She was very outgoing and had a boyfriend who owned a speedboat [ ] Erfan loved to ride in. Sarah, [ ] the youngest daughter, was constantly getting into trouble when she played near the lake. She had a shovel [ ] she loved to use to throw sand at people. One time, a neighbor [ ] in a boat next to the dock was thrown into the lake by Sarah, who had tipped the boat over. Erfan was really surprised [ ] her parents didn't scold her more. The Ripples also had a dog [ ] named Max. The ball [ ] Max loved to chase after was a dirty, soggy tennis ball. Erfan was never very happy to throw it, but he loved Max, so he would make the sacrifice.

Although life was very different for Erfan in the Ripples' house, he had a wonderful time staying with a family that treated him so well. He also learned a great deal about American culture. Still, he was happy when he finally got an apartment [ ] near campus so [ ] he could live alone again.

ACTIVITY 8.8

Possible answers:

1. A coffeemaker is a machine that makes coffee.
2. A bicycle is a means of transportation that has two wheels.
3. A monkey is an animal that likes bananas.
4. A library is a place where books are kept.
5. A butcher is a person who cuts up meat.

ACTIVITY 8.9

Possible answers: After; When; As; Before; After; while

ACTIVITY 8.10

Possible answers:

1. Meanwhile, back at the hall of the Justice League, Superman was talking to Batman.
2. Although blue tortilla chips are tasty, I don't believe in eating blue food.
3. When we reach the plateau, hit the brakes and do a spin-out.
4. Once we got to camp, we were able to wash our socks.
5. Since 1952, there have been twenty major earthquakes.

ACTIVITY 8.11

Possible answers:

A. 1. My mother wanted to know whose shoes were in the hall.
2. I wonder when there will be peace in the Middle East.
3. Amy asked Tom if he votes Republican.
4. Astrid replied that she was happy with her test results.
5. Katarina wondered whether adopting a baby would be a smart idea.
6. The caterer decided that two loaves of bread would be enough for the party.

ACTIVITY 8.12

Budget Meals for New Homeowners

Dixie Cups Filled with Sugar

This easy-to-prepare meal is not only economical, it is extremely popular with children, who find it gives them that extra energy boost they sometimes need, to stay awake for six days in a row.

Wedding Reception Food

If you go to any major hotel or country club on a weekend, you might find a large formal wedding reception going on, featuring people walking around who actually give away teeny little sandwiches with the crust cut off. This is an excellent source of food for you, the new homeowner. Looking like you are a close personal friend of either the bride or groom, help yourself to as many trays as you feel you will need during this particular mortgage payment period. To keep people from getting suspicious, stop from time to time and remark aloud, in a natural tone of voice: "I am a close personal friend of the bride! Or the groom!" [Dave Barry, *Homes and Other Black Holes*]

ACTIVITY 8.13

1. The Sears Tower, which is in Chicago, is the tallest building in the world.
2. Kathy, who went roller-blading, had a lot of work to do.
3. Maria, who is an aerobics instructor, has seven children.

ACTIVITY 8.14

(See Activity 8.1.)

ACTIVITY 8.15

Possible revision:

> The Tasaday tribe, whose name means "people of the caves" in the language of neighboring Filipino tribes, has twenty-seven members. They live in the rainforest of Mindanao, in three big limestone caves in a cliff overlooking a rushing stream.
>
> The Tasaday settlement is invisible from the air and even from a few yards away because dense forest growth hides the settlement. There are no roads in this part of the forest, so there is no way to reach the settlement except by helicopter. The Tasaday, who have been living in caves for possibly a thousand years, are certainly native Filipinos, since they have brown skin, high cheekbones, dark curly hair, and a slight build.
>
> The Tasaday have no chief or leader because they need none; they share their food and tools and compete with no one. They are a gentle, nonaggressive people who live in peace and harmony with one another and whose language has no words for anger, war, weapons, or hostility.
>
> In some of the families, which are made up of a man, his wife, and their children, a widowed mother or father stays with a son or daughter; then there are three generations living together in their part of the cave. Each family collects its own firewood and does its own cooking. If a child is hungry and his own meal is not ready, he feels free to wander over to another family and eat with them.
>
> The Tasaday have one serious problem: they may not marry anyone in their group, so they must find mates elsewhere. Although the Tasaday are very isolated, they do have occasional contact with groups deeper in the forest, from whom they get mates and to whom they probably give their own girls as wives.

Chapter 9

ACTIVITY 9.1

Relevant section of chapter is indicated in parentheses. Answers may vary.

1. I swam and canoed in the river and hiked in the forest. (9b)
2. Eating vegetables, drinking water, and exercising regularly are necessary for good health. (9d)
3. Louis XVI was king of France in the eighteenth century and was married to Marie-Antoinette. (9b)
4. Dogs and life in the wild are common subjects in Jack London's short stories and novels. (9b)
5. When Ed was in college, he was involved in karate, student government, and tennis. (9d)
6. (Correct as written; 9b)
7. It's amazing that cats can walk on thin fences and look down without falling off. (9b)
8. In tennis class, I improved my backhand and my serve. (9b)
9. Driving in Europe is just as expensive as taking a plane. (9e)
10. Buying a car and moving into a new apartment are her goals for next year. (9b)
11. (Correct as written; 9c)
12. Salespeople need to be both friendly and persuasive. (9c)

13. The hotel was not only dirty but also uncomfortable. (9c)
14. (Correct as written; 9c)
15. No eating, drinking, or smoking is allowed in the theater. (9d)
16. Hawks can catch mice as easily as lions can. (9e)
17. I would rather eat cake than ice cream. (9e)
18. I am excited to go to Paris, Brussels, and Barcelona. (9g)
19. I planned to buy a backpack, a map, and my plane ticket and leave for Maine. (9g)
20. My aunt's cat likes to hide behind the TV, under the bed, and under the stairs. (9g)

ACTIVITY 9.2

Possible answers:

1. My mathematics class is interesting but difficult.
2. During my three-week vacation, I'll go to Niagara Falls or Atlanta.
3. Jason hasn't come to class and hasn't done his homework.
4. Anita was born in Iran, yet she has lived in the United States since 1982.
5. When I was a child, I used to play in the park and fight with my brother.

ACTIVITY 9.3

Possible answers:

1. I've taken algebra and geometry, but I haven't taken calculus.
2. I can't wait to go to France and eat the delicious pastries.
3. My brother would enjoy a career in editing or publishing.
4. In 1990, I graduated from college, moved to Chicago, and got married.
5. I was very tired after my trip to Japan, but I was happy to be back home.

ACTIVITY 9.4

1. Nadine could study at either Northern Illinois University or Columbia University.
2. Most lawyers are both hardworking and dedicated to their clients.
3. He had neither the courage nor the stamina to join the navy.
4. Larry not only loved studying in a foreign country but also liked meeting new people.
5. Both Professor O'Gorman and her secretary are very patient with students.

ACTIVITY 9.5

Possible answers:

1. They wanted to go to a movie or see a play.
2. Both my mother and my father worked in a supermarket.
3. You can either buy a new car or lease one.
4. John didn't study for his statistics exam, yet he passed it.
5. I neither heard the explosion nor smelled the smoke.
6. Work productivity at Hutton Computers, Inc., has increased, but sales have dropped.
7. He should have quit his job a long time ago and worked in Japan instead.
8. Not only am I taking a physics exam tomorrow, but I'm also taking a statistics exam.

ACTIVITY 9.6

Possible answers:

1. kind	2. lock the doors	3. hiking	4. content
5. painting	6. hot	7. getting married	8. enthusiastic
9. went to two parties	10. strength		

ACTIVITY 9.7

Possible answers:

1. Swimming no longer interests me as much as lying on the beach.
2. European cities have many more outdoor cafés than American cities have.
3. Riding in an airplane is not more comfortable than taking a train.
4. Janine finds volleyball as interesting as Jim does.
5. Money is harder to earn than to spend.
6. I would rather travel than stay at home all summer long.
7. Running is as important as eating well for good health.

ACTIVITY 9.8

Possible answers:

1. C. Eating at restaurants in Chinatown
2. A. Less than $15,000
3. I. B. Shared bathrooms
    II. C. Saving money

ACTIVITY 9.9

1. Omit *You can* from the third item.
2. Change *Getting* to *Get* in the first item.

ACTIVITY 9.10

1. Before I left on vacation, I talked to the landlord and to the superintendent of my apartment building.
2. I believe that she is confident, she will find a job, and she will be successful.
3. She chose to stay in Bloomington, find a new job, and sign up for an art class.

ACTIVITY 9.11

(See Activity 9.1.)

ACTIVITY 9.12

Possible revision:

> The United States is a consumer society. The range in price, amount of goods available, and large selection make us the envy of the world. Appealing to the consumers is more important now than meeting their basic needs. The term *selling* suggests that the desire to buy must be created in the consumer, reinforced by values and social norms.

In the colonial era, there was little effort at selling and advertising because there was little need. Signs outside shops indicated both type of merchandise and cost. Basic commodities were sold in bulk. More exotic goods arrived by ship, but their availability was made known primarily through a newspaper notice of the ship's arrival. Sometimes not only the products' arrival time but also the quantity was printed in the newspapers.

Early retail selling was done both in shops and by peddlers. Peddlers sold a variety of items and traveled all over the countryside. Sales were governed by *caveat emptor*—let the buyer beware. A typical transaction might involve cash, credit, or bartering. There was no guarantee of quality, and price was subject to bargaining between seller and buyer. Through the years, it was found that many Americans would rather visit one store to buy everything necessary than go to several different shops.

Chapter 10

ACTIVITY 10.1

Relevant section of chapter is indicated in parentheses. Answers may vary.

1. The purchasing error that Julie made at work cost the company thousands of dollars. (10b)
2. (Correct as written; 10b)
3. The people in the dorm next to ours are having a party tonight. (10d)
4. Dedication is refusing to give up your hopes and dreams. (10c)
5. (Correct as written; 10c)
6. (Correct as written; 10f)
7. In my most interesting dream, I was flying in the air like a bird. (10c)
8. (Correct as written; 10e)
9. I didn't return your phone call yesterday because I didn't get home until after midnight. (10c)
10. Sabine's explanation for going to Florida was that she greatly needed a vacation. (10c)
11. (Correct as written; 10d)
12. The movie I rented last night was full of mystery and suspense. (10e)
13. (Correct as written; 10f)
14. The performer's jokes were distasteful, and his songs were off-key. (10f)
15. (Correct as written; 10f)
16. Amtrak is faster than Greyhound. (10f)
17. (Correct as written; 10f)
18. After I graduate, I will return to my native country. (10f)

ACTIVITY 10.2

Possible revisions:

1. Working on my paper until 3 A.M. meant I was tired this morning.
2. (Correct as written)
3. (Correct as written)
4. My sister attended Johnsley College, which is a local community college.
5. Working overtime last week meant I made an extra $75.

6. The book that you recommended is now a best seller.
7. (Correct as written)
8. Having completed her research paper early, she could relax for the weekend.
9. My husband drives eighty-five miles to work each day, which is a long way to commute.
10. (Correct as written)

ACTIVITY 10.3

Possible revisions:

1. It is imperative that Joan call the office by 5:00 P.M.
2. (Correct as written)
3. I was late for class this morning because my car broke down.
4. Alper's biggest dream is winning the lottery.
5. I recommend that your daughter take the chemistry class again.
6. (Correct as written)
7. I wish to become a teacher after I graduate.
8. My sister won't swim in the ocean because she is afraid of sharks.
9. My favorite childhood memory is visiting my grandparents' farm.
10. In the best romance novels, the two main characters fall in love.

ACTIVITY 10.4

1. The people who remained in the Canadian Arctic, Alaskan, and Aleutian areas were the Eskimos.
2. (Correct as written)
3. Some of the Asian immigrants traveled farther south than the Eskimos did.
4. (Correct as written)
5. The Indians who migrated to the Central Plains were similar in some ways to the Pacific Coast settlers.
6. (Correct as written)
7. (Correct as written)
8. Native American Indians who settled in the southwestern United States and northern Mexico were stable and skilled.
9. (Correct as written)
10. The American Indian culture was highly developed.

ACTIVITY 10.5

Delete *in* from sentences 2, 3, 5, 8, 9, and 10.

ACTIVITY 10.6

1. Your class is better than any *other* class I have taken at the university. (b)
2. I can talk more openly with my mother than *with* my father. (b)
3. When I finish this book report, *I* will go to the movies with you. (d)
4. *There* are 1,200 employees working at my father's company. (e)
5. My sister, Sharla, is more intelligent *than I*. (b)
6. Our physics *professor* and *our* biology professor should be at the graduation party this Saturday. (a)

7. (OK)

8. (OK)

9. In the small northern town, winter temperatures were cold and the wind *was* strong. (a)

10. My wife found *that* a puppy requires a lot of patience and energy. (c)

11. *I called* the telephone company to inquire about my outrageous phone bill. (d)

12. (OK)

13. In Boston *there* are many interesting historical tourist attractions. (e)

14. (OK)

15. In my English class *there* are people from eleven different countries! (e)

16. Unfortunately, at my first dinner party, my guests were late and the meal *was* cold. (a)

17. I love Korean food but dislike Japanese *food.* (b)

18. I think the course helped Paco more than *it helped* Donna. (b)

19. Erin's best friend and *her* neighbor will both be coming to her birthday party. (a)

20. *It is* interesting to watch how mother birds care for their young. (e)

21. I recently moved to a new city, but my job is interesting and my neighbors *are* friendly. (a)

22. (OK)

23. (OK)

24. The winter season in Wisconsin is colder *than in Florida.* (b)

25. Judy was proud *of* but surprised by the announcement of her scholarship. (a)

26. I enjoy studying English more than my roommate *does.* (b)

27. I understand *that* a second language is needed for a person to advance to a management position. (c)

28. *He hopes* to complete his degree in hotel management by December of next year. (d)

29. (OK)

30. (OK)

ACTIVITY 10.7

(See Activity 10.1.)

ACTIVITY 10.8

A painful experience at the dentist's office for many people is getting their wisdom teeth pulled. What purpose do wisdom teeth serve? These teeth serve a powerful purpose for dentists, who are paid to extract them. Otherwise, they are commonly regarded as useless to modern humans. However, a little investigation is necessary because nature rarely provides us with useless body parts.

Primitive people ate meals so tough that eating beef jerky feels like mashed potatoes in comparison. The reason for the extra molars in the back of the mouth, now known as wisdom teeth, is that they undoubtedly aided in our ancestors' chewing.

Modern human brains are larger than our ancestors'. In addition, the face position has moved farther downward and inward. About the time that primitive people started walking in an upright position, other changes in the facial structure occurred. The fact that the protruding jawbones of early humans gradually moved backward made the jaw itself shorter. Leaving no room for wisdom teeth meant that most people's jaws no longer had the capacity to accommodate these now superfluous teeth—teeth which cause many modern humans pain.

Chapter 11

ACTIVITY 11.1

1. about the life (Prepositional phrase); of Thomas Sawyer (Prepositional phrase)
2. which is in the southern part of Alaska (Adjective clause); very (Adverb); beautiful (Adjective)
3. to see (Infinitive phrase)
4. beautifully (Adverb); in *Les Miserables* (Prepositional phrase)
5. eating the banana (Participial phrase); biggest (Adjective)
6. lonely (Adjective); of the coyote (Prepositional phrase)
7. to the doctor (Prepositional phrase); after (Adverb)

ACTIVITY 11.2

Relevant section of chapter is indicated in parentheses.

1. Corado ate only breakfast yesterday. (11c)
2. Sharon told Cheryl to sneak quietly into the office. (11b)
3. Kwo arranged the flowers on the table. (11b)
4. Mick sat in the sun for almost five hours! (11c)
5. As I was driving quickly into the driveway, my car nearly hit the house. (11d)
6. To avoid being drenched in the rainstorm, we put up umbrellas. (11d)
7. Sheila decided to go quickly to the doctor. (11e)
8. I always try to eat lots of fruits and vegetables, if possible. (11e)

ACTIVITY 11.3

Possible answers:

1. In the afternoon, the teacher told us about the sinking of the *Titanic*.
2. The doctor attended to the little girl, who was screaming and crying.
3. Roberta batted away the spider dangling in midair.
4. Val asked Dino to go quickly to the store.
5. In his office, the lawyer gave us advice about suing people.

ACTIVITY 11.4

1. Rob had scarcely eaten his dinner when the phone rang.
2. Stephanie nearly paid $20,000 but decided it wasn't worth it.
3. John worked in the garden for almost six hours.
4. Sugu had eaten just two meals a day for a week, but she still gained weight.
5. The little boy hardly touched the crystal vase, yet it shattered.

ACTIVITY 11.5

Possible answers:

1. Because I was chewing the cereal loudly, my mother told me I sounded like a pig.
   Chewing the cereal loudly, I was told by my mother that I sounded like a pig.

2. When driving, you should keep your baby in a car seat at all times.
   When you are driving, the baby should be in a car seat at all times.
3. Turning circles in midair, the Flying Blue Angels amazed the children.
   When the Flying Blue Angels were turning circles in midair, the children were amazed.
4. Delighted by the snowfall, people were driving snowmobiles everywhere.
   People were delighted by the snowfall, and snowmobiles were everywhere.
5. Before registering for classes, you must pay your tuition.
   Before you register for classes, tuition must be paid.

ACTIVITY 11.6

1. (Not awkward)
2. They tried with all their might to prevent the accident, to no avail.
3. (Not awkward)
4. Wayne wanted to go quickly to the store before the game started.
5. It seems I am always forgetting to lock the door.

ACTIVITY 11.7

(See Activity 11.2.)

ACTIVITY 11.8

1. The corner of Main Street and Emerson Avenue will be the site of Bloomington's annual Town Parade and Festival. Workers have been setting up tents and booths for almost two weeks. Mayor O'Gorman wants to greet people early outside City Hall before the parade.
2. Because people are driving through the tree-lined streets at the south end of town, many pets have been injured or killed. Police are advising motorists to drive cautiously through this residential area.
3. The Bloomington Public Library will begin its lectures on money management this Monday night in Seminar Room B at 7:00 P.M. Financial adviser E. N. Farrow will give participants information about developing a personal budget.
4. Two young children were found trapped in a recycling dumpster late Monday morning. The police finally rescued the panicked children. Glenn Schuster and Nicky Ranger, both 12-year-olds from the South Side, were in the dumpster for almost four hours.

Chapter 12

ACTIVITY 12.1

Relevant section of chapter is indicated in parentheses.

1. Eloise did business with the new client. (12b)
2. The water isn't boiling yet. (12b)
3. The bus drivers demanded their fair pay. (12c)
4. (Acceptable as written; 12c)
5. Linnaeus was a famous botanist who studied plants. (12d)
6. Three dogs are destroying the carpet in my house. (12d)

7. (Acceptable as written; 12e)

8. All people should have medical insurance. (12e)

9. (Acceptable as written; 12f)

10. The model is thin and has a beautiful complexion. (12f)

ACTIVITY 12.2

1. do; make   **2.** make   **3.** doing   **4.** make   **5.** do

6. made   **7.** does   **8.** do   **9.** do; make   **10.** make; do

ACTIVITY 12.3

Paragraph 1: The other

Paragraph 2: another; another; each other/one another

Paragraph 3: another; each other/one another; other; other

Paragraph 4: another; other; other

ACTIVITY 12.4

1. He hasn't taken his car to the mechanic yet.

2. She's still waiting for her paycheck.

3. She hasn't paid the rent yet.

4. She still has two exams this week.

ACTIVITY 12.5

1. . . . and he still doesn't like to play tennis.

2. . . . but they already speak very well.

3. . . . but Dr. Matthews isn't here yet.

4. . . . and they are still complaining.

5. . . . but Tom is already tired.

6. . . . but he hasn't come yet.

7. . . . but it's here already.

8. . . . and he is still looking for a job.

ACTIVITY 12.7

1. its   **2.** whose   **3.** than   **4.** too   **5.** too

6. they're   **7.** live   **8.** clothes   **9.** it's   **10.** passed

11. Who's   **12.** their   **13.** raise   **14.** except   **15.** affects

16. number   **17.** well   **18.** Neither   **19.** fewer   **20.** were

ACTIVITY 12.8

Possible revision:

    Henry David Thoreau was an important writer and naturalist of the nineteenth century. He believed in the freedom of each individual and did not support a strong government because governments often destroy that freedom. He was a naturalist in many ways. He believed that individuals should live with nature and provide for themselves from nature to be happier. He even built a simple cabin for himself in the woods near Walden Pond in which to write about what he believed. Many people were impressed with Thoreau's ideas, and he remained their ideal after his death.

ACTIVITY 12.9

Words crossed out:

1. definitely
2. rather
3. absolutely, quite
4. relatively

ACTIVITY 12.10

Possible revision:

Oak Bridge police are deciding whether loud music from car stereos should be included under the city's current ordinance, which is used to stop noise from homes. Police officers are required to fine car owners driving vehicles with loud exhausts and squealing tires. However, no ordinance exists to prosecute those with massive speakers and amplifiers in their cars. Many people have complained about the noise from these cars. Forty-two complaints were filed in the past two weeks. Several guidelines were established by the council's transportation board members, and they intend to research the present ordinance and the complaints. Of course, many car owners believe there is nothing wrong with the stereo systems, and several options were suggested.

ACTIVITY 12.11

Possible revision:

Foreign students studying abroad face many problems, due primarily to language and cultural barriers.

English is one of the most difficult languages to learn because there are so many exceptions. Also, English has a very different word order from my native language, and there is so much slang!

Cultural barriers are a second problem. This problem is the biggest. The cultural barrier between Korea and the United States is very wide. We Asians respect our elders, whereas relationships in the United States are a lot different. This may really shock foreign students. Finally, loneliness can be a problem for foreign students. Loneliness can cause homesickness and make it difficult to study. These are only some of the problems faced by foreign students, but they are the biggest problems.

ACTIVITY 12.12

Answers and possible revisions:

1. b; Humans have inhabited the earth for thousands of years.
2. e; Mrs. and Mr. Sneeden are moving to Hoopestown, Illinois.
3. c; The dairy's driver drops off the milk and butter every Monday at 1:00.
4. b; Most people never forget the language of their homeland.
5. d; Ministers must be constantly aware of current events around them.

6. d; Every truck driver ought to know how to change the truck's oil.
7. a; The old woman who lives on the corner just got a puppy.
8. d; Everyone is required to carry identification at all times.
9. c, f; "Be a cowpoke for a day! Everyone is invited to the annual rodeo and square dance."
10. b; All people are created equal.

ACTIVITY 12.13

1. broad (N), woman (P)
2. drunk (N), tipsy (P)
3. cheap (N), bargain (P)
4. aging (N), mature (P)
5. unmarried (N), single (P)
6. skinny (N), slender (P)

ACTIVITY 12.14

Possible revisions:

1. The group of protesters gathered outside the capitol.
2. The chairperson's determination surprised all the members of the board.
3. She used to be tall and thin when she was in junior high school.
4. The workers asked their boss for a longer lunch period.
5. The schoolchildren excluded the new child from their kickball game.

ACTIVITY 12.15

(See Activity 12.1.)

ACTIVITY 12.16

Possible revision:

Verbal communication is one of the most studied human activities. From first grade through college, students are required to learn the structure of their written and spoken language. Nonverbal communication, on the other hand, is one of the least studied human activities. It is not yet considered important enough to be included in the public school curriculum. However, when we communicate, as much as eighty percent of the meaning of our messages is derived from nonverbal language.

Human communication cannot be reduced to words alone. If it could, we would have fewer communication problems. Telephone, radio, and television carry the human voice to the most remote corners of the earth; yet in this age of instant communication, the term *communication gap* has become commonplace. Why? We are nonverbal creatures who have learned to speak, but we do not trust words that we use during speech.

A conflict arises when people believe that their verbalizations should be accepted at face value. Of all the channels of communication available, however, verbalization often carries the least weight. We communicate with our entire bodies, and in situations of deep personal meaning and of great importance, body language is trusted more than words. Words count for very little when they conflict with the silent language of the body. Thus we may talk and talk, but until our nonverbal behavior agrees with our words, a credibility gap, not a communication gap, will exist.

Chapter 13

ACTIVITY 13.1

Relevant section of chapter is indicated in parentheses.

1. The force of the storm bent the tree right in half. (13b)
2. The burglar crept up behind the unsuspecting woman. (13b)
3. (Correct as written; 13b)
4. You won't believe what I saw! (13b)
5. The professor pointed out to Maryanne that light travels faster than sound. (13c)
6. The chairperson said it was time to get back to business. (13c)
7. It was almost time to pick her up at the airport. (13c)
8. (Correct as written; 13c)
9. (Correct as written; 13d)
10. I used to like spinach when I was little. (13d)
11. You could/might/should have told me you were coming to visit! (13d)
12. You should have gone to the doctor last week. (13d)

ACTIVITY 13.2

Paragraph 1: rose, woke, got, thought, was, was, was, lost, felt, remembered, sold, worked, bought, said, told, was, dreamed, could

Paragraph 2: was, came, called, was, was, fell, looked, crossed, said

ACTIVITY 13.3

A. 1. e   **2.** f   **3.** a   **4.** g   **5.** j   **6.** i   **7.** d   **8.** b   **9.** c   **10.** h
B. Possible answers:
1. The Sandersons thought they could get by on only the husband's salary.
2. My car broke down on the highway last week.
3. The paint on the house began to wear away.
4. After the meeting, Lon came away with a feeling of accomplishment.
5. Mario ran ten miles this morning without eating anything. Later, he passed out.
6. Someone broke into my car last week and stole my stereo.
7. Sometimes my younger brother Rob is permitted to stay up until three in the morning!
8. People were saddened to learn that the actress had passed away.
9. Sabine grew up in the Philippines, but she considers herself German.
10. The argument blew up when Ms. Bunson called the president an ugly name.

ACTIVITY 13.4

A. 1. f   **2.** k   **3.** h   **4.** b   **5.** a   **6.** g
    7. l   **8.** e   **9.** c   **10.** d   **11.** i   **12.** j

B. Possible answers:
1. Melissa always takes off her makeup before she goes to bed.
2. When Greg was looking through his closet, he came across a picture of his old girlfriend and decided to throw it away.
3. People who drop out of high school have difficulty finding jobs.
4. Rose looked over the rental agreement carefully before she signed it.
5. Chandra got off at the wrong stop.
6. Even though everyone is against him, I am going to stand up for my congressman.
7. We decided to put off building the deck because of the expense.
8. Mr. Plough handed out/gave back/passed out the quizzes to the students.
9. Cheryl is looking into buying a new car.
10. The terrorists decided to blow up the dam.

ACTIVITY 13.5

1. up **2.** by **3.** up with **4.** into **5.** up
6. back **7.** out/away **8.** ahead **9.** in on **10.** after

ACTIVITY 13.6

Possible answers:

1. I'm going to take her out to dinner.
2. Fred has always looked up to his sister.
3. George said he would take out the garbage. George said he would take the garbage out.
4. Look it up in the dictionary.
5. The photocopier ran out of paper.
6. Turn the radio on and let's dance! Turn on the radio and let's dance!
7. I might take up golf this summer. I might take golf up this summer.
8. The mayor decided to tear down the building. The historical society doesn't want him to tear the building down.
9. The children were sad until the clown cheered them up.
10. I checked the book out of the library. I checked out the book from the library.

ACTIVITY 13.7

1. My boss wanted to think about my proposal to start a textbook series.
2. The plan was to pick her up at the bus station and then go have dinner.
3. (Correct as written)
4. The robber broke into the house next door and stole practically everything.
5. Certain religions look down on living together as a couple before marriage.

ACTIVITY 13.8

Possible answers:

1. He ought to go to sleep. He should get some rest.
2. He had better take an umbrella. He should wear his raincoat.

3. He should study tonight. He had better review his lessons this evening.

4. She might join a club. She could take a trip to Europe.

5. She has to leave immediately! She must get out of there!

ACTIVITY 13.9

A. 1. I   **2.** I   **3.** F   **4.** F   **5.** I   **6.** F   **7.** F   **8.** I

ACTIVITY 13.10

A. 1. criticism   **2.** anger   **3.** desire   **4.** irritation   **5.** regret

B. Possible answers:

   1. You should have seen it.

   2. She should have told me.

   3. He/She could have told me.

   4. She shouldn't have worn them.

   5. He might have closed the garage door.

ACTIVITY 13.11

Possible answers:

Paragraph 2: could have

Paragraph 3: might

Paragraph 4: should

Paragraph 5: will

ACTIVITY 13.12

Possible answers:

   1. I will/am going to get a five percent raise.

   2. I might/may take the trip.

   3. I should/ought to/had better get a haircut.

   4. I will/am going to/must/go back to the store.

ACTIVITY 13.13

would/used to; used to; could; used to/would; used to/would; used to/would; could; could; used to/would; could; can

ACTIVITY 13.14

(See Activity 13.1.)

ACTIVITY 13.15

ought to: advisability

could: ability

used to: condition or state in the past

would: repeated action in the past

should: advisability

could: possibility

might: possibility

would: probability

could: possibility

would: probability

will: certainty

ACTIVITY 13.16

1. I should have gone to the store for Mom.
2. I used to be a farmer when I lived in Minnesota in 1976.
3. Anastasia should see a doctor for the headaches and weight loss she has experienced.
4. I would like some french fries with my hamburger.
5. You can make the trip from San Francisco to Sausalito by ferry in about thirty minutes.

Chapter 14

ACTIVITY 14.1

Paragraph 1: works, agrees, wants, sign, have been

Paragraph 2: is, get, go, resulted, caught

Paragraph 3: agreed, signed, arrived, realized, came, handed, drove

Paragraph 4: was given, was known, debated, do/did, awarded, was declared, decided, spends

ACTIVITY 14.2

1. d   2. h   3. f   4. a   5. g   6. b   7. c   8. e

ACTIVITY 14.3

1. is taking; takes
2. is having; has
3. is looking; looks
4. speaks; is speaking
5. reads; am reading
6. is seeing; sees

ACTIVITY 14.4

Paragraph 1: gives, has, are, elects

Paragraph 2: are facing, are preparing, are ending, are rising, demand, is holding

ACTIVITY 14.5

1. lived   2. hasn't voted   3. has worked   4. has studied
5. was   6. hasn't seen   7. have increased   8. didn't take

ACTIVITY 14.6

1. had spent/spent; worked/was working/had been working; organized; has held; has been doing/has done; had been directing/had directed/directed
2. has traveled/traveled; visited; moved; have been/decided; has been studying/has studied; has planned/has been planning

ACTIVITY 14.7

Paragraph 1: established, was, owned/had owned

Paragraph 2: is, has diminished/has been diminishing, expanded/expanding, remains, have attained/attained

Paragraph 3: has been, have achieved, has gone, has decreased/has been decreasing, has been diminishing/has diminished/is diminishing

ACTIVITY 14.9

1. closes; will go
2. will have given
3. will be paying off/will pay off
4. will have taught/will have been teaching
5. will come/is coming
6. will begin/begins; will end/ends
7. will be eating/will eat
8. take

ACTIVITY 14.10

1. André has worked/has been working at the department store since 1985.
2. Naoki needs to buy books for the fall semester.
3. The car engine will cool down if the radiator works/is working.
4. Park had skied/had been skiing/skied in Colorado every winter before he broke his leg.
5. Alessandro will have studied ten hours by daybreak.
6. Water turns to ice at the freezing point.
7. Kari went to Paris last year.

ACTIVITY 14.11

was; has; discussed; made; was affecting/affected; had passed; has continued; has become; will double/will have doubled; has made; is continuing/continues, needed; is growing/has been growing; will adapt

ACTIVITY 14.12

1. F
2. T

3. T (more than 85% of the sentences using passive voice are agentless)
4. T (e.g., born, rumor)
5. T (e.g., have, belong)

ACTIVITY 14.13

1. X; By the time Jan arrived, all the food had been eaten.
2. C
3. X; Written in 1847, the opera has never had success.
4. X; Betty began to cry when she realized her dress was torn.
5. X; The railroad station was built during the eighteenth century.
6. X; Champagne is used for celebrating on New Year's Eve.
7. C
8. X; The United Nations was founded in 1945.
9. C
10. X; The schoolchildren were taken to the zoo yesterday.

ACTIVITY 14.14

Possible revision:

In the early 1980s, the Ford Motor Company was in trouble. It was being said that the Ford name stood for "fix or repair daily." The need for dramatic changes was recognized, and these changes were incorporated in the project "Team Taurus." Rather than have the various tasks done sequentially by each unit, a team was established, consisting of planners, designers, engineers, manufacturing people, and even suppliers. Assembly-line workers were also involved in development: they were asked by management to describe difficulties had by them in assembling the parts and to make recommendations for improvements.

Other manufacturers' cars were studied and their best features were examined by Ford employees, instead of adopting a know-it-all attitude. For example, Toyota's accurate fuel gauge and BMW's good tire storage were noted. Various seats were also tested on male and female drivers of all ages. Through extensive market studies, customer preferences were learned about.

The team is credited for Ford's turnaround by the chairman, Donald Petersen. But the biggest risk in developing the new line of cars was taken by him. Authority was delegated by him down the organizational hierarchy to the ranks of the workers. "Management by wandering around" was practiced by Peterson. In other words, the workers were visited and listened to by him. Ford was put back in the running by this style of management.

ACTIVITY 14.15

Paragraph 1: had declined, began/has begun, ended/have ended, has intensified, is not, has been, has given, has been, held, include

Paragraph 2: was given, relocated, exist, enjoy, are performed, is

ACTIVITY 14.16

(See Activity 14.1.)

Chapter 15

ACTIVITY 15.1

Relevant section of chapter is indicated in parentheses.

1. If it had been raining, I wouldn't have been able to walk to school today. (15d)
2. Jim wishes that he had a bigger apartment. (15c)
3. Whenever I ride in an airplane, I get an earache. (15b)
4. If participation had been greater this year, money might have been raised for a new stadium. (15c)
5. (Correct as written; 15d)
6. If he had been there earlier, the director would have seen him. (15c)
7. Unless I finish my research paper by Tuesday, I won't be able to go to the concert. (15b)
8. (Correct as written; 15c)
9. (Correct as written; 15d)
10. More people would have come to the party if the invitations had been sent out earlier. (15c)
11. If you lost your credit card, what would you do? (15b)
12. Bob acts as if he were the director of the center. (15d)
13. If I hadn't dropped off that package by ten o'clock today, it wouldn't have arrived until Wednesday. (15c)
14. (Correct as written; 15d)
15. Provided that all children are immunized, the virus won't spread. (15b)

ACTIVITY 15.2

1. rains; won't be   2. sees; turns   3. catches; will give
4. will hire; receive   5. arrived; became

ACTIVITY 15.3

1. When Nathan quits the soccer team, Woody will take his place.
2. Unless I write to my mother very often, she isn't very happy.
3. On the condition that Danny promises not to have an accident, Shirley will let him borrow her van.
4. (Correct as written)
5. If cars are parked in the wrong places, they will most likely be given tickets by the university police.

ACTIVITY 15.4

Possible answers:

1. If people didn't learn foreign languages, international business would be at a standstill.
2. If all the males in the world suddenly became females, the world would be a friendlier place.
3. If I find strange hair in my cafeteria food, I take it back.

4. If my best friend were fifty pounds overweight, I wouldn't mention it.
5. If the sun rose in the west tomorrow morning, I would go back to bed and try again.
6. I could have slept until eleven o'clock this morning if the neighbors had decided to do the same.
7. If Gandhi had not been born, India might not be independent today.
8. We would all be rich if none of us had any bills to pay.
9. I wish traveling were cheaper so that I could do it more often.
10. I wish I had studied harder for the exam last week so that I could have impressed the professor.

ACTIVITY 15.5

1. If Greg and Peter play football in the house, someone will get hurt.
   If Greg and Peter had played football in the house, someone would have gotten hurt.
2. Amy will buy a new truck if she has enough money at the end of the month.
   Amy would have bought a new truck if she had had enough money at the end of the month.
3. John will go to Michigan State University if he finishes the statistics course at the community college.
   John would have gone to Michigan State University if he had finished the statistics course at the community college.
4. If Deana sees her cousin this weekend, she will ask him for his new phone number.
   If Deana had seen her cousin this weekend, she would have asked him for his new phone number.
5. If I find your watch, I will bring it to work with me on Monday.
   If I had found your watch, I would have brought it to work with me on Monday.

ACTIVITY 15.6

1. Had Harry enough money, he would buy a car.
2. Should you want to borrow money, see the loan officer.
3. Were I a millionaire, I would travel more.
4. Had I studied harder, I would have passed the exam.
5. Were it winter, I would go skiing.
6. Should the people arrive late, cancel their reservations.
7. Had you told me earlier, I could have helped you.
8. Should the present arrive early, hide it in the closet.
9. Were my dog human, she would talk to me.
10. Had I a new computer, I could work faster.

ACTIVITY 15.7

1. be	2. fill; is	3. do; were	4. is	5. were
6. were	7. claims	8. was	9. were	10. find

ACTIVITY 15.8

1. (Correct as written)
2. The manager recommended that all employees take a seminar in accounting.
3. It is important that the taxi be on time.
4. It was essential that the train leave punctually.
5. (Correct as written)

Possible answers:

6. A suggestion was made that the boss be fired.
7. My mother asked that I keep my room clean.
8. The football players demanded that the fans be kept off the field.
9. It is essential that you bring your raincoat.
10. I would prefer that you not open that present now.

ACTIVITY 15.9

(See Activity 15.1.)

ACTIVITY 15.10

Possible revision:

Many armchair historians are prone to speculation. They like to ask questions like "If Abraham Lincoln hadn't been assassinated, what would have happened after the Civil War?" or "If Kennedy hadn't been born, how would our world be today?" At times, I wish I were more knowledgeable in the study of history, but I still find it amusing to hear people carry on about such questions as if there were some great conclusion to be reached. If one were to continue speculating on the results of a certain person or event having never existed, one would eventually come to the same conclusion that I reached.

We must not question history. We all wish that we could relive the countless possibilities of our past, but we cannot. Unless we accept the reality of our own personal and collective past, we won't be able to concentrate on what is really important: our personal and collective future.

Chapter 16

ACTIVITY 16.1

Words in bold are corrected from the original text. Other underlined words are identified but not changed from the original text. Type of verbal is indicated in parentheses: gerund *(ger.)*, infinitive *(inf.)*, present or past participle *(pres. part., past part.)*.

To find *(inf.)* work in another country is never easy. Understanding *(ger.)*

what you are expected **to do** *(inf.)* in a strange new workplace is even more difficult. This is precisely what Larry was made to discover *(inf.)* after **arriving** *(ger.)* as a university instructor in Paris. One thing he liked, <u>having</u> *(ger.)* a close relationship with his supervisors, was nearly nonexistent. He was **surprised** *(past part.)* when they even let him see them. Of course, the positive side to this was that he was nearly always able **to do** *(inf.)* what he wanted **to do** *(inf.)* in the classroom without much interference. He appeared to <u>enjoy</u> *(inf.)* this at first. He found his teaching **exciting** *(pres. part.)*. But after a few months, it did become difficult to <u>continue</u> *(inf.)* without any guidance. He was never sure what **to teach** *(inf.)*. In the end, by <u>asking</u> *(ger.)* many questions, he was able **to take** *(inf.)* control of the situation. By the time he was about to <u>leave</u> *(inf.)*, he finally wanted **to stay** *(inf.)!*

ACTIVITY 16.2

1. to be: infinitive, adjective modifier
2. naming: gerund, appositive
3. deliver: infinitive with modal (*to* omitted)
4. to find: infinitive, adjective modifier
5. studying: gerund, object of a preposition
6. to be: infinitive, appositive
7. being: gerund, object of a verb
8. hand in: infinitive with *make* (*to* omitted)
9. To join: infinitive, subject
10. to help: infinitive, subject
    pay: infinitive with *help* (*to* omitted)

ACTIVITY 16.3

1. I can't imagine moving as often as Joy does. (Rule 4)
2. I forgot to buy milk at the store. (Rule 5)
3. (Correct as written; Rule 2)
4. I was about to go to the store when my aunt called. (Rule 3)
5. (Correct as written; Rule 6)
6. I expect to win the lottery. (Rule 4)
7. Kwon offered to help with the dishes. (Rule 4)
8. After considering the proposal, I accepted it. (Rule 3)
9. (Correct as written; Rule 4)
10. (Correct as written; Rule 1)

ACTIVITY 16.4

1. to extend
2. to drink
3. to run
4. Riding; To ride
5. to sleep
6. to give

7. writing
8. to increase
9. printing
10. to skate; skating

ACTIVITY 16.5

1. startled	**2.** confusing	**3.** surprising; amazed
4. doing; finished	**5.** annoyed; boring	**6.** frightened
7. Irritated	**8.** impressed	

ACTIVITY 16.6

Possible answers:

1. Excited about her new car, Corey drove it everywhere.
2. Jumping off the building, the boy landed on the trampoline below.
3. Running toward the train, Larry slipped on a banana peel.
4. The water surrounding the island is crystal blue.
5. The books on the table need to be removed.

ACTIVITY 16.7

(See Activity 16.1.)

ACTIVITY 16.8

I arrived in Perth with five dollars and a determination **to get** a job in the mines. I was too late. Every company, it seemed, had just recruited a small army of miners; the quotas were full. To face the urgent necessity of **finding** work that day, I went to the employment office and invented some agricultural experience. I wanted **to be** somewhere isolated, without the need or opportunity **to spend** my earnings. A farmer arrived and agreed **to collect** me when his wife had finished her shopping.

At seven-thirty the next morning, I was driving a tractor for the first time in my life, being taught **to plow** a straight furrow. These fields were huge—over a thousand acres apiece—and I felt, at first, **overwhelmed** by the desolate vastness of the place. We were miles from the nearest house, and every tree was a landmark, **stretching** almost featureless to a far horizon. It was poor soil, virtually sand, **exhausted** by the monoculture of wheat, **fertilized** by tons of superphosphate. In parts it was even **poisoned** by salinity.

Gradually, however, I began relishing the space, the scale, the shadow of the clouds passing across the enormous landscape. Alone on my tractor, I plowed around and around in ever-diminishing rings. I became proud of my expertise. I came **to know** where I might find an iguana, lurking like a miniature dragon in the shade of a rock, and I became accustomed to the harsh cawing of the flocks of red and gray birds.

Chapter 17

ACTIVITY 17.1

Relevant section of chapter is indicated in parentheses.

1. (Correct as written; 17b)
2. That silk shirt looks great with my skirt. (17b)
3. The children ask to watch cartoons every morning. (17b)
4. (Correct as written; 17c)
5. (Correct as written; 17c)
6. I am happy to be studying in this country. (17c)
7. (Correct as written; 17d)
8. My classmates are surprised at their test scores. (17d)
9. (Correct as written; 17e)
10. (Correct as written; 17e)
11. Sue might go to New Mexico over the semester break. (17e)
12. Joey's younger brother can eat so much. (17e)
13. (Correct as written; 17f)
14. (Correct as written; 17f)
15. The attention of young boys often wanders during long speeches. (17g)
16. Fishing, as well as camping, is my favorite thing to do in the summer. (17g)
17. Joon and Carlos always study together in the library. (17g)
18. Hot tea with lemon makes me feel better. (17g)
19. (Correct as written; 17g)
20. Each teacher and student wants a copy of the new schedule. (17g)
21. (Correct as written; 17g)
22. Kris or Paul has lost the telephone message. (17g)
23. (Correct as written; 17g)
24. My staff is willing to work overtime. (17h)
25. Every night, the audience shouts and begs the musician to continue. (17h)
26. (Correct as written; 17h)
27. (Correct as written; 17i)
28. There are many ways to get to my house from Washington Street. (17i)
29. (Correct as written; 17i)
30. Tom's biggest complaints about the movie were the price and a weak ending. (17j)
31. This restaurant's most famous dish is spaghetti and meatballs. (17j)
32. (Correct as written; 17k)
33. (Correct as written; 17k)
34. One hundred miles was the distance to the campground. (17k)
35. (Correct as written; 17l)
36. (Correct as written; 17l)
37. (Correct as written; 17l)
38. Some of the money has been spent on groceries. (17l)

39. (Correct as written; 17m)
40. (Correct as written; 17m)

ACTIVITY 17.2

A. 1. -*s*   **2.** does not end in -*s*
B. 1. writes   **2.** make   **3.** likes   **4.** swing   **5.** helps
       6. teaches   **7.** works   **8.** cost   **9.** assign   **10.** exercises

ACTIVITY 17.3

1. live   **2.** works   **4.** studies   **4.** speak   **5.** eat
6. look   **7.** love   **8.** visit   **9.** fly   **10.** swim

ACTIVITY 17.4

A. 1. am   **2.** is   **3.** are
B. Possible answers:
   1. He is a crazy guy.
   2. Your girlfriend is really ugly.
   3. My cat is hairless.
   4. They are the car wax specialists.
   5. Those books are based on films.
   6. We are listed under "Expensive Car Repairs" in the Yellow Pages.
   7. I am not a singer.
   8. You, however, are a singer.

ACTIVITY 17.5

A. Corrected words are in boldface.

   Let me tell you a little about my family. I **come** from a family of seven; I have three sisters and one brother. My father is a businessman. He **owns** a little jewelry store where he sells and repairs beautiful gold and silver pieces. My mother is a homemaker, but she often **helps** my father at the store on the weekends. My oldest sister, Cathy, **is** a nurse at the local hospital. I **admire** Cathy; she works full-time and also **cares** for her husband and two children. My sister Judy is an artist. Her specialty **is** watercolors, but she is also good with pen and ink. My brother, Paul, is an architect. Paul also **has** artistic talent, and he designs eye-catching buildings. Currently, his newest design is being considered by the city. And finally, my youngest sister, Sharla, is a high school science teacher. She **loves** her work and **plans** to teach for many years to come.

ACTIVITY 17.6

Corrected words are in boldface.

   The outerwear system you need **depends** on the weather conditions you anticipate. Experience **has** shown that design of the outerwear is very important in making your backpacking trip successful. Design includes everything from the fit to the hood closure to the number of pockets. Key considerations are as follows:

Outerwear should never **fit** tightly. You **need** room to wear a bulky sweater and pants underneath. Shell jackets intended for winter should accommodate a down sweater, too. Look twice before buying a jacket that doesn't **include** an attached hood. If you tend to overheat, your outerwear should ventilate easily. So-called "breathable" gear won't **keep** you cool when lumbering uphill with a heavy pack. We assume you'll be wearing a pack, so don't choose a short-waisted jacket that will **crumple** up under your waistbelt.

ACTIVITY 17.7

1. It was a beautiful day! The sun was shining, and the birds were singing. On cool spring days, I woke up at sunrise and walked my dog, Fido. Fido liked to sniff the wet ground. He also enjoyed watching the birds in the trees. Sometimes Fido saw a small rabbit in the bushes. He chased the frightened animal, but he was only playing. He never harmed the animals we encountered on our early morning walks.

2. My roommate and I will ride our bicycles each morning before our classes. We will see the countryside at its most peaceful moments. The roads will be free of traffic; the air will be clean. Then we will eat a healthy breakfast at the small diner on the corner of Main and Berkeley streets. Our day will begin in a wonderful way!

ACTIVITY 17.8

Changed verbs are in boldface.

1. The newsletter, as well as the booklet, has to be published this week.

2. My coworkers or Mr. Wald **has** the original file.

3. Chinese, Mexican, and Italian are my favorite ethnic foods.

4. The report by the committee and its board members **has** been reviewed and revised.

5. Robert, along with Susan and Anne, **attends** weekly discussion meetings.

6. A review of the tax proposals **was** conducted last week.

7. My mother or my father gives me $20 each week.

8. Confusion about subject-verb agreement and pronoun agreement causes many problems.

9. After each of the placement exams **is** corrected, the students receive their scores.

10. My wife and my mother each are excellent cooks!

ACTIVITY 17.9

Corrected verbs are in boldface.

1. Warm drinks like thick, sweet Turkish coffee **are** served in demitasse cups to whet the appetite. *Chay* (tea) has a special place in every Turk's heart. Small glasses of the carefully brewed beverage **are** sipped throughout the day. The tea leaves, grown on the Aegean or Black Sea coasts, **are** steeped in a small teapot perched atop a larger steaming kettle for fifteen minutes. The strong brew that results **is** tempered with hot water to the personal taste of the drinker. A tea-

spoon of sugar or a squeeze of lemon **adds** the final touch to the smoothest glass of *chay* in the world.

Before breakfast, it is common to take a brisk walk to the neighborhood baker to buy a fragrant, just-baked loaf of bread. For the morning meal, generous slices are topped with chunks of feta cheese, black olives, and juicy tomatoes. Homemade jams, boiled down from seasonal fruit combined with sugar, **are** served with butter churned from fresh milk.

2. Meet one of the world's largest land mammals, the common hippopotamus. Hippos **spend** most of their lives in the water, napping and relaxing. During dry seasons, they cool off in wallows, or mud holes. Then a coating of mud and dirt **protects** the animals' skin from the sun. Although the Greek word *hippopotamus* means "river horse," the hippo most **resembles** its cousin the pig.

The hippo may look awkward, but the river giant swims and dives with grace and ease. Underwater, the hippo's eyes narrow to slits and its ears flatten to form a seal. Pores in the hippo's skin **produce** a pink, sticky fluid that waterproofs the animal. Even the toes on its feet, which **aid** in paddling, are designed for its watery environment.

A calf, or young hippo, **is** born—you guessed it—underwater. Right away it can push off the bottom and rise to the surface to breathe. When in water it often rides on its mother's back. There it can breathe easy, safe from crocodiles.

ACTIVITY 17.10

1. Management; disagrees
2. The number; has
3. couple; is
4. A number; appear
5. members; debate
6. people; are
7. A number; live
8. team; needs
9. members; love
10. the number; has

ACTIVITY 17.11

1. are; people
2. was; no one
3. is; book
4. is; equipment
5. were; courses

ACTIVITY 17.12

1. is; shop
2. are; letters

3. is; vase

4. are; supplies

5. is; present

ACTIVITY 17.13

1. worry; is

2. game; is

3. Grades; are

4. item; is

5. interest; is

6. wife; seems

ACTIVITY 17.14

1. c; Two and one-half hours; is

2. b; *American Challenges;* is

3. c; ten dollars; was

4. a; series; was

5. c; Eighty miles; is

ACTIVITY 17.15

1. are   **2.** is   **3.** have   **4.** is   **5.** is   **6.** are
7. appreciates   **8.** was   **9.** has   **10.** becomes   **11.** is   **12.** are

ACTIVITY 17.16

1. Students are late for class. Students should enter the room quietly.
2. A bird migrates across the Gulf of Mexico. A bird is exhausted when it reaches the coast.
3. Birds migrate across the Gulf of Mexico. Birds are exhausted when they reach the coast.

ACTIVITY 17.17

1. This is one of those problems. Those problems are easy once you know the answer.
2. She is one of those women. Only one of those women is always punctual.
3. This is one of those problems. Only one of those problems is easy once you know the answer.

ACTIVITY 17.18

1. was   **2.** make   **3.** study; study   **4.** are
5. calls   **6.** wins   **7.** take   **8.** gives

ACTIVITY 17.19

(See Activity 17.1.)

ACTIVITY 17.20

Corrected verbs are in boldface.

In 1985, my friend and I **were** sent to Madagascar to look for an almost extinct form of lemur, called the aye-aye. Only a few of these animals **are** known to exist on a tiny island off the northeastern coast of Madagascar. This nocturnal animal, like everything else that **lives** on the island, **does** not **exist** anywhere else on earth. It **looks** a little like a large cat with a bat's ears, a beaver's teeth, a tail like a large ostrich feather, a middle finger like a long dead twig, and enormous eyes that **seem** to peer past you into a totally different world that **exists** just over your left shoulder.

When Madagascar broke off Africa and drifted into the Indian Ocean, it became isolated from all evolutionary changes that took place in the rest of the world. The major change that passed this island by **was** the arrival of the monkeys. They descended from the same ancestors as the lemurs, but they had bigger brains and **were** aggressive competitors for the same habitat. The monkeys were ambitious and interested in all sorts of things, especially twigs, with which they found they could do all kinds of things that they couldn't do by themselves—dig, probe, hit. The monkeys took over the world, and the lemur branch of the primate family died out everywhere—except on Madagascar. There **were** no monkeys for millions of years.

Then, fifteen hundred years ago, the monkeys finally arrived, or at least the monkeys' descendants—us. Thanks to astounding advances in twig technology, we arrived in canoes, then boats, and finally airplanes and started to **compete** for the same habitat. Today, the lemurs once again **are** fighting for survival.

Chapter 18

ACTIVITY 18.1

Relevant section of chapter is indicated in parentheses. Answers may vary.

1. My teacher, Mrs. Collins, asked Ali to pass out the papers for her. (18b)
2. (Correct as written; 18b)
3. My roommate goes to the library every night because she must complete a research paper. (18b)
4. (Correct as written; 18b)
5. My sister didn't come home for the holidays because she had research to do. (Correct as written; 18b)
6. A conscientious student must submit his or her papers on time. (18c)
7. (Correct as written; 18c)
8. Each employee should submit his or her health insurance questionnaire by Wednesday. (18c)
9. All people who see the movie will think about their relationship with their own father. (18c)
10. A cat or a dog is allowed in the apartment only if it is quiet and clean. (18d)

11. (Correct as written; 18d)
12. The reason my parents and brother called was that they wanted to wish me a happy birthday. (18d)
13. Anyone who has a question about his or her paper should see me after class. (18e)
14. (Correct as written; 18e)
15. Some of the instructors have office hours posted on their door. (18e)
16. (Correct as written; 18e)
17. (Correct as written; 18e)
18. My committee decided to revise the bylaws, but the revision took us about a month. (18f)

ACTIVITY 18.2

Corrected pronouns are in boldface.

Recently, I purchased one of your company's products, the Handy Dandy Kitchen Tool. The Acme Company advertised that a person doesn't need to spend **his or her** precious evenings cooking. Acme guaranteed that this product would save valuable time in the kitchen.

I am a working mother who wants to spend **her** free time relaxing with **her** children. When I bought your product, my husband laughed at me. **He** said that the product was a waste of money. I want to inform you that my husband was wrong! I use the Handy Dandy Kitchen Tool every day and have more time to spend with **my** children.

People should try your product. I think **they** will be pleasantly surprised.

ACTIVITY 18.3

Answers to item c may vary.

1. a. I believe that each citizen should volunteer to help clean up his or her neighborhood.
   b. I believe that citizens should volunteer to help clean up their neighborhood.
   c. I believe that each citizen should volunteer to help with neighborhood cleanup.
2. a. A teacher must have his or her credentials to teach in the public school system.
   b. Teachers must have their credentials to teach in the public school system.
   c. A teacher must have the necessary credentials to teach in the public school system.

ACTIVITY 18.4

Changes are required only in the numbered list, as follows (answers may vary):

1. All positions are posted on the Human Resources Bulletin Board.
2. If employees are interested in a position, they must complete an application form.

3. When applying for a position, each employee should bring his or her employment identification card.

4. Employees will be required to interview for the desired position, and their department manager will notify them of the outcome.

ACTIVITY 18.5

Words that have been changed are in boldface. Answers may vary.

1. My grandfather and grandmother were taught the meaning of hard work and honesty when **they were** young.

2. Aunt Helen and Uncle Gene sold the house in which **they** lived for over twenty years.

3. Neither dogs nor cats enjoy baths, even if they like water.

4. My mentor and friend is a hardworking person who enjoys **his** career immensely.

5. Roses or tulips are wonderful anniversary gifts because they are beautiful.

6. Employees and spouses will receive **their** invitation in the mail.

7. Waffles or an omelet is part of a good breakfast because **it contains** carbohydrates.

8. It is important that students receive an education so that **they** can be productive members of society.

9. Either my parents or my older sister will drive me to the airport when **she returns** from work.

10. My husband and son couldn't attend the party because they went to a baseball game.

ACTIVITY 18.6

Answers to item c may vary.

1. a. Anybody who knows how to cook should volunteer his or her time to the food drive.
   b. All the people who know how to cook should volunteer their time to the food drive.
   c. Anybody who knows how to cook should volunteer some time to the food drive.
2. a. Each of the students in this class will write his or her next paper using a computer.
   b. All of the students in this class will write their next paper using a computer.
   c. Each of the students in this class will write the next paper using a computer.
3. a. Anybody who has questions about the computer will have a chance to ask those questions as he or she works on his or her papers.
   b. All students who have questions about the computer will have a chance to ask those questions as they work on their papers.
   c. Anybody who has questions about the computer will have a chance to ask those questions while working on class papers.

ACTIVITY 18.7

Changed words are in boldface.

1. All of my sisters are coming home for the holidays; **they** will be traveling great distances.

2. Most of the books in the library are out of date; they do not provide the information needed to complete my research.

3. Much of my second language, Spanish, was taught by my mother; it was her native language.

4. None of the local television stations have female broadcasters; I wonder if **they are** violating the equal employment opportunity regulations.

5. Half of my breakfast remained on my plate; **it was** not very good!

6. Several journalists used their recorders during the press conference.

ACTIVITY 18.8

Monterey is a city with a long and brilliant literary tradition. It remembers with pleasure and some glory that Robert Louis Stevenson lived there. More recently in Carmel there have been a great number of literary men about, but there is not the old flavor, the old dignity of the true belles-lettres.

Where the new post office is, there used to be a deep gulch with water flowing in it and a little foot bridge over it. On one side of the gulch was a fine old adobe and on the other the house of a doctor who handled all the sickness, birth, and death in the town. He worked with animals too and, having studied in France, he even dabbled in the new practice of embalming bodies before they were buried. Some of the old-timers considered this sentimental and some thought it wasteful and to some it was sacrilegious since there was no provision for it in any sacred volume. But the better and richer families were coming around to the idea and it looked to become a fad.

ACTIVITY 18.9

Revisions may vary.

1. a; The car sped and turned from the dangerous oncoming vehicle, but the oncoming vehicle managed to pull away.

2. a; Dina and Bill decided to move back to Minneapolis, but the decision took them almost three months.

3. b; When André took his nephews to the Vail ski area, he knew skiing was something they would like to do again.

4. a; When Abdul went to Erfan's house for dinner, he told Erfan that he wasn't hungry.

5. c; Francisco thought about staying at his job in Seville or moving to Chicago, but he decided against moving to Chicago.

ACTIVITY 18.10

(See Activity 18.1.)

ACTIVITY 18.11

Changed words are in boldface. Revisions may vary.

Veteran robot expert Roy Morley, a senior development engineer in Peoria, Illinois, has been interested in **robots** since he was a robot in **his** fifth-grade Halloween parade. A certified robotic engineer, Morley has been with his company for twenty-seven years.

His first full-time assignment was to locate the best place for the company to install its first robot. At that time, the robot was required to work with a heat treatment furnace **which** got as high as 1,500 degrees Fahrenheit.

Getting the robot operational wasn't easy. Morley recalls having to rearrange the plant area to make room for **the robot** and planning **its** functions carefully. Intensive job analysis was another of **his** responsibilities. He not only wrote the programs for the robot but also trained the operators.

More than twenty years after the first installation, Morley is still enthusiastic about robots. Now that he's helping **his** daughter choose a college and a career, Morley suggests strongly that everyone who is considering working with robotics tour industrial plants, research labs, and manufacturing environments as much as possible while **he or she is** still in high school. **Morley** especially recommends summer career institutes in engineering like those offered by the Bradley Institute, which give young people a chance to take field trips and meet industry leaders.

He points out that new engineering graduates are rotated through company assignments for one to two years, and they take on a variety of company projects so that company managers can evaluate how well **the graduates** do on the jobs. "Every man and woman is rated on **his or her** initiative, desire, quality, and quantity of work," he says. "It's better to have as broad an engineering background as possible, rather than just a specialty in robotics."

Chapter 19

ACTIVITY 19.1

Relevant section of chapter is indicated in parentheses.

1. Boyd asked her to give him a break. (19b)

2. (Correct as written; 19b)

3. The person who will be president is she. (19c)

4. (Correct as written; 19c)

5. Sam was convinced that both he and they had played terribly in the baseball game. (19d)

6. (Correct as written; 19d)
7. The greatest fishermen, Rodney and I, caught more than twenty bass yesterday. (19e)
8. Save some food for your best friend, me. (19e)
9. (Correct as written; 19f)
10. It is clear that we liberals are a minority. (19f)
11. Mohammad can run faster than I. (19g)
12. (Correct as written; 19g)
13. Violet liked the man who was wearing the red hat. (19h)
14. (Correct as written; 19h)
15. Whom did you write to? (19h)

ACTIVITY 19.2

1. he   2. him   3. them   4. she   5. he

ACTIVITY 19.3

1. he; was; L   2. I; be; L   3. her; compelled; A   4. he; was; L
5. she; was; L   6. us; asked; A

ACTIVITY 19.4

Changed pronouns are in boldface.

1. Reynaldo and **I** are going to the movies tonight.
2. Just between you and **me,** the food tastes terrible.
3. After class, my friends and **I** went for a bite to eat.
4. (Correct as written)
5. My mother asked my sister and **me** to help her.

ACTIVITY 19.5

1. (Correct as written)
2. (Correct as written)
3. The coaches, Gloria and I, decided to replace the pitcher.
4. (Correct as written)
5. The director asked us, Carol and me, to lead the seminar.

ACTIVITY 19.6

1. we   2. us   3. us   4. We   5. We

ACTIVITY 19.7

Changed pronouns are in boldface.

1. **I** can.   2. **I** am   3. she envies me; **I** do   4. he is   5. I do; it annoys me

ACTIVITY 19.8

1. **a.** *who/whom* is a paleontologist
   b. he is a paleontologist

    c. subject
    d. who
2. a. *who/whom* he admired
    b. him (he admired him)
    c. object
    d. whom
3. a. *who/whom* people often showed fossils to
    c. him (people often showed fossils to him)
    d. object
    e. whom

ACTIVITY 19.9

1. who   **2.** whom   **3.** who   **4.** whom   **5.** Whoever

ACTIVITY 19.10

1. his   **2.** our   **3.** them   **4.** his   **5.** them

ACTIVITY 19.11

(See Activity 19.1.)

ACTIVITY 19.12

Changed pronouns are in boldface.

    The eldest daughter, Rose, is a big husky girl of twenty-one, the "big sister" of the family, the mother's constant companion and helper, a robust creature full of hilarity and vigor and warmth. **She** possesses a large and generous nature. She walks around the kitchen with the heavy steps of a pachyderm that make the dishes in the pantry rattle and jingle, and she hauls in the wash in huge baskets from the yard. When her favorite brother, **who** is Joe, comes home from **his** constant wanderings, she yells and chases **him** around the house. Joe is faster than **she.**

    The few boyfriends **whom** she goes out with are all big husky creatures like **her who** work on farms or drive trucks or handle the heavy work in factories. When one of them cuts his finger or burns his hand, she and **he** sit down and she administers the necessary aid and scolds **him** furiously. She is the first member of the family to get up in the morning, and the last in bed. As far back as **she** can remember, she has been a "big sister." At dusk, we, my other sister and **I,** can see her standing in the yard taking down her wash, packing it in baskets, and starting back to the porch.

Chapter 20

ACTIVITY 20.1

Relevant section of chapter is indicated in parentheses.

1. Annette does her work very well. (20b)
2. Since his accident, Darnell thinks differently about his life. (20b)
3. The dog went in the water, and now she smells bad! (20c)

4. (Correct as written; 20c)
5. Larry is bigger than Jeff. (20d)
6. (Impossible comparison; 20d)
7. (Correct as written; 20d)
8. (Correct as written; 20e)
9. I don't understand anything about nuclear energy. (20e)
10. Kaye always tells the truth. (20f)

ACTIVITY 20.2

A. The sun has just (adv.) gone down. I am sitting alone (adj.) on a smooth (adj.) log that is slightly (adv.) moist (adj.) from the previous (adj.) rainstorm. I sit quietly (adv.), taking in the sights around me. It is a place I often (adv.) come to at this time of the day. In front of me is a lake that is still (adj.), except for the few (adj.) ripples where fish are eagerly (adv.) eating their dinner. Suddenly (adv.), a bird calls out above me. It is the cry of a lonely (adj.) raven, perhaps looking for its mate. The sky is still (adv.), light (adj.), and the clouds are moving swiftly (adv.). There is a warm (adj.) glow that only (adj.) this time of day can provide. It is intensely (adv.) beautiful (adj.), and I am peaceful (adj.).

B. strikingly; special; surprisingly; constantly; unique; considerable; newly; quickly; different; interesting

ACTIVITY 20.3

1. smelled; A 2. smelled; L 3. touched; A
4. touched; L 5. tasted; A 6. tastes; L

ACTIVITY 20.4

1. sadly 2. bad 3. bad 4. really; good 5. well

ACTIVITY 20.5

slow/slower; fastest; likely; more slowly; faster

ACTIVITY 20.6

A. Sentences will vary but should include these terms:
    1. best food
    2. earlier event
    3. busier agenda
    4. (the) most luck
    5. leaking more slowly
B. Summaries will vary.

ACTIVITY 20.7

1. The backhand in tennis is an impossible swing.
2. *Dracula* is the scariest movie ever made.
3. Konishki is the fattest of all the sumo wrestlers.
4. My puppy was the worst of all the dogs in the park.
5. Peter was the happier of the two brothers.

ACTIVITY 20.8

Answers may vary.

1. Meaning: Erfan likes history; he prefers geography.
   Revision: Erfan isn't interested in history; he prefers geography.
2. Meaning: The weather usually gets above 30°C in London.
   Revision: The weather rarely gets above 30°C in London.
3. Meaning: Many people are going to the arts and crafts show.
   Revision: Nobody is going to the arts and crafts show.
4. Meaning: Kristin's son cleans his room.
   Revision: Kristin's son never cleans his room.

ACTIVITY 20.9

Revisions may vary.

1. The queen is wearing an impressive mauve satin evening gown to the ceremony.
2. The agent carefully opened the suspicious package.
3. My mother's scissors are seldom where she expects them.
4. The movie had a grotesque, slimy, small green alien in the beginning.
5. The uncomfortable small wicker chair is in the corner.

ACTIVITY 20.10

(See Activity 20.1.)

ACTIVITY 20.11

Most technological gizmos seem **extraordinary** for a time, then either go away because **nobody needs them** (electric knives) or blend into the world of things we take for granted (remote-control television). No one **is** amazed or troubled anymore (as people once were) by the implications of a horseless carriage, a transistor radio, or a personal computer. But isn't it **strange** how these **impressive, small, plastic** answering machines, which are over a quarter-century old, still make a lot of people act so funny?

Some callers are rendered speechless. For many, refusing to leave a message on the tape is a gesture of principle: they consider answering machines a symbol of the fact that the world is becoming less **personal.** These people believe that personal attention **is dead.** Then, too, there are people who experience stage fright when talking to an answering machine. Few other occasions in life call on you to sum up your thoughts and express them **clearly** and **concisely** and have them neatly saved on a recording device.

If talking to a machine makes some callers seem **rude** or **foolish,** programming the machine has **quickly** transformed normally reserved people into entertainers. For the time it takes to deliver their message, they have something that is **rare** even for professional actors: a **captive** audience, which sits waiting **patiently** and **politely** for a beep. And while it waits, this audience has the privilege of listening to whatever humorous routine the machine owner has programmed. Has any other **technological** invention made us act so **differently?**

Chapter 21

ACTIVITY 21.1

Relevant section of chapter is indicated in parentheses.

1. Illinois Wesleyan University has an average enrollment of 1,700 students (21d)
2. My mother prefers an umbrella rather than a raincoat. (21c)
3. When Gary swims for a couple of hours, he usually gets an earache. (21c)
4. Most people agree that touring Europe on the/a train is better than flying. (21h)
5. Kristie goes to church on Sunday morning and Wednesday night. (21h)
6. (Correct as written; 21d)
7. My professor suggested that I add an appendix to my research paper. (21e)
8. (Correct as written; 21f)
9. A credit card is not necessary for a university student. (21f)
10. A bridal shop is located on Michigan Avenue in Chicago. (21d)
11. An apple is a refreshing snack on a hot day. (21c)
12. Many elementary school students carry lunch boxes to school every day. (21g)
13. Did you turn in the homework that Professor Bach assigned for today? (21c)
14. Prague is one of the most beautiful cities in Europe. (21f)
15. AIDS is becoming one of the most common killer diseases. (21h)
16. (Correct as written; 21d)
17. The telephone was invented by Alexander Graham Bell. (21g)
18. In general, cats are much smarter than dogs. (21g)
19. I love to take walks on the beach when the moon is full. (21f)
20. Would you go to the store and buy some rice? (21e)

ACTIVITY 21.2

An; a; an; a; A; an; a; an; A; a; a; a; An; a; an; a

ACTIVITY 21.3

| 1. –; the | 2. The | 3. the; –; the | 4. –; the; – | 5. the |
| 6. the | 7. The | 8. –; the | 9. –; the | 10. –; –; the |

ACTIVITY 21.4

Additions are in boldface. Category descriptions may vary.

NONCOUNTABLE NOUNS	CATEGORY
biology, chemistry, economics, **music**	**subjects of study**
politics, pollution, violence, **education, weather**	general topics
air, oxygen, carbon dioxide, **smoke**	gases

rain, gravity, sunshine, **weather, darkness, lightness**	natural phenomena
rice, sand, sugar, **oatmeal, gravel, flour**	**fine-grained substances**
milk, water, coffee, **blood**	**liquids**
basketball, soccer, table tennis, **chess**	**sports and games**
chicken pox, flu, measles	**illnesses**
fruit, furniture, jewelry, **luggage, equipment, money, garbage**	groups of items
Arabic, Japanese, Russian	**nationalities and languages**
parking, smoking, studying, **learning, dancing**	**gerunds, activities**
sadness, happiness, anger	**emotions**
intelligence, courage, honesty, luck, **patience**	qualities

ACTIVITY 21.5

Changed words are in boldface.

TAKESHI: Professor Bird, can you tell me the **criteria** for completing my **theses**?

DR. BIRD: All you need to do is finish your research. How is it going?

TAKESHI: Well, I still don't understand the **formulae** that **measure** the **radii** of he **nuclei** of **atoms.**

DR. BIRD: Did you read my **articles** on the **analyses** of **those formulae** in the *Chemical Journal?* You can find **them** in the **indices.**

TAKESHI: No, I didn't know about **them.**

DR. BIRD: **They're** on the **shelves** over there.

TAKESHI: Thank you so much, Professor Bird.

DR. BIRD: You're welcome. Good luck, Takeshi!

ACTIVITY 21.6

1. 2, 5, 5, 5   **2.** 2, 3   **3.** 1

ACTIVITY 21.7

1. G   **2.** G   **3.** D   **4.** I   **5.** G   **6.** I   **7.** D

ACTIVITY 21.8

(See Activity 21.1.)

ACTIVITY 21.9

A. *Paragraph 1:* The; The; The; the; a; a; –; the; the; the; the
Paragraph 2: The; –; –; an; The; a; –; the; The; the; –; –; the
Paragraph 3: The; The; the; the; –; –; –

B. 1. An excellent dry cleaner is on Pennsylvania Avenue.
2. Each greenhouse gas has an influence on the greenhouse effect.
3. Jose went to a hospital in Tucson.
4. Many students ride bicycles in a university town.
5. Fahad saw an eagle on our field trip.
6. Recently, the market share of Coca-Cola has declined.

7. Alex tried the clams that Brian had recommended.
8. My roommate goes to church every Sunday morning.
9. Writing a research paper is a criterion for completing this course.
10. Mrs. Robbins had patience and she was very honest.

Chapter 22

ACTIVITY 22.1

Relevant section of chapter is indicated in parentheses.

1. (Correct as written; 22c)
2. (Correct as written; 22c)
3. Albert arrived in this country three days ago. (22c)
4. (Correct as written; 22c)
5. That behavior isn't consistent with our friendship. (22d)
6. (Correct as written; 22d)
7. My mother made a cake for me. (22d)
8. (Correct as written; 22d)
9. The concert was canceled because they were sick. (22e)
10. It is difficult to provide for families in Romania because of the low wages. (22e)
11. Please explain to me what you mean. (22e)
12. Talking to my boss is difficult. (22f)
13. (Correct as written; 22f)
14. The leg of the chair is unstable. (22g)
15. (Correct as written; 22g)

ACTIVITY 22.2

on; in; before/by/at; until; on; since; in; During; After; Before; until; for; by/before/at

ACTIVITY 22.3

on; onto; from; to; in; from; as far as; in/at; on; around; on; along/down/in; at/in front of; at; toward/against; at; next to; beside; on/above; over; toward

ACTIVITY 22.4

Answers will vary.

ACTIVITY 22.5

1. k	2. g/h	3. g/h	4. j	5. a	6. b	7. f	8. c
9. m	10. i	11. e	12. d	13. n	14. l	15. o	16. p

ACTIVITY 22.6

1. of	2. to	3. about	4. with	5. except (for)/but
6. for	7. for	8. from	9. despite	10. by

ACTIVITY 22.7

1. U; You could ride a bike, but a motorcycle will get you there faster.
2. W; Sometimes you are stuck in traffic for half an hour without moving.
3. O; Parents who punish their children by hitting them and not listening to them are often despised.
4. U; PepsiCo is moving aggressively into foreign markets, pushing harder to sell its soda brands such as Mountain Dew and Slice.
5. U; Ben did not come to class because he was sick.
6. W; Police are very strict about the speed limit.
7. O; Shelly believed in and donated to the Sierra Club.

ACTIVITY 22.8

Possible revisions:

1. It is difficult to get along with my mother.
2. George doesn't understand the subject of the book.
3. My friend recommended that I go to Hudson's to try on a dress.
4. Marilee's boyfriend came to her house to pick up the car.
5. Rhonda really needed to talk to someone.

ACTIVITY 22.9

Possible answers:

1. my brother's arm
2. the door of the car
3. Whiskers's toy
4. the claws of the eagle
5. Alex's stereo

ACTIVITY 22.10

(See Activity 22.1.)

ACTIVITY 22.11

Possible answers:

of; (out) of; by; during; of; with/upon/after; into; of; For/Over; of; of; of; of; from; to; At; of; into; of; until; by; in; for; of; to; of

Chapter 23

ACTIVITY 23.1

Relevant section of chapter is indicated in parentheses.

1. (Correct as written; 23b)
2. Most junior colleges do not have student housing; however, they do refer students to apartments. (23b)

3. (Correct as written; 23b)
4. (Correct as written; 23d)
5. My teacher told us that it is common to confuse the words "accept" and "except." (23d)
6. (Correct as written; 23b)
7. Mom always told us not to play ball in the house. (23d)
8. Most American students, in my opinion, are more serious than foreigners think. (23b)
9. The student who usually comes to class late is named Simon. (23b)
10. My mother-in-law's birthday is the same day as mine. (23c)
11. We told Michelle that she shouldn't worry about her upcoming exam. (23c)
12. (Correct as written; 23b)
13. You didn't think you could leave without saying good-bye, did you? (23b)
14. The private detective searched each lawyer's files for evidence. (23c)
15. Whenever a dog thinks it's time to go for a walk, it usually barks. (23c)
16. Did Michael actually say, "I need to know how much money you make"? (23d)
17. (Correct as written; 23b)
18. (Correct as written; 23c)
19. In several professors' opinions, the university needs better-qualified graduate students. (23c)
20. Art King, who ran for city council last August, is a good friend of mine. (23b)

ACTIVITY 23.2

Gandhi kept a day of silence once a week. No matter what happened or who came to visit, he would spend that day quietly. Most of us are unable to maintain an entire day of silence. However, we can establish regular periods of meditation.

There are as many forms of meditation as there are temperaments. Some of these forms of meditation are elaborate, some are simple, and some are unstructured. In alphagenetics, people select a number and count slowly; biofeedback monitors body processes with machines; transcendental meditation focuses on a personal mantra; and psychosynthesis uses visual images and guided daydreams.

Slow conscious breathing focuses our energy. When the mind slows down, it channels deep beneath the noise and surface clutter. After meditation, we emerge renewed, refreshed, and peaceful.

ACTIVITY 23.3

1. Glenora was very excited about her high school reunion, but she couldn't go.
2. Nuclear power is beneficial because it doesn't contribute to the greenhouse effect; on the other hand, it has many problems with safety and disposal issues. (Answer may vary.)
3. The newly established baseball team has a winning record, and the fans are going to the game in droves.

4. The water was found to be heavily contaminated in Cooperstown. As a result, the townspeople have to buy bottled water. (Answer may vary.)
5. The Johnsons could leave their puppy with us, or they could pay to leave it in the kennel.

ACTIVITY 23.4

1. Emily's dog, who always barks at strangers, is a golden retriever.
2. My friend Naomi, who lives in Japan, is coming to visit.
3. Sheila, running to catch the train, did not see the small rock.
4. The light at dusk, my favorite time of day, is perfect for taking moody pictures.
5. My professor, Dr. Moriarity, is famous for his research on pesticides.

ACTIVITY 23.5

1. (Correct as written)
2. Boulder, Colorado, is where Heather lives, not Denver.
3. "Your deadline," said my boss, "is August 28."
4. Their car all packed, the Wilsons left for a wonderful vacation.
5. "Yes, I will do my homework, I promise," the little boy told his mother earnestly.
6. The sea was very stormy, and it was difficult to navigate.
7. (Correct as written)
8. "I will hold your daughter," snarled the kidnapper, "until you bring me $325,000 in cash."
9. Sam caught a slimy, wet salamander and put it in his mother's closet.
10. (Correct as written)

ACTIVITY 23.6

On a wintry day in November 1823, a tall, beefy wanderer with a bland, open face like a rising sun stood with his scrawny wife, pudgy eleven-year-old son, and three hunting dogs in the western reaches of the new state of Louisiana. A straggler from Tennessee who had fled to avoid bankruptcy and jail, he was not pleased with what faced him.

"Don't mind the water; we can wade through it. Done so many times on our exploration, but I do worry about this next stretch between here and Texas."

"We'll get through," his red-headed wife mumbled. Reaching for her rather unpleasant son, she warned, "You're to stay close, Yancey. Help us load the guns if they attack."

The three were dressed in buckskin garments laboriously cut and sewn by the mother, who appeared to be responsible for all vital decisions; on the other hand, her husband thrashed about deciding issues which never seemed to matter. Each member of the family carried guns, an axe, pots, extra articles of clothing, and bundles of food. Useful items protruded from every angle of their body(,) so that they looked like three porcupines waddling through the woods.

ACTIVITY 23.7

1. I must prepare for my mother-in-law's visit.
2. The two weeks' delay will cost the company thousands of dollars.

3. The legs of the table are not very sturdy.
4. The bridesmaids' dresses are peach.
5. The committee's decision made the workers angry.
6. The book on the table is mine.
7. The time the play begins is anyone's guess.
8. The president of the United States' policy on abortion is controversial.
9. His computer is a Macintosh.
10. The back of the room is for standing only.

ACTIVITY 23.8

Dear Huong,

How are you? Things are okay here, but I'm a little upset about the writing class I'm taking. The teacher's grades are incredible. I received Cs on my first two compositions. I couldn't believe it. When I went to talk to her about it, she told me my writing was good, but I had to learn the proper format for papers in an American university. Also, she said I had to learn how to use the spelling checker on the computer as all of my *separate*'s and *accept*'s were spelled wrong. What's really frustrating is that I could barely read her comments because of her writing. Her *a*'s look more like *o*'s, and the handwriting is terrible. She's nice, though, and was helpful when I went to see her about my paper.

Now I'm working on a research paper about life in America in the 1960s. It's really interesting! Mostly I'm focusing on the big events that reflected the cultural attitudes of that time, like President Kennedy's assassination. I'm working hard to understand the style of writing research papers here. I didn't know there were so many rules, and it's so different from the way we write. Oh, well, I guess I'm learning!

Hope everything's well with you. Can't wait to see you in December. Write soon.

Love,

Hajin

ACTIVITY 23.9

1. In President Kennedy's inaugural address, he stated, "Ask not what your country can do for you; ask what you can do for your country."
2. Marius used the transitional expression "however" more than twenty times in his research paper!
3. Greg stared at Penelope, who looked away. "That's a lot of money to spend on a trip," Greg said.
4. "When will you be home?" asked Mrs. Cleaver. "Before supper," said Beaver. "I promise."
5. In his book *Dictators,* Jules Archer cites Karl Marx and Friedrich Engels: "Let the ruling class tremble at a Communist revolution. The proletarians have nothing to lose but their chains. They have a world to win. Working men of all countries, unite!" (17).
6. Paula stated defiantly, "I ate the turkey, mashed potatoes, and stuffing!" No wonder nothing remained for the other guests.
7. The *Wall Street Journal* article "Flooded by Refugees, Western Europe Slams Doors on Foreigners" was fascinating.
8. "Texans," replied Jake, "are a tough breed."
9. The actor was upset about the writer using "skinny" rather than "slender" to describe him.
10. Did the policeman say, "Please sign the warrant"?

ACTIVITY 23.10

1. ✓
2. Cheryl blurted out, "When my laundry is done, I'm out of here."
3. ✓
4. ✓
5. The little boy screamed to his mother, "Mindy did it!"

ACTIVITY 23.11

"When we have France," said Casson, "there will be no shortage—"
"Cash," said the Englishman. "Half in advance and half on completion."
"How much?" asked Rodin.
"Half a million."
Rodin glanced at Montclair, who grimaced. "That's a lot of money, half a million new francs—"
"Dollars," said the Englishman.
"Half a million dollars?" shouted Montclair, rising from his seat. "You are crazy!"
"No," said the Englishman calmly, "but I am the best, and therefore the most expensive."

ACTIVITY 23.12

(See Activity 23.1.)

ACTIVITY 23.13

It was two o'clock in the morning when Pilar waked him. As her hand touched him, he thought it was Maria, and he rolled toward her and said, "Rabbit." Then the woman's big hand shook his shoulder, and he was suddenly, completely, and absolutely awake. His hand was around the butt of the pistol that lay alongside of his right bare leg; he was as cocked as the pistol with its safety catch slipped off.

In the dark, he saw it was Pilar, and he looked at the dial of his wristwatch with the two hands shining in the short angle close to the top. Seeing it was only two, he said, "What passes with thee, woman?"

"Pablo is gone," the big woman said to him.

Robert Jordan put on his trousers and shoes. Maria had not waked.

"When?" he asked.

"It must be an hour."

"And?"

"He has taken something of mine," the woman said miserably.

"So. What?"

"I don't know," she told him. "Come and see."

In the dark, they walked over to the entrance of the cave, ducked under the blanket, and went in. Robert Jordan followed her in the dead-ashes, bad-air, and sleeping-men smell of the cave. He shined his electric torch so that he would not step on any of those who were sleeping on the floor.

Chapter 24

ACTIVITY 24.1

Relevant section of chapter is indicated in parentheses.

1. (Correct as written; 24c)
2. Boris ate thirty-five hamburgers at lunch! (24b)
3. I still remember the old Irish priest's words: "Let the sun shine warmly on your face." (24c)
4. Wayne had to contact the director (a woman who was also the chairperson of the Modern Language Association [MLA] and whom he had already met at the previous convention). (24g)
5. Anita's plane was scheduled to arrive at O'Hare International Airport at 3:00 A.M. (24c)
6. U.S. educators are concerned with the low scores on the Scholastic Achievement Test (SAT). (24e)
7. I tried to get French Open tickets for the men's quarterfinals and the women's finals. (24c)
8. You should contact your state senator and/or state assembly representative. (24h)
9. "Don't you think you should buy a foreign car instead?" my uncle asked me. (24b)
10. (Correct as written; 24c)
11. Her purpose—to win the race—was second only to the money. (24f)

12. The proportion of students to teachers is 15:1. (24c)
13. (Correct as written; 24e)
14. (Correct as written; 24h)
15. The ingredients for guacamole are as follows: avocados, tomatoes, garlic, and hot peppers. (24c)

ACTIVITY 24.2

Are you happy with your life? Have you been feeling worthless lately? How would you like to turn your life around? We have the answer:

JOIN

the School of Snappy Comebacks

Millions of people have turned their lives into successful, profitable, and happy ones! The School of Snappy Comebacks teaches you how to take charge of your life. No longer will you find bullies kicking sand in your face at the beach or your boss humiliating you in front of your clients. You will be well prepared with all kinds of interesting, humorous, and forceful comebacks to any situation!

Read the following quote from one of our clients:

"When I first arrived at the School of Snappy Comebacks, I had never been so low in my life. I was at the end of my rope. In just six short weeks, I was a new person! I got a new job and was recently promoted to vice-president of the company. It's unbelievable! I never could have done it without the help of your school."

If you call today, you will receive the first week's tuition absolutely free. Classes are offered in the A.M. and P.M. Don't hesitate to call. Isn't it time to turn your life around?

555-3333

ACTIVITY 24.3

1. The committee decided on two important recommendations: to raise taxes and to limit spending.
2. (Correct as written)

3. Don is currently reading *Peer Editing: What Do Students Really Think?*

4. I'll never forget my grandmother's words: "An apple a day keeps the doctor away."

5. Sue's son suffered a terrible injury: When he was out late at night, a piece of glass from a bottle flew into his eye. (May also be considered correct as written.)

ACTIVITY 24.4

Possible answers:

1. The time is 6:35.

2. Here's what my mother used to say: "You can eat sherbet with a spoon, but that doesn't make it soup."

3. Even though *The ABC of Style: A Guide to Plain English* was written three decades ago, it still provides good advice.

4. There are three reasons for the hot weather: the sun, the calm winds, and some old voodoo woman in Haiti who has a miniature of the earth that she is holding over a flame.

5. My favorite salad is simple: lettuce, tomatoes, and dressing.

ACTIVITY 24.5

1. Mustafa Kemal Atatürk, Turkey's dictator, was both a great man and a terrible man. "He freed Turkey from European colonialism—and burned alive tens of thousands of Greek civilians in Smyrna. . . ."

2. Mustafa Kemal Atatürk, Turkey's dictator, was both a great man and a terrible man. "He brought Turkey out of the Middle Ages . . . —and lived a personal life of barbaric depravity." (Dash may also be omitted.)

3. Mustafa Kemal Atatürk, Turkey's dictator, was both a great man and a terrible man. "He freed Turkey from European colonialism—and burned alive tens of thousands of Greek civilians in Smyrna, pitching their charred bodies into the harbor. . . . He preached for democracy for Turkey—and ruled as an absolute dictator, torturing and hanging his opponents.

ACTIVITY 24.6

Possible answers:

The British anthropologist Sir Edward Burnett Tylor introduced the term *culture* as scientists use it today. In his book *Primitive Culture* (1871), Tylor defined culture as "that complex whole which includes knowledge, belief, art, morals, law, custom, and any other capabilities and/or habits acquired by man as a member of society." Tylor's definition includes three of the most important characteristics of culture: (1) Culture is acquired by people—a process called *enculturation*. (2) A person acquires culture as a member of society. Social life would be impossible without understandings and practices shared by all people. (3) Culture is a complex whole. Its units are called *cultural traits*. They may include a customary place for the dead, a device (such as a plow), or a gesture (such as a handshake).

Culture must be in two places at once. First, it must be in the environment, where it appears as *artifacts*—things made by human beings—or as *behavior*.

Some of the culture in this environment—such as a gesture or the telling of a story—is short-lived. But other culture—such as a stone ax or a written story—lasts for a very long time. Second, culture must be in some person's mind as a set of ideas for understanding and evaluating artifacts and behavior. An artifact that nobody understands is incomplete culture.

Development of a culture can bring change. For example, a society may switch from food gathering to farming as a result of population growth and the disappearance of game. A still larger population, in turn, brings even greater specialization and division of labor. The United Nations Population Fund (UNPF) is now studying the effects of these changes in Third World countries. Whenever environmental changes or other pressures make new ways of doing things desirable, a culture changes.

ACTIVITY 24.7

(See Activity 24.1.)

ACTIVITY 24.8

A. 1. For the written character *P'u*, the first, the second, Which brings us to Pooh, As an illustration of the principle, But no matter how he may seem to others,
   2. natural, simple, plain, honest
   3. . . . wood; the second . . .
   4. He knew that one was right, . . .
   5. . . . power; this power . . .
   6. the "radical" or root-meaning one; the "phonetic" or sound-given one; Pooh, the Uncarved Block
   7. "What do you think, Pooh?"
   8. "Well,"
   9. especially those fooled by appearances,
   10. . . . right," "Well,"
   11. it's
   12. "I think it's more to the right"; "What do *you* think, Pooh?"; "Well,"
   13. "natural, simple, plain, honest"; "radical"; "phonetic"; "tree in a thicket"; "wood not cut"; "things in their natural state"; "uncarved block"
B. 1. The first introduces examples to explain the first independent clause; the second introduces a quotation.
   2. To set off important parenthetical information for emphasis
   3. To show that there is more to follow; to build suspense (Answers may vary.)

Chapter 25

ACTIVITY 25.1

Relevant section of chapter is indicated in parentheses.

   1. Meade High School will be hosting the track invitational this Saturday. (25b)
   2. "When you arrive at the airport," my sister said, "give me a call." (25b)
   3. Twenty-five thousand people marched in the parade last week. (25f)
   4. Kathy's grandparents came to the United States from England. (25e)

5. *Dallas* was a popular television drama. (25d)
6. I explained to the secretary that I had an appointment with my professor (25c)
7. I can't decide whether to take Art History 101 or Film Aesthetics 110 this semester. (25b)
8. Boat rides on the Mississippi River are more popular than ever. (25b)
9. (Correct as written; 25f)
10. The legal drinking age in most states is twenty-one. (25e)
11. Have you ever read a Shakespearean poem? (25b)
12. (Correct as written; 25b, 25d)
13. The governor asked Senator Bower to speak at the meeting. (25b)
14. The failed *coup d'état* jeopardized the lives of many people. (25d)
15. (Correct as written; 25e)
16. When told that the peasants had no bread, Marie-Antoinette retorted: "Let them eat cake!" (25b)

ACTIVITY 25.2

1. Correct as written, or lower-case *not:* An independent clause after a colon may or may not be capitalized.
2. Lower-case *doctor:* Capitalize only proper nouns.
3. Lower-case *with* and capitalize *my*: In titles, prepositions are lower-cased and pronouns are capitalized.
4. Capitalize *French* and *Germans:* Nationalities are proper nouns, which must be capitalized.
5. Capitalize *the:* A quoted sentence that follows a colon must be capitalized.

ACTIVITY 25.3

Possible answers:

1. Bob said, "Frank is an excellent linebacker."
2. P. T. Barnum got it right: there/There *is* a sucker born every minute!
3. Kleenex is my favorite brand of tissues.
4. I am taking English 201 with Professor Kaminski and Statistics 103 with Professor Gass.
5. My favorite musical is *The Phantom of the Opera.*

ACTIVITY 25.4

A popular dreamer was Professor John Chapman from Swaffam, England. He had three dreams that told him to journey to London and meet on London Bridge a man who would make him rich. He obeyed and met a man who asked, "What are you doing on this bridge?" He answered, "A dream has sent me here." The man remarked that a recent dream had instructed him to journey to Swaffam and dig up a jar of gold coins that rested under the only tree of John Chapman. Chapman kept quiet, went home, and became a rich man.

Sir E. W. Budge had a triple dream on the night before his fateful examination in Ancient Oriental Languages 101, between midnight and 2 A.M., showing him just what the test would be. He got up and studied the obscure material from 2 A.M. until it was time for the examination. His dream had been accurate in every detail, and he won the fellowship that made possible his career as keeper of Egyptian antiquities at the British Museum.

Abraham Lincoln was oppressed for two weeks by a dream that foretold his assassination. When Lincoln next looked into his Bible, he turned by chance to Jacob's dream and then discovered how much emphasis the entire Bible puts on dreams and visions. He remarked that in his day, dreams were regarded as very foolish, but if we believe the Bible, we must accept the fact that in the old days, God used dreams. Lincoln shared that observation shortly before he died, hoping that his dream would not come true.

ACTIVITY 25.5

Possible answers:

1. Professor Theodore Watt and Denny T. Driller, D.D.S., are meeting at IBM at 3:00 P.M.
2. Eco-terrorists, i.e., people who use violent means of protesting against environmental problems, are threatening to blow up the Hoover Dam.
3. Vada Marceau, M.S.W., whose office is at 65 Polk St., charges $65 per hour for counseling.
4. Robert Vassen III is the new director of the CIA.

ACTIVITY 25.6

1. *Washington Post; Titanic*
2. *The Catcher in the Rye*
3. *churritos*
4. *swallowed*
5. *The Firm; Today*

ACTIVITY 25.7

1. OK   2. peeled   3. many   4. alone
5. agri-   6. OK   7. massa-
   cultural   cred

ACTIVITY 25.8

Paragraph 2: ten-gallon; cowboy; football; ✓; fourteen and seven-eighths

Paragraph 3: ✓; top-forty; Raspberry; ✓; ✓

Paragraph 5: ✓; fly-fishing; self-respecting; fisherman; ✓; aerodynamic; ✓; ✓; overall

Paragraph 6: neckties

ACTIVITY 25.9

By the end of the eleventh century, shortly after the Norman Conquest, the total population of England seems to have been about 1.5 million. In the year 1500, there were about five million speakers of English, as against ten million speakers of German, twelve million of French, eight and one-half million of Spanish, and nine and one-half million of Italian. By 1700, the population of England stood at less than six million, but there were about eight million speakers of English. By the year 1790, when the first American census was taken, some four million persons were counted, ninety percent of whom were of British stock.

By 1900, the English population stood at 32.5 million. A total of 123 million people spoke English, outstripping German with eighty million, Russian with eighty-five million, French with fifty-two million, Spanish with fifty-eight million, and Italian with fifty-four million.

ACTIVITY 25.10

(See Activity 25.1.)

ACTIVITY 25.11

This article was first printed in the *Sunday Times* on May 4, 1974.

In September 1971, author George Feifer lent an impatient friend an advance copy of his novel, *The Girl from Petrovka.* He'd been reluctant, for it was a unique copy, bearing marks of intensive work. Major errors in the American proofs of the same book persuaded his New York editor to publish an Americanized version of the English edition—which itself had been specially Anglicized, since he was an American. His red marks, four or five to a page, indicated necessary changes (for example, *labour* to *labor* and *theatre* to *theater*). These marks gave the copy almost as much sentimental as practical value for him.

Within a week, his friend had lost it from his car in Bayswater. Frantic searches and proffered rewards failed. It was an oddly painful experience that seemed to jinx the book.

Twenty-six months later, in November 1973, Feifer traveled to Vienna to write an article about the novel's filming and quickly felt submerged in the haunted lives of the persons on whom the characters are based. Anthony Hopkins, a well-known actor who plays one of the strongest characters, told Feifer of a puzzling incident the previous summer.

Having signed to do the part, Hopkins went to central London to buy a copy of the book. Returning home after a fruitless trip, he noticed an abandoned book on a bench in the Leicester Square subway station. Turning it over, he read the title: *The Girl from Petrovka.* He was still confounded by the red marks scattered on most pages. "Might that copy," Hopkins asked Feifer, "have some personal meaning for you?"

One wonders how many journeys the book had made, in the nearly two years since it had been stolen, before it chanced to be abandoned in Leicester Square for the movie character, Anthony Hopkins.

Chapter 26

ACTIVITY 26.1

Corrected words are italicized.

Today, *environmental* problems, such as overpopulation, global warming, and acid rain, are important issues worldwide. Overpopulation is a problem primarily in the developing *countries,* where people lack *access* to education and medical facilities or where religious *beliefs* may prevent the use of birth control. Cultural traditions also may encourage large families as a source of *labor.* Some *governments* have established laws that families may not *exceed* more than one child.

When population grows beyond a *sustainable* point, there are bound to be *disastrous consequences.* More people means that more resources must be *developed* and ultimately used. Since the Industrial Revolution and the subsequent rise in population, problems from the burning of coal, oil, and gas have *occurred.* One *effect* has been an increase in the *temperature* of the earth. This increase could result in the melting of the polar ice cap, which would raise the sea level, and a change in *weather* patterns that could shift agricultural production. Another problem, acid rain, results from the burning of coal, which increases the acidity of precipitation. This acidity can have negative health consequences for humans and also damages aquatic ecosystems.

Can the earth adjust to these *incredible* changes? What's more important, will people be able to adapt their *behavior* to *lessen* the impact on the earth? *Regrettably,* we do not have any choice.

SECTION 26B

Answers may vary.

1. Ask a native speaker
2. Look in the dictionary
3. See if certain pronunciation rules apply

ACTIVITY 26.2

Corrected words are in boldface.

Dear Mrs. Polton:

I am writing to complain about the interaction I had with a member of **your personnel,** André, last Saturday afternoon, May 20.

I was in a **dilemma** about a gift to buy for my **niece.** I was **interested** in buying her a piece of **jewelry,** but I was financially a little bit strapped at the time. I explained my situation to André and told him that I **preferred** to stay within a certain price range. Well, he must not have been paying attention because he **proceeded** to bring out increasingly expensive items. I was **embarrassed** to keep telling him that I couldn't afford the items, and the situation became more and more **uncomfortable.** I could tell he was losing his **patience.** I repeated that I was looking for something a little less elegant, and he began to get angry. Then another customer **interrupted** us, and André **completely** ignored me and began to help the new customer.

```
I found André's behavior inappropriate and unnecessary.  I would appreci-
ate it if you would remind him that although some people may not have a lot
of money, they still deserve to be treated as valuable customers.  I would
also like him to apologize for his rudeness.  Thank you very much for your
attention to this matter.


Sincerely,



Gladys Kravitz
```

ACTIVITY 26.3

1. alter   **2.** fair   **3.** threw   **4.** accept   **5.** all ready
6. brake   **7.** advice   **8.** device   **9.** principal   **10.** than

ACTIVITY 26.4

Possible answers:

1. Tours of the capitol begin at one o'clock.
2. The capital of Minnesota is Saint Paul.
3. The word *bat* always precedes the word *batter* in the dictionary.
4. After the fire drill, the teacher told us to proceed with our studies.
5. Please bring your pencil to the exam.
6. I know you're going on vacation.
7. The cake is altogether too fattening.
8. Let's proceed all together to the door.

ACTIVITY 26.5

Paragraph 1: repatched, rule 7; pavement, rule 3; bracketed, rule 2

Paragraph 2: referred, rule 2; married, rule 4; beginning, rule 2

Paragraph 3: noticeable, rule 6; beige, rule 1; unbuttoned, rule 2; presentable, rule 6; succeed, rule 5

Paragraph 4: listened, rule 2; prettiest, rule 4; believed, rule 1

ACTIVITY 26.6

Corrected words are in boldface.

> I clearly remember when **it** all **began.** Just before he retired, a journalist **friend** of mine returned from the Austria-Hungary border in mid-September 1989, crying with excitement. "East **Germans** are crossing the border **by** the **thousands.** I didn't think I would **ever** live to see this." Neither did I. That is **how** you are trained in this part **of** the world, **not** to believe that change is pos-

sible. You **are trained** to fear change, so that when change eventually begins to take place, you are suspicious, afraid, because every change you ever **experienced** was always for the worst. Much as I desired the collapse of the **old** system, the ground was shaking beneath my **feet.** The world I had thought of as permanent, stable, and secure was suddenly falling apart **all** around me. It was not a **pleasant** experience.

ACTIVITY 26.7

(See Activity 26.1.)

Chapter 27

ACTIVITY 27.1

A. 1. F   **2.** T   **3.** F   **4.** F   **5.** T
B. 1. Is it interesting?
   2. Does it fit the assignment?
   3. Will I be able to find enough material on the subject?
C. 1. Magazines
   2. Newspapers
   3. Journals
   4. Interviews
   5. Questionnaires
   6. Books

ACTIVITY 27.2

 1. P   **2.** DQ   **3.** DQ   **4.** P   **5.** P

ACTIVITY 27.3

A. 1. a. Yes. b. It's statistical information.
   2. a. No. b. It is a fact that is not disputed.
B. 1. a. Yes. b. It's statistical information.
   2. a. No. b. This is a personal opinion or judgment that would not be disputed.
   3. a. No. b. It is a personal opinion, but it does need to be supported with evidence.

ACTIVITY 27.4

Possible answers:

  1. Changes the vocabulary (for example, *abundant* is changed to *plentiful*), changes sentence structure from active to passive, changes sentence word order, breaks one sentence into two
  2. Yes

ACTIVITY 27.5

1. a. Unacceptable
   b. The sentence structure is almost exactly the same, and the information follows in the exact same order. The writer does change some vocabulary words, but the style is not much different.
2. a. Acceptable
   b. The meaning is maintained, but the passage is written in a different style.
3. a. Unacceptable
   b. The original meaning is not maintained; the paraphrase does not convey the "cramped" feeling of the cemetery; it also gives information that the original doesn't ("one of the biggest").

ACTIVITY 27.6

Acceptable paraphrases:

1. In Africa, Asia, and Australia, the deserts are expanding. This process, called desertification, is caused by overgrazing by animals, planting too many crops in an area, and harvesting too much firewood, which leaves an area bare.
2. Gestures, which are used to accentuate conversations, to point out things or people, or to show words or ideas, sometimes serve instead of words. Italians use the most words and gestures; the French use somewhat fewer, the Americans much fewer, and the Japanese the fewest of all.
3. When you are buying auto or homeowner's insurance, check out as many plans as possible to get the best rate. Then select a higher deductible (your deductible is the amount you pay toward repairs), which involves more risk but generates greater savings. For example, if you are an adult driver of a 1981 Chevrolet Citation in Ohio and purchase auto insurance from Allstate, one option is to pay $208 for collision and comprehensive coverage with a $100 deductible. But if you take a higher deductible of $500, your payment is only $114. Unless you are a terrible driver, your savings will be more than the $400 you will have to pay after an accident.

ACTIVITY 27.7

Changed portions are in boldface. **[]** shows that text or punctuation should be deleted. *Italic type* identifies missing material that should be added.

> Drinking is a pervasive and deep-rooted feature of American life. In a survey of U.S. drinking behavior, a Gallup poll found that the proportion of adults 21 or older who drank at least occasionally rose from 65% of men and 40% of women before World War II to nearly 80% of men and 60% of women by the end of the 1960s (Calahan**[, 1988,]** 64). According to Olson, in his report on alcohol usage, the per capita consumption of pure alcohol in the United States is about $2 \frac{3}{4}$ gallons per year, which corresponds to approximately two drinks a day**[. (Olson,]** (32).
>
> Today the most severe problem caused by alcohol is traffic accidents. According to the National Highway Traffic Safety Administration (NHTSA), alcohol-related crashes are the leading cause of death for young Americans between 16 and 24 years of age (1). On the average, more than three Americans

are killed and eighty are injured by drunk drivers every hour of the day**[.]** (Starr**[,]** 34).

The effort of one grassroots organization, Mothers Against Drunk Driving (MADD), has had a tremendous impact on educating the public about this problem. Specifically, more police resources, such as roadblocks, have been directed against drunk drivers, penalties have been increased, and plea-bargaining has been cut in drunk driving cases**[.]** *[citation]*.

A MADD publication distributed worldwide describes the tragic story of how the organization began:

> **["]**A Los Angeles mother named Cindy Lightner had the misfortune of losing her lovely 13-year-old daughter Cari in an accident. By chance, Cari was walking to school in a bicycle lane when she collided with a hit-and-run drunk driver who had been arrested a few days before for a Driving Under the Influence (DUI) charge. Her death sparked the nationwide movement of MADD, which demands reform of the drunk-driving problem which Cindy Lightner has had to endure. **["]** (2)

ACTIVITY 27.8

1. Michener, James A. *Alaska*. New York: Random, 1988.
2. Cox, Robert B. "City under Grass." *Sierra* Sept.-Oct. 1993: 28-30.
3. Kostelnik, Marjorie, et al. *Guiding Children's Social Development*. 2nd ed. New York: DelMar Publ., 1993.
4. McCartney, Paul, and Ringo Starr. Personal interview. 7 Feb. 1993.
5. Brice-Heath, Shirley. "Inner City Life through Drama: Imagining the Language Classroom." *TESOL* 27 (1993): 173-93.
6. Many Britons Dream about Queen Elizabeth." *Lansing State Journal* 19 Sept. 1993, sec. A: 11.

CREDITS

Abbey, Edward. *Desert Solitaire*. New York: Ballantine, 1968. 55. (Activity 7.2)

Adams, Douglas, and Mark Cawardine. *Last Chance to See*. New York: Ballantine, 1990. 1–3. (Activity 17.20)

Alderson, William T. *American Issues: Understanding Who We Are*. Nashville, TN: American Association for State and Local History, 1976. 92. (Activity 9.12)

American Red Cross. *Advanced First Aid and Emergency Care*. Garden City, NY: Doubleday, 1979. 170. (Activity 4.9)

Anderson, Kelli. "Luke and Murphey Jensen." *Sports Illustrated* 21 June 1993: 56. (Activity 7.1)

Archer, Jules. *Dictators*. New York: Hawthorn, 1967. 17, 49. (Activity 23.9) (Activity 24.5)

Armstrong, David M. *Rocky Mountain Mammals*. Estes Park, CO: Rocky Mountain Nature Assn., 1975. 31. (Activity 4.8)

Aumond-Achard, Amaury. "The Middle East Crisis: President Bush's Crusade." *Monterey Review* Spring 1991: 19. (Activity 6.1)

Baedecker's Prague. Englewood Cliffs, NJ: Prentice, 1991. 94. (Activity 27.5)

Baker, Tim. "The Future: It Doesn't Work." *Baltimore Sun* 2 March 1992, sec. A: 7. (Activity 6.5)

Barry, Dave. *Homes and Other Black Holes*. New York: Ballantine, 1988. 40–41. (Activity 8.12)

Bohannon, Paul. Culture. *The World Book Encyclopedia*. Chicago: World Book. Vol 4, pp. 186–187.

Bone, Jan. *Opportunities in Robotics Careers*. Lincolnwood, IL: VGM Career Horizons, 1987. 49. (Activity 18.11)

Brosnahan, Tom. *Turkey*. Berkeley, CA: Lonely Planet, 1989. 62. (Activity 4.6)

Brown, Jan. "Making a Basket out of White Oak Splits." *The Foxfire Book*, ed. Eliot Wigginton. Garden City, NY: Anchor/Doubleday, 1968. 123–124. (Activity 6.6)

Brunvand, Jan Harold. *The Choking Doberman and Other "New" Urban Legends*. New York: Norton, 1984. 67. (Activity 4.11)

Bryant, Sir Arthur. *Leeds Castle*. London, Eng.: Jolly and Barber, 1989. 4. (Activity 22.11)

Buchsbaum, Ralph, and Mildred Buchsbaum. *Basic Ecology*. Pacific Grove, CA: Boxwood, 1987. 29–31. (Activity 4.2)

Celce-Murcia, Marianne, and Diane Larsen-Freeman. *The Grammar Book*. Rowley, MA: Newbury House Publishers, Inc. 1983. 324. (Activity 8.2)

Christopher, Robert C. *The Japanese Mind*. New York: Fawcett, 1983. 133. (Activity 4.3)

Clayton, John Jacob. *What Are Friends For?* Boston: Little, Brown, 1979. 203–04. (Section 23d)

Connell, Evan S. *Mrs. Bridge*. San Francisco: North Point, 1959. 152. (Activity 13.11)

Di Fiore, Ann L. "Hip, Hip Hippo!" *National Geographic World* May 1992: 19–20. (Activity 17.9)

Dillard, Annie. *Pilgrim at Tinker Creek*. New York: Harper, 1974. 14–15. (Section 24d)

Drakulic, Slavenka. *How We Survived Communism and Even Laughed*. New York: Harper, 1993. xiii. (Activity 26.6)

Dreher, Diane. *The Tao of Inner Peace*. New York: Harper, 1990. 42. (Activity 23.2)

Du Fresne, Jim. *Michigan State Parks*. Seattle: Mountaineers, 1989. 123. (Activity 4.3)

Erkanat, Judy. "Turkish Delight: Explore the Culinary Frontiers of Traditional Turkish Cuisine." *Vegetarian Gourmet* Spring 1993: 40. (Activity 17.9)

Feldman, David. *Why Do Clocks Run Clockwise? and Other Imponderables*. New York: Harper, 1987. 137. (Activity 10.8)

Forsythe, Frederick. *The Day of the Jackal*. New York: Bantam, 1971. 44. (Activity 23.11)

Friend, Jewell A. *Writing English as a Second Language*. Glenview, IL: Scott, Foresman, 1971. 119–20. (Activity 10.4)

Gass, Susan, and Natalie Lefkowitz. *Varieties of English*. Ann Arbor: University of Michigan Press, in progress. (Activity 4.3)

Handler, Barbara. *Positively Obedient.* Loveland, CO: Alpine, 1987. 39. (Activity 4.6)

Harris, Philip T., and Robert T. Moran. *Managing Cultural Differences.* Houston: Gulf, 1987. 43. (Activity 27.6)

Hemingway, Ernest. *For Whom the Bell Tolls.* New York: Scribner's, 1940. 360–61. (Activity 23.13)

Hillesum, Etty. *An Interrupted Life.* New York: Pocket, 1981. 74. (Activity 4.12)

Hoff, Benjamin. *The Tao of Pooh.* New York: Penguin, 1982. 11–12. (Activity 24.8)

Hood, Mary. "Why Stop?" *The Best American Essays, 1989.* Ed. Geoffrey Wolff and Robert Atwan. Ticknor & Fields, 1989. 179. (Activity 6.5)

Hughes, Langston. "Dream Variations." *Black Voices.* Ed. Abraham Chapman. New York: NAL, 1968. 427. (Section 25b)

Jenkins, Mark, and Steve Gorman. "Creating the Perfect Clothing System." *Backpacker* Sept. 1992: 44. (Activity 17.6)

Kerouac, Jack. *The Town and the City.* San Diego: Harcourt, 1945. 10. (Activity 19.13)

Ketchum, Richard M. *Great Historic Places.* New York: American Heritage, 1957. 345. (Activity 8.9)

Kingman, Daniel. *American Music: A Panorama.* New York: Schirmer, 1979. 75. (Activity 14.15)

Kohn, Howard. "Malignant Giant." *Twenty Years of Rolling Stone.* Ed. Jann S. Wenner. New York: Friendly Press, 1987. 233. (Activity 5.1)

Koontz, Harold, and Heinz Weihrich. *Essentials of Management.* New York: McGraw, 1990. 137. (Activity 14.14)

Kunzig, Robert. "Earth on Ice." *Discover* April 1991: 61. (Activity 5.9)

Lindskoog, Kathryn. *The Gift of Dreams.* New York: Harper, 1979. 125–26. (Activity 25.4)

Loftus, Simon. *A Pike in the Basement: Tales of a Hungry Traveler.* San Francisco: North Point, 1987. 75–76. (Activity 16.8)

Mandela, Nelson. *No Easy Walk to Freedom.* Portsmouth, NH: Heinemann, 1965. 189. (Sections 23d, 27b)

Marcus, Rebecca B. *Survivors of the Stone Age: Nine Tribes Today.* New York: Hastings House, 1975. 15–20. (Activity 8.15)

Michener, James A. *Texas.* New York: Random, 1985. 193. (Activity 23.6)

Millgate, Michael. "The Sound and the Fury." *Faulkner: A Collection of Critical Essays.* Englewood Cliffs, NJ: Prentice, 1966. 107. (Section 23d)

Naj, Amal Kumar. "Some Manufacturers Drop Efforts to Adopt Japanese Techniques." *Wall Street Journal,* 7 May 1993, sec. A: 1. (Activity 4.7)

Neiman-Marcus. *Pure and Simple.* Dallas: Neiman-Marcus In Circle, 1991. 145. (Activity 5.9)

Nelson, Christopher. *Mapping the Civil War.* Washington, DC: Starwood, 1992. 16. (Activity 5.8)

Otto, Simon. *Walk in Peace: Legends and Stories of the Michigan Indian.* Grand Rapids: Michigan Indian Press, 1990. 17–18. (Activity 8.3)

Pei, Mario. *The Story of the English Language.* Philadelphia: Lippincott, 1967. 70. (Activity 25.9)

The Phantom of the Opera. Playbill, Her Majesty's Theatre, London. (Activity 7.2)

Plath, Sylvia. *The Bell Jar.* New York: Harper, 1971. 1. (Section 27e)

Samuelson, Robert J. "The Way We Diaper." *Newsweek* 19 Mar. 1990: 46. (Activity 27.3)

Smith, Emily T. "The Global Greenhouse Finally Has Leaders Sweating." *Business Week* 1 Aug. 1988: 74. (Activity 27.3)

Stanley, David. *Eastern Europe on a Shoestring.* Berkeley, CA: Lonely Planet, 1989. 88. (Activity 20.2)

Steinbeck, John. *Cannery Row.* New York: Bantam, 1945. 43. (Activity 18.8)

Stern, Jane, and Michael Stern. *Encyclopedia of Culture.* New York: Harper, 1992. 19–20. (Activity 20.11)

Steves, Rick, and Gene Openshaw. *Europe 101: History and Art for the Traveler.* Santa Fe, NM: John Muir, 1990. 93. (Activity 21.9)

Strickland, Carol. *The Annotated Mona Lisa.* Kansas City, MO: Andrews and McMeel, 1991. 120. (Activity 6.6)

Tan, Amy. *The Joy Luck Club.* New York: Putnam, 1989. 91. (Activity 4.8)

Tarnes, Richard. *A Traveller's History of London.* New York: Interlink, 1992. 159. (Activity 5.6)

Terkel, Studs. *Working.* New York: Ballantine, 1974. xv. (Section 23d)

Thompson, James J. *Beyond Words.* New York: Citations, 1973. 1. (Activity 12.16)

Thoreau, Henry David. "On the Duty of Civil Disobedience." *Walden, or Life in the Woods, and On the Duty of Civil Disobedience.* New York: Signet, 1960. 230. (Section 24c)

Thurman, Judith. *Isak Dinesen's Africa.* San Francisco: Sierra Club Books, 1985. 58–59. (Activity 13.15)

Timberlake, Lloyd. "The Politics of Food Aid." *The Earth Report.* Ed. Edward Goldsmith and Ned Hilyard. Los Angeles: Price, Stern and Sloan, 1988. 27. (Activity 27.4)

Tobias, Andrew. *The Only Investment Guide You'll Ever Need.* New York: Bantam, 1987. 22. (Activity 27.6)

Turtle, Melina. "The Death Threat against Rushdie: A Case Study in Political Scapegoatism." *Monterey Review* Fall 1990: 4. (Activity 6.1)

Tyler, Anne. *Saint Maybe.* New York: Knopf, 1991. 1–3. (Activity 26.5)

United Nations. *Global Outlook 2000.* New York: United Nations, 1990. 6, 251. (Activity 4.4) (Activity 20.5)

Vaughn, Alan. *Incredible Coincidence.* New York: Ballantine, 1979. 95–96 (Activity 25.11)

Wagenknecht, Edward. *Nathaniel Hawthorne: The Man, His Tales and Romances.* New York: Ungar, 1989. 1. (Section 24e)

Wagner, Jane. *The Search for Signs of Intelligent Life in the Universe.* New York: Harper, 1985. 164. (Activity 2.3)

Walther, Ingo F. *Vincent van Gogh.* Köln: Taschen, 1988. 58. (Activity 5.9)

Zamel, V. "The Composing Processes of Advanced ESL Students." *TESOL Quarterly* 17 (1983): 177. (Epigrams, Chapters 1, 2, 3)

Zielinski, John M. *Amish Horsefarming across America.* Iowa City, IA: Amish Heritage, 1988. 43. (Activity 5.9)

INDEX

Abbreviations
  acronyms, 329–330
  initial, 329
  of Latin terms, 329
  with numbers, 328
  of organizations/companies/government
    agencies, 329
  periods with, 329
  in personal titles, 327–328
  practice with, 330
Absolute phrases
  commas with, 296
  nature of, 296
Acronyms
  examples of, 329
  parentheses in, 317
  practice with, 330
Action verbs, adjectives and adverbs with,
  250–251
Active voice, 78
  example of, 184
Address, numbers in, 336
Adjective clauses
  formation of, 90–91
  omitting relative pronouns, 89–90, 91
  particles in reduced clauses, 206
  relative pronouns in, 86–90
  use of, 91–92
Adjectives
  with action verbs, 250–251
  compared to adverbs, 248
  comparative and superlative forms, 251–254
  coordinate, 296
  cumulative, 296
  double negatives, 254–256
  identification in sentences, 247–248, 249
  after linking verbs, 249–250
  order in sentences, 256–257
  proper, capitalization of, 325
  regular and irregular forms, 247, 252
Adverb clauses
  participles in reduced clauses, 206
  subordinating conjunctions in, 92–94
  writing sentences with, 94

Adverbs
  with action verbs, 250–251
  compared to adjectives, 248
  comparative and superlative forms,
    251–254
  double negatives, 254–256
  identification in sentences, 247–248, 249
  order in sentences, 256–257
  regular and irregular forms, 247
Aircraft, italics for, 331
Antecedents, compound, and pronoun agreement, 230–231
Apostrophes
  with contractions, 301
  editing for usage, 302–303
  with plurals, 301–302
  with possessives, 298–301
Appositives, pronoun case in, 241
Articles
  a and *an*, 260–261, 268
  with common nouns, 263, 269–270
  correcting errors in usage, 259–260
  with countable and noncountable nouns,
    263–265
  definite, 259, 267–268
  with definite nouns, 267
  as determiners, 260
  with generic nouns, 267
  indefinite, 259
  with indefinite nouns, 267
  with indefinite common nouns, 268
  with proper nouns, 261–263
  use in sentences, 268
Artworks, italics for, 330
Audience, 17–20
Auxiliary verbs, 131. *See also* Modals

Be, subject-verb agreement with, 211–212
Book titles
  italics for, 330
  MLA style documentation, 367–368
Brackets
  inserting in paragraph, 318–319
  uses of, 317–318

Brainstorming, to narrow topic, 9–10
British spelling, 351

Capitalization
    editing sentences for, 326
    I and *O,* 325
    inserting in paragraph, 327
    in poetry, 323
    proper adjectives, 325
    proper nouns, 323–325
    in quotations, 325
    text after colon, 312, 323
    in titles, 325–326
    writing sentences with, 326–327
Causative verb, 131
Cause and effect pattern, 56–58
Chronological organization, 54–55
Citations, parentheses in, 317
Classification pattern, 56–58
Clauses
    adjective, 86–92
    adverb, 92–94
    commas with, 293–294
    noun, 94–96
Coherence
    demonstratives, 46–47
    repetition of words/phrases, 45
    revising for, 47
    and transitions, 43–45
Collective nouns, subject-verb agreement with,
        217–218
Colons, 311
    capitalization with, 312, 323
    editing for use of, 313
    with quotation marks, 305
    with *the following* and *as follows,* 312
    uses of, 312, 313
    writing sentences with, 314
Commas
    with absolute phrases, 296
    in compound sentences, 81
    with contrasted elements, 296
    with coordinate adjectives, 296
    with cumulative adjectives, 296
    with dates, 296
    with direct address, 295
    editing for, 297
    with independent clauses, 293–294
    with interjections, 296
    with introductory elements, 292, 293
    with items in series, 292
    in numbers, 297
    with participle phrases, 295
    with places, 297

    with prepositional phrases, 294
    with quotation marks, 305
    with quotations, 296
    with restrictive and nonrestrictive elements,
        294–295
    to set off parenthetical elements, 295
    with tag questions, 296
    in titles, 297
    with *yes* and *no,* 295
Comma splice
    nature of, 85
    revision of, 86
Common nouns, 263
    articles with, 269–270, 275
Company names, abbreviation of, 329
Comparative form, 251–252
    choosing correct form, 253
    editing for, 254
    writing sentences with, 253–254
Comparison and contrast, 56–58
Comparisons
    ambiguity in, 118
    parallelism with, 107
Complex sentences, 81, 86
    clauses in, 86–96
    forming with coordination, 81–82
    forming with subordination, 86–96
Compound constructions, pronoun case in,
        240–241
Compound sentence
    comma in, 81
    conjunctive adverb in, 81–82
    coordinating conjunction in, 81
    formation of, 83–85
    semicolon in, 81
Compound subjects, subject-verb agreement
        with, 215–216
Compound words, hyphenation of, 332–333
Computer spelling checkers, 352–253
Conciseness, in word choice, 138–140
Conclusions
    elements to avoid, 66
    identification of, 66–67
    writing of, 67
    writing techniques for, 64–66
Conditional sentences
    example of, 189
    identification of, 189–190
    verb forms with, 190–191
    writing of, 191–192, 193–194
Conjunctive adverbs
    in compound sentence, 81–82
    identifying functions of, 83
    listing of, 82

Connotation of word, 143–144
Contractions
 apostrophes with, 301
 compared to possessives, 302
Coordinate adjectives, commas with, 296
Coordinating conjunctions
 in compound sentence, 81
 identifying functions of, 83
 parallelism with, 102–104
Coordination in sentences, 81–86
 complex sentence formation with, 81–82
 meaning of, 81
 rules of, 82
Correlative conjunctions
 listing of, 104
 parallelism with, 104–106
Countable nouns
 changing to plurals, 266–267
 nature of, 263
Cubing process, 11–12
Cumulative adjectives, commas with, 296

Dangling modifiers
 correction of, 126–127
 identification of, 126
Dashes
 inserting in paragraph, 318–319
 quotation marks with, 305
 uses of, 317
Dates
 commas in, 296
 numbers in, 336
Definite articles, 259
 criteria for use, 267–268
Definition pattern, 56–58
Definitions, quotation marks with, 305
Definite nouns, articles with, 267
Demonstratives, 46–47
Denotation of word, 143
Description, 56–58
Details, 53
Dialogue, quotation marks with, 304, 307
Direct address, commas with, 295
Direct object, relative pronoun as, 87, 88
Direct quotations, 78
 MLA documentation for, 365–366
 nature of, 303
 quotation marks, 303, 306
 in research paper, 358–359
 shifts in discourse, 78–79
Division and analysis, 56–58
Documentation of sources, 359–360, 364–370.
  See also Modern Language Association
  documentation

decision making about, 359–360
 endnotes, 365
 footnotes, 365
 in-text citations, 365
 Modern Language Association, 364–370
 types of information for, 359
Double negatives, 254
 examples of, 255
 and frequency adverbs, 255
 revising sentences with, 255–256
Drafting process, 21–22

Ellipses
 adding to passage, 316
 for interrupted speech, 315
 in quotations, 314–315
 to show omissions, in poetry, 315
Elliptical constructions, 117–118
Emphasis, italics for, 331–332
Emphasis-oriented organization, 55–56
Endnotes, 365
End-of-line word division, hyphenation, 332
Evaluation of writing, peer review, 29–36
Exclamation points, 310
 adding to sentences, 311
 quotation marks with, 305
Expletives, in sentences, 140

Films, italics for, 331
Footnotes, 365
Foreign words, italics for, 331
Fractions
 form in writing, 336
 hyphenation of, 333
Fragments. *See* Sentence fragments
Freewriting, 10
Frequency adverbs, 255
Fused sentences
 nature of, 85
 revision of, 85–86
Future perfect progressive tense, 182
Future perfect tense, 182
Future progressive tense, 182
Future tense
 future perfect progressive, 182
 future perfect, 182
 future progressive, 182
 simple, 181
 subject-verb agreement with, 214
 use in sentences, 182–183

Gender, and pronoun agreement, 228
Generic nouns, articles with, 267
Gerunds, 96, 199, 200

Gerunds (*Continued*)
function of, 200
identification of, 201, 203–204
nature of, 200
pronoun case with, 244–245
rules for use, 201–202
Government agencies, abbreviation of, 329

Helping verbs, 131. *See also* Modals
subject-verb agreement with, 213–214
Homonyms
identification of, 346
listing of, 341–345
writing sentences with, 347
Hyphens
compound modifiers, 333
compound words, 332–333
division of words at end of line, 334
end-of-line word division, 332
fractions and numbers, 333
practice with, 334–335
prefixes and suffixes, 333
suspended, 333
Hypothetical sentences
example of, 189
identification of, 189–190
and inverted word order, 194
verb forms with, 192
writing of, 193

Imperative mood, 77, 195
Incomplete sentences
ambiguous comparisons, 118
correction of, 119–121
elliptical constructions, 117–118
missing expletives, 119
missing subjects, 119
omission of *that*, 118–119
Indefinite articles, 259
criteria for use, 268
Indefinite nouns, article with, 267
Indefinite pronouns
listing of, 221
pronoun agreement with, 232–233
subject-verb agreement with, 221–222
Indicative mood, 77, 194–195
Indirect quotations, 78
nature of, 303–304
quotation marks, 303–304
shift in discourse, 78–79
Infinitives, 96
function of, 200
identification of, 201, 203–204
nature of, 199–200

rules for use, 201–202
split, 127–128
verbals, 199, 200
Information sources, 20
Initial abbreviations, 329
Intensifiers, in word choice, 139–140
Interjections, comma with, 296
In-text citations, 365
Intransitive phrasal verbs, 153, 154, 155–156
Introductions
elements to avoid, 64
identification of, 66–67
parts of, 59–61
purpose of, 59
thesis statement, 61–63
writing of, 67
writing techniques for, 63–64
Introductory elements, commas with,
292, 293
In which errors, 116–117
Irregular nouns, plurals of, 265–267
Italics
for emphasis, 331–332
foreign words, 331
practice with, 332
spacecraft/ships/airplanes/trains, 331
titles of works, 330–331
words as words, 331

Journalistic questions, 11
Journals, italics for, 331
Journal writing, benefits of, 14–15

Language
excessive humility, 140–141
sexist, 141–143
Latin terms, abbreviation of, 329
Limiting modifiers
correction of, 125–126
identification of, 125
Linking verbs
adjectives after, 249–250
pronoun case after, 239–240
subject-verb agreement with, 219–220
Lists, parallelism in, 109

Magazines, italics for, 330
Main idea, support of, 53
Manuscript preparation, research paper, 370
Mapping, to narrow topic, 12–13
Mechanics
abbreviations, 327–330
capitalization, 323–327
correcting errors in, 322

hyphens, 332–335
italics, 330–332
numbers, 335–336
Misplaced modifiers, 123–125
Mixed constructions, 121
    identification of, 112–113
    in which errors, 116–117
    mixed grammatical construction,
        113–114
    mixed meaning, 114–115
    pronoun subject repeating noun subject,
        115–116
Mnemonic device, for spelling words, 350
Modals, 160
    for ability, 168–169
    correcting sentences with, 169–170
    for degrees of certainty, 167
    for giving advice, 163–164
    identification of, 169
    logical meanings of, 166
    for past events, 168–169
    perfective, 164, 165–166
    periphrastic, 161, 162–163
    for permissions and requests, 164–165
    for social interaction, 162
    subject-verb agreement with, 213
    true, 161–162
Modern Language Association (MLA)
        documentation, 364
    acknowledgment of paraphrases, 366
    for direct quotations, 365–366
    example citations in, 367–368
    in-text citations, 365
    Works Cited list, 368–370
Modifiers
    compound, hyphenation of, 333
    dangling, 126–127
    limiting, 125–126
    misplaced, 123–125
    in sentences, 122–123
    squinting monitor, 124
Money, form for writing, 336
Mood
    imperative, 77, 195
    indicative, 77, 194–195
    shifts in, 77
    subjunctive, 77, 189, 195–198
Musical works, italics for, 330

Narration pattern, 56–58
Newspapers, italics for, 330
No, comma with, 295
Noncountable nouns
    identification of, 263–264

nature of, 263
    that are countable, 265
Noun clauses
    types of, 94–95
    writing sentences with, 95–96
Nouns
    common, 263
    plurals, 265–267
    possessives of, 298–299, 298–300
Numbers
    abbreviations with, 328
    commas in, 297
    forms to use in writing, 335–336
    hyphenation of, 333
    practice with, 336
    and pronoun agreement, 227
    shifts in, 75–77

Objective case, 237
    pronoun in, 238, 239
Object of preposition, relative pronoun as, 87
Object of sentence, verbal, 202–203
Organizational patterns, 54–58
    chronological, 54–55
    emphasis-oriented, 55–56
    spatial, 54
    types of development of, 56–58
Organizations, abbreviation of, 329
Outlines, 13–14
    parallelism in, 108–109

Paragraphs
    beginning new, 42
    coherence in, 43–47
    demonstratives in, 46–47
    headings of, 42
    length of, 49–50
    organizational patterns, 54–58
    repetitions in, 45–46
    sentence variety, 47–49
    topic sentences, 39–42
    transitions in, 43–45
    unity of ideas, 42–43
Parallelism
    with comparisons, 107
    with coordinating conjunctions, 102–104
    with correlative conjunctions, 104–106
    finding errors in, 101–102
    with items in series, 106–107
    in lists, 109
    nature of, 101
    in outlines, 108–109
    repetition of words in parallel structures,
        109–110

Paraphrasing in research paper, 358–359, 361–364
  acknowledging paraphrases, 366
  avoiding plagiarism, 362
  recognizing methods of, 361–362, 363
  writing of, 364
Parentheses
  and acronyms, 317
  inserting in paragraph, 318–319
  uses of, 316–317
Parenthetical expressions, commas with, 295
Participle phrases, commas with, 295
Participles, 96
  nature of, 200, 204
  as reduced adjective and adverbial clauses, 206
  use in sentences, 205
Particle, with phrasal verbs, 153, 158–159
Passive voice, 78
  forms of, 184
  situations for use, 184–185
  use in sentences, 185–186
Past perfect tense, 179
Past progressive tense, 178
Past tense
  past perfect progressive, 179
  past perfect, 179
  past progressive, 178
  present perfect, 176–177
  present perfect progressive, 178–179
  simple, 176
  subject-verb agreement with, 214
  use in sentences, 176–178, 180–181
Peer review, 29–36
Perfective modals, 164, 165–166
Periods
  in abbreviations, 329
  adding to sentences, 311
  end of sentence, 310
  with quotation marks, 305
Periphrastic modals, 161, 162–163
Person
  and pronoun agreement, 227
  shifts in, 75–77
Personal titles, abbreviations in, 327–328
Phrasal verbs
  intransitive, 153, 154, 155–156
  listing of, 154–155
  nature of, 153
  particle with, 153, 158–159
  transitive, 153, 154–155, 157–158, 159–160
Places, commas in, 297
Plagiarism, 359, 361, 362

Planning for writing
  and assignment, 8
  audience for piece, 17–20
  choosing topic, 9–13, 14–15
  good topic, characteristics of, 8
  information sources, 20
  outline, 13–14
  purpose for writing, 15–17
Plays, italics for, 330
Plurals
  apostrophe with, 301–302
  of countable nouns, 266–267
  irregular nouns, 265–267
  regular nouns, 265
  singular subject in plural for, and subject-verb agreement, 220–221
Poetry
  capitalization in, 323
  ellipses for omissions in, 315
  italics for title, 330
Possessive case, 237
Possessives
  with animals, 285
  choosing *of* or possessive *'s*, 284–286
  formation of, 300–301
  with inanimate objects, 285
  of nouns, 298–299
  of personal pronouns, 300
  relative pronoun as, 88
  with things possessed, 285
Prefixes
  hyphenation with, 333
  and spelling, 348
Prepositional phrases, commas with, 294
Prepositions
  be and adjective/noun and, 287
  choosing *of* or possessive *'s*, 284–286
  editing of, 276
  ending sentences with, 283–284
  identification of errors with, 282–283
  of logical relationships, 281–282
  most commonly used, 277
  of space, 279–281
  of time, 278–279
  verb and preposition combinations, 286
Present perfect past tense, 176–177
Present perfect progressive tense, 178–179
Present progressive tense, 174–175
Present tense, 177
  present progressive, 174–175
  simple present, 173–174
  use in sentences, 175–176, 180–181
Primary information sources, 20

Process pattern, 56–58
Pronoun agreement
  with compound antecedents, 230–231
  editing for, 228
  and gender, 228
  identification of, 226–227
  with indefinite pronouns, 232–233
  and number, 227
  and person, 227
  and sexist language, 229–230
Pronoun case
  in appositives, 241
  in compound constructions, 240–241
  editing for, 237–238
  before gerund, 244–245
  identification of, 239
  after linking verbs, 239–240
  objective case, 237, 238, 239
  possessive case, 237
  subjective case, 237, 238, 239
  with *than* and *as,* 242–243
  we and *us* before noun, 241–242
  with *who, whom, whoever, whomever,*
    243–244
Pronunciation, and spelling, 338–340
Pronoun reference
  editing for, 235
  examples of, 234
  identification of, 226–227, 234
Pronouns
  antecedent of, 226
  nature of, 226
  possessives of, 300
Proper adjectives, capitalization, 325
Proper nouns
  articles with, 261–263, 274
  capitalization, 323–325
Punctuation
  apostrophes, 298–303
  brackets, 317–318
  colons, 311–314
  commas, 292–298
  correcting errors in, 291–292, 309–310
  dashes, 317
  ellipses, 314–316
  exclamation points, 310
  parentheses, 316–317
  periods, 310–311
  question marks, 310
  quotation marks, 303–307
  semicolons, 292–293, 298
  slashes, 318
Purpose for writing, 15–17

Question marks
  adding to sentences, 311
  quotation marks with, 305, 310
Quotation marks
  adding in sentences, 306–307
  colons with, 305
  commas with, 305
  with dashes, 305
  with definitions, 305
  with dialogue, 304, 307
  direct quotation, 303, 306
  with exclamation points, 305
  indirect quotation, 303–304
  for ironic use of words, 305
  period with, 305
  with question marks, 305, 310
  for quotation within quotation, 304
  with semicolons, 305
  for titles, 304
  for words used as words, 304
Quotations. *See also* Direct quotations; Indirect
    quotations
  capitalization in, 325
  commas in, 296
  direct, 78
  ellipses for omissions in, 314–315
  indirect, 78
  shifts between direct and indirect,
    78–79

Redundancy, in word choice, 138–139
Regular nouns, plurals, 265
Regular verbs, 150
Relative pronouns, 90
  in adjective clauses, 86–87
  as direct objects, 87, 88
  as objects of preposition, 87
  omitting in clauses, 88–89, 91
  as possessives, 88
  as subjects, 87, 88
  subject-verb agreement with, 223–224
Repetition of words/phrases, 45
Research paper
  characteristics of, 357
  direct quotations in, 358–359
  documentation of information, 359–360,
    364–370
  manuscript preparation, 370
  paraphrasing in, 358–359, 361–364
  and plagiarism, 359, 361, 362

Revision
  for coherence, 47
  for content/purpose/audience, 24–29
  large-scale, 23–24
  small-scale, 24
Rote learning, of spelling words, 350

Secondary information sources, 20
Semicolons, 292–293
  in compound sentences, 81
  with independent clauses, 293–294
  with items in series, 292
  with quotation marks, 305
  use in sentences, 298
Sentence fragments
  correction of, 97–98
  examples of, 96–97
  intentional fragments, 97
Sentences
  clauses in, 86–96
  comma splices, 85–86
  complex, 81, 86
  compound, 81–82
  conditional, 189–192
  coordination in, 81–86
  coordination and subordination errors, 80–81
  fragments, 96–98
  fused, 85–86
  hypothetical, 192–194
  incomplete, 117–121
  mixed construction, 112–117
  modifiers in, 122–123
  simple, 81
  subordination in, 81, 86–96, 98–99
Sentence variety, 47–49
Series
  commas in, 292
  parallelism with items in, 106–107
  semicolons in, 292
Sexist language
  correction of, 142–143
  editing for, 230
  examples of, 141–142
  and pronoun agreement, 229–230
Shifts
  between direct and indirect quotations, 78–79
  in mood, 77
  in number, 75–77
  in person, 75–77
  in tense, 73–75
  in voice, 78
Ships, italics for, 331
Simple future tense, 181
Simple past tense, 176
Simple present tense, 173–174

Simple sentence, 81
Slashes
  inserting in paragraph, 318–319
  uses of, 318
Spacecraft, italics for, 331
Spatial organization, 54
Spelling
  American versus British, 351
  commonly misspelled words, 340–341
  computer spelling checkers, 352–353
  correcting misspelled words, 338, 345–346,
    352–353
  dictionary as aid, 351–352
  homonyms, 341–345, 346–347
  and pronunciation, 338–340
  rules for, 347–348
  strategies for improvement, 349–351
Split infinitives
  correction of, 128
  identification of, 127
Squinting monitor, 124
Stative verbs, 174–175
Subject complement, nature of, 239
Subjective case, 237
  pronoun in, 238, 239
Subject of sentence
  adding missing, 119
  relative pronoun as 87, 88
Subject-verb agreement
  basic rule for, 210
  with be, 211–212
  in clauses beginning who, which, that,
    222–223
  with collective nouns, 217–218
  with compound subjects, 215–216
  editing for, 216–217
  with future tense, 214
  with helping verbs, 213–214
  identification of, 208–209, 216
  with I and you as subject, 210–211
  with indefinite pronouns, 221–222
  with linking verbs, 219–220
  nature of, 208
  with past tense, 214
  with relative pronouns, 223–224
  in sentences beginning with prepositional
    phrase, 219
  in sentences beginning with there, 218–219
  singular subjects in plural form, 220–221
  for subject following verb, 218
Subjunctive mood, 77, 189, 195–198
  adjectives with, 195
  identification of, 189–190
  nouns with, 195
  situations for use, 195

use in sentences, 196–197
verbs with, 195, 196
Subordination in sentences
clauses in, 86–96
meaning of, 81
rules of, 98–99
Subordinating conjunctions
in adverb clauses, 92–94
listing of, 92–93
use of, 93–94
writing sentences with, 94
Suffixes
hyphenation with, 333
spelling rules related to, 348
Superlative form, 251–252
choosing correct form, 253
editing for, 254
writing sentences with, 253–254
Support, for topic, 52–53
Suspended hyphens, 333

Tag questions, comma with, 296
Television programs, italics for, 331
Tense. *See* Verb tense
That, 86–89
Thesis statement
critiquing of, 61–63
guidelines for, 61
writing of, 63
Time, numbers and words for, 335
Titles
capitalization of, 325–326
commas in, 297
italics for, 330–331
MLA style documentation, 367–368
quotation marks for, 304
Topic
brainstorming, 9–10
characteristics of good, 8
cubing process, 11–12
details related to, 53
freewriting, 10
journal, use of, 14–15
journalistic questions, 11
mapping, 12–13
support for, 52–53
Topic sentences, 39–42
evaluation of, 39
matching to paragraphs, 40–41
recognition of, 41
writing of, 41–42
Trains, italics for, 331
Transitions, common transitional
expressions, 44

Transitive phrasal verbs, 153, 154–155,
157–158, 159–160
True modals, 161–162

Unity of ideas, 42–43

Verbals, 96
editing sentences with, 203
gerunds, 199, 200
identification of, 199–200, 201, 204
infinitives, 199, 200
participles, 204–206
verbal objects, 202–203
Verbs
auxiliary, 131
causative, 131
helping, 131
identification of errors in form, 149
irregular, 150–152
modals, 160–170
phrasal, 153–160
regular, 150
stative, 174–175
use in sentences, 152–153, 187
voice, 184–187
Verb tense, 171–188
editing sentences for, 183
English system, 172
future, 181–183
past, 178–181
present, 173–178
shifts in, 73–75
use in sentences, 171–172, 183–184, 187
Voice
active, 78, 184
passive, 78, 184–186
shifts in, 78

Which, 86–89
Who, 86–89
Word choice. *See also* Language
already, yet, still, 133–135
another and *other,* 132–133
commonly confused words, 136–137
conciseness, elements of, 138–140
connotation of word, 143–144
correct word, identification of, 137–138
denotation of word, 143
do and *make,* 131–132
incorrect word, identification of, 130
intensifiers, 139–140
redundancy, 138–139
there and *it,* 140
usage errors, 135–138

Words as words
  apostrophe in, 302
  italics for, 331
  quotation marks for, 304
Works Cited list, MLA style, 368–370
· Writing process. *See also* Planning for writing
  composing, 4–7
  drafting, 21–22
  revision, 23–29
  writing in different languages, 4–5
  writing situations, 3–4

Yes, comma with, 295